Iraq Endgame?

Surge, Suffering and the Politics of Denial

Also by Geoff Simons

Are Computers Alive?: Evolution and New Life Forms

The Biology of Computer Life: Survival, Emotion and
Free Will

Eco-Computer: The Impact of Global Intelligence

Is Man a Robot?

Evolution of the Intelligent Machine

Libya: The Struggle for Survival

The United Nations: A Chronology of Conflict

Korea: The Search for Sovereignty

UN Malaise: Power, Problems and Realpolitik

Cuba: From Conquistador to Castro

The Scourging of Iraq: Sanctions, Law and Natural Justice

Vietnam Syndrome: Impact on US Foreign Policy

Saudi Arabia: The Shape of a Client Feudalism

Imposing Economic Sanctions: Legal Remedy or
Genocidal Tool?

Iraq: Primus Inter Pariahs – A Crisis Chronology 1997–98

Indonesia: The Long Oppression

Targeting Iraq: Sanctions and Bombing in US Policy

Future Iraq: US Policy in Reshaping the Middle East

Iraq: From Sumer to Post-Saddam

Libya and the West: From Independence to Lockerbie

Colombia: A Brutal History

The Ethnic Cleansing of Palestine

Nuclear Nightmares

They Destroyed Iraq and Called It Freedom

Iraq Endgame?

Surge, Suffering and the Politics of Denial

Geoff Simons

POLITICO'S

First published in Great Britain 2008 by
Politico's Publishing, an imprint of
Methuen Publishing Ltd
8 Artillery Row
London
SW1P 1RZ

10 9 8 7 6 5 4 3 2 1

A CIP catalogue record for this book is available from the British Library.

ISBN 978-1-84275-221-0

Set in Bembo by SX Composing DTP, Rayleigh, Essex
Printed and bound in Great Britain by Butler and Tanner, Frome

To Christine

she knows all the reasons why

Contents

Preface

I well remember Madeleine Albright, then US ambassador to the United Nations and later Secretary of State, acknowledging on the CBS *60 Minutes* television programme (12 May 1996) that the draconian sanctions imposed on Iraq had by the mid-1990s killed half a million Iraqi children. She responded with the words '*we think the price is worth it*' in pursuit of American political objectives. The monstrous nature of this statement haunts me still. Now it seems that what Denis Halliday, former UN humanitarian co-ordinator in Iraq, called a sanctions genocide serves as a clear precedent for what has been inflicted on Iraq since 2003.

There are at least two independent estimates – one academic[*] and one corporate[†] – that put the number of Iraqi dead since the US-led invasion at not less than one million, of which hundreds of thousands, if not a majority, were children. This suggests at least a similar number of wounded. I wrote parts of this book during the period when the British and Portuguese media were obsessed with the harrowing plight of an English family who had lost a young and beautiful daughter. And yet I had to search the media for the barest mention that the British and American governments were complicit in the deaths, injuries and disease suffered by perhaps a million Iraqi children. Many of these were young and beautiful daughters. It all happened, we were righteously told, because the United States and Britain were bringing freedom and democracy. *They think the price is worth it.*

Geoff Simons
January 2008

[*] Dr Gideon Polya (Chapter 2).
[†] Opinion Research Business (Chapter 9).

Introduction

Allow the president to invade a . . . nation, whenever he shall deem it necessary to repel an invasion, and you allow him to do so whenever he may choose to say he deems it necessary for such a purpose – and you allow him to make war at pleasure.

Abraham Lincoln, letter to William H. Herndon,
15 February 1848

This book charts the principal events of 2007 that bear on the Iraq issue. Within the framework of a detailed chronology, particular attention is given to the main American strategic initiative of this period – namely, the US military 'surge' designed as a troop escalation to clear and hold Baghdad and other areas – and its impact. The congressionally approved *Iraq Study Group Report*, published in late 2006, made seventy-nine recommendations, variously cherry-picked by the Bush administration, to be followed by the less prestigious *Iraq Commission Report* in Britain. Neither of these reports substantially deflected President George Bush or Prime Minister Tony Blair (or Prime Minister Gordon Brown) from policy courses already determined – an escalation of US troops in Baghdad and a gradual drawdown of British troops in southern Iraq – though efforts were made to implement recommendations that may have been adopted for other reasons (for example, talking to Iran and encouraging a greater role for the United Nations). In the same way, the mixed assessment of military and political progress given in the Petraeus–Crocker report of September 2007 did little to influence a Bush regime already seemingly determined to maintain a long-term military presence in Iraq. The different political postures in the United States and Britain coupled with the shifting tone of the Brown administration inevitably created tensions between Washington and London, which in early 2008 are not yet resolved.

In this book the military character of the surge is set against the impact of war on Iraqi civilians, the growing congressional divisions in the US, the evolving posture of the Brown administration, the role of the Iraqi government, the activities of Iraqi sectarian groups, the issue of human rights and other aspects. Finally, an attempt is made to draw the various themes together; noting in particular the international ramifications of the Iraq question, and the regional and global significance of the war.

No political situation can be understood without some knowledge of its antecedent events (see below) or the wider context (see Chapter 11). In principle earlier events, each of them simultaneously causes and effects, are infinite in number, and so the best we can do here is to briefly highlight a few of these, selected for their seminal significance.

The Western involvement in Muslim affairs did not begin with the Crusades but this is not a bad starting point. Today we should not ignore how the historical encroachment of foreign armies into Muslim lands is buried deep in the folk memories of many countries. It is no accident that some of the insurgent groups in Iraq, stimulated in part by Bush's crass reference to a 'crusade' against America's enemies, often broadcast their successes with talk of destroying 'crusader forces'. A Western journalist (see Chapter 9) described the US embassy in Baghdad, a vast fortress, as resembling the crusader castles that once dominated the Middle East.

When the Crusades were launched in 1094 they were advertised as a holy war against Islam, but it soon became clear that a principal aim, as now, was to establish control over the riches of the Middle East and beyond. The Christian forces were inspired as much by dreams of plunder as by religious zeal, with the inevitable concomitants of imperial conquest. A modern Lebanese writer, Amin Maalouf, describes the character of the Christian advance:

> Wherever they passed, they were heard to proclaim that they had come to exterminate the Muslims, although they were seen to

plunder many a Greek church on their way . . . [they] passed through several villages . . . and commandeered the harvests, which had just been gathered, mercilessly massacring those peasants who tried to resist. Young children were even said to have been burned alive.[1]

In *The Misery of Christianity* Joachim Kahl quotes an eye witness testimony on what happened when the Christians conquered Jerusalem in 1099:

> Soon . . . all the defenders were leaving the walls and running through the city. Pursued by our men, who drove them along, cutting them down and killing them . . . there was such a blood-bath that our men were wading ankle-deep in blood . . . Then, happy and indeed weeping for joy, our men went to venerate and pray at the sepulchre of our Redeemer.[2]

Such events have not faded from history but have helped to shape Muslim perceptions of all later Western invasions. In Iraq, according to the Commission on International Religious Freedom, a US watchdog, the invasion of Iraq was one of the reasons why the presence of 'ancient Christian communities that had lived on these same lands for 2,000 years' may be ending. The resurgent Islamists, perceiving a fresh 'crusader' invasion, were no longer prepared to tolerate the established Christian presence that had been acceptable to Saddam Hussein's Ba'athist regime.

As early as 1798 Britain dispatched a permanent agent to Baghdad, a modest response to Napoleon's supposed intention to march across Mesopotamia to India; in 1836 the British government decided to fund an expedition to explore the possibility of using a steamboat to navigate the Euphrates; and by the 1850s the possibility of expanding railway communications in the region was being considered. However, it was the collapse of the Ottoman Empire and the assigning of regional mandates to Britain and France by the League of Nations after the First World War that led to a massive expansion of Western influence in the Arab world.

On 21 December 1915, in anticipation of the Ottoman collapse, François Georges-Picot and Sir Mark Sykes met to plan a French–British carve-up of the Middle East. According to the subsequent Sykes–Picot agreement, France was to be given a greater Lebanon and an exclusive influence over Syria. A sphere of French influence would also extend to Mosul, while Britain would be handed the two Mesopotamian provinces of Basra and Baghdad. A compromise was reached on Palestine: Britain was to be given the ports of Acre and Haifa, and also a territorial region that would facilitate the building of a railway to Mesopotamia, while the rest of the country was to be given some sort of international administration. The Sykes–Picot agreement was kept secret for some time, so as not to inflame Arab nationalism, but the scene was set. The French had no intention of allowing an Arab Syria to emerge from the ruins of the war, and what had originally been the Ottoman province of Syria was now divided up into four political entities – Palestine, Lebanon, Transjordan and a much-reduced Syria – for the benefit of Britain and France. Britain quickly expanded its influence in the part of Mesopotamia that came to be known as Iraq, installed a puppet monarch, and brutally repressed Arab and Kurdish tribes struggling for independence.

Thus Winston Churchill, then Secretary of State for War and Air, sought advice from Hugh Trenchard, a pioneer of air warfare. Would it be possible for Trenchard to crush any resistance, 'perhaps using some kind of asphyxiating bombs calculated to cause disablement of some kind but not death . . . for use in preliminary operations against turbulent tribes'? Churchill was in no doubt that gas could be profitably employed against Arabs and Kurds (as well as against other colonial peoples), as revealed in the Trenchard Papers, David Omissi's *Air Power and Colonial Control* and other sources: 'I do not understand this squeamishness about the use of gas. I am strongly in favour of using poisoned gas against uncivilised tribes.' The use of gas as a 'scientific expedient' should not be prevented 'by the prejudices of those who do not think clearly'. In the event gas was used against the Iraqi rebels in 1920 with 'excellent moral effect'.

Iraqis interviewed in the 1990s remembered the British suppression of the tribes by means of gas, air strikes, incendiaries (the forerunners of napalm) and air-to-ground missiles. Wing-

Commander Arthur Harris (later 'Bomber' Harris of WWII) rejoiced that 'within forty-five minutes a full-size [Iraqi] village can be practically wiped out and a third of its inhabitants killed or injured'. It was an easy matter to bomb and machine-gun tribespeople with no effective means of defence.

The Iraqi monarchy, reliant on British military power, survived until 14 July 1958, when two hundred 'Free Officers' took power, heralding further *coups d'état* that would eventually facilitate the emergence of Saddam Hussein as the head of the Iraqi Ba'ath Party. On 17 July 1979 Saddam proclaimed himself President of Iraq, and thereupon set about a terror purge of the party in closed session to consolidate his power. The world had long known the character of the new Iraqi ruler, at least from the early 1960s, when Saddam was helping to create the Jihaz Haneen (the so-called 'instrument of yearning'), a special security body modelled on the Nazi SS and designed to protect the Ba'ath Party by targeting the 'enemies of the people'. A subsequent army coup against General Abdul Karim Kassem, who had toppled the monarchy, was supported by both Saddam and the CIA. Thus Ali Saleh Saadi, minister of the interior, said: 'We came to power on a CIA train.'[3] The CIA, quick to secure the terrain after the coup and the murder of Kassem, prepared comprehensive lists of people to be murdered to ensure that the old power factions could not regroup. The victims of the CIA-orchestrated death squads, embarking on gruesome missions of torture and killing, included those who continued to resist and also a wide range of educated Iraqis (lawyers, teachers, professors, doctors and others) judged to be a possible threat to the new regime and Western interests. Saddam was one of several Iraqis happy to add names to the CIA death lists, so confirming his support for US ambitions. In such a fashion the United States worked to support a course of events that would set Saddam firmly on the road to power, and then to consolidate a pragmatic alliance with him that would last nearly three decades.

Iraq had a number of persistent grievances against Iran, which in part would propel the countries to war. Some of these, like much of Iraq's case against Kuwait, were rooted in historical territorial

disputes; and the Islamic overthrow of the Shah of Iran – who had
served as a conduit for Israeli and US arms to the northern Kurds
– did nothing to improve relations between Tehran, now run by
ayatollahs, and a secular Baghdad.

Following the outbreak of the Iran–Iraq War in 1980, the US
had access to intelligence reports confirming Iraq's 'almost daily' use
of chemical weapons, but proclaimed a bogus neutrality towards the
conflict. On 19 December 1983 Donald Rumsfeld, as President
Reagan's special envoy to the Middle East, visited Saddam Hussein,
shook his hand and concluded – at a time when Saddam was known
to be using chemical weapons – that the Iraqi leader 'was not
interested in making mischief in the world'. Saddam's invasion of
Iran, given in 2002–3 as one of the reasons for toppling the Saddam
regime, was of no concern to Rumsfeld in 1983 – quite the reverse,
since Washington, openly committed to a pro-Saddam coalition,
was aiding the aggression. The US, along with other countries,
supplied Iraq with weapons, satellite intelligence and other means
of support for its war effort – to the extent that the US became an
active belligerent, bombing Iranian oil platforms in the Gulf and
killing Iranian service personnel.

There were plenty of other reasons for indicting Saddam for
genocide and committing crimes against humanity: in particular,
the dreaded Anfal campaign against the Kurds in the late 1980s
and the suppression of the Shi'ite and Kurdish revolts after the
1991 Gulf War. Unfortunately, Western hands were steeped in
the same blood. The US and other countries had supplied Saddam
with the weapons used in the Anfal atrocities; and the Pentagon
even published a 1990 study, *Iraqi Power and US Security in the
Middle East*, stating that it was Iran, not Iraq, that had been
responsible for the Halabja massacre.[4] Moreover, the 1991 revolts
were stimulated by American promises of support that never
materialised, with Saddam's helicopters even being allowed to fly
through coalition lines to attack his Iraqi enemies. In the event,
after a farcical trial, Saddam Hussein was hanged in December
2006 by a baying Shi'ite lynch mob.

Soon after the eight-year-long war, on 12 April 1990, Saddam
Hussein met with five US senators – Dole, Simpson, Metzenbaum,

McClure and Murkowski – in what was clearly an amiable encounter. Senators Dole and Simpson went so far as to denounce the Western press for presuming to criticise Saddam; and Senator Metzenbaum commented to Saddam that he was 'a strong and intelligent man and that you want peace'. Despite the placatory tone of this meeting, on 18 June 1990, Saddam complained on Baghdad Radio that Kuwait and other states, with US support, were waging an economic war against Iraq by manipulating their volume of oil production: 'War is fought with soldiers and harm is done by explosions, killing and coup attempts, but it is also done by economic means sometimes . . . this is in fact a kind of war against Iraq.' At the same time Saddam referred to traditional border disputes with Kuwait, whereupon US ambassador April Glaspie made the much-quoted comment to Saddam 'We have no opinion on Arab–Arab conflicts like your border disagreement with Kuwait' – and acknowledged that from 'the Iraqi point of view' actions taken by the United Arab Emirates were 'tantamount to military aggression against Iraq'. The historic 'green light', subsequently a matter of much speculation, had been given to Saddam for his invasion of Kuwait.

The resulting Gulf War, supposedly deriving authority from UN Security Resolution 678 (29 November 1990), led to hundreds of thousands of Iraqi casualties, many of them helpless conscripts incinerated in the desert; various subsequent cruise missile attacks on Iraq; and the deaths, according to UNICEF and the Iraqi Ministry of Health, of around 1.5 million Iraqi civilians through economic sanctions – in violation of many instruments of international law. However, the US deemed all this to be insufficient and, under the administration of George Bush, decided at some time after his inauguration – probably before the events of 11 September 2001 – on a unilateral invasion of Iraq, using the pretext of removing Saddam's weapons of mass destruction (WMD) but with no pretence at UN authorisation (the legalistic White House 'spin' and the brief Goldsmith apologetics, after he had produced a detailed sceptical analysis, were widely regarded as spurious).

The circumstances of this aggression have been copiously discussed and do not need to be rehearsed here. It is enough to

note that the episode came to mark the Bush and Blair
administrations as at best guilty of appallingly poor judgement and
at worst responsible for deliberate lies and copious violations of
international law. On 22 March 2002 Sir Peter Ricketts, political
director of the Foreign Office, warned that US 'scrambling to
establish a link between Iraq and al-Qaeda is so far frankly
unconvincing';[5] and a much-quoted memorandum, dated 23 July
2002, from MI6 head Sir Richard Dearlove declared that 'the
intelligence and facts [about WMD] were being fixed around the
policy'.[6] In December 2002 CIA chief George Tenet had
famously and absurdly declared to Bush in the Oval Office: 'Don't
worry [about Saddam's possession of WMD]. It's a slam dunk
[meaning it would be easy to present the case for war].' On 29
June 2007, with Resolution 1762, the UN Security Council
finally terminated the mandates of UNMOVIC and the IAEA, the
weapons inspectors in Iraq, at last explicitly admitting the futility
of their work: as the Saddam regime had consistently asserted,
there were no WMD in Iraq.

In short, the United States, with British acquiescence, was
inventing facts to 'justify' an invasion of Iraq. On 22 February
2007 Lord Butler of Brockwell, who had already produced a
damning report on Tony Blair's manipulation of intelligence,
declared in the House of Lords that neither the UK nor the US
had intelligence to 'prove conclusively' that Iraq had WMD, and
that Blair 'was disingenuous about that':

> The United Kingdom intelligence community told him on 23 August
> 2002 that we 'know little about Iraq's chemical and biological
> weapons work since late 1988'. The Prime Minister did not tell us
> that. Indeed, he told Parliament only just over a month later that the
> picture painted by our intelligence services was 'extensive, detailed
> and authoritative'. These words could simply not have been justified
> by the material that the intelligence community provided to him.[7]

There were other reasons why the US and Britain decided to
attack Iraq: the sort of deranged arrogance, fed by religious bigotry,
described by Lord (David) Owen in *The Hubris Syndrome* (2007);
the self-interested pressures from arms manufacturers and other

companies linked to the Bush administration; the permanent imperial struggle for strategic advantage; the US interest in abolishing Ba'athist socialism, just as Yugoslavian socialism had been ravaged in the Balkans; the little-publicised dollar–euro war, after Saddam declared his intention to join the euro (see Chapter 11); and the urgent quest for adequate energy supplies – mainly oil.

In 2001 US Vice-President Dick Cheney, discussing oil depletion in a speech in London, declared: 'The Middle East with two-thirds of the world's oil and lowest cost is still where the prize ultimately lies'; on 6 January 2003 Jack Straw, the British Foreign Secretary, addressing 150 ambassadors in London, pinpointed secure energy sources as a key priority of British foreign policy; in June 2003 Paul Wolfowitz, US deputy Defense Secretary, declared at an Asian security summit in Singapore: 'The . . . difference between North Korea and Iraq is that we had virtually no economic options with Iraq,'[8] implying that Saddam's oil reserves were strategically important, hampering US economic leverage; and Alan Greenspan, former head of the US Federal Reserve, wrote in his book *The Age of Turbulence* (September 2007): 'I am saddened that it is politically inconvenient to acknowledge what everyone knows: the Iraq war is largely about oil.'[9] It was equally significant that Washington and London orchestrated and approved a hydrocarbon law, to be adopted by the Maliki regime and which favoured foreign oil companies, before Iraqi legislators were allowed sight of it.

Bearing such details in mind, it is difficult to avoid the conclusion that both President Bush and Prime Minister Blair lied to Congress and the House of Commons, and that British and American legislators were prepared to endorse such mendacity without adequate scrutiny of what their leaders were telling them. For example, it emerged that Hillary Clinton, a leading Democrat presidential candidate in 2007–8, had voted for the war without bothering to read the full text of the 2002 National Intelligence Estimate, which was full of equivocations about Saddam's purported weapons. Jeff Gerth and Don Van Natta Jr commented: 'She did not do enough homework on the decision she has called the most important of her life . . . She chose to make statements to justify her vote for war that were not supported by the available intelligence.'[10] Her fellow parliamentarians were seemingly afflicted with the same reluctance to do homework.

Lord Goldsmith, the British Attorney General, at first had serious doubts about the war and then mysteriously changed his mind a few days later. On 7 March 2003 he offered Tony Blair detailed legal advice on the option of invading Iraq, which was at first marked 'Secret', then partially leaked and finally made public under mounting pressure for its release. The document is remarkable in its copious caveats and qualifications, all of which were subsequently omitted by Goldsmith ten days later.

In Paragraph 3 the Attorney General dismissed the American eagerness to launch a pre-emptive attack on Iraq, declaring that 'there must be some degree of imminence'. He acknowledged that Washington had been arguing for the right to use force to prevent danger in the future, but rejected this posture: 'If this means more than a right to respond proportionately to an imminent attack (and I understand that the doctrine is intended to carry that connotation) this is not a doctrine which, in my opinion, exists or is recognised in international law.' In Paragraph 9 Goldsmith argues that the international community disagrees with the US view that individual states are entitled to take action without the authorisation of the UN Security Council; and he later states (Paragraph 27) that 'the safest legal course would be to secure the adoption of a further resolution [after the adoption of Resolution 1441] to authorise the use of force'. Finally he concludes that, while Saddam Hussein could be legally removed from power if this was necessary to secure the disarmament of Iraq, 'regime change cannot be the objective of military action'. This means that when Blair evinces pride at having 'removed Saddam Hussein' he should remember that the British Attorney General advised him that regime change was illegal.

Goldsmith's later advice to Blair, made public on 17 March 2003, contained none of the careful reasoning that characterised the earlier document. Where the original report contained thirty-six detailed paragraphs extending to more than a dozen pages, the new submission sanctioning war comprised nine brief paragraphs on one page. This gross disparity invited the suspicion that the Attorney General, an intimate friend of the Prime Minister, had been pressured into authorising a war to which Blair and the Bush administration were already committed. (Goldsmith was subsequently rewarded with a $2 million-a-year job with the American law firm Debevoise & Plimpton.) Philippe Sands, professor of law at University College London, expressed a widespread view:

> The publication of the March 7 document [under protest from Blair] makes it clear that the Prime Minister was willing to play fast and loose with the presentation of legal advice. It also makes clear the fact that the Attorney General was willing to go along with this, and as such it raises concerns of the greatest constitutional significance.[11]

Goldsmith had carefully highlighted the ambiguities of Resolution 1441 (8 November 2002) to leave open the possibility that it might be legitimately used to 'revive' the authorisation for war contained in Resolution 678 (27 November 1990), but this option was vulnerable to two major objections: 1) Resolution 678 required the Security Council to judge what measures were 'necessary' to evict the Iraqi forces from Kuwait, and this judgement was never given; and 2) All the members of the Security Council declared on 8 November 2002 that Resolution 1441 was not intended to authorise war. John Negroponte (for the US) and Sir Jeremy Greenstock (Britain) said, in almost identical language, that the resolution contained no 'hidden triggers' or 'automaticity' with regard to war, and that if Iraq was in further breach of UN resolutions the matter would be returned to the Security Council for discussion. Other members of the Security Council – France, Mexico, Ireland, Russia, Bulgaria, Syria, Colombia, Cameroon and China – took pains to emphasise that this was also their understanding of the resolution; and on the same day Russia, France and China, all permanent members of the Security Council, issued a joint statement confirming that Resolution 1441 did not authorise force and that if necessary the matter would be returned to the Council. The Syrian statement, made immediately after the adoption of the resolution, conveyed the unanimous view on that day:

Syria voted in favour of the resolution, having received reassurances from its sponsors, the United States of America and the United Kingdom, and through France and Russia through high-level contacts, that it would not be used as a pretext for striking against Iraq and does not constitute a basis for any automatic strikes against Iraq. *The resolution should not be interpreted…as authorising any State to use force. It reaffirms the central role of the Security Council in addressing all phases of the Iraq issue* [emphasis added].

In short, Security Council Resolution 1441 did not authorise or justify the 2003 invasion. Washington and London only decided to use the resolution to justify war when it was plain that the second war-enabling resolution could not be obtained. The US and Britain had lied and dissembled in order to prosecute an illegal war.

Moreover, according to Alastair Campbell's diaries (2007), the British Cabinet had severe doubts about Blair's planned invasion of Iraq – and, with the exception of Foreign Secretary Robin Cook, kept quiet about them. In much subsequent commentary, in both the US and Britain, there were frequent references to 'lies', 'incompetence', 'mendacity', 'dishonour' and the like – and all this was before the full catastrophe of the bloody occupation had unfolded for all the world to see.

There is now a substantial literature on the 2003 invasion and its aftermath, much of it shocking and deeply harrowing – descriptions of the overflowing Baghdad morgue; death squads linked to the Iraqi government roaming hospitals looking for victims; the razing of whole communities; the stream of headless bodies found in the street; the desperate fleeing of thousands of families; the targeting of civilians by sectarian factions and the US military; the growing incidence of torture perpetrated by Iraqi personnel and American guards; the hell of Iraqi prisons and Abu Ghraib; and so on. The American interrogator Tony Lagouranis tells us how interrogation typically escalated into torture – mostly involving tens of thousands of innocent Iraqi victims;[12] Lawrence Anthony notes how Iraqis were 'pink misted',[13] vaporised at huge distances by the marvels of modern American firepower; we learn that Iraq had become, like all battle zones, a vast experimental laboratory in which, for example, the Pentagon exercised some 4,000 robot vehicles and other hi-tech devices throughout the country; and Jeremy Scahill reminds us that US-funded mercenaries had become the second largest military force in Iraq, despite a 1989 UN convention banning all mercenary activity.[14]

General Sir Michael Rose, speaking from vast military experience, used his impressive book *Washington's War* to draw analogies between the American forces fighting in the War of Independence to crush a British imperial occupation and the Iraqi forces today struggling to end a US occupation of their country:

> As [an aide] said at the end of the American War of Independence, 'though the people of America might be conquered by well disciplined European troops, the country of America is unconquerable'. *These words provide as fitting an epitaph for the folly that was Britain's war in North America in the eighteenth century as they do today for Bush and Blair's ill-judged war in Iraq* [emphasis added].[15]

On 5 July 2007 the *Los Angeles Times* recorded that George Bush also saw similarities between the Iraq War and the American war for independence, with the US troops in Iraq (having invaded a foreign country) mysteriously equated with the American revolutionaries who had 'picked up their muskets [in their own country] to fight for liberty'. On other occasions George Bush transmuted himself into a sometimes unpopular Harry Truman determined to crush Adolf Hitler (maintaining a foreign occupation in Europe), just as Saddam Hussein had to be extirpated from Iraq (his own country). In August 2007 David Halberstam, commenting in *Vanity Fair* that Bush's 'history' was based on 'wishful thinking, arrogance, and a total disdain for the facts', highlighted the widespread perception of the American president's ignorance, if not his tenuous grip on reality.

The behaviour of the Bush and Blair administrations inevitably raised the question of legal accountability. The Nuremberg Declaration had declared: 'To initiate a war of aggression . . . is not only an international crime, it is the supreme international

crime differing only from other war crimes in that it contains
within itself the accumulated evil of the whole.' (In addition,
there was a plethora of legal violations of the sort highlighted by
former US Attorney General Ramsey Clark in connection with
the 1991 Gulf War.) The UN secretary general, Kofi Annan, had
declared that the US-led invasion of Iraq was inconsistent with the
Charter of the United Nations and in consequence illegal. So
should the principal architects of the war be arraigned before an
appropriate court – for example, the International Criminal Court
(ICC), the International Court of Justice (ICJ) or a specially
constituted UN tribunal, as with Rwanda and the Balkans? On 24
April 2007 *The Times*, under the heading 'Does Blair deserve to
be in the dock?', discussed recent theatrical and television
depictions of the British Prime Minister being brought to legal
account for his alleged crimes.

The US had not recognised the ICC and would dispute the
jurisdiction of the ICJ; but Tony Blair and his erstwhile colleagues
could in principle be taken before the ICC, and there was the
precedent – namely, the case of Nicaragua in the 1980s – of
the ICJ overruling US claims regarding jurisdiction (in 1986 the
ICJ delivered a multifaceted conviction of the US for terrorist acts).

Moreover, there was the possibility of taking legal action
against George Bush, Tony Blair and their ministers under
domestic legislation. In both countries the option of impeachment
had been widely discussed. On 7 May 2007 *The Nation* published
an article, headed 'Impeachment fever rises', on the possibility of
holding 'lawless presidents' to account; and on 15 May the
Washington Post ran an advertisement from fifty-six members of
the 1982 Harvard Law School class, of which Attorney General
Alberto Gonzales had been a member, chastising him for his
'failure to stand for the rule of law' in carrying out various actions,
including 'sweeping aside the Geneva Conventions in order to
justify torture', removing habeas corpus from constitutional
protections, claiming power to wiretap US citizens without
warrants, and for firing US attorneys on political grounds. It is
hard to imagine that such charges – all of them directly or
indirectly relevant to Iraq – could not form the basis of legal action
against Gonzales and other members of the Bush administration.

On 30 May 2007 Maine became the eleventh US state legislature to introduce a petition for the impeachment of President Bush and vice-President Dick Cheney. Already fourteen state Democratic parties had passed resolutions supporting impeachment, as had some eighty-five cities and towns, either by public vote or by a vote of the local government, or both. The possibility of legal action being taken in the future against Bush, Blair and others for war crimes, crimes against humanity and genocide cannot be ruled out. In this context one other important consideration should not be forgotten. There can be no doubt that the behaviour of Washington and London over Iraq has severely damaged the moral authority of the US and Britain around the world. One obvious way to begin rebuilding that authority would be for those countries to acknowledge the enormities committed in their name and to bring those responsible for such copious legal derelictions to account.

This book presents detailed information that bears on these topics. It was impossible to deal with the many aspects exhaustively, but sufficient month-by-month information is included to convey the character of the Iraq War and the shifting politics that surround it. Attention is given to the legality of the war (see above), the nature of the military occupation, the parts played by governments and the overwhelming signs that this ill-considered and brutal conflict is moving into a decisive endgame (Chapters 1 to 10). Finally (Chapter 11), some of the lies associated with the launching of the 2003 invasion and its aftermath are indicated and brief attention included about the regional scene. The Iraq War has implications that reach far beyond the principal actors in this catastrophe.

It is in the nature of war that many social and political questions, formerly dormant, are freshly paraded for scrutiny, and that 'unintended consequences' are generated, often to the deep disquiet and alarm of the belligerents. The Iraq conflict has encouraged examination of, for example, the role of private companies in modern war-making, media responsibilities in informing people what is being perpetrated in their name, the relevance of established legal instruments for the protection of civilians and combatants, the constitutional provisions of sovereign states intending war, how individuals and states can be made accountable for their legal and ethical derelictions, and the wider global ramifications of military interventions in sovereign countries.

The matter of 'unintended consequences' should be approached with caution. It is unlikely that the social and political chaos in Iraq, with the further consequence of a Greater Iran emerging from the ruins, was intended by the Washington strategists, but at least one pillar of American society is benefiting hugely from the further carnage and destruction in a foreign country: the abundant shareholders of the major and minor corporations. This goes far beyond the ambitions of such oilmen as Bush, Baker, Cheney, Rumsfeld and others (Condoleezza Rice was formerly on the board of Chevron and an oil tanker bore her name), extending to vast swathes of free-enterprise America. It also reaches far beyond the arms manufacturers, obvious beneficiaries of war, extending to countless construction companies, transport providers, food delivery enterprises, communications firms, computer companies, mercenary providers (one of them claiming 'to have more generals than the Pentagon') and the rest. Many of these corporations, hedging their bets, enthusiastically fund both Republican and Democrat candidates, thus buying political influence where it matters.

Little need be said about the American arms manufacturers: in many sectors the factories are humming, employment is secure and the shareholders are being suitably rewarded; but Iraq does not encourage the production of cruise missiles, as it did through the 1990s. American factories are brimming with huge inventories of intelligent guided bombs, crammed with state-of-the-art technology, and needing to be tested 'in the field'. If evasive insurgents in Sadr City and Baghdad are not suitable targets, where else could such impressive weapons be used to good effect? Are there signs that American foreign policy is preparing the ground for a congenial depletion of cruise missile inventories?

The apparently unintended consequences of the Iraq War also include encouragement for a resurgent Islamism, necessitating, in some Western perspectives, the so-called 'war on terror'. Here we should tread with care. Do governments with authoritarian instincts have their own secret objectives? Do they regard the occasional terrorist attacks in Western and other countries as a worthwhile price to facilitate the gradual erosion of domestic human rights? Do they feel uncomfortable with real freedom and genuine democracy? How does real political power operate in society? Social turmoil, such as war, invites many such questions.

The main purpose of this book is to chart a seminal phase in an Iraq conflict that in fact began in 1990. The long Western war on Iraq has a grim continuity.

1

Surge: a new way forward?

By early 2007 it had become plain to all sections of international opinion that the US-led invasion of Iraq in March 2003 had degenerated into an unmitigated disaster. The original reasons for war – Iraq's alleged possession of weapons of mass destruction and its alleged links with al-Qaeda – had been exposed as at best mistaken assumptions and at worst unconscionable lies. And the declared aims of establishing a liberal democracy in Iraq, where the rule of law and human rights would be observed and which would serve as a beacon of freedom in a region unaccustomed to democratic values, were in shreds. For months, perhaps years, the United States had been engaged in a damage limitation exercise, but the comprehensive damage being inflicted on the Iraqi people was not the issue. What was important was the need to salvage something of America's international reputation, to avoid a Vietnam-style military defeat and to sustain something of the *realpolitik* goals of the illegal invasion.[1]

On 15 March 2006 members of both parties in the US Congress supported the creation of the bipartisan Iraq Study Group, to be co-chaired by James A. Baker III and Lee H. Hamilton, which would review the deteriorating situation in Iraq and to propose strategies for the way forward. For more than eight months the group met with military officers, regional experts, academics, journalists and high-level government officials from the US and abroad.[2] In the event the group's report, published in December 2006,[3] contained some seventy-nine recommendations, all of them relevant to US policy and intended to support American interests.[4] In the following months some of the report's recommendations would be ignored by the Bush administration, others implemented. Perhaps the main virtue of the report was to highlight, albeit in general terms without much detail, the appalling state of Iraq after more than three years of American occupation. The situation in Iraq was 'grave and deteriorating',[5] and the Iraqi people were being subjected to 'great suffering':

> There is no guarantee for success in Iraq. The situation in Baghdad and several provinces is dire . . . The government is not adequately advancing national reconciliation, providing basic security, or delivering essential services. The level of violence is high and growing. There is great suffering and the lives of many Iraqis show little or no improvement. Pessimism is pervasive.[6]

The report's acknowledgement of a deteriorating situation and the suffering of the Iraqi people did nothing to disguise the principal focus of the document. In the conclusions to the assessment of the situation in Iraq, details were given of the cost to the US of the American involvement, with no comparable statistics provided of the cost to Iraq. Thus the report noted that, as of December 2006, nearly 2,900 Americans had been killed, 21,000 had been wounded, roughly $400 billion had been spent on the war, and some estimates of 'tail costs' suggested that the war would cost the US as much as $2 trillion in total.[7] Hence it was left to other enquiries and other reports to attempt estimates of the scale of the catastrophe that had been visited on the Iraqi people.

The Human Rights Office of the United Nations Assistance Mission for Iraq (UNAMI), empowered by Security Council Resolution 1546,[8] was providing regular reports about the human rights situation in the country to assist the Iraqi government in its 'ultimate aim' of 'ensuring lasting stability and security'. In reality the US-supported Iraqi regime was completely incapable of providing security and often seemed unwilling or incapable of providing UNAMI with requested information. Thus, following the publication of a UNAMI report of 16 January 2007, the Iraqi

Prime Minister's office declared that the mortality figures contained in the report were exaggerated, although they were in fact official figures compiled and provided by a government ministry.[9] The new report noted that it was 'a matter of regret' that the Iraqi government refused to provide UNAMI with access to the Ministry of Health's overall mortality figures for the reporting period,[10] thus encouraging speculation that the US 'surge' policy was causing escalating civilian casualties that the American authorities and the Iraqi regime were keen to disguise. Already independent estimates suggested that the invasion and occupation were responsible for the deaths of at least tens of thousands of Iraqi civilians and at most a million.[11] And in every other area of human rights the situation in Iraq was appalling and deteriorating.

The United Nations High Commissioner for Refugees (UNHCR) had revealed that an estimated 736,422 people had been forced to flee their homes since the bombing of the al-Askari shrine in Samarra on 22 February 2006. Of these, more than 200,000 had been displaced since December 2006,[12] and there was evidence that the US surge was forcing many more people to flee from the mounting violence. UNAMI was able to provide evidence of the continuing impact of car bombs and other attacks on the civilian population. On 22 January 2007 two bombs exploded in the Bab al-Sharki market in central Baghdad, killing an estimated eighty-eight people and wounding 160 others.[13] UNAMI also noted armed groups competing for territorial domination, members of the Mahdi Army militia hanged on lamp posts, random firings in Haifa Street, and the failure of the Iraqi special forces to prevent kidnappings, murders and other crimes. On 11 January eleven employees of the Minister of Oil were abducted by an armed group; and on 27 January eight employees working for al-Qimmah Computer Company in al-Karrada district were abducted from company headquarters, allegedly by gunmen wearing police uniforms.[14]

At the beginning of January up to fifty or more unidentified bodies were being found on a daily basis in Baghdad alone, with scores more in such areas as Mosul and Suwayra; in the first week of January the police reported finding 168 corpses in various parts of Iraq. And many of the casualties were being caused by joint coalition–Iraqi operations, such as the massacre of 260 people in the village of al–Zarka in the province of Najaf on 28 January, caused by actions by the Iraqi security forces and coalition aerial bombing.[15] In addition, UNAMI has also highlighted attacks on educational institutions, such as the firing of mortar rounds at Maysaloon High School in the Hay al-Yarmuk district of Mosul on 10 January, wounding four female students and also two women and three children who lived nearby; and on 28 January a mortar attack on al–Khulud School for Girls in Baghdad's Hay al-Adl district, killing five students and wounding twenty-one other people.[16]

On 11 January Professor Kamel Abdul-Hussein at Mosul University's Faculty of Law was shot dead by unknown gunmen on his way home; two days later Sheikh Yunis Hamid al-Sheikh Wahib, deputy head of the Association of Salahuddin Scholars and imam of the Awlad al-Hasan mosque, was gunned down at his home in Samarra; and on 17 January Professor Majid Nasser Hussein of Baghdad University was shot dead in the Adhamiya district. On 28 March Sami Sitrik, the acting dean of al-Nahrain University's Law College, survived an assassination attempt. Sometimes targeted academics were given an opportunity to flee the country. Thus on 27 January a Basra University professor, his name withheld for security reasons, at first went into hiding and then left the country. The professor reported to UNAMI that a group calling itself the Doctrine Battalion (*Saraya Nusrat al-Mathhab*) had sent him an AK-47 bullet enclosed with a letter referring to him as a 'criminal atheist', accusing him of cooperating with the occupation forces and ordering him to leave Basra on pain of death. The front door of his apartment had been marked with an X and the word 'Wanted'.[17]

UNAMI has also recorded the arrest and killing of journalists, the targeting of religious and ethnic minorities, the plight of Palestinian refugees, the displacement of the civilian population and the gross abuse of women's rights. The many disastrous consequences of the occupation included an escalation of 'honour' killings and alleged attempted female suicides through burning. Typical cases concerned a woman who sustained 40 per cent burns to her body on 24 January, claiming that this was caused by a baking accident in the kitchen; a woman from Irbil who sustained 60 per cent burns from an alleged accident involving an exploding water boiler; and the charred remains of an unidentified woman, also in Irbil. The killing of women for alleged violations of Islamic law was also commonplace,[18] as were rapes, beatings and prolonged incarcerations. In January 2007, according to the Iraqi Ministry of Human Rights, there were 30,622 detainees in Iraq, mostly men but including thousands of women.[19] UNAMI has summarised the abuses of human rights that the system of incarceration involves: 'UNAMI remains concerned about procedures followed by the CCCI [Central Criminal Court of Iraq] and other criminal courts in Iraq, which consistently failed to meet minimum fair trial standards. Such trials are increasingly leading to the imposition of the death penalty.'[20]

The various 'serious pre-trial irregularities' included failure to bring defendants to court in a reasonable time, failure to apprise defendants of the reasons for their arrest, delays in access to legal counsel, the appointment by the courts of legal counsel unknown to the defendants and lacking knowledge of their clients' cases, and the failure to guarantee continuity of representation (so a defendant's trial counsel was often totally ignorant of what had transpired during the investigative phase). Detainees held by the occupation forces (the multinational force) were denied all access to legal counsel during the first sixty days of internment. Where defendants were eventually brought to trial the procedure was brief: the entire trial typically lasted fifteen to thirty minutes, even in complex cases that ended with a sentence of life imprisonment or the death penalty. Defendants, usually inadequately represented, often became aware of their right of appeal only after the deadline for submission had passed.[21]

Early January also witnessed widespread responses to the execution of Saddam Hussein on 30 December 2006 – in effect a lynching by baying Shi'ites following a rigged trial in a kangaroo court.[22] The images, taken on a mobile phone, of the Iraqi dictator's final moments also showed him being taunted by Shi'ite hangmen and witnesses, hooded executioners shouting at him to 'go to hell' and chanting 'Muqtada', invoking the name of Muqtada al-Sadr, the Shi'ite leader of the Mahdi Army.[23] The final video image showed Saddam with the noose around his neck as he recited the Muslim *shahada*, the last testimony, but before he could finish he was dropped through the floor to the sound of a trapdoor crashing open. The following day the Iraqi government ordered an investigation into how guards had taunted Saddam with 'inappropriate' slogans and filmed him as he was hanged.[24] On 3 January a spokesman for the US occupation forces, Major General William Caldwell, sought to absolve American personnel from the conduct of the execution, though admitting that the US military had transported witnesses to the hanging. Later Egypt's President, Hosni Mubarak, claimed that the 'revolting and barbaric' scenes at the execution had turned Saddam into a martyr.[25]

President George Bush slept through the execution in a seeming attempt to distance himself from the killing as the war was becoming increasingly unpopular in the US. Before he went to bed at 9 p.m. he left instructions that he was not to be disturbed and that a brief statement was to be released after Saddam's death, calling the execution an 'important milestone' but predicting further trouble in Iraq: 'Many difficult choices and further sacrifices lie ahead. Yet the safety and security of the American people require that we not relent in ensuring that Iraq's young democracy continues to progress.'[26]

The reactions throughout the Arab world were mixed, some welcoming the end of a tyrant and others outraged at the killing of a heroic opponent of Western 'crusaders'. One Iraqi Shi'ite cleric, Sayed Hassan Moussawi, performing the hajj in Saudi Arabia, declared that the ritual of 'stoning the devil' had acquired extra significance that year: 'We were also stoning Saddam.' Official Saudi sources said that many observers disapproved of the execution because it had taken place during the holy month of Dhu al-Hijjah and on the first day of Eid al-Adha, when Muslims slaughter sheep to commemorate the prophet Abraham's willingness to sacrifice his son for God. By contrast, Saad bin Tifla al-Ajmi, former information minister of Kuwait, commented:

'This [the execution] is the best Eid gift for humanity.'[27] Hundreds of Palestinians in the West Bank took to the streets to mourn Saddam's death and held a mock funeral in Jenin, chanting 'Death to Bush', 'Death to [Iraqi Prime Minister] al-Maliki' and 'Death to al-Sadr'. In Jordan, Palestinian Fatah demonstrators issued a statement describing Saddam as 'a martyr who was killed by the Americans and their allies in the Iraqi government'.[28]

While Bush was celebrating Saddam's killing, the British government was more circumspect. Deputy Prime Minister John Prescott denounced the manner of the execution as 'deplorable',[29] an adjective echoed by Chancellor Gordon Brown four days later.[30] But there was no attempt to denounce the fact of the execution, merely how it was carried out – and Prime Minister Tony Blair, the leader of a country with a supposedly principled opposition to capital punishment, remained silent. Peter Kilfoyle, a former Labour defence minister, urged Blair to break away from his holiday in Florida and make a statement; Alan Simpson, a leading Labour left-winger, spoke of the 'morally vacuous position that Tony Blair now occupies'; and Glenda Jackson, a former junior transport minister, commented that Blair's silence was 'amazing'.[31] It was left to a Tory parliamentarian, Boris Johnson, to condemn in the most vigorous terms the travesty of justice with which both Washington and London were plainly complicit:

> Was this what we fought for? . . . This wasn't justice. This was a sectarian lynch mob. This was a snuff movie. How dare the Prime Minister pretend that it is somehow nothing to do with him . . . It is ridiculous to pretend that a silence is somehow tactful because this 'is a matter for the Iraqis'. The trial itself was a farce.[32]

On 7 January Downing Street, increasingly sensitive to mounting criticism of the Prime Minister's silence, issued a statement declaring that the execution had been 'wrong and unacceptable', and a spokeswoman added that Blair 'does believe that the manner of execution was completely wrong, but that shouldn't lead us to forget the crimes that Saddam committed'.[33] Eventually, at a press conference on 9 January with the Japanese Prime Minister, Shinzo

Abe, Blair broke his silence to enlarge upon this theme: the manner of the execution of Saddam was 'completely wrong' but that 'should not blind us to the crimes he committed against his own people, including the death of hundreds of thousands of innocent Iraqis, one million casualties in the Iran–Iraq War and the use of chemical weapons against his own people, wiping out entire villages'.[34]

Here there was no principled opposition to the use of the death penalty, only a criticism of how it had been carried out. Moreover, Blair made no reference to the crime for which Saddam Hussein had supposedly been convicted in the Iraqi court, namely the killing of more than a hundred Dujail villagers in 1982. *Instead Blair cited the many alleged crimes which had never been tested in any court of law.* We need not dwell on such inconvenient details as Western complicity in Saddam's alleged crimes, the US-supported coalition designed to strengthen Iraq in its war against the Iranian ayatollahs, or the Pentagon's initial insistence that it was Iran, not Iraq, that had used chemical weapons against the Halabja victims. Here we need only emphasise that Blair's attempt to gloss over the fact of the execution by citing a plethora of alleged crimes is disreputable in a lawyer who should know better. Are people to be executed for mere allegations that are never tested by judicial due process? In a sense the question is academic. Saddam was judged to be guilty of all charges, whether aired in court or not, before the farce of the Iraqi judicial process commenced. The simple cliché of *victor's justice* was never more applicable.

Some desultory efforts were made to save Saddam's co-defendants from the gallows: for example, the United Nations secretary general, Ban Ki-Moon, and the European Union presidency appealed against the imminent executions of Saddam's half-brother Barzan Ibrahim and Awad Hamed al-Bandar, the former head of the revolutionary court, but to no avail. The executions were carried out, as with Saddam, after wholly inadequate court procedures. And the resulting accidental decapitation of al-Bandar was taken as further evidence of the incompetence of the Iraqi executioners. Now the Iraqi state was set to develop as one of the world's most enthusiastic supporters of the death penalty – a posture with which the supposedly anti-capital-punishment Tony Blair was directly complicit.

*

The execution of Saddam Hussein, the manner of its implementation and the aftermath invited many questions – not least concerning the indifference of the Bush–Blair axis to the rule of law. It was clear that the dramatic nature of the killing had served to obscure, albeit briefly, the impact of the war and occupation on the lives of ordinary Iraqi families. While Tony Blair was cataloguing Saddam's alleged crimes the UNHCR was claiming that the hundreds of thousands of Iraqis fleeing their violent homeland made up the largest long-term population movement in the Middle East since the founding of Israel in 1948. The UNHCR then launched an appeal for $60 million to help the 40,000 to 50,000 Iraqis now abandoning their homes each month, on top of the 3.7 million already displaced. With about a hundred Iraqis being killed every day, there was no prospect of an end to this 'massive and escalating displacement'.[35]

It was estimated that about one in eight Iraqis was displaced, though some had already fled before the US-led invasion of March 2003. Out of a population of 26 million, about 1.7 million were internally displaced, putting massive pressures on the moribund national infrastructure, while two million had fled to nearby states. Syria had taken in about a million Iraqis, Jordan 700,000, and Lebanon and Egypt between 20,000 and 40,000 each. Some Iraqis had fled to Turkey, others to Sweden and other European countries.[36] In September 2006 the US had laid down a quota of 500 Iraqi refugees for 2007, a totally inadequate number which was duly criticised by humanitarian groups.[37] Already the UNHCR was collating information on the escalating numbers of women forced into prostitution and the increasing exploitation of children, as a result of the destitution caused by the forced exodus.

The deteriorating situation in Iraq, signalled not least by the mounting US casualties, was inevitably impacting on the morale of the American political establishment, the Iraqi government and troops on the ground. It was anticipated that the newly installed Democrat-controlled Congress, following the Republican reversals in both the Senate and the House of Representatives in the November elections, would challenge afresh how the Bush administration was handling the war. It was thought that President Bush was about to announce a new escalation of the war, a 'surge' of an extra 30,000 troops, and to demand an additional $100 billion to fund the war through 2007. In early January even some Republicans, estimates suggested about a dozen, anticipating the 2008 elections, seemed increasingly reluctant to support an escalation of the war. Thus the Republican senator Chuck Hagel commented: 'I'm absolutely opposed to sending any more troops to Iraq. It is folly.'[38]

Senator Joseph Biden, a Democrat from Delaware, announced that he intended to hold three weeks of hearings on the war; and Stuart Rothenberg, the publisher of a Washington newsletter, commented: 'I think the White House will be answering lots of questions. There will be a blizzard of paper and I think we are in for a year of examination of administration policy.'[39] In the same vein, Tom Lantos, the chairman of the House of Representatives International Relations Committee, said that he would call the co-chairmen of the Iraq Study Group, James A. Baker III and Lee H. Hamilton, to aid his investigation of the war. The American opponents of the administration's Iraq policies, sensing that the political climate was moving strongly in their favour, were taking heart. They could not know how soon their hopes would be dashed.

On 3 January 2007 the Iraqi Prime Minister, Nouri al-Maliki, tired of trying to bring security to his country, revealed in a published report that he wished he could quit and that he would not seek a second term. It was 'impossible', he declared in a *Wall Street Journal* interview, that he would seek such a term:

> I wish it [his premiership] could be done with even before the end of this [four-year] term. I would like to serve my people from outside the circle of senior officials, maybe through the parliament, or working directly with the people. I didn't want to take this position. I only agreed because I thought it would serve the national interest, and I will not accept it again.[40]

Here was the plain recognition that the Iraqi Prime Minister had an impossible role. The US was constantly demanding that the

Iraqi regime 'step up' to its responsibilities for security, reconstruction and basic administration. But Iraq had a government only
in name: the regime, cloistered in the 'Green Zone' fortress, had
no control over what was happening on the streets, long
surrendered to Shi'ite militias, Sunni death squads and criminal
gangs. The Iraqi police and security forces, comprehensively
infiltrated by insurgent and other elements, could not be trusted.
The remit of the Maliki regime did not extend beyond the fortress
walls. If the US military could not impose peace and security, even
on Baghdad, what was their impotent placeman expected to do?

Al-Maliki's poor morale was increasingly reflected in the
attitudes of the US military, which was suffering extended tours
of duty and growing casualties, and becoming more and more
sceptical about its role in Iraq. General James Conway, the head
of the Marines, expressed a widespread concern that the American
public, disenchanted with the war, would not give the military the
time it needed in Iraq to stabilise the country: 'I fear there are two
timelines out there. One is how long it's going to take us to do
the job. One is how long the country [the United States] is going
to allow us to do the job. And they're not synching up.'[41]

The authors of *The Iraq Study Group Report*, presumably James A.
Baker III and Lee H. Hamilton, agreed with the goal of US policy
in Iraq, as stated by the President: an Iraq that can 'govern itself,
sustain itself, and defend itself'. But they judged it necessary to
propose 'a new way forward' to achieve the declared objective.[42]
Among the 'Alternative Courses' included for consideration the
option of 'more troops for Iraq', akin to the Bush administration's
planned 'surge', was considered – and rejected as a realistic policy:

> Sustained increases in US troop levels would not solve the
> fundamental cause of violence in Iraq, which is the absence of national
> reconciliation . . . Adding US troops might temporarily help limit
> violence in a highly localised area . . . Past experience indicates that
> the violence would simply rekindle as soon as US forces are moved.[43]

Moreover, the United States' military capacity was already
'stretched thin' and it would not be practical 'to make a

substantial, sustained increase in our troop presence'. To attempt any such troop increase in Iraq would necessarily hamper military efforts in Afghanistan and the ability to respond to other crises around the world.[44] The alternative was to increase the number of US troops 'embedded in and supporting Iraqi Army units' as a prelude to moving combat forces out of Iraq and 'restoring the US military'.[45]

There was nothing here that supported the idea of a troop surge to reduce the levels of violence in Baghdad and elsewhere. The Iraq Study Group, having deliberated for more than eight months, had produced its recommendations (ten out of the seventy-nine dealt with military matters) but President Bush, who proudly declared that he had read the report (a slight document of fewer than one hundred small-format text pages), was not about to implement fresh measures that pulled against his preconceptions. The report emphasised above all that, in the deteriorating situation of Iraq, 'a new approach' be adopted, and that this did not mean a simple escalation of military conflict.

Moreover, there were many problems associated with the idea of a troop surge. Where would the troops come from? Already morale in the US military was being seriously affected by sending soldiers back to Iraq for more tours than they had expected, and by denying them the customary period at home between tours. And how could faith be placed in an escalation of policies that had already failed? Was a troop surge really the 'new approach' that Baker and Hamilton, and many others, had emphasised was essential to improve the worsening situation in Iraq? And there was also the question of the Shi'ite-led Iraqi regime itself. Did it really want what the Bush administration was seemingly advocating: a multiethnic, multisectarian Iraq in which the Sunni minority would have a real stake in power? Or did the Shi'ites, now they had cast off decades of subservience, prefer a fragmented, possibly federal Iraq, in which the Sunnis were marginalised and powerless? Would the troop surge be working to an American agenda oblivious to the instincts of what Washington was happy to call the 'democratically elected government' of Iraq? And then there was the matter of practicalities.

It seemed that the surge would involve a decentralisation of US military power. Troops would be expected to forsake the relative safety of the heavily fortified bases and to fan out from localised entrenchments in Baghdad to expand the areas of security. The plan was fraught with hazard. Since the American troops would be more exposed, there would be more casualties – which would play badly back at home with an increasingly restless public and political class anticipating the 2008 elections. The execution of Saddam Hussein had coincided with the American fatality total reaching 3,000. Would Bush's troop surge mean another 3,000 American dead?

It now appeared that the new plan was even opposed by the US military as it, with the American public, turned against the war.[46] The news weekly *Army Times*, carrying a devastating criticism of the war, led an edition with the headline 'About-face on the war: after 3 years of support, troops sour on Iraq' and highlighted a poll that found for the first time that 'more troops disapprove of the president's handling of the war'.[47] Only a third of the service members surveyed in a *Military Times* poll approved of Bush's handling of the war, while 42 per cent disapproved. Only half of the troops believed that success in Iraq was likely, signalling poor morale. It was not difficult to see the reasons for such pessimism. As the University of Maryland's David Segal, director for the Center for Research on Military Organization, observed: 'They [the US troops] are seeing more casualties and fatalities and less progress.'[48] The *New York Times*, along with much of the American media, had at last been driven to acknowledge the enormity of what was being perpetrated in Iraq:

> On New Year's Day, readers of the *New York Times* could see the excruciating photo layout of the latest 1,000 American service members to die in Iraq. As in all wars, most of them were young. Many of them were smiling in the photos. All of them died unnecessarily. The war has been an exercise in futility and mind-boggling incompetence . . . [It is] as if the US had fallen into some kind of bizarrely destructive trance from which it is unable to awaken.[49]

Here, as in the vast bulk of American commentary, there is no attempt to indicate the scale of Iraqi casualties. It is acknowledged that the 'ordinary Iraqis' were paying the 'most grievous price of all' for 'this insanity', but in a long article the most abundant victims of the carnage, tormented in their own country, merit only one cursory sentence.[50] And in this context what should the 'ordinary Iraqis' themselves expect from George Bush's troop surge?

There would be more Iraqi deaths and injuries as troops swept through regions of the city, calling in tanks and air strikes where necessary, in an attempt at pacification. This in turn would be counter-productive, throwing more legions of the bereaved and infuriated into the arms of the insurgency. And once an area had seemingly been pacified, what then? The US troops, thin on the ground in a vast metropolis and with fresh missions to accomplish, would not hang around to police it. They would move on, expecting the Iraqi army and security forces, massively infiltrated by militia and death-squad elements, to maintain the peace. Perhaps an effort would be made to establish 'gated communities', with ordinary Iraqis required to show passes as they moved about their city, as in the manner of Fallujah. In such a fashion would the troop surge bring peace and tranquillity to anarchic chaos? The entire plan seemed grotesquely fanciful.

In addition to the surge, President Bush had other plans, not least a shuffling of military and diplomatic staff to minimise opposition to the planned troop escalation.[51] Lieutenant General David Petraeus,[52] who was head of the US Army's Combined Arms Centre at Fort Leavenworth and helped oversee the drafting of a military manual on counter-insurgency, was to be named as the top American military commander in Iraq, replacing General George Casey. Petraeus, who led the 'Screaming Eagles' of the 101st Airborne Division during the 2003 invasion of Iraq, was to be charged with the task of implementing the troop surge and reporting in September 2007 as to its success. Admiral William Fallon, the top US admiral in the Pacific, then commanding 300,000 personnel from the army, navy, air force and marines, was expected to replace General John Abizaid as the head of

Central Command, which oversees both Iraq and Afghanistan. It was known that both Casey and Abizaid were deeply sceptical about the troop surge. Since the Iraq problem seemingly had little to do with naval matters, Fallon's appointment also encouraged speculation that the Bush administration was keen to counter Iran's growing power in the region.

The then ambassador to Iraq, the Afghan-born Sunni Zalmay Khalilzad, was to be moved to the UN and replaced in Baghdad by Ryan Crocker, a veteran of Middle East diplomacy, formerly ambassador to Syria, Kuwait and Lebanon and at this time the envoy to Pakistan. Retired vice-admiral Mike McConnell was appointed to take over as director of national intelligence from John Negroponte, who was moving to the State Department as Condoleezza Rice's deputy. And Bush also accepted the resignation of Harriet Myers, his White House counsel, thought to be insufficiently robust to handle the anticipated Democrat onslaught. A senior Bush administration official commented: 'The idea is to put the whole new team in at roughly the same time, and send some clear messages that we are trying a new approach.'[53]

On 5 January 2007, for the first time in twelve years, the Democrats took control of both houses of Congress,[54] and Nancy Pelosi became the first woman speaker of the House of Representatives. When handed the speaker's gavel, she received a standing ovation. 'I accept this gavel in the spirit of partnership, not partisanship,' she commented, but she put the President on notice that the American people opposed an open-ended commitment to the Iraq War. Harry Reid, the new Democrat leader of the Senate, made the same point. But it seemed clear that Bush would ignore calls from the Democrats and some Republicans for a 'responsible withdrawal' from the country. Thomas Mann, a congressional scholar at the Brookings Institution, commented: 'His [Bush's] apparent decision to surge US forces in Iraq will be wildly unpopular, in the country and in Congress. The ensuing battles [between Democrats and Republicans] are likely to diminish any chance of cooperation on domestic issues.'[55] There was growing speculation that Senator Joseph Biden, the new chairman of the

Senate Foreign Relations Committee, was preparing to put forward a resolution explicitly opposing the sending of more troops to Iraq. The surge, he suggested, was a means of postponing disaster so that the next President would be 'the guy landing helicopters inside the green zone taking people off the roof'[56] – a reference to America's panicky exit from its embassy in Saigon at the end of the Vietnam War.

The terms of the anticipated Bush announcement were clear. The surge, it was assumed, would be accompanied by a handover of many provinces to Iraqi government control and would be intended to herald 'victory' in Iraq, however that was to be defined. Again it was being reported that up to 20,000 extra troops would be deployed in Baghdad and Anbar province, which the Pentagon had claimed were the location for 54 per cent of all attacks in Iraq through 2006. An unnamed senior defence source commented: 'Most Iraqi provinces are pretty calm and where they're not, our presence is probably causing the trouble.'[57]

According to Major General William Caldwell, a military spokesman, all Iraqi army divisions would be under Iraqi command by the summer of 2007, and all provinces would be under Iraqi control by the autumn. Dan Goure, a military analyst at the Lexington Institute in Virginia, suggested that the accelerated timetable for handing everything over to the Iraqis would 'look like the beginning of a withdrawal'.[58] There was debate also about the likely size of the planned surge, with some observers suggesting that a small surge would be totally counter-productive. Thus Senator John McCain, enthusiastic for the plan, said: 'The worst of all worlds would be a short, small surge. This surge must be significant and sustained. Otherwise don't do it.'[59] As a gesture to the Iraq Study Group, largely ignored, the plan also included a doubling of the number of US troops embedded as trainers and advisors with Iraqi forces.

Bush was also expected to set the Iraqi government a series of tough benchmarks as a means of shifting responsibility from the US military to the Baghdad regime, and to include elements of a broader economic package. One suggestion was that the Sunnis should have a greater role in the political process, while oil revenues could be more fairly distributed throughout the regions.[60] It was thought that a renewed reconstruction package costing up to $1 billion would be offered[61] – though in the context of previous funds disappearing through endemic corruption, abandoned projects, and foreign companies fleeing the country, any suggestion of more aid for reconstruction was an empty promise. The troop surge itself, following discussions between the Bush administration and Nouri al-Maliki, would involve a troop increase of up to five combat brigades to supplement the 130,000 American troops already on the ground and would be matched by a rise in Iraqi army numbers.

Some Democrats seemed determined to exploit their position in Congress to promote anti-war policies, but already there were signs that the Democrat leadership did not relish a battle with the White House. Pelosi and Reid had written to Bush saying that they were opposed to any policy of troop increases and that soldiers should begin to be brought home in four months' time, but it remained to be seen how far the Democrats would be prepared to push such opposition. The Bush administration was already arguing that any restriction on funds for his new strategy, now called 'A New Way Forward', would be a betrayal of the troops on the ground, and the Democrats seemed unclear how to counter such a charge.

On 7 January 2007 Pelosi declared that the Democrats would refuse to give Bush 'a blank cheque with no oversight, no standards, no conditions'; if he intended to escalate the war 'in his budget request, he is going to have to *justify* it and this is new for him' (emphasis added).[62] Commentators were quick to emphasise that, even though the Pelosi statement cast a cloud over the possibility of a trouble-free cross-party approach, it was far from an unambiguous pledge to block fresh funds for reinforcements. The Democrats, who by virtue of their congressional majority controlled the purse strings, were not planning a constitutional confrontation with the President, the US Commander in Chief. Already it seemed that – even against the wishes of Congress, the recommendations of the Iraq Study Group and public opinion – Bush's surge policy was under no serious threat. What 'justification' would satisfy Pelosi and the other leading Democrats? Would it be sufficient for Bush simply to read out carefully drafted rhetoric about 'the need to support our troops in the field', 'the American patriotic duty' and 'defeat not being an option'?

On 8 January the *Washington Post* reported Iraqi Health Ministry figures showing that 22,950 Iraqis met violent deaths in 2006, with 17,310 having died in the previous six months – indicating the mounting sectarian and other tensions in the country. The reported figures were almost double those claimed by the Iraqi Interior Ministry for the same year. Hakim al-Zamily, the deputy health minister, refused to confirm his ministry's figures but said: 'I have heard there is an increase in the number of victims.'[63] This was the context in which Bush was due to announce the troop increase.

It was clear that individual Democrats were prepared by any means possible to oppose a troop increase. On 9 January, a day before the expected Bush speech, Senator Edward Kennedy proposed legislation denying the President the requested billions needed to fund the surge without congressional approval:

> The American people ought to have a voice and a vote and members of Congress should be held accountable. We ought to take this step and stop the surge. The best immediate way to support our troops is by refusing to inject more and more of them into the cauldron of a civil war that can be resolved only by the people and government of Iraq.[64]

With no guarantee that such a bill would reach the full Senate, it was intended to serve as a rallying point for robust opponents of the war. Reid was saying that the Democrats would 'look at everything' in their power to curb the war, short of cutting money for troops already in the field, and that the surge would only be considered if Bush started to withdraw troops within six months. And in the same vein Carl Levin, chairman of the Senate Armed Services Committee, declared that 'the only way' to focus the attention of the Iraqi government on its own responsibilities was to tell it 'that we're going to redeploy our forces in four to six months'.[65] John Edwards, seeking the Democrat presidential nomination, had distanced himself from his fellow candidates Hillary Clinton and Barack Obama by calling for an immediate withdrawal of US troops. Thus, interviewed by the *New Yorker*, he said: 'Let's start leaving. We've devoted enormous resources, human and otherwise . . . We've reached the place . . . where the Iraqis are going to have to take responsibility.'[66]

On 10 January Bush announced in a widely anticipated and carefully scripted televised speech that he would send 21,500 additional troops to Iraq, claiming that it had been a mistake that more US troops had not been provided earlier.[67] He emphasised that the new policy would help America 'succeed in the fight against terror', and added: 'If we increase our support at this crucial moment and help the Iraqis break the current cycle of violence, we can hasten the day our troops begin coming home.'[68] Dan Bartlett, a White House counsellor, was now blaming the Maliki government for putting certain districts of Baghdad off limits: 'Military operations were handcuffed by political interference by the Iraqi leadership. They [the Iraqi forces] are going to have more boots on the ground. They're going to be the ones doing the knocking on the door.'[69]

The new security plan had been discussed with al-Maliki, though many observers doubted his ability to deliver. He remained unable to enforce any legislation passed in the Iraqi parliament or to command any armed forces. In the words of the English journalist Simon Jenkins, 'to tell [al-Maliki] to "bring the militias to heel" is like telling a junior cop to arrest Al Capone'.[70] And the extra US troops would fare no better. All that could be expected was a more comprehensive slaughter, the use of unassailable American firepower to lay waste yet more communities, and the consequent efforts of the US military to muzzle honest reportage.

The new policy, ignoring much of *The Iraq Study Group Report*, was a clear admission that the US was failing in Iraq: casualties on all sides were mounting; the country was in chaos; the militias held sway in many regions; and reconstruction aid had been swallowed by mendacity and corruption. An unnamed Bush administration official acknowledged that the previous strategy of 'clear, hold, build' – clearing the areas and remaining there to facilitate reconstruction – had failed: 'We cleared but did not hold and the build never arrived.'[71] The surge would increase US troop levels from 132,000 to 154,000, with no end date in sight, but even these bald figures disguised a piece of propaganda spin. It was being pointed out that in fact Bush would not be sending extra fresh troops into the conflict, since there were hardly any combat units in reserve. Some exhausted units would be ordered to stay in Iraq for months after their normal tours were over, and previously planned deployments would be brought forward – all creating the illusion of a statistical troop surge, but in circumstances where the army chiefs were already complaining that their forces were overstretched. Thus General Abizaid had told Congress that troop levels could be increased by 20,000 temporarily but 'the ability to sustain that commitment is not something we have right now with the size of the army and the marine corps'.[72] The new Defense Secretary, Robert Gates, was ordering a permanent increase in the size of the US army and marine corps, at a likely extra cost of $15 billion per year, but it was obvious that the new troops would not be immediately available for service. Earlier recruitment campaigns had not met targets, and in 2006 the maximum age for recruits was raised from thirty-five to forty, and then to forty-two; visible tattoos above the neck were no longer prohibited; and candidates who were overweight or who suffered from attention deficit disorder were no longer turned away. General Petraeus, newly installed in Iraq after his previous experience in Mosul, was being asked to report when he had attempted for some months to implement the new policy. It seemed obvious – with Congress, much of the military and the American people dissatisfied with Bush's policies – that the President would need an unambiguous return from his gamble.

The Bush administration was not helped by indications of British intentions to reduce its troop contingent in the country. Over Christmas 2006 the British forces had stormed the headquarters of the corrupt Serious Crimes Unit based at the police station in the Jamiat district of Basra and then blown up the building. Some members of the provincial council felt that the action had been unnecessary and done without authorisation. Such events were helping to undermine any attempts to 'win hearts and minds' as a route to success in the country.

Members of the Mahdi Army were now issuing fresh threats against the foreign troops in the area, forcing the British contingent to spend much of its time in relatively secure barracks. Despite the much-hyped Operation Sinbad the British patrols were accomplishing little, apart from offering the insurgents new opportunities for target practice. The 1,200 British troops at Basra Palace and the 1,000 at the Shatt-al-Arab Hotel were facing a daily onslaught of mortar and rocket attacks, including twenty-three bombardments in the first week of January. Much of the region had been surrendered to the local Shi'ite militias and their bloody contest for power, rendering any thought of British-imposed security and effective training of non-sectarian Iraqi forces illusory. What, wondered many British personnel, were they doing camped in army bases while conflict raged around them?

However, it was still necessary to maintain the propaganda front. Thus a defence source said that the British presence was filling the security vacuum and that power would have to be handed over effectively to the Iraqi army and police 'to ensure that the vacuum is filled by an organisation that will deliver security legitimately and democratically'[73] – as if a *de facto* surrender of power to 'illegitimate' Iraqi factions was not already taking place.

President Bush's speech announcing the administration's 'new way forward' had been greeted with general scepticism. The US military had formerly declined to enter Sadr City, the stronghold of the main Shi'ite militias, in force and there were widespread doubts that the extra troops would be sufficient to encroach significantly on Muqtada al-Sadr's territory. However, on 11 January Defence Secretary Gates made it clear that earlier military restraint would not apply in the new situation: 'All parts of Baghdad are going to be involved in this campaign, including Sadr City.'[74] A battle between the US military and the Mahdi Army in Najaf in 2003 had not been followed by further American attacks on Shi'ite factions, but now it seemed that the US forces would be targeting all insurgent groups, Shi'ite and Sunni.

Supporters of the surge were suggesting that Fallujah and Tal Afar,[75] scenes of huge Iraqi casualties and massive destruction, were examples of what might be achieved in Baghdad. While the capital could not be cut off entirely, separated from the rest of the country, it was hoped that gated communities could be created, with entry controlled by fences, gates and security staff. This policy, reminiscent of how the Israeli army prevented Palestinians from free movement around their own villages and towns, was intended to establish safe zones that would spread 'like ink blots' to wider communities. Iraqi residents would be issued with ID badges and movement from and to the secured zones would be logged as a prelude to creating an accurate census of those people in the area. But even the US military had doubts about the plan. Thus a senior defence source commented that such a plan might have worked in 2003 or 2004, 'but it is probably too late now'.[76]

Other military observers were sceptical whether the highly sectarian Iraqi army, drafted into the Bush plan, would be capable of confronting the Shi'ite militias; or even whether Iraqi politicians, themselves dependent on militia support, would be willing to encourage such a policy. In fact the US military had orchestrated earlier initiatives – Operation Forward Together and Operation Forward Together II – that similarly envisaged Iraqi troops taking a lead role in pacifying Baghdad, but only two of six battalions promised by the Iraqi government actually turned up for action. In the new plan American troops would be embedded in Iraqi units with the aim of stiffening their resolve. Prime Minister al-Maliki, George Bush had implied, would be in trouble if the plan did not work out – and so, it seemed, would Bush. Immediately after the President's televised address a *Washington Post*/ABC poll showed that 61 per cent of Americans opposed the plan, while just 36 per cent backed it. Another poll, by Associated Press and Ipsos, indicated 70 per cent of respondents against sending more troops to Iraq.[77]

Bush had also declared that Syria and Iran were allowing 'terrorists and insurgents' to move in and out of Iraq, and that the US would 'seek out and destroy the networks providing advanced weaponry and training to our enemies in Iraq'.[78] Did this herald military strikes against Iraq's neighbours? For months, citing Iran's nuclear programme, the Bush administration had been hinting at the likelihood of attacks on Iran. How would the newly Democratic Congress respond to this enhanced possibility?

In Iraq the insurgents responded with their own comment on the planned troop surge: Bush's 22,000 new troops would be sent home in body bags. Thus Abu Moath, an insurgent with the National Front for the Liberation of Iraq, declared:

> Twenty thousand soldiers will never be able to achieve what 140,000 have failed to achieve so far, and the fate of the new soldiers will not be any better than for those who were here before them. They came here to kill innocent Iraqis so they should all be killed the same way.[79]

In the same vein Ahmed al-Hassani, of the militant group Ansar al-Sunna, said: 'We will keep going in our war that does not accept any mid-way solutions. Either they pull out of our country or the war will continue until we achieve victory.'[80] The Mahdi Army, while not expecting a massive confrontation throughout Sadr City, was reportedly ordering every man aged between fifteen and forty-five to register for combat against the US troop surge.[81] Again it seemed that the Iraqi government had little appetite for a full-on confrontation with the powerful Shi'ite militia factions. Thus one Maliki aide told *The Times* that the fresh Baghdad offensive would first concentrate on outlying Sunni insurgent strongholds that were choking the city:

> [Al-Maliki] argues that the way to deal with the Mahdi Army is to bring down the level of terrorist attacks so ordinary Shia don't feel the need for the Mahdi. Right now they think the Mahdi is bad, but without them they would be killed by al-Qaeda and the others.[82]

In addition there were also other signs that al-Maliki, as well as lacking the requisite powers to impose security, was out of sympathy with various aspects of American policy:

- In December 2006 the Maliki government invited several Iranian officials to Baghdad, whereupon the US military arrested them.
- In November al-Maliki ordered US forces to lift roadblocks they had put in place to help track down a missing American soldier.

- The Iraqi authorities pressed ahead with the execution of Saddam Hussein, despite American demands that it be delayed for political reasons.
- On 24 October 2006, when Zalmay Khalilzad and General George Casey announced a new timetable for establishing security, al-Maliki denied that he had agreed to any such plan and emphasised Iraqi sovereignty.
- On 25 October, when US and Iraqi forces raided Sadr City, al-Maliki said that he had not been consulted and 'that it will not be repeated'.
- When US forces embedded with Iraqi units urged actions against the Shi'ite militia, al-Maliki overruled them.
- Al-Maliki condemned the Israeli attack on Lebanon in July 2006 and arranged a high-level meeting with Iran's President Mahmoud Ahmadinejad in Tehran, to the anger of the United States.[83]

Already the policy rifts between the Bush administration and the Maliki government were plain.

In the United States the new policy continued to attract criticism, though largely from predictable sources. Harry Reid, branding the surge 'a serious mistake', commented that President Bush was now 'virtually standing alone', and predicted that the Senate would vote overwhelmingly to reject the policy in a non-binding resolution; Chuck Hagel, speaking at Senate hearings after Bush's speech and addressing Condoleezza Rice, declared: 'It [the surge policy] is morally wrong. It's tactically, strategically, militarily wrong. We will not win a war of attrition in the Middle East. This speech given last night by this President represents the most dangerous foreign policy blunder since Vietnam. I will resist it.'[84] These comments were greeted by applause from the public gallery; while by contrast remarks by Rice were greeted with shouts of 'You lie! More lies! Stop lying! Stop the war!'[85] A protester was escorted away.

In Iran, Foreign Ministry spokesman Mohammad Ali Hosseini denounced the surge as a 'continuation of occupation, to be condemned', a policy which would 'extend insecurity, danger and tension'. In Syria the Vice-President, Farouk al-Sharaa, said that the American troop increase was 'not a positive step'; while a Syrian MP and former deputy Foreign Minister, Suleiman Hadad, said that the US plan was 'an escalation devoid of any signs of peace'. In France Philippe Douste-Blazy, the Foreign Minister, was sceptical of any military solution: 'It is through a comprehensive approach, through a political strategy, that Iraq will regain stability.' In Russia defence spokesman Vladimir Shamanov said that additional troops 'would not be able to radically change the situation' and ensure peace and security. And in Germany Karsten Voigt, a senior foreign office spokesman, commented that the US President had in the past often proved to be 'too optimistic' about US policies.[86] It was now clear that, in the teeth of domestic and international opinion, the Bush administration was escalating failed policies. Prime Minister al-Maliki had been put under political pressure in the past, but to no avail. Now Zalmay Khalilzad, leaving Iraq to become ambassador to the UN, insisted that the Iraqi Prime Minister was facing a 'last chance' to end sectarian divisions and to create a properly functioning government. The threat was plain: '[Al-Maliki] has pledged this to the President of the US. There will be no sanctuary. He has said to me that he has given sanctuary a chance with the militias. Now we have to do whatever is necessary.'[87] In such a fashion any lingering pretence of Iraqi sovereignty was stripped away. And Muhammad Bashar al-Faydi, of the pro-insurgency Muslim Scholars Association, emphasised the futility of expecting al-Maliki to implement the new security policy: 'Those who are on the ruling side today have taken the path of exclusion, or marginalisation and pursuit of others. There are no links between the Sunnis and those participating in the political process.'[88]

Hence al-Maliki could be expected neither to confront the Mahdi Army in Baghdad nor to build the reconciliation with the Sunni communities that the Bush policy demanded. The scene was set for nothing more than further carnage and destruction, even though the surge would be of limited duration. To the dismay of military strategist Jack Keane, a former army vice-chief of staff, who had proposed an eighteen-month surge,

Robert Gates was telling congressmen that the surge would only last 'a matter of months'. Keane commented:

> 'We need all five [extra] brigades in Baghdad as soon as possible. It will take three to four months to clear neighbourhoods of death squads and insurgents, and at least the rest of the year to establish proper security for the population. If you only wanted to stage a clearance operation, you could do that in a few months. But if we left then, the militia would just return as they have in the past.[89]

Again it seemed clear that President Bush was 'virtually standing alone' in advocating the surge policy. The international opposition was obvious, and the domestic opposition had many aspects – from the straightforward opposition represented in Congress and public opinion polls to the strategic opposition signalled in *The Iraq Study Group Report* and much military opinion. In January 2007 there was nothing resembling a pro-Bush consensus on the wisdom of a troop surge or how such a policy should be implemented. It remained to be seen whether world and American opinion would shift as the surge, in whatever form, was imposed on Iraq.

It was plain that Paul Wolfowitz's focus on the oil factor (see Introduction) typified the attitude of the US government. The Bush administration, motivated by this consideration and strategic interest, clearly intended American corporations to benefit from the Iraqi energy resource – a fact that determined the shape of company negotiations over oil. Thus *The Iraq Study Group Report* emphasises the need for the US to 'encourage investment in Iraq's oil sector . . . by international companies'; to 'assist Iraqi leaders to reorganise the national oil industry as a commercial enterprise'; to 'urge the Iraqi government to post all oil contracts, volumes, and prices on the Web' for the benefit of outside observers; to press Iraq in conjunction with the International Monetary Fund (IMF) to reduce subsidies in the energy sector and to adopt market pricing; to support 'the World Bank's efforts' to shape Iraq's contracting procedures;[90] and to provide personnel to run every aspect of the Iraqi oil industry.[91]

Such US-orchestrated initiatives, guaranteeing American corporate control over Iraqi oil, were intended to bolster US company negotiations.

Under such American ambitions the Iraqi government was being pressured to pass a law giving Western oil companies the right to exploit the country's massive oil reserves – an estimated 115 billion barrels waiting to be extracted. The Iraqi law, under American scrutiny, had passed through various drafts and was ready to be presented to the Iraqi Cabinet. Its provisions – under a system known as production-sharing agreements (PSAs) – represented a radical departure from the norm for developing countries, not least by allowing such oil majors as BP and Shell in Britain, and Exxon and Chevron in the US, to sign deals for up to thirty years.[92] The PSAs, allowing Iraq to retain legal ownership of its oil but guaranteeing massive profits to the international investing companies, would be an innovation in the Middle East. Both Saudi Arabia and Iran, the world's leading oil exporters, both tightly control their industries through state-owned companies, as do most members of OPEC (Organization of the Petroleum Exporting Countries). Iraq was to be allowed no such right.

The new Iraqi legislation had been drafted with the assistance of BearingPoint, an American consultancy firm hired by the US government and with a representative working in the American embassy in Baghdad. The various drafts had been shown to the US government, the major oil companies and the IMF; but, of twenty Iraqi MPs interviewed, only one had seen the proposed legislation. No restrictions would be placed on foreign companies taking their profits out of the country, and no taxes would be imposed on such activities. Some 20 per cent of the profits would be extracted once the investment costs had been recouped, with 10 per cent regarded as the norm. The generous terms have been compared to deals signed by Russia in the 1990s when the country was bankrupt and in chaos, though scarcely as anarchic as Iraq in 2007. James Paul, of the advocacy group Global Policy Forum, pointed out that Iraq was in no position to negotiate: the Iraqi authorities were 'a government under occupation, and it is highly influenced by this. The US has a lot of leverage . . . Iraq is

in no condition right now to go ahead and do this.' He
commented also on the argument that the US-friendly PSAs were
a legitimate protection against risk:

> It is relatively easy to get the oil in Iraq. It is nowhere near as
> complicated as the North Sea. There are super giant fields that are
> completely mapped . . . there is absolutely no exploration cost and no
> risk. So the argument that these agreements are needed to hedge risk
> are specious.[93]

On 18 March 2003, with the invasion imminent, Tony Blair had
said in the House of Commons that the oil revenues would be put
in a UN-administered trust fund for the Iraqi people – a pledge
that came to nothing.

It now seemed clear that, even though the official version of the
draft law had not been published, most of Iraq's oil resources
would be handed over to foreign corporations under PSA
schemes. Kamil Mahdi, an Iraqi academic at the University of
Exeter, expressed a widespread view: the draft oil law 'must not
be allowed to pass during these abnormal times . . . before peace
and stability return'.[94] The law had been discussed behind closed
doors and considered by the US government, but it had not been
released to the Iraqi public. The US and its allies were plainly
intent on privatising and selling off Iraq's oil resources, so
reversing Law No. 80 (December 1961), which recovered most
of Iraq's oil from foreign control. It remained to be seen how the
Iraqi public would respond to the PSAs once the occupation of
their country was over.

On 11 January 2007 the US military detained five Iranians, and
confiscated computers and documents, in a raid on Tehran's
diplomatic mission in Irbil, hours after George Bush had accused
Iran and Syria of aiding militants in Iraq. In Tehran the foreign
ministry summoned the ambassadors of Iraq and Switzerland,
which represents US interests in Iran, and demanded an explanation, while Mohammad Ali Hosseini commented that the US
was aiming to create tension between Iraq and its neighbours.
Bush had reportedly signed a clandestine directive ordering US

forces to launch a military offensive against Iranian personnel in Iraq.[95] The raid on the diplomatic mission came less than two weeks after a senior Revolutionary Guard commander, known by his alias, Chizari, and allegedly involved in military operations in Iraq, had been seized in a raid near Baghdad. He was later released at the insistence of the Iraqi government, again signalling the extent of Iran's influence in Baghdad.

The United States was now making various claims of Iranian involvement in Iraqi affairs. The Revolutionary Guard's Quds (Jerusalem) Force was said to be active in terrorist activities and in the growing struggle between Iran and Saudi Arabia for influence in the region. Documents captured along with Chizari allegedly revealed the Quds Force's plan for attacks, telephone numbers connected with Sunni insurgents and evidence of involvement with Shi'ite militias. Iran had reportedly set up a network of fake import-export companies in Iraq's Anbar province to channel funds to Sunni fighters, and had allegedly worked with al-Qaeda groups.[96] Alireza Jadarzadeh, an Iranian exile leader, had compiled a dossier detailing the vast Quds Force network in Iraq, with operations centred on Basra and Najaf to support militia and other groups. Thousands of Shia militiamen had allegedly travelled to Iran for training and indoctrination, while British and American officials had identified Iran as the likely source of the increasingly effective roadside bombs.[97]

The American detention of five Iranians, termed 'diplomats' by Tehran and 'insurgent activists' by the US, was continuing to exacerbate tensions. Stephen Hadley, the National Security Advisor, said that the US had the authority to detain anyone who put 'our people' at risk in Iraq: 'We know . . . that Iran is supplying elements in Iraq that are attacking Iraqis and attacking our forces . . . These are activities that are going on in Iraq that are unacceptable. They put our people at risk ...We will interdict their operations, we will disrupt their supply lines, we will disrupt these attacks.'[98]

It was significant also that the US was concerned not only to stabilise Iraq but to remain a powerful regional player. Iran, Defense Secretary Robert Gates signalled, was mistaken if it believed that US power in the region was waning. As the first surge reinforcements began arriving in Iraq he commented to journalists in Brussels:

> The Iranians clearly believe we are tied down in Iraq, that they have the initiative, that they are in a position to press us in many ways. We are simply reaffirming . . . the importance of the Gulf region to the US and our determination to be an ongoing strong presence in that area for a long time into the future.[99]

In fact few observers doubted Iran's growing influence in Iraq and the region. Tariq al-Hashemi, one of the two Iraqi vice-presidents, expressed the widespread view that Iran was becoming a 'major player' with 'deep influence' in Iraq: 'Wherever you go in Iraq you see their fingerprints.'[100]

Iran was reportedly laying plans, mainly through the deep penetration of Basra's security network and political parties, for the complete domination of southern Iraq when the British withdrew. Already British commanders were saying that a withdrawal would bring an immediate confrontation between the weak Iraqi army and the Iranian-backed Basra militias, with the likelihood that the Shi'ite factions would win power in the area.[101] Iran had found it relatively easy to build alliances with fellow Shi'ites, who form the majority in southern Iraq, and one important consequence of the US-led invasion was the probable emergence of a Greater Iran absorbing the Basra territory and extending north towards Baghdad – an outcome that was alarming Saudi Arabia and other Sunni states in the region.

On 16 January, after meeting Condoleezza Rice in Riyadh, the Saudi Foreign Minister, Prince Saud al-Faisal, expressed support for the surge strategy but urged a radical change of heart by the Baghdad leadership. Already the Saudis had been dismayed to witness Shi'ite Muslims, many of them beholden to Tehran after years of exile, assuming power in Baghdad after the overthrow of Saddam Hussein; and had suggested ways in which Iraqi Sunnis could be helped to defend themselves against Iranian-backed Shi'ite militias. In this vein Sheikh Musa bin Abdulaziz, editor of the Saudi *Al Salafi* magazine, said that Iran had become 'more dangerous than Israel itself' and that the Iranian revolution had come 'to renew the Persian presence in the region . . . the real clash of civilisations'.[102]

The Bush administration's new security policy for Iraq now appeared to be facing mounting opposition from congressional sources, forcing the President to invite leading Republicans to Camp David to rally support. At the same time George Bush was driven to acknowledge past errors and to concede ground to his US opponents: 'Well, no question, decisions have made things unstable . . . We could have done things better. No question about it.'[103] One newspaper article described him as '"disappointed" with the circumstances surrounding the execution [of Saddam]. It was like a sectarian "revenge killing".'[104]

On 17 January Representative Jerrold Nadler (a Democrat representing New York's 8th Congressional District) introduced a bill, the Protect the Troops and Bring Them Home Act, to prevent the allocation of funds to Iraq – except to protect US forces, to begin their withdrawal after one month and to end by 31 December 2007, to provide assistance to the Iraqi security forces, to provide reconstruction aid and to fund diplomatic consultations: 'We must save American lives by bringing them home as soon as possible.'[105]

Representative Sam Farr (a Democrat representing California's 17th Congressional District) was now introducing legislation to repeal the Authorization for Use of Military Force against Iraq Resolution and to force the President to begin the withdrawal of troops: 'Too many troops have died, too many have been wounded, and Iraq has descended into a violent civil war . . . The solution to the crisis is political and will not be reached by keeping our troops in harm's way.'[106] With the likelihood of Republican opposition and the prospect of a presidential veto, neither bill was expected to become law.

The Iraqis were now reaping the first fruits of George Bush's surge policy. For days Abu Hamed had been trapped with his two blind daughters, without water or electricity, in one room in Baghdad's Haifa Street. 'Is this the new paradise that the Americans said they would give us when they invaded our country. When is this nightmare going to end?'[107] About a thousand US and Iraqi troops smashed their way into the area, helicopters raking the rooftops with rocket and machine gun fire, F-18 jets swooping low over the buildings, and tanks and other fighting vehicles taking up positions around people's homes as Iraqi families cowered inside.

At the end of the military operation Iraqi officials claimed that fifty insurgents had been killed, just as the area – less than a mile from the fortified Green Zone – had been cleared many times previously, before the US troops returned to their bases and allowed the insurgents to filter back. The difference now was that the US military intended to set up twenty-seven mini-bases, known as joint security stations, across the city. The American troops would eat and sleep there alongside Iraqi forces, with the aim of denying the insurgents the chance to return. And the various sectors would be 'gated'. Thus Stephen Biddle, an advisor to Bush and a senior fellow at the Council on Foreign Relations, said: 'They [the US troops] can't be commuters. There is going to be a heavy emphasis on a high-density presence.'[108] It was unclear how a mere 20,000 American soldiers and their poorly motivated sectarian Iraqi allies would be able to provide a 'high-density presence' in the vast metropolis of Baghdad; Sadr City alone comprised two million people mostly hostile to the foreign occupation.

The Iraqi civilian death toll was continuing to mount – a detail that was never factored into the Bush administration's surge calculations. As always, the numbers were uncertain, though no estimate put the toll of civilian dead in 2006 at less than 12,000.[109] Gianni Magazzeni of UNAMI emphasised that the UN's figures, among the highest estimates, were based on reports from various sources. The UN report implied that the Shi'ite-dominated government was allowing the Shi'ite death squads to operate with relative impunity:

> The root causes of the sectarian violence lie in revenge killings and lack of accountability for past crimes as in the growing sense of impunity for on-going human rights violations. This leads people to take the law into their own hands and rely on action by militias or criminal gangs.[110]

In these circumstances – with an ineffective Iraqi government allied to an even more aggressive US posture – the Iraqi civilian population was continuing to suffer. The death squads, militias and criminal gangs were wreaking their daily carnage, and the Bush surge seemed likely only to add to the scale of slaughter and misery. On 16 January 2007 at least sixty-five university students, most of them women, were killed at Mustansiriya University, in a Shi'ite district of Baghdad, and more than a hundred injured by two suicide bombs. The students were slaughtered as they emerged from classes for the day, the explosions clearly designed to cause maximum damage.[111] These events, with other outrages throughout the country, again brought the number of daily Iraqi dead to more than one hundred.

The bombings and other attacks typically left more wounded than dead, and the ill-equipped and understaffed hospitals had no way of coping with the constant inflow of bleeding and limbless victims. On 19 January a letter, signed by nearly one hundred eminent doctors and sent to Downing Street via International Development Secretary Hilary Benn, highlighted the plight of children dying in Iraqi hospitals; and a group of lawyers emphasised that the conditions described in the letter amounted to a breach of the Geneva Conventions that require the US and Britain, as the occupying powers, to protect human life.[112]

The desperate shortages, sometimes of items costing less than a pound, were causing 'hundreds' of children to die:

> Sick or injured children who could otherwise be treated by simple means are left to die in hundreds because they do not have access to basic medicines or other resources. Children who have lost hands, feet and limbs are left without prostheses. Children with grave psychological problems are left untreated.[113]

Babies were being ventilated with a plastic tube in their noses and dying for want of an oxygen mask, while others were dying for lack of sterile needles costing about 95 pence. Fatal infections were spreading from baby to baby because of the lack of surgical gloves, costing about 3½ pence a pair. There was film evidence of dead babies being dumped in cardboard boxes, and in one hospital there were three babies to a single incubator held together by tape and bits of wire. The doctors, British and Iraqi, called on the British government to account properly for the $33 billion in the Development Fund for Iraq, which should have supplied the means for hospitals to treat children, and said that more than half the money had vanished through corruption, theft and payments to mercenaries. The Save the Children charity estimated that up to 230,000 Iraqi children might have died since the 2003 invasion.[114]

Benn responded to the letter by saying that it made 'very sobering reading', but of course he remained a supporter of the war and occupation. He admitted that there were 'problems' over the 'weak' financial controls of the development funds, and promised to stop the money intended for health care being lost through incompetence and corruption. The matter would be raised with the Iraqi authorities: 'They have sole control over how these funds are managed and spent. It [the Development Fund for Iraq] is overseen by an expert committee appointed by the government to ensure that oil revenues are governed transparently and for the benefit of the Iraqi people.'[115] The terrible conditions prevailing under the US-led occupation were, Benn emphasised, the fault of Saddam Hussein.

There were now further signs of discord between the Iraqi government and the Bush administration. On 17 January Prime Minister al-Maliki said that America's refusal to give the Iraqi security forces sufficient guns and equipment had cost a great number of lives, that the insurgency had been bloodier and prolonged because of Washington's policy. If the US military released the necessary arms, the Americans could 'drastically' cut their numbers within three to six months. The charge had some weight: the Americans had been reluctant to release arms to the Iraqi security forces because they were likely to end up with the insurgents. Moreover, al-Maliki criticised the US for suggesting that the Iraqi government was living on 'borrowed time', an attitude that boosted the extremists and indicated 'some kind of crisis situation' in Washington.[116] He admitted that mistakes had been made over the hanging of Saddam Hussein, but he countered Italian Prime Minister Romano Prodi's criticism of Iraq's capital punishment laws by citing the Italians' summary execution of Benito Mussolini at the end of the Second World War.[117]

There was further evidence also that widespread corruption had deprived the Iraqi armed forces of arms, money and troops. In order to attract extra funding Iraqi officials had swelled the army ranks with 'ghost soldiers' who did not exist; one Iraqi brigade commander, General Khalid Juad Khadim, had been removed after selling weapons and fuel on the black market; and Lieutenant General Nasier al-Abadi, deputy chief of staff for the armed forces, claimed that Iraqi Ministry of Defence (MoD) officials were supporting the terrorists. Similarly, Lieutenant Colonel Jabour Ahmed Sabih, stationed in Fallujah, said that 'someone' was receiving the salaries of 'ghost soldiers' but he could do nothing about it: 'These people who work in MoD, some of them support terrorism. This doesn't mean only to kill innocent people . . . they work for their personal benefit . . . The problem in the MoD is corruption.'[118] The Iraqi Interior Ministry claimed that 7,700 police officers, suspected members of death squads, had been sacked; of these, fewer than 10 per cent were in jail awaiting trial.

It was plain that the divisions in Iraqi society were reflected in the government and the armed forces, making it unlikely that the US surge plan, for all its brutality, would be translated into effective security on the ground. With no real efforts being made at national reconciliation the sectarian war was continuing, with religious and ethnic minorities being persecuted wherever they could be found. The Christian exodus was gathering pace and even the Sunni Palestinians living in Iraq were being told that if they did not leave the country immediately they would be killed by the Shi'ite militias. Already more than 600 Palestinians had been murdered by the militias as a prelude to driving out the 20,000-strong Palestinian community, formerly protected by Saddam and offered housing, money and free education.[119]

As the US death toll reached 3,044 an opinion poll by *Newsweek* magazine found that 68 per cent of respondents opposed President Bush's surge policy, with only 26 per cent in support. It was clear also that this attitude to government policy was increasingly reflected in the political establishment. The Republicans Chuck Hagel and Olympia Snowe had signalled their willingness to support one of the Democratic resolutions against a troop increase (Hagel: 'To feed more American troops into this bloodbath is wrong').[120] American citizens, including Iraq War veterans, were congregating in Tacoma, near Washington, to participate in the Citizens' Hearing on the Legality of US Actions in Iraq.

On 19 January 2007 General Anthony Zinni, a supporter of the surge plan, rejected Bush's new policy as a confused and timid plan that was 'too little, too late'. He declared that the policy did not go far enough: 'I thought he'd come out with a bolder policy.' The plan appeared to be 'just doing more on security with inadequate troops'. And in the same vein Frederick Kagan, an academic whose Iraq Project Group (IPG) report provided the intellectual foundation for the surge policy, said that holding back some of the new troops in reserve was 'antithetical' to his surge plan: 'Other elements of the administration's plan are also significantly at variance with the proposals on the IPG, especially the administration's emphasis on putting Iraqis in the lead at all levels.'[121] Even so, the US troops were paying a heavy price. As about 3,200 paratroops of the 2nd Brigade, 82nd Airborne Division, were deployed as the first element of the surge taskforce, the US military announced that twenty-five American troops had been killed, including twelve when a helicopter crashed north of Baghdad, in one of the bloodiest days of the war; and on 22 January a suicide bomb killed at least eighty-eight people in the Bab al-Sharji market in northern Baghdad – again indicating that neither the Iraqi government nor the US forces could guarantee security. Prime Minister al-Maliki was now proposing a timetable for the withdrawal of US forces as part of the price for ending a Muqtada al-Sadr boycott of the Iraqi parliament.

On 23 January Lieutenant General David Petraeus, about to receive Senate confirmation of his role as ground commander of US forces in Iraq, admitted that the situation was so bad that he could not guarantee the success of Bush's new war plan. Iraq was now becoming a 'failed state' dominated by sectarian militia, international terrorists, Sunni insurgents and interference from neighbouring countries: 'The situation in Iraq is dire. The stakes are high. There are no easy choices. The way ahead will be very hard. But hard is not hopeless.'[122] The irony that it was the US that had created the 'failed state' and that it was the principal 'interfering country' escaped Petraeus. Now the Senate Foreign Affairs Committee was giving the go-ahead for a resolution condemning Bush's surge policy, saying that the troop increase was 'not in the national interest'. Nor, US commentators rarely bothered to point out, was it in the interest of the Iraqi people.[123]

The American public was plainly opposed to the war. Two-thirds believed that the surge policy was mistaken; more than 70 per cent thought that Bush had no clear plan for the war; a majority thought that invading Iraq was a mistake; and almost two-thirds thought that Congress had not been assertive enough in challenging the Iraq policies of the Bush administration. A BBC poll showed that 73 per cent of people in twenty-five countries opposed Washington's Iraq policies. Juan Cole, a Middle East expert, reported on 26 January that the Green Zone had taken mortar fire that had wounded six people: 'That nearly four years into the war, the US HQ in Iraq is subjected to rocket fire just underlines how helpless Gulliver is before the supposed Lilliputians.'[124]

2
One million deaths and counting

The possibility of a troop surge in Iraq had been discussed for months before the new contingents arrived in Baghdad. The Iraqis, not least the insurgent leaders, had been given weeks to prepare for the exact date when the new security plan would be put into effect.[1] In such circumstances it was hardly surprising that many death squad and militia leaders fled Baghdad to avoid capture or killing by American and Iraqi forces before the start of the new crackdown in the capital.[2] It seemed obvious that even if the surge was successful in reducing the amount of sectarian and other violence in Baghdad the problems would simply shift elsewhere. What *was* remarkable was that Prime Minister Nouri al-Maliki had reportedly encouraged the Shi'ite militia leaders to flee and that weapons belonging to Muqtada al-Sadr's Mahdi Army had allegedly been hidden inside the Iraqi Interior Ministry to prevent confiscation.[3]

Such allegations, made by a former Iraqi minister who did not want to be named for security reasons, clearly raised further questions about al-Maliki's reliability as an ally of the United States. Whose side was he on? It was known that his political position was dependent upon Shi'ite factions linked to the militias, and that al-Sadr had only consented to abandon a boycott of the government in return for al-Maliki pledges on agreeing a timeline for a US withdrawal.

It was hard to avoid the conclusion, already reached months ago by many observers, that the ineffectual Iraqi government was deploying its limited powers to aid the insurgency. The United States could do nothing. Had not the Maliki regime been democratically elected? Washington had no choice but to maintain the fiction that the Iraqi government was a reliable ally in the new security plan. This was just one of the many absurdities that were guaranteeing the ultimate collapse of the new US expansion of the war. But before this could be fully admitted by a disenchanted Congress and the ultimately decisive American public, tens of thousands of Iraqi and US victims would be forced to pay the price of folly.

Iraqi families were being forced by terror to become refugees in their own country and abroad, although through such mounting demographic and other pressures Iraqis were finding themselves increasingly unwelcome throughout the Middle East and elsewhere.[4] Nearly four years after the US-led invasion Iraq was increasingly descending into bloody chaos. Kidnappings, killings and criminal extortion were fragmenting Baghdad and other parts of the country along religious and ethnic lines – to an extent reminiscent of the ethnic cleansing of Rwanda, Sudan and the former Yugoslavia.

The case of Khaled's family is one among thousands. One night six men, armed with AK-47 assault rifles, smashed down the door of the family home, hitting the 54-year-old Khaled on the head with the butts of their rifles and dragging him into a car for imminent execution as a Sunni Muslim. On this occasion Khaled's Shi'ite neighbours managed to intervene, proclaiming that he was a good neighbour and managing to secure his release. But it was assumed that the gunmen would return and that a second neighbourly intervention would not be possible. Within hours Khaled had gathered his family and fled, abandoning his home and possessions, to learn the next day that a Shi'ite family connected with the militia had moved into his house:

> We have no rights any more in our own country . . . at least we are together and alive. So many people are being killed every day . . . My country was never like this. Mixed marriages were common. My daughter is a Sunni and she was married to a Shi'ite. But last year after the Sunnis bombed the holy Shi'ite mosque in Samarra, her husband divorced her immediately and has abandoned her and her daughter.[5]

It is impossible to overemphasise the enormity of the Iraqi population displacement, involving perhaps six million people – a crisis
that international aid organisations were saying that Britain and
the United States were ignoring. The Americans were expecting
to spend $100 billion on war and security in Iraq in 2007, and a
mere $20 million on migration and refugee assistance; in
September 2007 Britain deported twenty-seven Iraqi refugees
back to their country, and in early 2007 there had been plans to
send more back. Andrew Harper, coordinator for the Iraqi unit of
the United Nations High Commissioner for Refugees
(UNHCR), graphically summarised the situation in a word: 'Iraq
is haemorrhaging.'[6]

The United Nations continued to highlight the scale of the
carnage and human rights abuses throughout the country. In early
February various media sources reported a surge in the incidence
of killings, with fifty mutilated bodies found in Baghdad on 5
February and a further 140 elsewhere; but by the end of the
month the Iraqi authorities were announcing that because of
the new security plan the number of such killings had decreased –
to about twenty-five bodies being found on some days.[7]

On 1 February 2007 two suicide bombers at a crowded market
in al-Hilla killed up to seventy people and injured another 125;
two days later a truck packed with a ton of explosives detonated
in the Baghdad district of al-Sadriya, killing 135 people and
injuring 339 more; on 12 February two bombs exploded in
Baghdad's Shorja market, killing seventy-six people and injuring
more than 155 others and setting stalls, shops and a nearby high-
rise building on fire; four days later car bombs in the Baghdad
al-Jadida shopping centre killed sixty-two people and wounded
129 others; and on 24 February a bomb killed more than
fifty people, including five children, outside a mosque in al-
Habbaniya.[8]

On 13 February the Maliki government announced new
emergency procedures designed to coincide with the beginning of
the troop surge. There was no mention of any measures designed
to protect human rights and judicial due process rights. Instead
arrests without warrants were authorised and suspects could be

interrogated with no limit on how long they could be detained. In addition, the new regulations also provided that suspects accused of various offences – murder, rape, theft, abduction, the destruction of private and public property and other crimes – would be punished in accordance with the 2005 anti-terror legislation, which provides the death penalty for all the listed crimes.

The UN also noted that 'the use of torture and other inhumane treatment in detention centres under the authority of the Ministry of Interior and the Ministry of Defence continues to be of utmost concern' and emphasised the 'urgent need to establish an effective tracking mechanism to account for the location and treatment of all detainees from the point of arrest'.[9] In short, the US military and the Iraqi security forces were authorised to arrest people and to torture them in undeclared locations for indefinite periods.

Many Iraqis were being rounded up in the dead of night and taken to unspecified interrogation centres without access to legal protection or family visits; relatively few of these cases were recorded by the UN and other agencies. In a typical case, on 19 February armed men wearing Iraqi special forces uniforms abducted Mahmoud Sa'id Salih, a Palestinian, from his home in al-Yusufiya, and his fate remained unknown.[10] Some abductees were released on the payment of ransoms, while the bodies of many others were dumped in Baghdad and other cities across the country. There were also numerous attacks and assassination attempts, many successful, against former Ba'ath Party members, other prominent political figures, and professionals such as journalists, university lecturers and medical staff. Thus on 4 February the journalist Suhad Shakir al-Kinani, who worked for the Council of Representatives in Baghdad, was allegedly killed in her car in crossfire between the US military and an armed group;[11] on 12 February Mohan Hussein al-Dahr, editor of the daily *al-Mashreq* newspaper, was shot dead as he tried to escape gunmen; and on 20 February the bullet-riddled body of the journalist Abdul-Razzaq al-Khakani was found at the Medico-Legal Institute.[12] On 26 February a bomb was timed to explode at the Ministry of Municipalities to coincide with a visit by Vice-President Adel Abdul-Mahdi to attend a staff award ceremony; ten people were killed and eighteen injured in the blast.[13]

The UN was also monitoring the attacks on religious and ethnic minorities that were continuing 'unabated' in most areas of Iraq – in the context of the Iraqi government's inability 'to restore law and order, together with the prevailing climate of impunity'.[14] On 15 February, after two men from the minority Yezidi sect had been found in a car with a Kurdish woman, dozens of Kurds from the Mizori tribe attacked the Yezidi district of Shaikhan in Nineveh province. The Kurdish woman was then killed by her husband for 'dishonouring' her family – one of many killings prompted by the growing swing towards cultural and Islamic primitivism. Tensions between the Yezidi and Kurdish communities were running high and calls for revenge were being made in Yezidi towns and villages.

In anticipation of the surge impact, the US military and the Iraqi authorities were now expanding the detention facilities to accommodate several thousand new inmates. There were already some 34,992 detainees, mostly uncharged and without legal representation, and the numbers were expected to increase in the weeks and months ahead.[15] The United Nations Assistance Mission for Iraq (UNAMI) had learned that various Iraqi government officials had given assurances that judicial orders for the release of prisoners, where these could be obtained, would be respected, and that detainees would be held only in officially recognised facilities. Previous pledges of this sort had rarely been respected, and 'the absence of effective monitoring and accountability mechanisms' was doing nothing to engender confidence in the new commitments.[16]

By the end of February, following the launch of the troop surge and the associated security plan, hundreds of people had been arrested. Five Ministry of Defence brigade headquarters in and around Baghdad were being used as initial holding centres prior to the transfer of detainees to Ministry of Justice facilities. The procedure was far from transparent: UNAMI said that no detailed information was available regarding the extent of judicial involve-ment in the process.[17] The Iraqi government had failed to address issues relating to detainee abuse: there was a lack of transparency, and the authorities had yet to demonstrate the political will to bring suspected torturers to account. Again UNAMI emphasised 'the climate of impunity' that was undermining official efforts to restore law and order.[18] The US military refused to disclose how many of the 16,931 detainees held at the end of February were classified as security internees being held for prolonged periods without charge or trial, and UNAMI judged that the current legal arrangements at the detention facilities 'do not fulfill the requirement to grant detainees due process'.[19]

While Iraqis continued to resist, flee and die in their hundreds of thousands, the massive funds supposedly intended to ease their plight were being squandered through corruption, inefficiency and other forms of waste. This was not a judgement made only by factions opposed to the US-led occupation, but also by official American bodies working to uncover the scale of financial abuse. Thus a congressional investigation team set up to examine the billions of dollars spent on reconstruction in Iraq, and reporting quarterly, had fifty-five auditors and investigators in Iraq, with seventy-eight investigations under way into fraud, waste and abuse of funds.

On 31 January 2007 the last of the team's reports indicated something of how the funds were being mismanaged. One example was the police training camp at the Adnan palace in Baghdad, provided with a $51.6 million budget for the camp and $36.4 million for equipment. For security reasons the camp and the equipment had never been used. Noting that the State Department had paid about $43.8 million to the Virginia-based DynCorp contractor 'for manufacturing and temporary storage of a residential camp that has never been used, including $4.2 million for unauthorised work [including an Olympic-size swimming pool and twenty VIP trailers, ordered by the Iraqi interior ministry] associated with the residential camp', the congressional report recommended that the US government seek reimbursement from the company.[20]

The report also concluded that weapons and other equipment may have gone missing: 'DoS [the State Department] may have spent another $36.4m for weapons and equipment . . . that cannot be accounted for because invoices were vague and there was no back-up documentation or property book specific to items purchased'; moreover, the audit cited 'weak and sometimes non-existent contract administration'.[21] Stuart Bowen, the special inspector general for Iraq reconstruction, who headed the audit team, judged that the billions spent in Iraq on security had had limited effect. And in the same vein Lee Hamilton and Edwin Meese III, who had been members of the Iraq Study Group (ISG), told a Senate investigation that the United States had botched the training of the Iraqi police. Giving the task to the State Department and private contractors who 'did not have the expertise or the manpower' and then to the Defense Department had left Iraq with little if any law enforcement on the street. This meant, for example, that thirty to forty people were being kidnapped daily in Iraq for subsequent torture and execution, while thousands more were being forced to flee their homes. The Brookings Institution noted that ransoms averaging $30,000 for abductees were being demanded, and that about 300 foreigners had been kidnapped since the war began. On 1 February two bombers wearing suicide belts attacked the Shi'ite city of al-Hilla, killing forty-five people and wounding 150 others.

On 2 February the US National Intelligence Estimate, to which all sixteen US intelligence agencies contributed, noted that the Iraq conflict had the hallmarks of a civil war (a description avoided by the Bush administration): 'The term "civil war" accurately describes key elements of the Iraq conflict, including the hardening of ethno-sectarian identities, a sea change in the character of the violence, ethno-sectarian mobilisation, and population displacements.' The agencies assessed 'that the overall security situation will continue to deteriorate', but that a hasty withdrawal of US forces would trigger 'spiralling violence and political disarray'.[22]

This was part of the American paradox. There was widespread acknowledgement in the United States that Iraq was in chaos. Neither the US military nor the Iraqi forces, such as they were, were able to establish security and stability. The cost, in both lives and treasure, was escalating by the day, and yet the Bush administration and most American pundits were resisting any calls for a speedy American withdrawal. There were already 'spiralling violence' and 'political disarray' – as shown by the six million internal and external refugees and perhaps a million dead (see below). All that the US forces were bringing to the conflict was prodigious firepower – the ability to continue the slaughter and to lay waste entire neighbourhoods. The mythical weapons of mass destruction were a distant dream and 'regime change' had been accomplished; but all hopes of establishing a liberal democracy and respect for human rights had seemingly evaporated. Why were the American troops still in the country?

On 3 February a suicide truck bomber struck at a busy food market in a predominantly Shi'ite area of Baghdad, killing at least 140 people and wounding more than 300. Victims, many of them mutilated, were dragged from the devastated wreckage of shops and stalls. At the Ibn al-Nafis hospital in the central Kerrada district the hallways overflowed with the wounded as volunteers offered what help they could and friends and relatives of the victims screamed for help. In the ethnically mixed city of Kirkuk, a string of car bombs killed at least four civilians and wounded thirty-seven more. Two of the bombs were detonated outside the offices of the two main Kurdish parties, the Kurdistan Democratic Party and the Patriotic Union of Kurdistan. Police, claiming that insurgents were trying to take over Mosul, were placing the city under curfew as battles with militants occurred in several districts.

Such daily events were failing to convince the Bush administration that the American presence was doing nothing to establish a tranquil democratic state. On 5 February George Bush asked Congress for an extra $250 billion for the war, even though he was facing a no-confidence Senate vote on his surge policy. The proposed increase would take the total cost of the Iraq and Afghanistan wars since 11 September 2001 to almost $750 billion which – allowing for inflation – exceeds the cost to the United States of the Vietnam War over a much longer period. Before the invasion of Iraq in March 2003 the Bush administration pledged that war costs would be limited to $100 billion.[23]

On 4 February Rob Portman, the White House budget director, conceded that about 90 per cent of the new money was for Iraq, not least to replace equipment destroyed in combat or worn out by harsh conditions. It was now also being admitted that four US helicopters that had crashed in the previous fortnight had been downed by enemy fire, indicating the growing ability of the insurgents to attack American aircraft; on 7 February a fifth helicopter crashed north of Baghdad. Did the insurgents now have anti-aircraft missiles?[24] Some twenty Americans, including sixteen soldiers and four civilians working for a security company, died in the helicopter crashes.

Democrats were also increasingly concerned about a White House proposal to raise the Pentagon's core budget by 11 per cent, bringing the department's annual spending to nearly $500 billion in addition to Iraq War costs. However, the Bush propaganda was still effective: even the dissident Democrats could not be seen to be 'undermining the brave boys in the field'. On 4 February Harry Reid, the Senate majority leader, emphasised that the US troops would be 'provided with everything they need'.[25] Already the Democrats had agreed to a softening of the anti-surge resolution, so allowing current funding for the war to be maintained, in order to maintain the fragile alliance between the Democrat sponsors and a handful of sceptical Republicans. Half-a-dozen Republican senators were backing the resolution, with a further six said to be wavering, but the compromise drafting was also counter-productive: some Democrats were considering voting against the resolution because, in guaranteeing war funding, it served to prolong the conflict. In any event, it seemed impossible to achieve a sufficient vote to avoid the presidential veto.

The US forces were already learning the practicalities of the surge campaign. After an operation troops were no longer required to seek refuge in the large heavily fortified American bases but were expected to remain in the field, living with Iraqi soldiers closer to the sectarian conflict. One such advance base comprised a cluster of fortified houses on the edge of the war being fought by Sunnis and Shi'ites in the district of Ghazaliya in west Baghdad. Here US soldiers, trapped in what they had dubbed 'the Alamo', had no water or heating and only the most primitive latrines. One hot meal was brought in daily by armoured vehicle, and every window was sandbagged. They were forced to sleep in close proximity to each other, and the nights were invariably punctuated by gunfire and explosions. One private summarised the general attitude: 'It sucks.'[26]

The plan was to establish about two dozen such bases, 'joint security stations' (JSSs), in vital parts of Baghdad, staffed by some of the extra surge troops who would be required to suppress local fighting, to train their Iraqi army colleagues and to enlist local people in the fight against the Shi'ite militias and Sunni death squads. But how realistic was the plan? The small Ghazaliya base, occupied by a mere 100 US soldiers, was only five miles from the Green Zone but, as the journalist Martin Fletcher found, it took much of a day to traverse the distance: three hours waiting for a helicopter to travel to the airport on the edge of Baghdad, and three hours waiting for a convoy of Humvees to travel to the base.[27]

Fletcher contrasted visiting friends in Ghazaliya in 2003 with what he found in February 2007 – the fruits of nearly four years of US occupation:

> Then it was a pleasant suburb with wide streets of palm-shaded villas. Now I found abandoned homes, shuttered shops and rubble-strewn streets barricaded against marauding gangs of killers. I drove past lakes of sewage and acres of rubbish. Local services have collapsed. There is an hour of electricity a day. Most schools are closed. One headmistress who defied the terrorists was beaten, raped, tied to a bed and electrocuted, then cut up.[28]

The JSS was ringed by blast barriers and coiled razor wire – to protect the US troops of C Company, 2nd Battalion, 12th Cavalry living in two knocked-through houses and the Iraqi soldiers living in a second pair. The last two houses were regarded as useful buffers against incoming fire. Already the station commander, Captain Erik Peterson, claimed to be succeeding in his task, as his men patrolled daily in Humvees and on foot, adopting the innovatory practice of talking to Iraqis instead of kicking their doors in. He said that fewer corpses were being found on the streets and that local people were beginning to offer high-grade information about the 'bad guys' in their midst: 'We are fighting a counter-insurgency campaign and you need different tools from the old-style knock-down-doors campaign.'[29] Peterson judged that his Iraqi contingent had a 'lot of potential', but his men criticised its sloppy habits, lack of discipline and trigger-happy behaviour.

The United States and the Iraqi government, continuing to accuse Iran and Syria of fomenting the insurgency, were seemingly oblivious to the irony of suggesting that 'foreign' personnel had no right to interfere in Iraqi affairs. In the aftermath of the attack on the Baghdad market that killed 135 Shi'ites, the Iraqi spokesman, Ali al-Dabbagh, said that Syria must bear heavy responsibility for the loss of life in Iraq: 'Fifty per cent of murders and bombings are by Arab extremists coming from Syria. They come from Syria, we have evidence to prove it.'[30] The comments were predictably rejected by Damascus, which accused pro-American factions in the Iraqi government of attempts to disrupt diplomatic negotiations. The ISG had proposed talks with both Iran and Syria but the Bush administration was resisting the suggestion, instead trying to crush domestic opposition to the surge policy.

Seven Republicans were now backing the anti-surge resolution, five of whom were facing re-election in 2008. Five others said they were leaning towards a bipartisan compromise, and five more said that they opposed the surge but were unsure how they would vote. There was now the prospect that a few senators would vote to support George Bush even though they opposed any troop increase, what some journalists dubbed 'an exquisite example of Senate flip-floppery on a crucial matter of war and peace'.[31] Part of the problem facing the vacillating senators was that the surge was already under way, a *de facto* circumstance that posed a dilemma for those men and women struggling with their anti-war sentiments.

Already, with the creation of the first JSS and an influx of new troops, the situation on the ground was changing. Security had been intensified, with fresh roadblocks and checkpoints set up in the east of Baghdad on the approaches to the Shi'ite stronghold of Sadr City. Lieutenant General Abboud Qanbar, a Shi'ite once decorated by Saddam Hussein, was officially leading the joint US–Iraqi security operation, since Washington judged that an Iraqi figure in nominal charge of Operation Imposing Justice would have an obvious propaganda advantage. Bush had not waited for appropriate congressional approval: he had begun his surge, a manifest expansion of the war, and then dared the US political establishment to withdraw financial support from US troops already engaged on a dangerous mission. It would soon emerge that the Democrats and their handful of Republican dissidents had no stomach for any such action.

Efforts to quantify the scale of the Iraq catastrophe usually focused on the number of American or British casualties,[32] with less attention given to the Iraqi dead and wounded. It was known that there were millions of displaced persons but figures were vague and rarely publicised. And what was the impact of perhaps two million internal refugees on the life support systems of other parts of Iraq? But there was little statistical information or speculation about the associated consequences of the war for the Iraqi people as a whole. Since none of the estimates of Iraqi fatalities put the figure at less than tens of thousands of dead, what were the knock-on effects of this carnage? For every Iraqi killed there were sure to be many bereaved, not only immediate family members but also members of the local community. And in circumstances where hospitals and psychiatric facilities had all but collapsed what could be said about the impact of trauma on the Iraqi people?

In early February 2007 the Association of Iraqi Psychologists (API) said that the violence had affected millions of children, raising serious concerns for future generations. Thus API's Marwan Abdullah told IRIN, the UN-funded news agency, that Iraqi children were 'seriously suffering psychologically with all the insecurity, especially with the fear of kidnapping and explosions'; and that in some cases they were found 'to be suffering from extreme stress'.[33] In the same vein Sherif Karachatani, a psychology professor at the University of Suleimaniya, said: 'Every day another innocent child is orphaned or sees terrible things children should never see. Who is taking care of the potentially enormous damage that is being done to a generation of children?'[34] The 'relentless bloodshed' and the lack of psychiatric help meant that Iraq's children were growing up either deeply scarred or so habituated to violence 'that they keep the patterns going as they enter adulthood'.[35]

Many of Iraq's best doctors had either fled the country or been killed, and parents were often reluctant to take their children to any residual medical facilities for fear of social stigma. Karachatani said: 'They don't bring their children in for treatment, fearing that they will be labelled as mad.'[36] The continuing conflict, social attitudes and the collapse of medical facilities were combining to produce a generation of disturbed children, with untold consequences for the future. In December Harith Hassan, a prominent child psychologist, had been shot dead as he drove to work. Such agencies as UNICEF, Save the Children and the Iraqi Red Crescent Society were either maintaining only a minimal presence or were closing their operations for security reasons. The Iraqi Red Crescent had been forced through lack of funding to suspend a programme for children suffering from war trauma.

There were signs also that the war was impacting on social programmes in the United States. In early February George Bush was planning to slash medical care for the poor and elderly to meet the soaring costs of the war – which meant that $66 billion would be cut from Medicare, the health care scheme for the elderly, over five years and $12 billion would be cut from the Medicaid health care scheme for the poor. As in Iraq, the war was having a drastic impact on the health of a nation, including children. Bush commented: 'Our priority is to protect the American people. And our priority is to make sure our troops have what it takes to do their jobs.'[37] It was left to the *New York Times* to note that the cost of the war would have paid for universal health care in the United States, nursery education for all three- and four-year-olds in the country, immunisation for children around the world against a host of diseases – and still leave half the money for other purposes.[38]

The United States and Britain were reluctant to publish statistics on the number of Iraqi fatalities since the 2003 invasion but they could not disguise the scale of the slaughter that their policies had brought to a national people. The estimates varied but by

February 2007 none, not even the conservative Iraq Body Count survey, put the number of deaths at less than 50,000. The celebrated *Lancet* survey[39] judged that in excess of 650,000 Iraqis had died as a result of the war, and one estimate put the number of excess deaths at a total of one million.[40]

Dr Gideon Polya, a Melbourne scientist, summarised the costs of the Iraq War as at February 2007. He noted:

- the total accrual cost to the United States was $2.3 trillion;[41]
- there were 3.7 million Iraqi refugees;[42]
- the post-invasion excess deaths (avoidable deaths, deaths that did not have to happen) totalled one million (see below);
- post-invasion deaths of under-fives totalled 600,000;[43]
- there were 1.7 million excess Iraqi deaths associated with the Western-imposed 1990–2003 sanctions war;[44]
- there were 1.2 million under-five deaths during the sanctions war;[45]
- the deaths among the US-led forces total about 3,360.

The estimate that one million deaths were caused by the war derives from data supplied by medical scientists at Johns Hopkins University and the UN Population Division (UNPD). Thus the scientists noted an 'annual death rate per 1,000 of population' of 13.3 (post-invasion Iraq) as compared to (a) 5.5 (for pre-invasion Iraq after twelve years of crippling sanctions) and (b) 4.0 (for Iraq's resource-poor but peaceful neighbours, Syria and Jordan). The UNPD noted that the 'post-invasion excess death rate/1000 of population was 13.3 - 5.5 = 7.8 (comparison a) or 13.3 - 4.0 = 9.3 (comparison b). Assuming an average population of 27 million, the 'post-invasion excess deaths' total (over four years) either (a) 7.8 × 2,700 × 4 = 842,000 or (b) 9.3 × 2,700 × 4 = 1,004,400 (i.e. in excess of one million deaths).

Put simply, if the Iraq death rate before and after the 2003 invasion is compared with that of peaceful Syria and Jordan – a not unreasonable comparison – then the war has caused about one million deaths.[46]

Polya went further. If the number of Iraqi casualties – deaths and refugees – caused by the sanctions war are added to the number of deaths caused by the 2003 invasion and occupation then the United States and Britain are responsible for an Iraq genocide comparable to 'the WW2 Jewish Holocaust (5–6 million victims) and the "forgotten" WW2 British-caused Bengali Holocaust (4 million victims)'. Hence the total excess Iraqi deaths (1990–2007) come to 2.7 million, and the post-invasion excess deaths in occupied Afghanistan total 2.2 million, with Afghan refugees totalling about 3.7 million. In these circumstances it is hard to avoid the conclusion that President Bush, Prime Minister Tony Blair and others should be arraigned before a suitable court on charges of genocide, war crimes and crimes against humanity.[47]

In reality the Bush administration intended to use the law to support aggressive war. On 5 February Lieutenant Ehren Watada faced a court martial for refusing to deploy to Iraq and for making public statements against the war – the first US officer to be prosecuted for criticising George Bush's war policy:

> It would be a violation of my oath because this war to me is illegal in the sense that it was waged in deception, and it was also in violation of international law. Officers and leaders have that responsibility to speak out for the enlisted and certainly when we do so it comes with more consequences, which is what a leader should do. A leader can't just go with the crowd.[48]

Already a number of enlisted men, citing conscientious objection, had refused to serve in Iraq. Thirteen had sought political asylum in Canada, and thousands more had gone absent without leave. In 2006 six senior generals, including some who had served in the invasion and occupation of Iraq had demanded that the then Defense Secretary, Donald Rumsfeld, stand down.

Now the US military was launching the first stage of the new security strategy in Baghdad, hours after Bush had won a temporary victory against congressional opposition to his surge policy. Several moderate Republicans, acting in alliance with the Democrats, had backed a motion urging the President to reconsider 'all options', but were unable to obtain the sixty preliminary votes needed to back a full debate. Senate majority leader Harry Reid commented that the American people did not support an escalation of the war and wanted a change of course; the Republicans 'should not run from this debate': 'If they believe we should send thousands of our young soldiers into the maws of this wretched civil war, they should at least have the courage to stand up and defend their position.'[49] As noted, the new Baghdad command centre to supervise the troop surge and the associated security plan was to be led by an Iraqi soldier, Lieutenant General Abboud Qanbar, approved by the US military after the Americans rejected Prime Minister al-Maliki's first choice for the job. As always, the United States was running the show.

On 6 February 2007 the Pentagon declared that it would take no further action against the US pilots whose 'friendly fire' attacks on British tanks in 2003 had killed a soldier, Lance Corporal of Horse Matty Hull, and wounded four others. A graphic cockpit video and voice transcript evidence had been leaked, forcing Washington to hand over the evidence to the Oxfordshire assistant deputy coroner, Andrew Walker, on the condition that the material was seen only by him and the Hull family. The affair was widely interpreted as further evidence that the United States had little interest in cooperating with its allies when controversial matters arose.[50] At the same time thousands of delegates at an anti-war conference in Malaysia launched the Kuala Lumpur War Crimes Commission for the trials of George Bush and Tony Blair. The former Malaysian Prime Minister Mahathir Mohammed acknowledged that the tribunal would not be able to implement its verdicts: 'History should remember Blair and Bush as the killers of children or as the lying prime minister and president. What Blair and Bush have done is worse than what Saddam has done.'[51]

The United States was again ratcheting up tensions with Iran when a senior Iranian diplomat in Baghdad was kidnapped by gunmen in Iraqi army uniforms, allegedly acting under US 'supervision';[52] Iraq's deputy Health Minister, Hakim al-Zamili, was also arrested – on suspicion of corruption and helping to funnel millions of dollars to Shi'ite militiamen. A Pentagon official claimed that the arrest of al-Zamili by US and Iraqi forces showed that the Maliki government was prepared to take action against anyone during the security crackdown, but Health Minister Ali al-Shammari gave a different version of events. He had been with Prime Minister al-Maliki when the news of the raid broke. Al-Maliki, al-Shammari claimed, had denounced the action as illegal, a violation of Iraq's sovereignty, and Abdul Qadar Obeidi, the Defence Minister, pointed out that the Iraqi troops involved in the raid were special forces who came under US command.[53]

The failure of the US and Iraqi forces to impose security was leaving thousands of families with no choice but to flee the country. The story of 'Mohaned', a Sunni, was typical. At first he had experienced no financial problems since he was working both as an anaesthetist and a translator, and he could afford two generators, but he was compelled to leave his home. 'Neither he nor his family had yet been killed. He wanted to keep it that way.'[54] He had at last been prevented from going to work since, with the Shi'ites now controlling the hospital, he would be killed either there or at the checkpoints manned by Mahdi militiamen 'looking for Sunnis to kill'.[55] Mohaned paid $100 for the necessary documents and then left his home at 6 a.m., taking care to avoid the US military convoys, whose rear gunners typically fired at anyone who came near. Eventually he managed to reach the border with Syria, paying a $500 bribe to avoid the queue of Iraqis trying to leave their country, and acquired a fifteen-day visa in Damascus from the Syrian authorities that could not be renewed unless he found a job. 'I don't even want to think about returning to Iraq. I know very well that will be like walking back to hell, and I will be finished.'[56]

The American task of providing security for both Sunnis and Shi'ites seemed totally unrealistic. The US onslaught, involving the destruction of all the social and political institutions of the state, had generated levels of violent anarchy that were unprecedented in Iraqi history. General David Petraeus was continuing to cite Fallujah as the model for what might be achieved in other communities:[57] in effect, the razing of a city, the destruction of 36,000 homes, the obliteration of Fallujah's infrastructure, the eviction of three-quarters of the city's population into makeshift desert camps lacking basic amenities, and the imposition of gated compounds to accommodate authorised Iraqis carrying biometric

ID cards. Some observers compared the destruction of Fallujah with the wanton murder and destruction associated with the cities of Guernica in the 1930s and Grozny in the 1990s : 'This decade's unforgettable monument to brutality and overkill is Falluja, a textbook case of how not to handle an insurgency, and a reminder that unpopular occupations will always degenerate into desperation and atrocity.'[58] Is this what Petraeus intended the surge to mean for Baghdad?

An unnamed senior US defence official confirmed that the aim was to establish several 'gated communities' in Baghdad to provide extra security for Sunnis and Shi'ites: 'There are certain areas in Baghdad where we will have to control access with checkpoints because otherwise there will be people trying their best to blow them up.' Nowhere in the capital would be off limits although 'we're not going to rush straight into Sadr City'. The objective would be to keep the areas secure, 'and Fallujah is the best example, a gated community with ID cards for all the residents'; there 'would have to be more [such] gated communities' in Baghdad to ensure security.[59]

Even now, the mood in Washington was far from confident, with Defense Secretary Robert Gates seemingly planning for a failure of the surge policy: if the new strategy did not succeed he was prepared to move American troops 'out of harm's way . . . I would be irresponsible if I weren't thinking about what the alternatives might be.'[60] Petraeus himself judged that the way ahead would be 'hard but it is not hopeless'.[61] Some of the forward bases, JSSs like the 'Alamo' (see above), would be sited in fortified clusters of houses, others in abandoned police stations. American troops would be expected to live cheek by jowl with their Iraqi counterparts, but this itself presented security problems. Thus Captain Ramiro Roldan, from the 1st Cavalry in East Baghdad, said: 'We can't for sure say that all of the Iraqi elements . . . are completely on our side.'[62] The ubiquitous problem of insurgent infiltration existed in the JSSs, as in all Iraqi units supposedly allied to the US military. In addition, the familiar question of Iraqi motivation was also evident in the early stages of the surge. Thus the launch of the new security policy was delayed for several days because not enough Iraqi soldiers turned up for duty[63] – casting further doubts on the likelihood that security could be handed over to the Iraqi forces in a matter of months.

The early results from the surge suggested that murders had been reduced in some parts of Baghdad, though the violence had migrated elsewhere and before long fatalities in the capital, not least those of American troops, would again be rising. The US military continued to assert that the surge was not yet being fully implemented and that some months would be needed to judge its success. On 7 February a US helicopter crashed in Iraq, killing all seven people on board, after being hit by an anti-aircraft missile; a few days later a series of large explosions in central Baghdad killed at least seventy-six people – a further blow to the Maliki regime and the US troop surge, struggling to impose order on the capital.

Iran was now being blamed for fuelling the insurgency by smuggling armour-piercing weapons and other arms to the militants in Baghdad and elsewhere.[64] Tehran, the US military charged, was responsible for much of the continuing violence in Baghdad and elsewhere. On 12 February a succession of car bombs shattered a city centre market, killing seventy-five people and wounding more than 160 others, apparently to mark the anniversary of the previous year's destruction of the Golden Shrine in Samarra. One witness, Wahiq Ibrahim, said: 'Paramedics were picking up body pieces and human flesh from the pools of blood on the ground and placing them in small plastic bags.' Amid the shattered stores and market stalls survivors of the blasts screamed: 'Where is the government? Where is the security plan?'[65]

It was now being reported, though contested by senior members of the Mahdi Army, that Muqtada al-Sadr, the Mahdi leader, and his senior commanders had fled Iraq to seek sanctuary in Tehran, where al-Sadr had family. The US military had said that the Shi'ite militias would be targeted, and Prime Minister al-Maliki had declared that he could not guarantee al-Sadr's safety.[66] Then Lieutenant General Abboud Qanbar, the Iraqi commander of the security offensive, announced on state television that the Iraqi authorities were closing the land borders with Syria and Jordan for seventy-two hours and extending the night-time curfew in Baghdad by three hours, beginning at 8 p.m., as part of the security plan to stop insurgent operations. However, this also meant that Iraqis struggling to flee the country would be trapped for days on the border, unable to reach a peaceful haven and unable to return to their abandoned homes.

Again the involvement of Iran in the insurgency seemed obvious. An unnamed high-level Iraqi official commented: 'Over the last three weeks, they [Iran] have taken away from Baghdad the first- and second-tier military leaders of the Mahdi Army' to 'prevent the dismantling of the infrastructure of the Shia militias' in the Iraqi capital. The strategy was 'to lie low until the storm passes, and then let them return to fill the vacuum'. It was clear that the Iranian authorities, anticipating the US troop surge, were 'playing a waiting game'.[67] Karim Moussawi, a senior figure in the Mahdi Army, confirmed the reports: most of the militia leaders had gone to Iran but on their own initiative, without being ordered by al-Sadr or enticed by Tehran. They were, he suggested, simply seeking sanctuary from the expected targeting by American troops.[68] Some observers suggested that the Mahdi leaders would not be wasting their time in Iran: they would be offered training and access to the sophisticated weaponry that was reportedly causing so much trouble for the US forces.

A new *USA Today*/Gallup poll revealed that nearly two-thirds of American citizens opposed the troop surge and wanted congressional action to set a timetable for bringing the troops home. It was now expected that the House of Representatives would adopt a non-binding resolution that

> disapproves of the decision of President George W. Bush to deploy more than 20,000 additional US combat troops to Iraq . . . Congress and the American people will continue to support and protect the members of the US armed forces who are serving or who have served bravely and honourably in Iraq.

In short, the Democrats were preparing a clear betrayal of the American people. The House would declare its 'disapproval' and then decline to take any effective action: the first units of surge troops were already in place, and there was no way that the Democrats would take steps to jeopardise their funding. Nancy Pelosi, the speaker of the House, highlighted the impact of the war – the 'thousands of deaths, tens of thousands of casualties, costing hundreds of billions of dollars and damaging the standing of the US in the international community' – and declared that a vote of disapproval would 'set the stage' for additional Iraq legislation. There was, Pelosi declared, 'no end in sight';[69] but it was becoming increasingly obvious that the Democrats had no stomach for a protracted battle with the White House.

On 15 February, as an important stage in Operation Imposing Justice, American and British troops enforced a security plan on Baghdad and Basra aimed at restoring order. In Baghdad, US and Iraqi troops supported by helicopters searched the Sunni insurgent bastion of Dora to the sound of exploding projectiles in the district. The Iraqi Interior Ministry claimed that four large districts were being searched for militants and weapons, but two car bombs exploded on a route leading to Shi'ite areas south of Baghdad, killing at least four civilians and wounding fifteen more. Later, another car bomb in Sadr City killed three and wounded seventeen; and a fourth bomb in the Baghdad district of Jamiya wounded two Iraqi soldiers.

In southern Iraq more than 2,000 Iraqi soldiers, supported by 1,200 British troops, cordoned off Basra and closed two border crossings with Iran at al-Sheeb and Shalamcha, blocking the gates with large metal containers while expanding the coastal patrols to monitor maritime traffic. In this massive operation, codenamed Troy, every vehicle on eight routes into and out of the city was checked in coordination with the US surge operation in Baghdad. Captain Ollie Pile, a spokesman for the 19th Light Brigade in southern Iraq, described Operation Troy as being conducted 'in partnership with the Baghdad security plan and other security operations being conducted throughout Iraq' and serving as 'another step along the way towards the Iraqi authorities taking responsibility for the security of Basra'.[70]

The UN was now appealing to the European Union to do more to protect the refugees fleeing from Iraq. Madeline Garlick, speaking in Brussels for the UNHCR, declared that the humanitarian situation in the country was 'grave and deteriorating', and that states 'should respond to the needs of asylum seekers on their territory'. By mid-February 2007 the largest number of Iraqis fleeing to EU countries had reached Sweden, followed by the Netherlands, Germany, Greece, Britain and Belgium.[71] Some 20,000 refugees had fled to Sweden, even though it took good connections and up to $15,000 to travel from Baghdad to Stockholm; and Sweden was bracing itself to receive a possible 35,000 Iraqis in 2007. The country's policy was unusual in that it allowed entry to any Iraqis who could prove they had just fled central and southern Iraq, no matter what their political involvement. Thus there were many 'Iraqis in Sweden . . . who are fleeing Sunni militia' alongside 'Sunnis who for decades belonged to the Ba'ath Party and supported Saddam's regime'.[72] The Swedish migration minister, Tobias Billström, stressed that more countries should be accepting Iraqi asylum seekers; and urged EU states to help Syria, Jordan and Iran, then hosting hundreds of thousands of Iraqi refugees. The United States had recently said that it would accept 7,000 Iraqis in 2007, out of the two million refugees – an increase for the US from the 202 Iraqis granted refugee status the previous year. Nasser Judeh, the Jordanian government's chief spokesman, noted that 7,000 Iraqi refugees 'is just 1 per cent of the number we have'. However, the EU initiatives were not always welcomed by Iraqi activists. Arkan Hanna, a priest representing some 40,000 Iraqi Christian refugees in Syria, commented: 'We are against the dispersal of the Iraqi refugees into a diaspora. We want the Americans out of our country. We want to go back to our country in a normal way.'[73]

On 16 February 2007 the US House of Representatives decided by 246 votes to 182 to condemn George Bush's policy of sending more troops to Iraq. The vote was non-binding but was considered to have immense symbolic weight, not least because seventeen Republicans had defied Bush and voted to rebuke him; two Democrats, from Georgia and Mississippi, voted against the resolution. Nancy Pelosi commented: 'The stakes in Iraq are too high to recycle proposals that have little prospect for success. The passage of this legislation will signal a change in direction in Iraq that will end the fighting and bring our troops home.' And, conscious of much recent White House rhetoric on Iran, she also urged legislation to curb Bush's power to launch a military strike on that country without first seeking congressional approval: 'There is no previous authority for the President, any President, to go into Iran.'[74]

The significance of the House vote remained to be seen. Few observers doubted that it represented the will of the American people, but Bush and most Republicans were seemingly indifferent to such a consideration. And already the Republicans were mounting opposition to the thrust of the resolution. Eric Cantor, the Republicans' chief deputy whip, suggested that Islamic radials would be inspired to continue the conflict by a Congress that said it would support the troops but not their mission; and John Boehner, the Republican leader, denounced any intentions 'to eliminate funding for our troops that are in harm's way'.[75] White House spokesman Tony Snow warned Congress not to move beyond a non-binding resolution to an attempt to cut off Iraq funding. President Bush made no immediate comment on the vote but his intention to expand the war was not in doubt.

In the United States there were also other controversial matters – relating to the treatment of members of the US military, particularly those wounded veterans returning home. On 18 February the *Washington Post* ran a devastating article describing the appalling conditions in which Iraq and Afghanistan veterans were expected to live in the Walter Reed Army Medical Center in Washington.[76] Here the journalists Dana Priest and Anne Hull described what they encountered in the hospital's Building 18 ('a rodent infestation issue'), the quarters of Jeremy Duncan, suffering from a broken neck, a shredded left ear and massive blood loss: 'mouse droppings, belly-up cockroaches, stained carpets, cheap mattresses'.[77] One case manager was so disgusted that she decided herself to buy roach bombs for the rooms; mousetraps were handed out, but made little difference. A broken garage door allowed unmonitored entry to the hospital, causing veterans suffering from 'schizophrenia, PTSD [post-traumatic stress disorder] and traumatic brain injury' to feel especially vulnerable. One veteran said he had been close to mortars and 'held my own pretty good . . . But here . . . I think it has affected my ability to get over it . . . dealing with potential threats every day'.[78]

It was widely assumed that Walter Reed was the 'crown jewel of military medicine', but Priest and Hull described a scene in which the 'wounded manage other wounded', where psychologically damaged soldiers were put in charge of inmates 'at risk of suicide', and where 'disengaged clerks, unqualified platoon sergeants and overworked case managers' were fumbling with simple needs.[79] George Bush had commented before Christmas 2006 that the United States owed the veterans 'all we can give them', but now it was plain they were suffering appalling levels of neglect and abuse. Thus when Staff Sergeant John Daniel Shannon arrived at Walter Reed, his eye and skull shattered, he was handed a chart of the hospital and told to find his own room. He stumbled around, sliding against walls, trying to keep himself upright, and asking anyone he encountered for directions.[80]

The scandal impacted on a Bush administration that was already discredited, seen to have launched a war on at best inadequate intelligence and at worst a pack of lies. President Bush himself was forced to respond, if only to create the impression that he cared about US military personnel (see also Chapter 3).

On 18 February a double car bomb attack in Baghdad killed at least sixty people, ending the brief lull in violence since the start of the American and Iraqi security operation. A Reuters photographer witnessed the bodies strewn in the street between the two blasts: 'I saw a man about 50 years old. He was carrying a dead boy who looked about 10. He was holding him by one arm and one leg, and screaming.'[81] A third car bomb explosion in Sadr City killed at least one person and injured ten more, and the US military reported two more soldiers killed – one when an insurgent hurled a grenade, and another when a patrol came under fire. Now the British were being forced to acknowledge the realities on the ground, and in consequence to plan for further reductions in troop levels. Anthony Cordesman, of the Center for Strategic and International Studies in Washington, commented that the British would simply hand more power to the Islamist groups backed by neighbouring Iran: 'The British cuts will in many ways simply reflect the political reality that the British "lost" the south more than a year ago.'[82]

A day later, insurgents launched an attack on a US combat post, killing two soldiers and wounding seventeen others; eleven people were killed by a mortar attack on a Shi'ite enclave; five people were killed when an insurgent detonated a bomb-rigged belt on a bus heading for Karradah in central Baghdad; roadside bombs killed three policemen in the Shi'ite area of Zafraniyah in south-east Baghdad and five civilians in an open-air market; and on 25 February a suicide bomber killed at least forty people and wounded thirty-five at a Baghdad business college. Prime Minister al-Maliki had welcomed the evident reduction in the violence – by as much as 80 per cent, according to Iraqi spokesman Brigadier General Qassim al-Moussawi – but it seemed his comments were premature.

On 27 February American troops bombarded a residential district of Ramadi in Anbar province with 'precision guided munitions', killing at least twenty-six Iraqi civilians, including women and children. A six-hour firefight with insurgents had begun when American troops were ambushed by Iraqis with small arms and rocket-propelled grenades, causing the US military to call in air strikes to flatten a number of buildings allegedly being used by the Iraqi gunmen. Residents managed to pull two small boys out of the rubble, and a Ramadi hospital doctor, Hafidh Ibrahim, confirmed that neighbours had salvaged twenty-six bodies from the ruins. Also, the American forces were preparing for a fresh offensive against Ramadi as part of the second phase of the surge.[83] Following the loss of a Black Hawk helicopter the previous day, another American helicopter crashed north of Baqubah, the ninth to be shot down since 20 January; US military spokesman Major General William Caldwell admitted that it had almost certainly been brought down by small-arms fire and rocket-propelled grenades.

The latest wave of violence had begun a day after the UN Development Programme (UNDP) criticised US-backed policies aiming to transform the Iraqi economy into a 'free market'. In a new study, *Unsatisfactory Basic Needs Mapping and Living Standards in Iraq*, the UNDP emphasised that the lifting of subsidies and the further dismantling of Iraqi state industries at such a time would plunge more people into poverty. Paolo Lembo, the UNDP's Iraq director, commented that the study, based on a sample size of 21,000 households in Baghdad, would aid policy makers and development planners, and he urged the international community to join the Iraqi people in restoring 'the real potential of the country – not only for the Iraqis but for the future of the world'.

On 21 February Tony Blair announced that an operation to put local Iraqi forces in charge of Basra was now complete, indicating the likelihood of significant British troop withdrawals from Iraq. He would not be drawn on reports that troop numbers could be cut from 7,100 to around 4,000, but praised the recent Operation Sinbad in Basra province: 'As the Iraqis are more capable down in Basra of taking control of their own security we will scale down [but] you've got to make sure you have sufficient forces in support and in reserve.'[84] *The Guardian* had reportedly learned that the British government, taking on board the message coming from military chiefs, intended to pull out all British troops by the end of 2008, starting with the withdrawal of up to 1,500 by early summer 2007.[85]

For months army commanders had been arguing that the presence of British troops on the streets of Basra was doing more harm than good, and urging much bigger cuts in numbers than either London or Washington was prepared to accept.[86] Now under the terms of Operation Zenith some 1,600 troops would be withdrawn when the 1st Mechanised Brigade began deploying in April with fewer troops than originally intended. However, the British government was continuing to insist that an unconditional timetable for withdrawal would be a disaster since it would enable the insurgents to plan their response. And despite the Prime Minister's hints on withdrawal there were evident plans to maintain at least 4,000 British troops in the country for another five years – 'for at least until the Americans leave Iraq'.[87]

★

On 25 February the Kurdish authorities, under pressure from the international oil corporations, agreed a draft law to manage Iraq's vast oil wealth. Here the oil giants were offered several methods by which to invest, including the production-sharing agreements which would hand the US and other international companies a massive slice of the oil revenues to recover their initial investments and then allow them substantial tax breaks. The Iraqi government would sign away the right to exploit its own untapped fields in so-called exploration contracts, which could be extended for more than thirty years. On the same day Ruth Tanner of War on Want commented: 'Iraq is under occupation and its people are facing relentless insecurity and crippling poverty. Yet . . . multinationals are poised to take control of Iraq's oil wealth.' And the matter no longer seemed to be an issue of dispute. Thus a British Foreign Office minister, Kim Howells, admitted in a written answer in the House of Commons that the government had discussed the proposed Iraqi law with Britain's oil corporations ('British oil companies have valuable perspectives to offer'), confirming a general suspicion. Alan Simpson, a Labour MP, said: 'This confirms the view of those who have said all along that the war in Iraq was not about weapons of mass destruction, but the control of the levers of mass production.'

The following day Iraqi leaders approved the draft oil law, opening the country's reserves to foreign investors on immensely favourable terms. Already Sunni Muslims, who live mainly in oil-poor areas, were arguing that the oil and gas profits would be likely to benefit only the Shi'ite majority – and now, under the terms of the new law, even this assumption seemed questionable. The Iraqi government and Washington continued to insist that the new law represented a fair sharing of Iraq's oil revenues through the various regions, giving no publicity to the favoured role of the international oil corporations; but even the Western press had to concede the character of the new legislation – 'Many Iraqis fear that the measure will hand the country's major natural resources over to foreign oil companies.'[88] In Washington, White House spokesman Tony Snow praised the new law.[89]

★

With growing concern among Shi'ites that the US military was preparing to attack Sadr City, Muqtada al-Sadr, who had toyed with a pragmatic support for the surge (thinking that it would focus on Sunni communities), declared it was not working. An al-Sadr aide said: 'There is no benefit in this plan because it is controlled by the occupiers,' and because the American forces were 'watching car bombs explode, taking the souls of thousands of innocent Iraqi people'.[90] This was a clear blow to American and Iraqi government policies. If Prime Minister al-Maliki was no longer able to rely on the integrity of the Iraqi parliament, with its Shi'ite majority, then any pretence at national government would be immediately exposed. It was already plain that the new Iraqi constitution, drafted in part by the Americans, had served to consolidate sectarian divisions and to intensify the low-grade civil war. If now the sectarian divide among the Iraqi legislators had been allowed to rupture an already ineffectual parliament, then what was left of the 'democratically elected' government? It seemed that Iraq's 'burgeoning democracy' consisted of no more than various squabbling sectarian groups confined to the Green Zone fortress within easy reach of American officials.

On 26 February the Sunni Vice-President, Tariq al-Hashemi,[91] declared that the new security plan, nominally an Iraqi initiative but in reality inspired and controlled by the United States, was failing to observe proper legal procedures. The rights of Iraqis were not being respected, just as human rights had not been observed in two earlier security operations the previous year: 'This is surely regrettable.' Al-Hashemi complained that the military operations had focused almost exclusively on Sunni areas – the converse of the Shi'ite objections. It was now possible to evaluate the surge's initial impact. Few military or security gains had been accomplished and the Iraqi commitment, such as it was, was faltering. The reliability of Iraqi troops, in terms of morale and competence, remained highly questionable; and some prominent Sunnis and Shi'ites, focusing on their own communities, were expressing concerns that the security plan was being implemented in a divisive manner.

Washington continued to advertise the surge as a fresh initiative that would succeed but there were signs of desperation in the

Bush administration, not least the US decision to participate in 'ice breaker' talks with Syria and Iran – both, according to the United States, 'pariah states' – in Baghdad.[92] This followed the specific recommendation in *The Iraq Study Group Report* that 'the United States should engage directly with Iran and Syria' to seek their help over the Iraq issue; and to this end the US should be prepared to consider 'incentives, as well as disincentives'.[93] Put another way, Washington was desperate to find a way of ending a catastrophic war and should not only threaten Iraq's neighbours in order to gain their support.

At the end of February 2007 American policies were in disarray. There were growing political divisions at home and a deepening crisis of morale in the US military, with troops uncertain about their objectives, and soldiers, veterans and their families not getting much-needed psychological help, because the military health system was overwhelmed with the mounting level of demand. Thus a report by the American Psychological Association cited a 40 per cent vacancy rate in active-duty psycho-logists in the US army and navy, family counsellors deprived of adequate resources, and weak support for veterans leaving the army. It was estimated that three out of every ten soldiers met the criteria for a mental disorder but fewer than half of these were seeking help, often because such help was not available. In addition, morale problems were also affecting the overburdened army psychologists: there were high levels of 'burn-out' and twenty-seven per cent reported 'low motivation for their work'. Even the magazine *Time* was forced to admit that the facts on the ground in Iraq were 'dismal' and that the 'near impossibility' of the surge mission was 'already apparent'.[94] On 27 February a truck bomb killed at least six women and twelve children playing football in the al-Warar district of Ramadi.

Such events were combining to destroy any credibility that the surge might have had. The additional American contingents were too small to have any appreciable impact on the security situation, and there were already doubts that enough Iraqi troops would turn up to support the US soldiers. Moreover, two of the Iraqi brigades expected to help the Americans were Kurdish, who rarely spoke Arabic and tended to dislike Arabs – which meant that any hopes of enlisting local support and achieving sectarian reconciliation were undermined from the start. Kurds and Arabs were already fighting in the oil city of Kirkuk, and it seemed likely that this element in the Iraq chaos would be imported to Baghdad. At best the surge policy would involve 'a long hard slog'.[95] And then what would happen? What did Washington's military planners imagine would transpire when the US surge troops abandoned their JSSs and left poorly trained Iraqis, with low morale and their own sectarian agendas, to police Baghdad?

3

'No moderate centre in Iraq'

By March it was increasingly clear that many factors were combining to produce an inexorable defeat for the US policy in Iraq. The scale of the social collapse and the resulting anarchy, shaped by freshly fuelled ethnic and sectarian divisions,[1] could never be adequately addressed by the size of the American forces in the country and the value system that coloured their presence. From the outset it had been foolish to assume that a proud Arab people at the heart of the Muslim world would tolerate, much less welcome, a permanent alien occupation of their country. But it had taken an enormous sacrifice of young American soldiers and capital for the basic realities to penetrate the ideological carapace of the Washington political establishment.

An elite team of officers advising General David Petraeus had concluded that they had only a few months to win the war in Iraq – or face a Vietnam-style collapse in political will and public support that would plunge the US military into a humiliating defeat.[2] The team, known as the 'Baghdad brains trust',[3] was struggling with a range of seemingly intractable problems that were preventing the United States from achieving its declared goals.[4] A former senior administration official, aware of the team's work, commented: 'They know they are operating under a clock. They know they are going to hear a lot more talk in Washington about "Plan B" by the autumn – meaning withdrawal. They know that the next six-month period is their opportunity. And they say it's getting harder every day.'[5]

Five main areas of difficulty were identified:

- There were too few troops on the ground – a charge that had been made by US army commanders from the beginning, against the 'lean war-making capacity' advocated by former Defense Secretary Donald Rumsfeld.

- As one member peeled off after another, the international 'coalition of the willing' was collapsing, giving weight to insurgent propaganda that the occupation was being maintained primarily by only one 'crusader' nation without international support.
- The likely withdrawal of the British forces from southern Iraq over the following year had implications for both US morale and the scale of the task facing the US military: would there be more violence in the south, caused in part by the displacement of insurgents from Baghdad by the US troop surge, or would a degree of security be imposed by Shi'ite militias comfortable in a Greater Iran?
- Morale in the US military was deteriorating as casualties increased, with little compensation being derived from the continuing slaughter of Iraqis and the wasting of their cities.
- Such factors, allied to the increasing unpopularity of the war throughout the United States, were contributing to what might emerge as a decisive failure of political will in Washington and Baghdad.[6]

The former official described what he saw as an atmosphere of mounting panic and despair: team members working round the clock in a 'very tense' scene, having endless cups of coffee with the Iraqis and trying to figure out what to do. President George Bush was expecting progress, but it was not clear what he meant: 'The plan is changing every minute, as all plans do.'[7] Lieutenant Colonel John Nagel, who, with Petraeus, had written the US military's revised counter-insurgency field manual, emphasised the need for more troops, particularly in the light of the planned British withdrawal.[8] Perhaps, said the former official, the situation would get 'really tough' in the next few months, and what then would happen to congressional opinion? One unnamed Pentagon official, while giving reasons for optimism, said that it was too early to judge whether the new policy would succeed and admitted that 'the military alone are not going to solve the problem'. There was also a need for a civilian surge: 'The Iraqis have to do it themselves.'[9]

It seemed clear at this stage that neither the military surge nor the envisioned civilian surge was making much progress. The coalition casualties continued to mount, with the increased exposure of the US troops leading to more fatalities. In early March the media reported the death of another British soldier, Rifleman Daniel Coffey, who had volunteered to return to Iraq for a second tour of duty. This casualty was significant in part because it was the first to occur in one of the army's new Bulldog armoured personnel carriers, thought to be more robust than Snatch Land Rovers.[10]

Iraqis were continuing to die in the sectarian war and through 'conventional' criminal activity involving abductions for ransom and other purposes; the US military was maintaining sporadic but heavy bombardments of 'suspected insurgent positions'; more and more civilians were being rounded up to swell the detainee populations; and the American raids on homes and other properties, sometimes in the dead of night, were continuing unabated. In late February US and Iraqi forces raided the head offices of the General Federation of Iraqi Workers, the country's national trade union centre. They arrested one of the union's security staff, destroyed furniture and confiscated a computer and a fax machine. Two days later they repeated the operation, causing more damage to the union headquarters – indicating, more than counter-insurgency activity, a political agenda in American efforts to establish a free-market economy.

It was evident also that US policy was impacting on human rights in various ways throughout Iraq. For example, MADRE, an international women's rights organisation, released a detailed report at the United Nations revealing that gender-based violence had been largely overlooked in Iraq since the 2003 invasion.[11] Houzan Mahmoud, of the Organisation for Women's Freedom in Iraq, commented: 'Before the US occupation, Iraq was a dictatorship. It was not perfect, but there was security. Women could go to work, could go out. What little protections there were for women before the occupation are now gone.' Furthermore Yifat Susskind, the author of the MADRE report, argued that, despite its legal obligations under the Hague and Geneva conventions, the Bush administration had 'decisively traded women's rights for cooperation with the Islamists whom it boosted to power'.[12] And no one doubted that the Islamists saw the subordination of women as a top priority. (In addition, the US military itself was guilty of a massive degree of sexual harassment of its own female personnel, often leading to assault. One survey conducted by the US Veterans Association revealed that 30 per cent of female veterans had been victims of sexual assault, 14 per cent had been gang raped, and another 20 per cent raped more than once. The rate at which females in the military were being sexually assaulted ranged anywhere from three to ten times that for female civilians.[13]

Save the Children, the last major charity working in Iraq,[14] was now pulling out after fifteen years in the country because the security situation made it impossible to protect staff. Paul Roberts, the charity's programme director, said that it had become more and more difficult for staff to travel round the country and their safety had been jeopardised: 'In practical terms it just became impossible.'[15] He had been based in Jordan with other international staff and had been making monthly trips into Iraq to monitor Save the Children's work with local partners, but now the charity could no longer meet the children that needed help. A 'huge humanitarian issue' was being masked by the US focus on conflict and 'terrorism', with around 8 per cent of children – 4 per cent of the entire Iraqi population – already suffering from acute malnutrition.

There was now mounting evidence that the British forces in southern Iraq were inadequately resourced and suffering low morale. On 6 March Air Chief Marshal Sir Jock Stirrup, the head of the armed forces, joined his fellow chiefs in the Ministry of Defence by echoing concerns that the UK forces were being asked to do too much. They were 'very stretched' and there had been a 'skill fade' with troops on counter-insurgency operations for the previous five years: the 'harmony guidelines' (allowing the troops two-year rests between operations) had been breached and soldiers had been forced to redeploy 'sooner than we would have liked . . . We can't keep doing this for years. We do have the capability for certain emergencies but they are pretty limited.'[16]

★

The United States, increasingly desperate for a way forward, was pressing ahead with plans for a regional conference that would include the 'pariah' states of Iran and Syria. The American U-turn was plain. Having denounced Tehran and Damascus for supporting terrorism and aiding the insurgency, Washington was now keen to enlist their support in efforts to bring stability to an increasingly anarchic country that the United States had comprehensively devastated. Philip Gordon of the Brookings Institution commented that the 'big reversal' in US policy reflected what almost everyone had to acknowledge – 'a failure of [American] foreign policy'.[17]

At first Iran was weighing up its possible participation in such a conference. Thus Ali Larijani, the secretary of Iran's Supreme National Security Council, said that 'we will attend the conference if it is expedient',[18] 'if it is in Iraq's interest'.[19] Syria had already said that it would send Ahmed Arnous, an aide to the Foreign Minister, as its representative. Iraq's Prime Minister, Nouri al-Maliki, had embraced the idea of a regional conference, perhaps hoping that a substantial Arab and Muslim presence would influence US policy, and had invited Saudi Arabia, Jordan, Kuwait, Turkey, Iran, Syria, Bahrain and Egypt – in addition to the five permanent members of the UN Security Council, the Arab League and the Organization of the Islamic Conference. Hoshyar Zebari, the Iraqi Foreign Minister, hoped for an 'ice-breaking' event that would lead to other meetings in the future.

American support for the proposed conference was confirmed by Condoleezza Rice at Senate hearings in late February, when she and Defense Secretary Robert Gates were pressed to explain what progress was being made in the Baghdad security crackdown and how soon US troops would be coming home. Senator Robert Byrd of West Virginia, the Appropriations Committee chairman, decried the expenditure of $10 billion a month in Iraq and Afghanistan: 'There is no end, I say, no end in sight.'[20] And Patrick Leahy, another Democrat, asked Gates to predict how soon Iraq would be stabilised. 'The honest answer to your question is I don't know,'[21] Gates replied.

American policy in Iraq was now attracting widespread domestic and international criticism, reflected in congressional divisions and in most informed commentary in the United States and elsewhere. Timothy Carney, the new US coordinator for Iraq's economic development, told National Public Radio that US policy following the 2003 invasion to exclude Iraqis from governing their country in the first two years of the American occupation was 'an enormous foolishness' which contributed to the collapse in security and the length of the conflict. 'We don't need to go into detail on that, but I think words such as incompetent, foolish, dubious . . . are the most charitable way to look at that period.'[22]

There were early signs that the troop surge was having an impact, with 'many Iraqis'[23] saying that the visible increase in the number of US soldiers, Iraqi troops and police on the streets was making them feel safer and worry less about checkpoints manned by insurgents or criminal elements. The skyline of Baghdad was still scarred by columns of smoke rising from bombings, and there remained the persistent doubt that Iraq's new security forces – hitherto crippled by low morale, corruption and insurgent infiltration – would be able to hold the districts cleared by the overwhelming American firepower.

Militia activity had diminished, but everyone knew that the Mahdi Army had simply melted away, biding its time. It was assumed that some of the militiamen had crossed the border into Iran, where they may have expected further training and resupply; others had simply merged with the civilian population, observing US and Iraqi army deployments as a prelude to action in the future. Colonel Doug Heckman, senior advisor to the 9th Iraqi Army Division in East Baghdad, said: 'A lot of bad guys are lying low. The difference between last time and this is stability. It's going to be a lot more boots on the ground. And we are not going to leave. We know last time we petered out. We are not going to make that same mistake again.'[24] But how sure was he? He well knew the unpopularity of the war among the American public and the growing congressional divisions: 'If we were going to be here for another five years I would be confident that things would turn around the right way. But we are not, so the uncertainty is right there.'[25]

There were also continuing tensions and disagreements between the US military and the Iraqi authorities. It was well known that Washington had doubts about Prime Minister al-Maliki's staying power and his ability to deliver on the security plan, and some of the problems derived from competing priorities. On 2 March Baghdad's mayor, Sabir al-Isawi, condemned the United States for huge spending on litter collection and tree-planting while the city still struggled without electricity. Speaking at a meeting in the Green Zone the mayor told US officials that the new renovation schemes were 'not what the people want'.[26] The United States had failed to deliver a single major power plant in four years of occupation, and Baghdad residents were annoyed at only receiving an average of two hours of electricity a day. Furthermore, a high-ranking American official admitted that the capital would have to wait until 2013 before it had a 24-hour electricity supply. Al-Isawi said that the US projects were 'overlapping and so badly planned', and that the workers hired were 'ineffective'.[27]

The scale of financial corruption in Iraq was now clearly emerging. Thus Hazen Shaalan, a small businessman who had become a minister in the interim government that ran Iraq from 2004 to 2005, had presided over the looting from the Defence Ministry's account of what came to be called 'one of the largest thefts in history'. The missing money was part of $8.8 billion of shrink-wrapped American cash that was flown into Iraq but which then disappeared. When eventually located in Jordan, Shaalan said that the missing money had nothing to do with him: 'These $800 million were never at any time received by the Ministry of Defence', but documents seen by the *Sunday Times* suggested otherwise.[28]

In the midst of the chaos of corruption and poorly managed reconstruction the American casualties were continuing to mount – affecting morale in the US military and the United States itself. Moreover, there were morale problems among injured veterans, not simply because of their wounds but because of their treatment when they returned home.[29]

In early March 2007 the scandal continued to rage about the treatment being given to Iraq veterans at the Walter Reed Army

Medical Center (see also Chapter 2), where some of the 50,000 sick and wounded US veterans of the Iraq War were being treated.[30] Injured veterans and their families had praised the level of medical care at the medical centre, but claimed that squalid conditions, bureaucratic chaos and insensitive regulations had hampered the process of recovery. One veteran, Latseen Benson, recovering from a double amputation, was forced to tolerate conditions in the hospital described by his mother: 'I wasn't bothered by the rats, although there were a lot running around outside, but I wanted his room to be swept and kept clean. You couldn't get people to mop the blood and urine from the floor.'[31] One amputee, Marine Sergeant Ryan Groves, wondered where the people were 'back here' who should have been giving him 'an easy transition'.[32]

One problem was the sheer flood of wounded veterans that the hospital was expected to handle: one doctor commented that he had seen 3,000 young men and women coming through Walter Reed and he did not know whether he could take any more.[33] It was plain that Walter Reed was suffering from grossly inadequate funding and lamentably poor management, and that President Bush's wars had produced many more American casualties than had been anticipated.

The articles in the *Washington Post* about the dreadful conditions in the 'other Walter Reed'[34] had forced Bush, speaking in his weekly radio broadcast on 3 March, to say how appalled he was and to promise a nationwide inquiry into veterans' care. The revelations prompted the resignation of the hospital commander, Major General George Weightman, and forced Robert Gates to demand the resignation of Francis Harvey, the Army Secretary. On 6 March Bush, desperate to create the impression that he cared for American troops, set up a 'wounded warrior' commission – to be led by Bob Dole, the former Senate majority leader, and Donna Shalala, the Secretary of Health and Human Services under President Clinton – to investigate the growing scandal. Now attention was being given to the adversarial process for determining the disability benefits of veterans, with military review boards trying to limit costs by claiming that certain brain injuries had been 'pre-existing'.[35] Bush noted the 'obligation' to provide the best possible care for the men and women who had served the country, because they 'deserve it . . . and they are going to get it'[36] – four years into the Iraq War.

In Iraq the carnage continued. In early March an insurgent group affiliated to al-Qaeda posted an online video showing the execution of eighteen kidnapped government security personnel in retaliation for the rape of a Sunni woman by members of the Shi'ite-dominated police. The blindfolded men, some in military uniform, their hands tied behind their backs, were shown in three rows lined up before a screen; the men in the front row were kneeling. Behind them, masked men were shown pointing machine guns at the captives. During the course of the video the insurgents chanted in Arabic, 'At your service, sister,' a presumed reference to the raped woman. Another voice denounced the refusal of the Maliki government to hand over the three officers who had allegedly committed the rape. Finally, two of the militants fired from handguns into the backs of the men's heads, while a third carried a black banner. The execution was accompanied by chants of '*Allahu Akbar!*' ('God is the greatest!').[37]

Prime Minister al-Maliki, under American pressure, was now preparing a Cabinet reshuffle that could further exacerbate sectarian tensions. Washington was urging al-Maliki to get rid of the six government ministers loyal to Muqtada al-Sadr and to create a 'moderate' coalition government bringing together 'non-violent' parties from across Iraq's ethnic divide.[38] On 4 March, as a further strike against 'extremist' power, hundreds of US troops entered the Shi'ite stronghold of Sadr City in the first major push of the troop surge. The usual house-to-house searches were conducted, terrorising ordinary Iraqi families but failing to detect significant evidence of militant activity. An American commander, Lieutenant Colonel David Oclander, commented that 'a lot of the really bad folks' had gone into hiding. Again a general paradox was plain. Al-Maliki had clearly come to power on the backs of his Shi'ite militia supporters. Could he now be expected to bend to American pressure, banning Shi'ite ministers and sanctioning punitive sweeps by the US military into Shi'ite communities? In fact Iraq's security forces were reportedly receiving orders from high-level Iraqi politicians to conduct raids in which Sunni Muslims were intimidated as part of the sectarian cleansing in Baghdad[39] – a manifest violation of the White House conditions specified to the Maliki government for the sending of additional troops to the country. A classified map of Baghdad seen by the *Daily Telegraph* showed substantial gains by the Shi'ites, and only a few areas consolidated by the Sunnis, in the sectarian war. It seemed obvious that the Maliki government was tolerating, if not encouraging, a dramatic redrawing of the Baghdad terrain in the interests of the Shi'ite communities.

In the event, despite US doubts about al-Maliki's commitment and his manifest Shi'ite loyalties, he seemed willing to support the American troop incursions, emphasising that security measures were necessary only against those Iraqis who rejected the language of reconciliation and dialogue and insisted on 'restoring the past': 'We present in our hand a green olive branch, and in the other hand we present the law – Operation Imposing Justice – started in Baghdad. It will cover every inch of Iraq.'[40]

The Iraqi government was now launching its own investigation into a recent British–Iraqi raid – on the National Iraqi Intelligence headquarters in Basra – that had captured an alleged death-squad leader and found thirty prisoners, including one woman and two children, some of whom showed signs of torture. More than 200 British troops and an unknown number of Iraqis had been involved in the operation, but there were local concerns that the raid had violated Iraqi sovereignty. Al-Maliki, again with an eye on his Shi'ite constituency, pledged that 'those who carried out this illegal and irresponsible act' would be punished.[41] But again there were signs that Washington was losing faith in the Maliki regime. On 14 March unnamed Iraqi officials said that the United States would topple the Maliki government if it failed to deliver on the hydrocarbon law handing Iraq's oil wealth to foreign multinationals.[42] This was a further graphic indication of Washington's main strategic priority in Iraq.

In Baghdad the troop surge was having at least some predictable effects. Formerly stable areas, once under the control of particular sectarian factions, were now being contested by US troops, sometimes with Iraqi forces support, on the ground. One consequence was formerly congested public zones were denuded of Iraqis, fearful for their lives in the new situation of local conflict. For example, the Al Adel Shopping Centre in Baghdad, accustomed to middle-class families wandering all around its four levels, was now sparsely populated by insurgent gunmen and American snipers on the roof. The 'darkened shell' of the shopping centre, now situated on a 'fault line' between Shi'ite and Sunni communities following sectarian cleansing, had been converted into a command outpost. A fortified tower was being used 'to direct operations by US soldiers, the Iraqi army, paramilitary national police squads and the regular Iraqi police'.[43] The shopping mall was now a battleground, its original function long abandoned.

The car bombers often targeted people leaving mosques, as a way of maximising the number of casualties, with the result that sometimes whole families were killed. In the same way crowds of pilgrims were seen as especially vulnerable. Thus on 6 March an estimated 120 pilgrims on their way to Karbala were slaughtered by a car bomber[44] – a typical form of sectarian murder. An unnamed witness described what he had seen: 'I saw one of the suicide bombers . . . He blew himself up and I saw parts of bodies flying around. I watched a second bomber run into the crowd . . . Everyone around him was shredded to pieces.' On 19 March a series of explosions targeted the Tis'deen quarter, a Turkmen district of Kirkuk; on 25 March a series of attacks between Sunni and Shi'ite armed groups in Iskandariya and Haswa in northern Babil province led to four more deaths and the burning of mosques on both sides; two days later, truck bombs – one reportedly carried by a vehicle distributing flour on behalf of a humanitarian organisation – targeted a Shi'ite crowd in Tal Afar, killing seventy-five people and wounding 185 more; and on 28 March, according to the director of Tal Afar hospital, about sixty people from the Sunni neighbourhood of al-Wahda in Tal Afar, shot in the back of the head, were brought into the hospital, while forty others were abducted by armed militia.[45]

Even relatively quiet areas were suffering from mounting tensions, targeted murders and the activities of conventional criminal gangs. On 23 March the Iraqi deputy Prime Minister,

Salam al-Zaubai, escaped an assassination attempt at his home, with one of his security guards allegedly involved in the suicide attack. Nine people were killed, including the deputy Prime Minister's brother Abdul-Rahman al-Zaubai, his cousin, his secretary and his advisor.[46] Various ethnic and sectarian minority groups were continuing to flee their homes. Thus by late March about a thousand Palestinian families from the Hay al-Amin, al-Nidhal Street and al-Baladiyyat areas of Baghdad were seeking protection in makeshift camps on the border between Iraq and Syria.[47] The security sweeps by US and Iraqi forces were swelling the ranks of detainees, typically incarcerated without charge or legal protection. By the end of March, according to the Iraqi Ministry of Human Rights, there were 37,641 detainees across the country.[48]

The failure of the US troop surge to quell the violence was prompting speculation about yet another military escalation. One suggestion was that President Bush, seeking to bolster the new security plan, might send another 7,000 troops to Iraq. The American deputy Secretary of Defense, Gordon England, revealed to the House of Representatives Budget Committee that army commanders were already requesting reinforcements beyond the 21,500 personnel already earmarked for the surge: 'At this point, our expectation is the number of . . . troops could go above 21,500 by about 4,000, maybe as many as 7,000.'[49] Bush was keen to talk about 'encouraging signs' in the security situation, but the feeling was that the surge would not be able to accomplish its objectives. On 5 March nine American soldiers were killed by explosions in Sunni areas north of Baghdad, bringing total US fatalities since March 2003 to at least 3,185. Such news was unlikely to heal congressional divisions.

On 8 March the Democrats threatened to cut off billions of dollars for US troops in Iraq unless Bush set a timetable for withdrawal, but it remained to be seen whether the House of Representatives would translate this bold gesture into effective legislation for a withdrawal of combat troops by August 2008, which would entail a start to withdrawal by March of that year. The Democrat aim seemed to be to attach the timetable ultimatum to a funding bill in which Bush was seeking another $100 billion for the wars in Iraq and Afghanistan. Nancy Pelosi, the Democrat speaker of the House, declared at a press conference that this was the first time that the party had specified 'a date certain' for troop withdrawal. In addition, it was proposed that the withdrawal deadline be brought forward if Prime Minister al-Maliki failed to deliver on his pledges to provide more troops and to begin sectarian reconciliation.

In terms of domestic US politics the strategy was risky: would the Democrats be accused of abandoning the troops 'in harm's way'? With this question in mind, the Republicans at once accused the Democrats of indicating to the Iraqi insurgents a time when American troops would leave the country, and by implication of making the task of the US military more difficult. Thus John Boehner, the leader of the Republicans in the House, accused the Democrats of 'telegraphing to our enemy a timetable', and declared: 'General [David] Petraeus should be the one making the decisions on what happens on the ground in Iraq, not Nancy Pelosi or John Murtha [another anti-war Democrat].'[50] At the same time Petraeus was saying at a press conference in Baghdad that there was no military solution and calling for talks with some insurgent groups – this latter a significant departure for US military policy. He declared that political progress would require talking to 'some of those who have felt the new Iraq did not have a place for them'.[51]

It was expected that the Democrats would vote for the House Appropriations Committee to authorise the full House of Representatives to debate the issue the following week, with the assumption that the Democrats would win the vote there but, with their small majority, struggle in the Senate. Pelosi had suggested that the bill specify more funding for injured soldiers, a sensitive issue after the Walter Reed revelations, but it remained unclear whether any Republican senators would feel able to support a clear legislative criticism of the Bush administration.

On 11 March Bush, confirming expectations, asked Congress for an extra 8,000 troops, on top of the surge reinforcements, for the wars in Iraq and Afghanistan. This followed comments from senior US officers in Iraq who had witnessed a 30 per cent increase in violence in Diyala province – a consequence of efforts to expel Sunni insurgents from Baghdad and Anbar province. Overall violence in Iraq was not being quelled, but simply being encouraged to migrate. Gordon Johndroe, a spokesman for the US National Security Council, said that extra military police would be needed to handle the rise in the number of suspects detained as a result of the Baghdad clampdown – which, in harsh reality on the ground, meant that hundreds more Iraqi families would be terrorised, often in the dead of night, their menfolk bound and blindfolded before being carted off for indefinite incarceration.

Bush made the demand to Pelosi from Air Force One while he was on a tour of Latin America: 'This revised request would better align resources based on the assessment of military commanders to achieve the goal of establishing Iraq and Afghanistan as democratic and secure nations that are free of terrorism.'[52] This statement, a familiar mantra, was immediately taken as a provocative suggestion to legislators already opposed to the 21,500-troop escalation. If Congress was already opposed to a defined troop expansion how could Bush expect to win support for a further escalation of the Iraq and Afghanistan wars?

American and Iranian representatives had attended the planned Baghdad conference, though nothing of substance had been agreed. According to Muhammad Ali Hosseini, an Iranian foreign ministry spokesman, the meeting had been constructive; and Zalmay Khalilzad, the US ambassador to Iraq, spoke of 'business-like exchanges'. However, nothing was revealed about any detailed discussions that took place, though perhaps it was remark-able that US and Iranian delegates were willing to sit at the same table after a non-speaking gap of nearly four decades. It was left to Condoleezza Rice to say that she would attend a follow-up conference, also involving Iran, to discuss ways of reducing the violence in Iraq and to stop it spreading.

The predictable diplomatic language did nothing to disguise the growing American despair about the bloody chaos in Iraq. Now the Pentagon was reportedly drawing up plans, 'fallback positions', to withdraw combat troops and shift to a training and advisory role if the surge strategy were to fail.[53] Based on what the

Los Angeles Times and other commentators referred to as the 'El Salvador model',[54] the plan would be to withdraw most of its 150,000-plus troops and to replace them with a few hundred, or few thousand, military advisors. Andrew Krepinovich, a strategic analyst who was advising the Pentagon, said that the El Salvador model was being actively discussed, but he did not know whether it was being taken seriously. He questioned whether support could be given to a government in Iraq that lacked the necessary 'legitimacy and loyalty'. In the same vein Winslow Wheeler, a senior fellow at the Center for Defense Information, commented that the El Salvador model would not be viable in Iraq since any effort to train indigenous forces had to assume they were willing to die for their government: 'There is no moderate centre in Iraq for which people are willing to die.'[55] A related option was that the US military would retreat inside the heavily fortified Green Zone and the similarly protected airport on the outskirts of Baghdad – according to Wheeler, akin to the humiliating US pullout from Saigon: any retreat into the Green Zone would be tantamount to 'bringing in the wooden steps for helicopters to take us out. That is just the final stage before the failure becomes apparent.'[56]

All this seemed to confirm the increasing recognition in Washington, if not by Bush, that the game was lost, that simply piling more troops into the quagmire would do nothing to realise the declared US goal of establishing in Iraq a free-market democracy on Western lines. Thus an unnamed advisor familiar with discussions inside the Pentagon said that there was great 'pessimism' about whether the troop surge would work, and that military planners were being forced to study a range of alternatives.

In the United Kingdom two final acquittals were delivered after a controversial court martial investigated the alleged abuse of nine Iraqi civilians by British soldiers (four other soldiers were acquitted the previous month). This generated criticism of the Attorney General, Lord Goldsmith, for deciding to prosecute the troops in a trial that cost £20 million. The prosecution had alleged that Iraqi detainees were handcuffed, hooded with sacks, deprived of sleep and forced to maintain 'stress positions' – backs to the wall, knees bent and arms outstretched. When they tired and dropped their arms they were allegedly beaten, and one prisoner alleged that he was forced to urinate into a bottle which was then poured over him. The violence culminated with the killing of 26-year-old Baha Mousa in a detention centre controlled by the Queen's Lancashire Regiment.

Phil Shiner, the British lawyer representing Mousa, described the trial as a 'travesty' which 'gave the victims nothing', and he said: 'Mr Justice McKinnon found that the evidence was clear that these injuries were "sustained as a result of numerous assaults over 36 hours by unidentified persons".' Shiner commented that 'none of these soldiers has been charged with any offence simply because there is no evidence against them as a result of a more or less obvious closing of ranks'[57] and he concluded: 'It is a matter of public record that these Iraqis were abused, beaten, tortured, hooded and stressed. The outcome is a travesty.'[58] The Ministry of Defence declined to make any comment about the alleged hooding and stress positions, both of which are prohibited by the Geneva Convention and the laws of armed conflict.

In Iraq the bloody turmoil continued in circumstances of mounting political tension. The Maliki government was now under fresh threat from a new 80-seat parliamentary coalition – embracing the 44-seat Sunni Tawafuq bloc – formed by Iyad Allawi, the former Iraqi Prime Minister and former Ba'athist whose secular party enjoyed American support. Falah al-Naqib, an Allawi confidant who was once Interior Minister, said that he thought Allawi would be Prime Minister if the new grouping took charge of the government. The 15-seat Shi'ite Fadhila party had walked out of the government the previous week, whittling the Maliki alliance down to 113 seats, and now Allawi was also courting the Kurds, whose 55 seats would give the new grouping a working majority in the 275-member parliament. Al-Naqib said: 'We'll form a government and save the country.'[59]

Now, seemingly unconcerned by Iraqi anarchy and political tensions, Royal Dutch Shell and a group of Turkish companies, following discussions that included the United States, intended to bid for a licence to produce natural gas in Iraq and pipe it to

Ceyhan, the Turkish Mediterranean oil port. The turmoil within
Iraq had served to deter substantial investment in the country but
several independents were drilling wells in Kurdistan, near the
Turkish border. But even such enterprise seemed increasingly
hazardous: tensions between the Kurds and Turkey were again
growing, and the possibility of another Turkish invasion of
northern Iraq could not be ignored.[60]

It was now clear that the problems in Iraq were still not
sufficient to compel the US Democrats to consolidate serious
opposition to the Bush administration. The proposed resolution
in the House of Representatives for a withdrawal of American
troops by March 2008 failed to attract enough support to force a
vote in the Senate. The supporters of the Bill were unable to
muster the 60-vote majority needed to overcome procedural
hurdles – and even if the legislation had been approved by the
Senate the President was set to veto it. Senator Robert Byrd
denounced an invasion and occupation that was earning the
United States 'only hatred – with no end, no end, no end in sight';
but such commentary was doing nothing to alter US policy. Anti-
war activists were now rounding on the Democrats for failing to
use their power to cut funding for the occupation, and Gael
Murphy, a co-founder of the Code Pink anti-war group, was
arrested with ten other activists while attempting to interrupt the
Appropriations Committee as it voted to approve a $124 billion
emergency spending bill.

Now Iraqi and US generals, noting a fall in the number of
Baghdad kidnappings and murders, were claiming that the
month-old surge had saved lives; but it was also admitted that
the spate of car bombs and roadside bombs had not abated, and
that the months ahead would be critical. Brigadier General
Qassim al-Moussawi, an Iraqi spokesman, said that the number of
civilians killed had fallen to 265, compared with 1,440 from mid-
January to mid-February, but there was no way to verify the
figures. American spokesman Major General William Caldwell
declared that in Baghdad there had been a 50 per cent reduction
in the number of murders and executions since Operation
Imposing Justice (Operation Fardh al-Qanoon) began, but US
and Iraqi forces were still facing about 200 attacks each day. On

17 March the insurgents demonstrated that they were prepared to
use chemical warfare: after chlorine-filled devices were exploded
at sites near Fallujah and Ramadi, eight Iraqis were killed and 350
civilians and six US soldiers were treated for the choking and
burning effects of the gas. This change in insurgent tactics came as
no surprise. American soldiers had recently found a factory in
Fallujah where chlorine was being used to make bombs,
indicating that the insurgents were prepared to use weapons that
had brought terror to the trenches of the First World War ninety
years before.[61]

In mid-March 2007 an opinion poll of 5,019 Iraqis over the age
of eighteen, carried out by Opinion Research Business (ORB), a
respected British research company, produced some predictable
results and others that were unexpected. Some 400 interviewers
had fanned out across the country to find, amongst other things,
that the Iraqis' sense of security had improved since the beginning
of the troop surge. About a half of Iraqis thought that the country
was in a state of civil war or close to it, with a fifth believing that
Iraq would never reach civil war.

More than a quarter of the people had had a close relative
murdered, but about a half thought that life was better now under
Prime Minister Nouri al-Maliki than under Saddam Hussein;
some 26 per cent thought that life had been better under Saddam
Hussein; and 16 per cent said that the two leaders were as bad as
each other. The poll suggested a significant increase in support for
al-Maliki – from only 29 per cent supporting him in an ORB
survey a year before. Some 53 per cent of Iraqis nationwide
believed that the security situation would improve once the
international forces had left the country; only 26 per cent thought
that it would get worse.[62]

The poll indicated a degree of optimism that was remarkable in
the circumstances. The occupation itself had provided opportunities for diverse groups of foreign terrorists and domestic
criminals, as well as stimulating the efforts of an indigenous
resistance. The scale of Iraqi casualties, even in the most
conservative estimates numbering hundreds of thousands, was
supplemented by the millions of refugees and internally displaced

families.[63] On 23 March 2007 the office of the UN High Commissioner for Refugees (UNHCR) said that in 2006 Iraqis topped the list of asylum seekers in industrialised countries, with some 22,000 Iraqis applying for asylum in Europe, North America and other parts of the industrialised world – terrorised by the growing turmoil that the invasion and occupation had brought to Iraq. Ron Redmond, a UNHCR spokesman, said: 'We fear that the situation in Iraq is going to get worse before it gets better.'[64]

Much of the violence derived from murderous groups that had sprung directly out of the occupation. The occupation forces themselves numbered in excess of 150,000 troops; there were more than 50,000 contracted foreign mercenaries in the country; the Iraqi regime was funding 150,000 Facilities Protection Services forces, controlled by the US military and engaged in death-squad activities, according to al-Maliki; the US-trained Iraqi army and police forces numbered about 400,000; there were six secret US-controlled Iraqi militias; and hundreds of private kidnap gangs were active throughout Iraq.[65] In summary, including the thousands of militia and resistance fighters, there were 'about two million actively organised armed men in the country'.[66]

At the time of the fourth anniversary of the March 2003 invasion there had been 3,217 American combat fatalities and tens of thousands of wounded US troops taken to Walter Reed and other hospitals. In Iraq, considering the dead, injured, bereaved, traumatised and dispossessed, the victims of the war were numbered in the millions. On 13 March 2007 police found the decapitated bodies of nine policemen with their hands bound and bearing evidence of torture – a typical event in Baghdad. General Petraeus declared in an interview with the BBC that there were 'encouraging signs' in the capital but said that he did not want to get 'overly optimistic'. Several hundred families had been able to return to homes abandoned in the sectarian war, but the map of Baghdad was still being redrawn as sectarian communities clustered together in search of security. In yet another sign of shifting opinion in Baghdad Kadhim al-Jubouri, who had rejoiced in helping to topple the 20ft bronze statue of Saddam Hussein in Firdos Square, declared: 'I really regret bringing down the statue. The Americans are worse than the dictatorship. Every day is worse than the previous day.' Saddam 'was like Stalin, but the occupation is proving to be worse'.[67] A comprehensive poll of 2,212 Iraqis in Anbar, Sadr City, Basra and Kirkuk, carried out for the BBC, revealed that only a minority of Iraqis believed that life was better now than under Saddam Hussein; and 51 per cent, compared with 17 per cent in early 2004, believed that violence against US forces was acceptable.

On 18 March the *Morning Star*, under the headline 'Iraq death toll hits 1 million',[68] quoted the chief prosecutor of the International Criminal Court (ICC), Luis Moreno-Ocampo, as saying that President Bush and Prime Minister Blair could be arraigned for war crimes at The Hague: 'Of course that could be a possibility. Whatever country joins the court can know that whatever country commits a crime in their country could be prosecuted by me.' Thus, in this interpretation of ICC law, if Iraq were to sign up to the court Bush and Blair could face war crimes charges.

In the United States demonstrators took to the streets to mark the fourth anniversary of the invasion. Several thousand anti-war protesters crossed the Potomac River from the Lincoln Memorial in Washington to rally against the war in an echo of the 1967 protests against the Vietnam War.[69] Cindy Sheehan, who had lost her son in Iraq and was now a prominent activist, said: 'We're here in the shadow of the war machine. It's like being in the shadow of the Death Star [in *Star Wars*]. They take their death and destruction and export it around the world. We need to shut it down.'[70] In Los Angeles the 59-year-old Vietnam veteran Ed Ellis hoped that the demonstrations would be the 'tipping point' against a war that had killed more than 3,200 American troops and engulfed Iraq in a deadly cycle of violence. Other rallies were held in San Francisco, San Diego and Hartford, the capital of Connecticut, where more than a thousand demonstrators rallied at the old state house.

Speaking at a rally outside the Pentagon, anti-war protesters denounced both the Bush administration and the Democrats for not moving swiftly to cut off the funds for the war. Thus Michael Letwin, a New York trade union activist, condemned the 'bipartisan war', saying that the Democratic Party could not be trusted to end it. Five people were arrested after walking onto a bridge that had been closed; then they were released after being summonsed to appear in court. In Madrid some 400,000 Spaniards called for the United States to withdraw from Iraq and to close the US concentration camp at Guantanamo Bay. The Spanish film director Pedro Almodóvar declared that he was protesting against 'the barbarities they [the Americans] have been committing in Iraq for the past four years' and against the 'disgrace for civilisation' that Guantanamo represented.[71] About 2,000 people gathered in Barcelona and 500 in Seville; and similar protests at the American occupation were held throughout the world: some 3,000 protesters rallied in Istanbul, about 1,000 in Athens and more than 2,000 in central Tokyo. On 20 March BBC News reported that media around the globe saw no reason to celebrate the fourth anniversary of the invasion: 'Most commentators believe the war has been a disaster for the Bush administration and Iraq.'[72] Here the BBC quoted from two dozen international media commentaries, including ones from Iraq, on the anniversary of the invasion. The following are typical (all from 20 March 2007):

Four years have passed since the US President promised Iraqis a life of prosperity. However, Iraqis have found themselves in resuscitation wards and morgues.

(Al-Diyar television, Iraq)

Iraqis have not attained the promised freedom . . . They have lost security and safety and become fuel for war and daily killing.

(Al Jazeera)

On this sombre anniversary, civil society organisations are holding mass [anti-war] demonstrations in most parts of the world, from as far as Chile to South Korea . . . as well as in America and Britain . . . However, the Arab capitals keep silent, even more silent than the grave.

(Muhammad al-Masfar, Al-Quds Al-Arabi, Britain)

There is consensus that the US occupation has been a mistake.

(Al-Ahram, Egypt)

It is an anniversary not to celebrate, but to lament. How much longer before Mr Bush sees reason?

(*Age*, Australia)

The failure of the US invasion of Iraq represents the failure of self-righteous US unilateralism.

(*Hankyoreh Shinmun*, South Korea)

Four years ago on 1 May, Bush announced proudly to the world: The Iraq war has been won! Today . . . in the face of national opposition to the war, Bush has had no choice but to retreat to Camp David and wrack his brains for an exit strategy.

(Li Xuejiang, *Renmin Ribao*, China)

Iraq is a country brought to its knees without any indication that the US objective is being achieved.

(*Cape Argus*, South Africa)

In Iraq there was overwhelming evidence to justify such commentary. On 21 March Iraqi insurgents used two children as decoys to smuggle a car bomb past a military checkpoint in the mainly Shi'ite area of al-Shaab in Baghdad before detonating the vehicle, killing the children and eight other people and wounding twenty-eight more in the blast. According to Major General Michael Barbero, an official with the Pentagon's joint staff, the children were in the car to create the impression of a harmless family: 'Children in the back seat lower suspicions. We let it move through. They park the vehicle. The adults run out and detonate it with the children in the back.'[73] This is one graphic example of the insurgents' increasing use of children to launch attacks on American soldiers.[74] Lieutenant Colonel Christopher Garver, a US military spokesman in Baghdad, said that children were being employed as part of the insurgent war: 'We know that children as young as 12, 10 years old, are often paid to emplace IEDs [improvised explosive devices]. I believe the going rate is $125 per IED, which is dangerous work. If we see people emplacing IEDs at night, we may engage that person, not knowing if it is a child.'[75]

On 22 March an insurgent rocket penetrated deep inside the Green Zone, shaking the office where the UN secretary general, Ban Ki-Moon, and Prime Minister al-Maliki were holding a press conference to announce that the security situation was improving. Ban had just noted the improvement, saying that he was considering increasing the UN presence in Iraq, when the rocket landed. The secretary general, looking terrified, immediately crouched behind the wooden podium as scraps of plaster fell from the ceiling. About 50 yards away, a 3ft-wide crater marked where the rocket had landed, causing minimal damage but achieving an immense political impact. This was not the first rocket attack on the vast US fortress in the heart of Baghdad, but again it signalled that after four years of military occupation the Americans were not even able to secure their headquarters in the country.

On 28 March Shi'ite gunmen – acting in revenge for a double lorry bombing in Tal Afar which killed around seventy-five people and wounded 180 more – rounded up, bound and shot dead at least forty-five Sunni men in an orgy of violence in the city, once cited by President Bush as a shining example of US success in quelling sectarian violence. A doctor in the main hospital in Tal Afar said: 'I wish you could come here and see all the bodies. They are lying in the grounds. We don't have enough space in the hospital. I've never seen such a thing in my life.'[76] Now there were signs that Washington was trying to shift the blame for the violence onto the Iraqi government. On 26 March Zalmay Khalilzad, the outgoing US ambassador, said that the Bush administration's patience was wearing thin and urged the Maliki regime to stem the bloodshed. Then King Abdullah of Saudi Arabia, speaking at a summit of the Arab League in Riyadh, launched an unprecedented public attack on America, condemning the 'foreign occupation': 'In beloved Iraq, blood flows between brothers in the shadow of illegitimate foreign occupation and hateful sectarianism, threatening a civil war.'[77]

Now the United States was also struggling to prevent a Turkish invasion of northern Iraq to root out separatist Kurdistan Workers Party (PKK) guerrillas, said to be 3,800 strong and massing for attacks in south-eastern Turkey. The Bush administration was frequently complaining about Iraq's insecure borders, referring in general to what it alleged were Iranian and Syrian incursions to support the war against US troops, but it rarely publicised the insecurity of the Iraqi–Turkish border, accustomed to frequent Turkish incursions to attack supposed PKK positions, on occasions leading to a temporary but substantial occupation of large swathes of Iraqi territory.

It was obvious that this further American predicament derived from its traditional support for the Kurds as allies against the Iraqi Ba'athists and its long alliance with Turkey, receiving arms and diplomatic cover, as the only Muslim member of NATO. There was frequent media commentary on the manifest insecurity of Baghdad and other Iraqi cities, and of Iraq's borders with 'terrorist' states, but little attention given to Iraq's traditional problems with Turkey.

The course of events in Iraq – in particular the escalating spend of US lives and money – had become the major consideration in American politics, but it still seemed unclear what would be done to rein in the reckless adventurism and callous indifference of a discredited President. On 23 March the House of Representatives for the first time defied the threat of a presidential veto by passing binding legislation requiring the withdrawal of all American combat troops from Iraq by 31 March 2008. The vote, 218 to 212, resulted in the passing of a $122 billion war funding bill on the condition that US combat operations would cease before September – or earlier if the Iraqi government failed to meet security and other benchmarks.

George Bush immediately called a press conference at the White House, declared that the bill had no chance of becoming law, and said that the only consequence of the vote would be to 'delay vital resources for our troops' and 'score political points' for the Democrat majority in Congress. Nancy Pelosi commented that Americans had lost faith in the President's conduct of the war: 'The American people see the reality of the war. The President does not.'[78] Four days later, the Senate approved the bill by a 50-to-48 vote, largely on party lines, signalling a hardening of attitudes between the Bush administration and the legislature. A final Senate vote on the full spending bill was expected the following week. The Democrats had won a resounding victory by securing an anti-war resolution, even though it was subject to Bush's veto. It remained to be seen whether they would have the courage to vote against the comprehensive appropriations bill and so end the war.

4

Talk of 'reposturing': British retreat?

In late March and early April, in an echo of the American Walter Reed controversy, there was growing concern and anger about the treatment of injured British soldiers returning from Iraq and Afghanistan. The concern was mounting ahead of the closure of the Royal Hospital Haslar in Gosport, the last of the military hospitals, prompting questions about how well the NHS would be able to cope with wounded service personnel in a mixed environment.

The specific details related to such matters as service personnel with mental health problems being put on long waiting lists, inadequate attention being given to physical injuries, and wounded personnel being treated in squalid conditions. The cases included that of Jamie Cooper, a nineteen-year-old Royal Green Jackets rifleman who had suffered stomach wounds in a mortar attack. After being admitted to the Queen Elizabeth Hospital in Birmingham he was allegedly left in his own faeces after his colostomy bag was allowed to overflow. Then he was transferred to Selly Oak Hospital, where he twice contracted MRSA and developed sores after being left on a deflated air mattress.

In the same hospital another wounded soldier had been confronted by an irate Muslim who accused him of killing his 'brothers' in Afghanistan. One wounded paratrooper said that soldiers were treated as 'second-class citizens' in Selly Oak. The nurses, he alleged, were not interested in looking after soldiers, and he himself had cleaned a soiled mentally handicapped man after the hospital staff had ignored the patient: 'Afterwards I threw the dirty cloth on the desk and said, "Next time do it yourselves." . . . Their attitude was appalling.'[1]

These and other examples prompted David Borrow, a Labour MP on the Defence Select Committee, to demand an urgent inquiry to find out whether such cases were 'symptomatic of a wider malaise': 'If this had happened to a constituent of mine, I would be demanding a full explanation and apology from the chief executive of the hospital.'[2] In the same vein Mike Hancock, a Liberal Democrat member of the committee, declared himself 'shocked' and 'appalled' at the situation. The government, he declared, was sending young people into harm's way, was refusing to meet the families of those who had lost their lives, and was failing to look after those who had been wounded in action: 'We should be ashamed of how they have been treated. They should be given the highest priority of care.'[3] Liam Fox, the shadow Defence Secretary, suggested that the military covenant that used to exist between the government and the armed forces had been shattered.

Now another controversy was focusing on the spending of what was nominally the UK aid budget for Iraq. In early April, following a parliamentary question from Liberal Democrat MP Norman Baker, Foreign Office minister Kim Howells revealed that Britain had spent £165 million on hiring private security companies in Iraq over the previous four years – amounting to a quarter of the entire aid budget. This and other evidence[4] revealed, among other things, that Britain and the United States were diverting huge amounts of money from humanitarian and reconstruction resources to deal with the deteriorating security conditions in both Iraq and Afghanistan. The UK had spent around £145 million on security guards to protect British assets, with a further £20 million being allocated to police training and security advisors to the Iraqi government. Thus substantial sums had been diverted to such firms as the New York-based risk consulting company Kroll and the UK companies ArmorGroup and Control Risks. ArmorGroup, chaired by the Conservative MP Sir Malcolm Rifkind, had earned 50 per cent of its £129 million revenues from Iraq in 2006. Baker, in response to the parliamentary answer, commented:

It's an awful lot of money and shows how the security situation is out of control . . . There is also an accountability issue here . . . These people are employed from a shadowy world that is known to have engaged in deniable activities. We need to know more about their training and the rules of engagement they operate under.[5]

It was equally significant that parts of the Department for International Development's aid budget – as much as £6 million in the 2005/6 financial year – had also been diverted to security funding.

The matter also raised legal and human rights questions. The employment of effective mercenaries in a battle situation meant that large numbers of combatants were not subject to military discipline or the nominal rules of war. This had led to the killing of many civilians in Iraq by hired gunmen who were unaccountable to any military or political authority. In the Iraq turmoil such accountability was clearly insufficient to guarantee the protection of civilians,[6] but the removal of all such accountability from a large number of highly armed foreigners had added a fresh dimension to the bloody conflict.

The tensions and the casualty toll were mounting. The Iraqi government was trying to resettle thousands of Arab families who had been moved north to the oil-rich Kirkuk by Saddam Hussein in an attempt to 'Arabicise' the city and ethnically cleanse it of Kurds. It was no surprise that the new resettlement policy was popular with the Kurds – who had threatened to withdraw from the government if the plans were not implemented – but bitterly opposed by Sunni Arab nationalists. The aim was to give the relocated Arabs about $15,000 and land in their former home towns, but many remained reluctant to move. Such policies tended to exacerbate racial tensions and remind the world that the Iraq conflict included substantial elements of both ethnic and sectarian cleansing.

On 2 April in Kirkuk, outside an Iraqi police station being visited by US soldiers and close to a primary school, a suicide bomber detonated a lorry laden with explosives hidden by sacks of flour. At least fourteen children and adults, and also a newborn baby, were killed in the blast. One of the children, ten-year-old Buthayna Mahmud, described seeing the bodies of her classmates in flames: 'Everyone I saw was wearing the blue school uniform drenched with blood. Some of their dresses were torn. When we rushed out of the school, we saw pupils on the ground, some of them burning.' Another girl, Naz Omar, saw two of her classmates sitting near the window: 'They fell on the floor drenched in blood. They could not speak. I was terrified. I said, "God is Great. I need my mother. I need my father,"'[7]

At the same time about two dozen Shi'ite market workers were ambushed, bound and shot dead north of Baghdad, at a market visited the day before by John McCain, a US Republican presidential candidate. Other car bombs took their predictable toll of victims in Baghdad and in a Shi'ite town north of the capital, while a roadside bomb killed an Iraqi soldier and wounded seven others near the Iranian border. The US announced the deaths of six more of its soldiers in recent days, and noted that some 600 Iraqis had been killed over the previous week, most of them by truck bombs outside Baghdad. In Basra a British soldier, eighteen-year-old Rifleman Aaron Lincoln, was shot dead by a sniper. McCain said that the situation was improving and blamed the media for painting a pessimistic picture.

On 4 April insurgents opened fire on a minibus carrying power plant workers in a Sunni area west of Kirkuk, killing six men. On the same day gunmen abducted twenty-two shepherds from Karbala, also taking sheep and vehicles, when they were in the vast desert area around Amiriyah, 25 miles west of Baghdad in the Sunni-dominated Anbar province. And a suicide bomber and mortar attack hit a police station in Sadr City. Such events, commonplace in Iraq under occupation, indicated that the new security policy was failing in its purpose, and now even the US military itself was expressing doubts that the troop surge was succeeding in quelling the levels of violence in the country as a whole. Thus military spokesman Major General William Caldwell acknowledged that the military remained 'extremely concerned' about high-profile bomb attacks that had killed more than 300 people in recent weeks: 'There has been a drop in overall casualties in Baghdad, but when you look overall at the country at large, you have not seen a great reduction that we had wanted to see thus far.'[8]

On 5 April two women – a nurse from Queen Alexandra's Royal Army Nursing Corps and a member of the Intelligence

Corps – were among four British soldiers killed in Basra, along with a civilian interpreter, when their Warrior armoured vehicle was torn apart by a 'colossal' bomb; a fifth soldier, 'very seriously injured', was treated in a military hospital. Iraqis, rejoicing at the killings, were shown waving one of the soldiers' battered helmets, while children held aloft fragments of the vehicle as trophies. This was the first time that two British women had died in the same incident on the front line, bringing the total number of female fatalities to five, out of the 140 British dead since the 2003 invasion.[9]

Prime Minister Tony Blair, commenting on the deaths, contrasted the rejoicing over the release of fifteen Royal Navy sailors taken prisoner by the Iranians with the 'sober and ugly reality' of the killings in Iraq – and then he chose to link Iran to attacks in the south of the country. It was far too early, he declared, to link Iran with this 'particular terrorist act' but the 'general picture' was that there were 'elements at least of the Iranian regime that are backing, financing, arming, terrorism in Iraq'.[10]

Unnamed military sources had disclosed that there were 'very strong grounds' for believing that Iran had been training insurgents and equipping them with highly effective bombs; and military analysts had warned that deadly 'explosively formed projectiles', sophisticated and well machined, were set to proliferate in Iraq. The suddenness of the appearance of such devices suggested 'access to foreign expertise and complete weapons systems rather than indigenous development'.[11] It was well known that Iran was the paymaster for numerous Shi'ite parties operating inside its neighbour, notably the powerful Supreme Council for Islamic Revolution in Iraq. The leading Shi'ite cleric in Iraq, Grand Ayatollah Ali al-Sistani, was born in Iran and spoke Arabic with a strong Persian accent. In these circumstances, with Iran having a permanent interest in southern Iraq, it was reasonable to suppose that the Iraqi insurgents' new weapons, needing a sophisticated machining capability, were supplied from across the border.[12]

The British troops in Iraq were likely to face further problems in the coming months. Some commanders were already warning that plans to withdraw the British forces to just one base in Basra

– Basra Palace, a mile from the city centre and then home to about
a thousand soldiers – would lead to a significant increase in
casualties. The troops would be hemmed into an isolated location
and would face a relentless series of concentrated attacks over the
summer, launched by insurgent groups increasingly confident of
final victory. One senior unnamed officer said:

> We have been bombed out of every base we have been in so far and
> the prediction is that the same will happen when we are based only in
> the Basra Palace. Withdrawing to just one base will enable the
> insurgents to concentrate their forces against us. They can attack us
> with indirect fire from within the city, by firing rockets and mortars
> into the compound, they can ambush us with IEDs [improvised
> explosive devices] when we are travelling in vehicles and they can
> snipe at us when we are on foot patrol. It is only going to get worse.[13]

It now seemed clear that the planned withdrawal was part of Blair's
reluctant 'reposturing' plan, outlined in the House of Commons in
February and requiring British troops to 'hand over' areas of Basra
to the Iraqi police and army while they themselves relocated from
three separate bases to just one. The fighting in Basra was already
escalating, with virtually every British military control coming
under attack – usually within minutes of leaving the relative safety
of their bases – from automatic rifle fire, rocket-propelled grenades
or roadside bombs. The movements of British troops were being
monitored by so-called 'dickers', a term that originated in Ulster
and was then used to denote Iraqis who relayed information to the
insurgents by mobile telephones as a prelude to fresh attacks. Even
the shortest journeys were becoming major operations, with the
'vulnerable points' on routes having to be cleared by army dog
handlers. Even then, virtually any attempt to move British troops
would be sure to bring them under fire.

Here any British pretence of winning 'hearts and minds', or of
training responsible Iraqi police and security forces, was fanciful.
The relatively small British force was in retreat, working above all
to protect itself from further casualties. The much-hyped
handover was nothing more than an admission that in the south
of the country the Iraqis themselves – the Shi'ite militias, the Iraqi

security forces riven by sectarianism, non-political criminal gangs and corrupt local politicians[14] – were assuming power.

In the same vein the Americans, despite a 'hearts and minds' element in the new security plan, were struggling simply to contain a deteriorating situation and to minimise their own escalating casualties. The US military were desperately rounding up more and more Iraqis for detention – as if Washington would win Iraqi support by incarcerating tens of thousands of ordinary men and women, all of whom had family members who were being taught to hate the foreign occupiers of their country. And the mass imprisonment was also counter-productive in other ways. The US-run high security prisons had become, according to former inmates and Iraqi government officials, 'terrorist academies'[15] for the most dangerous militant groups. The relative shortage of suitable US prison guards meant that militant inmates, separated on sectarian grounds, were left largely to run their own blocks – and ordinary Iraqis were being thrown into this closed world. Inmates from Camp Cropper, the US prison at Baghdad airport, have described seeing al-Qaeda terrorists club to death an inmate suspected of being an informer; while other prisoners exacted retribution with razor wire stolen from the fences.[16] On 6 April American officials said that they were investigating the suspicious death of another Camp Cropper inmate.

It seemed obvious that new inmates, already bitterly resentful at their treatment, were being turned into insurgents by the hundred. Thus Saad Sultan, the Iraqi Human Rights Ministry's official for prisons, said that Camp Cropper looked like a 'terrorist academy': 'There's a huge number of these "students"; they study how they can kill. And we protect them, feed them, give them medical care. The Americans have no solution to this problem.'[17]

One case concerned Abu Tibeh (not his real name) and his colleagues – four Sunnis and four Shi'ites – wrongly arrested by a US patrol after the sort of bogus tip-off that meant virtually anyone could be rounded up and imprisoned. They were then put into Camp Cropper's sectarian halls, each containing about eighty-five inmates, the Sunni hall controlled by the imam Abu Hamza, linked to al-Qaeda, and the Shi'ite hall under the authority of a Sayyid Adnan al-Enabi, a Mahdi Army commander.

Tibeh said that he had been 'terrified', and one of his colleagues suffered a minor heart attack. Hamza gave daily lectures on the evils of the Iraqi government and the need for armed resistance; Tibeh, his own party often attacked, was forced to keep his identity secret. One of his colleagues, here called Abu Usama, witnessed a group of al-Qaeda enforcers beat a man to death with rocks. New recruits would quickly be recruited by the *takfiris*, or Sunni fundamentalists; or they would be forced by the Shi'ites to attend prayer sessions and lectures. When one Shi'ite refused to bow to the pressure, other inmates told the US guards that he was planning to escape, whereupon the Americans put him in a metal punishment box, 6ft by 4ft and known as 'the coffin', and kept him there for several days.

This was analogous to what was happening on the streets of Baghdad and other Iraqi towns and cities: men with a grudge would report to the Americans that their neighbour was a subversive, and the US military, desperate for 'intelligence', would take action. The incarcerations and killings that followed were useful for the statistics – yet more 'suspect insurgents' removed from the streets. And ordinary Iraqis faced many other hazards.

Thousands of family members – men, women and children – were being taken from their homes and workplaces or simply snatched off the street, then bound and driven away for ransom or a more gruesome fate. Bodies were being found every day in ditches, by the roadside, on wasteland or on rubbish dumps, many of the corpses with holes drilled in their limbs and eyes, and with bullet holes to the head. One case was that of 22-year-old Rasha Sebai, who lost her husband (who was beheaded), mother, father, brother and two uncles to Iraq's death squads. Rasha and her sister Huda, after frequent visits to the mortuary, had eventually found a photograph of their murdered mother. Huda said: 'My dead mother's face was staring me in the eye. Her face was all bloodied as if she'd been hit on it and then shot.'[18] Rasha, as a pregnant woman with no support, was refused entry to Jordan as an 'undesirable', and she yearned to die in childbirth: 'I long to die in labour. I cannot live alone like this. I want to join Ali [her husband] and Mama.'[19] Eventually, she fled to Damascus and, without family, began a lonely existence.

To Rasha the American troop surge was of no consolation. The leader of the death squad that had killed her husband had disappeared briefly to Tehran but had returned; according to neighbours, his men were openly living in the Sebais' houses and driving their cars. The surge had failed to quell the violence. The civilian body count was again rising – from 1,646 in February to 1,869 in March. When the surge began, only three bodies were being found every day around Baghdad, but in early April the figure had climbed to about nineteen.

The fresh American troop deployments, involving massive firepower, had achieved no more than intensifying the conflict in some districts of Baghdad and displacing elements of sectarian violence to others. In late 2006, following a US redeployment, the insurgents had taken control of the Diyala River valley outside Baqubah, but at the end of February 2007 the Americans again began patrolling the valley. On 24 March the US military began a massive onslaught on Qubah, a village on the edge of the valley, using seven Chinook helicopters, four Black Hawks, two Apache gunships and a convoy of Humvees and Bradley armoured vehicles. After prolonged street fighting, the Americans secured Qubah and then began marking numbers on the necks of detained men and on the hands of detained women to keep track of residents during the planned lockdown. The Americans said that they had killed about seventy insurgents and 'suspects', for the loss of four soldiers, but acknowledged that some insurgents had fled to other villages in the area. It was judged by US officers that 'clearing operations' in Baqubah 'could take months' and might require an increase in the number of troops available. And without the emergence of a functioning pro-US local government for the valley, the area would be unable to escape the control exercised by the insurgent forces. Colonel David Sutherland, the US commanding officer in the province, said: 'I can kill all day long. It will do no good.'[20]

In early April a report published by the International Committee of the Red Cross (ICRC)[21] began receiving significant publicity in the Western media. Here the ICRC indicated that Iraqi civilians were experiencing 'immense suffering' because of a 'disastrous' security situation, deepening poverty and a worsening humanitarian crisis. Thus Pierre Krähenbühl, the ICRC director of operations, commented at the group's Geneva headquarters: 'The suffering Iraqi men, women and children are enduring today is unbearable and unacceptable.'[22] John McDonnell, a Labour leadership contender, said that the report proved 'conclusively that our predictions about the invasion of Iraq were right. The people of Iraq were paying with their lives for Bush and Blair's grab for oil.' In the same vein the Stop the War Coalition chairman, Andrew Murray, stressed that the ICRC had highlighted what millions of Iraqis already knew, 'which is that life under the occupation is going from bad to disastrous on every measure – millions of Iraqis demonstrated at the weekend for the withdrawal of US and British troops and the government should now heed those voices because it is clear that the military occupation is failing to solve a single problem.'[23] Kate Hudson, CND chairwoman, said that Iraq was 'clearly a human tragedy on an extraordinary scale . . . We had all thought we had seen terrible things that could not get any worse, but as this report shows, there is now a deterioration on a daily basis . . . The presence of troops is making the situation worse.'[24]

More than 100,000 families had been forced to leave their homes in the previous year because of the shootings, bombings, abductions, murders and military operations. 'Every day dozens of people are killed and many more wounded. The plight of Iraqi civilians is a daily reminder of the fact that there has long been a failure to respect their lives and dignity.'[25] One humanitarian worker described the scene after a bomb blast when he witnessed a four-year-old boy sitting beside his mother's body, which had been decapitated by the explosion: 'He was talking to her, asking her what had happened.'[26] One woman begged for the bodies littering the street in front of her home to be collected since it was 'unbearable' to face them every morning on the way to school, but nobody dared touch or remove them. Moreover, the ICRC saw no signs that the American troops surge, the new security plan, was bringing relief to the capital. Hospitals were still having to cope with mass casualties, as malnutrition, as well as power and water shortages, became more frequent across the country. The

US military, presiding over social collapse, took comfort in an apparent rupture between erstwhile allies – Sunni insurgents and al-Qaeda forces. At least two al-Qaeda commanders had been killed by Iraqi insurgents and others forced to flee after the Sunnis reportedly passed intelligence to US and Iraqi commanders.[27]

On 3 April 2007 President George Bush set Congress a deadline of mid-May to pass the war funding bill, after which the problems facing troops in Iraq and their families would become acute. The aim was to secure the necessary money – $100 billion in emergency funding – without any qualifications attached, with no timetable specified for a troop withdrawal and with no other limitations on the war policies of the Bush administration. It remained to be seen whether the Democrat majority in the Senate would call the President's bluff and pull the plug on the war.

The challenge was plain. In a White House press conference Bush urged Congress, then in recess, to send him their legislation – so that he could veto it. He had pledged to block the Senate version of the bill, after which Congress would be pressured to 'get down to the business of funding our troops without strings and without delay. . . . They need to come off their vacation, get a bill to my desk.'[28] Even by mid-April, Bush claimed, there would be problems if Congress failed to submit a satisfactory bill, with the army being forced to cut back on equipment, repairs 'and quality of life initiatives for our guard and reserve forces'.[29] By mid-May, if the funding bill was not signed into law, Bush claimed that the problems would 'grow even more acute', including 'curtailing of training for active duty forces . . . Some of our military families could wait longer for their loved ones to return from, and others could see their loved ones heading back to the war sooner than they need to.'[30] The president clearly believed that the Democrats were vulnerable on the 'need to support our troops' issue. How could they fail to provide the necessary support for the brave men and women 'in harm's way'?

Already many families were being drastically affected by the Bush policies and the dispute between Congress and the White House.[31] Thus Robert Burgos, working as a communications specialist with the National Guard, had never expected to fight in a war but was now serving his second tour of duty in Iraq. His wife Mirian, 'always alone', said how her heart did not stop racing when she heard about fresh casualties, until she could speak to her husband; and she wondered whether he would be able to cope with a third term. Mirian applauded Democrat efforts to end the war, but her main concern was that her husband should not have to serve yet another term of duty: 'That's what I think now [that the Democrats must try to end the war]. But maybe I'd say [if Bush refused a withdrawal timetable]: "Just pay for the bill so that he can come home."'[32]

The Democrats' dilemma was how to oppose the war while not to be seen as undermining such families – a charge levelled against them in the Vietnam era. As one ploy, they had attached a $20 billion package of extra spending to the war funding bill, which included money to improve military medical services – after the Walter Reed scandal – and other measures, such as grants for peanut and spinach farmers, which had been ridiculed. Would such measures be sufficient for the Democrats to win public support for a bill that approved funding but also stipulated a withdrawal timetable?

The Democrats also took the surprising step of excluding the phrase 'global war on terror' from the draft war funding budget, arguing that it was a propagandist term designed to boost the President's claim that the Iraq conflict was a war of necessity. In Pentagon documents the term had its own acronym – GWOT – and was indelibly enshrined in most American discussion about US military operations around the world. It was inevitable that the Republicans would at once cite the exclusion as further evidence that the Democrats were weak on defence. Thus John Boehner, the Republican minority leader in the House of Representatives, said that it was no wonder they did not like the phrase 'global war on terror' since they had completely failed to take the threat seriously. The Republicans were aware that the public mood was increasingly hostile to the war, and this perception was affecting the attitudes of the presidential candidates.

On 8 April Pope Benedict XVI gave the traditional Easter address in St Peter's Square and declared, in an implicit rebuke to George Bush and Tony Blair, that 'nothing positive' was coming out of Iraq, a country 'torn apart by continual slaughter': 'How many wounds, how much suffering there is in the world. Peace is sorely needed.' On the same day the presidential candidate John McCain, an enthusiastic supporter of the surge plan who had recently given a rosy assessment of the security situation in Baghdad, felt compelled to disavow his optimistic statements. In excerpts released ahead of a CBS *60 Minutes* interview, McCain said that he had 'misspoken' when he said, on the eve of his departure for Baghdad, that the surge had made Iraqi neighbour-hoods safe.[33] In his visit to a Baghdad market he was obliged to wear a bullet-proof vest and was guarded by a hundred US troops and two military helicopters. Nonetheless he declared: 'I can tell you that if it had been two months ago and I'd asked to do it [go to Baghdad], they would have said: "Under no circumstances whatsoever." I view that as a sign of progress.'[34]

He asserted also, while admitting that his view of the war was not shared by most Americans, that the United States could succeed in Iraq: 'Failure will lead to chaos. Withdrawal will lead to chaos.'[35] A few days later McCain decried how the Democrat leaders had 'smiled and cheered' after securing the resolution setting a withdrawal timetable: 'A defeat for the United States is a cause for mourning, not celebrating.' A withdrawal, he said, would create a 'Wild West for terrorists' plotting future attacks on America and would abandon the Iraqis to a genocide worse than that in Rwanda.[36] The Pentagon was now announcing that it was extending the tours of duty in Iraq from twelve to fifteen months, reflecting the growing strains on the US military – a consideration that appeared not to affect White House thinking. On 17 April President Bush met Democrat leaders to increase the pressure for a war funding bill without conditions: 'I hope the Democratic leadership will drop their unreasonable demands for a precipitous withdrawal.'[37]

On 8 April Muqtada al-Sadr urged the Iraqi forces to stop cooperating with the United States, and told his guerrilla fighters to concentrate their attacks on US troops rather than on fellow Iraqis: 'You, the Iraqi army and police forces, don't walk alongside the occupiers, because they are your arch enemy. God has ordered you to be patient in front of your enemy and unify your efforts against them, not against the sons of Iraq.' The following day hundreds of thousands of Shi'ite Muslims, waving the national flag, marched through the holy city of Najaf and poured along the road to nearby Kufa. Some of the demonstrators burned American flags and spray-painted slogans, including 'Death to America', 'May America fall' and 'Bush is a dog'. The Iraqi authorities banned cars from the streets of Baghdad, and General David Petraeus, now the most senior US officer in the country, issued a public letter on the Central Command website:

> 'On this April 9th, some Iraqis may reportedly demonstrate against the coalition force presence in Iraq. That is their right in the new Iraq. It would only be fair, however, to note that they will be able to exercise that right because coalition forces liberated them from a tyrannical, barbaric regime that would never have permitted such freedom of expression. Our soldiers sacrificed greatly to give the Najafis the freedom, however imperfect they may be, that they enjoy today.[38]

(The right to march in protest was of course protected in the United States and Britain – on the implicit understanding that governments were never obliged to pay any heed to such demonstrations of mass opinion.)

The Iraqis, Petraeus said, must reject those who were trying 'to drive a wedge between people [Sunnis and Shi'ites] who had in the past lived in harmony in the Land of the Two Rivers'. Only in this way, he declared, could they make the best of the opportunity that the Iraqi and US forces were striving to give them. It was obvious that the Petraeus communication had no effect whatever on the marching crowds in Najaf. The protests, orchestrated by al-Sadr, ended peacefully after three hours, signalling that although he was keeping a low profile he was a force to be reckoned with. His whereabouts were uncertain – was al-Sadr in Iran? – and many of the Mahdi Army leaders were hiding or in US custody, their difficulties leading to fractures in the movement. The army's members had been ordered to stand down at the start of the US troop surge in Baghdad, but many were eager to fight the occupiers in such places as Diwaniyah, where Shi'ites had been confronted by American and Iraqi forces. Abu Haidar, a Mahdi fighter, said that the movement had intelligence on criminals and Sunni 'terrorists', implying that militant action was still being taken by Shi'ites in the sectarian war. Some thirty Mahdi Army members had reportedly been executed in the past five months for abusing their positions.[39] According to Haidar, some Mahdi hit squads were still abducting suspected Sunni extremists for hasty tribunals, torture and execution. Once they had been kidnapped, the victims were carried in the boots of cars: 'Our guys buy cars according to the size of the boot. The Toyota Crown Super saloon is a favourite. You can get four people in the boot.'[40]

The Shi'ite Cabinet ministers allied to al-Sadr were now threatening to quit the government in protest at Prime Minister Nouri al-Maliki's refusal to set a timetable for the withdrawal of the occupation forces – a threat to his already fragile administration.[41] Al-Maliki had declared that he saw no need for a withdrawal timetable ('We are working as fast as we can. Achievements on the ground will dictate how long troops remain'), despite the huge demonstrations two days before in Najaf and elsewhere demanding full national self-determination. According to the Sadrists, considering the option of leaving the Maliki administration, the government had not 'fulfilled its promises to the people' – who had clearly demonstrated their opposition to the foreign military occupation. A week later, six ministers loyal to al-Sadr resigned from the national unity government, citing as a reason al-Maliki's refusal to commit to a timetable for the withdrawal of US troops.[42]

On 11 April a force of 400 British troops in Warrior and Bulldog vehicles entered the Shia Flats area of Basra to search for hidden weapons and other evidence of insurgent activity. At first the operation went smoothly and then the atmosphere changed when Iraqi children began 'to speak into their mobile phones and point at us'. It seemed clear that the militia forces were massing for some kind of attack: as the troops assumed defensive positions Iraqi gunmen carrying AK-47 rifles and rocket-propelled grenades could be seen running along rooftops and down streets, while there were reports that the British forces were being approached by militiamen from other parts of the city. The ensuing battle lasted for two hours before the British, after killing two dozen gunmen, managed to fight their way back to their base in Basra Palace. It seemed likely that a number of civilians had been killed. Lieutenant Colonel Kevin Stratford-Wright, a British spokesman in Basra, said:

> While we may regret that such incidents [the killing of civilians] have to take place, we will not allow militia gunmen to control parts of Basra. There are no "no-go" areas . . . Security is our responsibility . . . This will inevitably involve taking on the rogue militia who blight the lives of people in Basra.[43]

However, it seemed unclear what the British operation had accomplished. The troops had been compelled to fight off a determined attack, killing two dozen 'terrorists' and probably a number of civilians, before being forced to retreat to their base. There was no suggestion that the British forces were now occupying and in charge of the area that they had invaded, and the Shi'ite militiamen were presumably back in control. Again it was clear that the British forces in Basra were doing little more than struggling to survive. On 23 April a roadside bomb penetrated a Challenger 2 tank, the British Army's heaviest weapon, wounding the driver, who was later recovering in hospital after both of his legs had been amputated.

Already, according to three new foreign policy reports – which Downing Street predictably rejected – Britain's reputation had suffered greatly because of its involvement in the invasion and occupation of Iraq.[44] Oxfam was accusing Tony Blair of squandering British interests in a conflict that was now out of control and that Britain, by implication, had helped to create. There had been immense damage to Britain's prestige in the Middle East and the wider world, with an inevitable impact on British foreign policy. Perhaps Britain might have expected credit for such achievements as debt relief in Africa, but this was largely eclipsed by Blair's role in Iraq. In the same vein the Oxford Research Group, a prestigious think tank, said that US and British strategies in Iraq and elsewhere were fuelling support for Islamic radicals, emboldening dictatorial regimes and seriously harming the prospects for a Middle East peace.

A new report from the ICRC found that every aspect of life in Iraq had been disastrously affected by the collapse of security.[45] Families had been 'torn apart' and hundreds of thousands of people had been forced to flee their homes; the country's health care system was in ruins, with more than half its doctors having left the country; the morgues were overflowing with unclaimed bodies; and public health was further damaged by the scarcity of such necessities as electricity and safe water. The ICRC judged that ordinary Iraqis, Whitehall mandarins and the leaders of American and British foreign policy had all been damaged by Iraq's burgeoning civil war; but Pierre Krähenbühl, the ICRC director of operations, said there was a chance that the recent troop surge might improve the situation.

The invasion and occupation of Iraq had been a 'terrible misadventure', but it would be 'disastrous if that failure led the UK and other governments' to ignore other difficult conflicts. On 18 April, in one of Baghdad's most dreadful days of slaughter, nearly 200 people were killed and another 200 wounded in a spate of bomb attacks. In the worst of five large explosions a car bomb in the Shi'ite district of Sadriya in central Baghdad killed at least 140 people and wounded around 150 more, some of them rebuilding a marketplace after an earlier bomb attack. One worker, 28-year-old Salih Mustafa, was waiting for a bus home when the explosion occurred: 'I saw three bodies in a wooden cart, and civilian cars were helping to transfer the victims. It was really a horrible scene.' Another witness said that he had seen dozens of bodies in the street and that more victims had been burned alive in their vehicles: 'There were pieces of flesh all over the place. Women were screaming and shouting for their loved ones who died.'[46] In such circumstances it seemed likely that al-Sadr, who had already ordered his six ministers to quit the Cabinet, would feel free to order his fighters back onto the streets in the guise of 'protecting' the Shi'ite communities. One militiaman commented: 'Washington calls us the greatest threat to peace in Iraq. But who is defending our citizens from al-Qaeda and the *takfiris*?'[47]

These events seemed to make nonsense of Prime Minister al-
Maliki's declaration that Iraqi forces would assume control of all
eighteen provinces by the end of the year, though the levels of
carnage and destruction varied throughout the country. Even the
US Secretary of Defense, Robert Gates, was forced to
acknowledge the 'determined strategy' of the insurgents, though
claiming that there was nothing surprising about it:

> We have anticipated from the beginning . . . that as the Baghdad
> security plan [including the troop surge] began to take hold in
> Baghdad, that the terrorists, al-Qaida, the insurgency and others
> would attempt to increase the violence in order to make the plan a
> failure or to make the people of Iraq believe the plan is a failure.[48]

Gates did not comment on widely voiced suggestions that the US
troop surge *was* a failure. On the same day as the coordinated
bomb attacks, British forces were transferring control of Maysan
province, making it the fourth of eighteen to be eventually
handed over to Iraqi control. Maysan, often dubbed Iraq's 'Wild
West', was a region of fiercely independent tribes of Marsh Arabs
in the south-east of the country who straddled but refused to
respect the Iran–Iraq border, smuggling in weapons, contraband
and people. It had now become plain that the British presence was
only exacerbating the violence. Thus an unnamed British officer
commented that if people in the region were drifting away from
al-Sadr's Mahdi Army it was 'because we're not there [the UK
forces having withdrawn from some areas] and they're not being
paid to attack us'.[49]

The families of six Iraqis who were killed by British soldiers in
2003 – including Baha Mousa, already considered – were now
appealing to the House of Lords in the hope of winning the right
to sue the government under European laws. Thus Shami
Chakrabarti, the director of the human rights group Liberty,
commented: 'If we win this case, there will be a human rights
obligation on our government to ensure an independent investigation into these issues. This is not about holding the military to
higher standards than they should be subject to anywhere. It's

about accountability.' It remained to be seen whether the Appellate Committee of the House of Lords would decide that under the European Convention on Human Rights and the British Human Rights Act the families of the Iraqi civilians who had been killed by British troops would have claims against the British authorities; a decision that can be summed up as follows:

- Does the right to life in Article 2 of the European Convention on Human Rights cover civilians in British-occupied Iraq?
- Can the families of the Iraqi civilian victims bring claims under the Human Rights Act in British courts?
- Has Britain complied with the 'procedural obligation' under Article 2 to conduct an effective investigation into deaths at the hands of the state?

It was significant that Article 1 of the European Convention required the state signatories to 'secure' its provisions for 'everyone within their jurisdiction' – a stipulation that is essentially but not exclusively territorial. Rabinder Singh QC, acting for the Iraqi families, argued that Britain had jurisdiction over southern Iraq while it was under occupation by the British between May 2003 and June 2004, whereas Christopher Greenwood QC, acting for the government, disputed crucial jurisdiction claims, nor did he accept that Baha Mousa's family had the right to bring proceedings under the Human Rights Act in the British courts. One legal observer, Joshua Rozenberg of the *Daily Telegraph*, commented: 'I would expect the law lords to rule that the Human Rights Act applies and that a further inquiry should be held into Mr Mousa's death alone.'[50]

On 18 April, after a long preamble, two men – David Keogh and Leo O'Connor – were tried for allegedly breaching the Official Secrets Act in connection with a memorandum detailing sensitive talks on Iraq between George Bush and Tony Blair. Keogh, a Cabinet Office civil servant, was said to have passed the memo to his friend, O'Connor, a political researcher working for Anthony Clarke, Labour MP for Northampton South,[51] in the hope that it would reach the public domain.

However, after Clarke, who had opposed the Iraq War, received the memo he responded by calling the police. David Perry QC, prosecuting, said that the document contained 'high-level strategic discussions between world leaders' and that the Official Secrets Act existed to protect the state:

> We are not talking about what may be embarrassing, a betrayal or act of disloyalty . . . The prosecution say the unauthorised disclosure of information in this case is likely to prejudice the capability of the armed forces either to carry out their tasks or lead to the loss of life or the possibility of loss of life or injury.[52]

Details of the memorandum, which was marked 'secret, personal', were not disclosed in court and some of Perry's opening speech was put to the jury in camera, with media personnel excluded from the hearing.[53] The trial lasted about two weeks and both men were found guilty: Keogh received a six-month sentence and O'Connor was sentenced to three months in prison.

There was mounting evidence that the US military had not managed to establish security in *any* part of Iraq. On 12 April a suicide bomber blew himself up in the very heart of the massively fortified Green Zone, the site of the Iraqi parliament and the huge US embassy. Eight people were killed, including three members of the parliament – two Sunnis and a Shi'ite,[54] and two dozen others were wounded. This attack came hours after a truck bomb destroyed the Sarafiyah steel girder bridge in northern Baghdad, constructed by the British in the 1930s. The explosion blasted vehicles into the river Tigris and sent a huge cloud of smoke over the city. In such a fashion the insurgents were demonstrating the failure of the troop surge and the associated Iraqi security plan to quell the violence in the capital. Khalaf al-Ilyan, a Sunni MP, voiced the widely shared perception: the new attack 'underlines the failure of the government's security plan . . . The plan is 100 per cent a failure.'[55]

The parliament bomber, believed to be an MP's bodyguard, managed to reach the assembly's cafeteria by evading the massive security measures – checkpoints, sniffer dogs and body searches –

in and around the Green Zone compound. The parliament itself was housed in bomb-proof concrete, and there were seven checkpoints – variously manned by Georgian, Peruvian and Iraqi guards – leading up to the nearest compound entrance. Mohammed Abu Bakr, a parliamentary spokesman, said: 'I saw two legs in the middle of the cafeteria and none of those killed or wounded lost their legs – which means they must be the legs of the suicide attacker.'[56] Reports that a security scanner checking pedestrians near the entrance was not working were being checked by the Iraqi police. Later, two other bombs were found near the cafeteria and were safely detonated, but further attacks seemed likely. The al-Qaeda-linked Army of Islam, claiming responsibility for the cafeteria bombing, posted a message on its website declaring that all those people cooperating with 'the occupier and its agents' would be targeted: 'We will reach you wherever you are.'[57]

It had been demonstrated several times that the Green Zone, home to 15,000 Iraqi civilians and many other people, was insecure. In October 2004 two suicide bombers killed six people in the zone; in March 2007 a mortar exploded only yards from a press conference attended by Ban Ki-Moon; and two weeks before the April bombing, American troops found two suicide bomb belts abandoned near an internal checkpoint. The US authorities were now admitting that the Green Zone was not safe, that nowhere in Baghdad was safe. Thus the US military spokesman Lieutenant Colonel Christopher Garver commented that the international zone was 'not safe . . . it is just safer than the rest of the city' and in Washington Condoleezza Rice commented: 'We know that there is a security problem in Baghdad. This [security crackdown] is still early in the process, and I don't think anyone expected that there wouldn't be counter-efforts by terrorists to undermine the security presence.'[58] President Bush emphasised the importance of dealing with the 'type of person' who is willing to kill 'innocent life . . . innocent Americans'.[59]

There were now signs that the bombing had united the disparate Iraqi legislators, with MPs from all sides condemning the suicide attack and vowing to press forward with the political process to isolate the extremists. Moreover, it seemed that rifts were developing between the Sunni insurgents and their erstwhile al-Qaeda allies – which suggested a fresh source of factional conflict rather than a reduction in violence. Thus Alaa Makki, a Sunni MP, said: 'They [Sunni insurgents] have realised that those people [al-Qaeda-linked groups] are not working for Iraq's interests. They realised that their operations might destroy Iraq altogether.' And one unnamed commentator suggested that the relationship between the Sunni and Shi'ite MPs was better after the bombing than before, 'because now they have agreed to fight terrorism together'.[60]

In the same vein the government had reportedly been rallying the tribes of Anbar province in the western desert against al-Qaeda, not least because of its targeting of tribal leaders who had been reluctant to join the bombing campaign against Shi'ite civilians. One result had been a wave of clan-based violence against the al-Qaeda network in the Sunni heartland, which was welcomed by the US military, still forced to confront the growing frustration in Muqtada al-Sadr's ranks as the Maliki regime continued to demonstrate its subservience to the Bush administration.

On 16 April Amnesty International warned that the Middle East was on the verge of a new humanitarian crisis and urged the European Union, the United States and other countries to take concrete measures to assist the more than three million people displaced by the Iraq War. Thus in a briefing released in advance of an international conference being convened by the United Nations High Commissioner for Refugees in Geneva on 17–18 April 2007, Amnesty called for states to provide urgent help to alleviate the suffering of the Iraqi refugees who had flooded into Syria and Jordan, particularly since the February 2006 attack on the Samarra shrine.

Malcolm Smart, the director of Amnesty's Middle East and North African Programme, declared that there must be a limit to which Syria and Jordan could continue 'to bear the brunt of the refugee exodus so far . . . in the face of the continuing surge of Iraqis desperate to escape the conflict'. Other governments should 'now step in and deliver – not just pledge – direct assistance in order to ensure that the refugees are adequately housed and fed, and have access to health care and education, in Syria, Jordan and the other countries which are now helping bear the consequences of the disaster in Iraq.'[61] In Syria, for example, the massive influx of Iraqi refugees had brought rising prices and overcrowding, and Syrian landlords and businesses were extorting money from Iraqi families desperate for any secure place to live. The crisis was escalating every day, and suburban trucks commonly hired by Iraqis to flee from Baghdad were lining many Damascus streets. Adnan, a merchant in the Bab Touma district, said: 'Bush is responsible for all of this. He burnt the Middle East and caused this suffering. We support the Iraqis here, but he is ultimately at fault.'[62]

Amnesty was calling on the US, the EU and other states to establish generous resettlement programmes to assist the refugees, especially the most vulnerable, to start new lives away from the war zone; and to afford all refugees and rejected asylum seekers effective protection. Smart said:

> The UK government and others which persist in returning failed asylum seekers to Iraq, arguing that the Kurdish north is relatively peaceful, should desist from this practice forthwith. Iraqis' lives should not be put at risk in order for governments to demonstrate to a domestic audience that they can be tough on asylum seekers – this is just playing with other people's lives.[63]

And the hundreds of thousands of Iraqis who had become internally displaced should also be helped – most specifically by redoubled efforts from the US, other states and regional political and religious leaders to find a political solution to the crisis, so that the Iraqis could return to their homes and live in peace.

On 20 April Amnesty issued a report stating that the Iraqi authorities were increasingly imposing the death penalty, including after pre-trial televised 'confessions', uninvestigated allegations of torture and unfair trials – making Iraq the world's fourth highest executioner after China, Iran and Pakistan.[64] Since capital punishment was reinstated in mid-2004 nearly 300 people had been sentenced to death and at least 100 had been executed. Smart commented that the dramatic increase in death sentences ('this cruel, inhuman and degrading punishment') represented 'a dangerous slide into the brutal errors of the past . . . Rising violence on Iraqi streets suggests that its reinstatement may simply have contributed to the brutalisation of Iraqi society.'[65]

At the same time the US military was working, against orders issued by the Maliki administration, to achieve the 'ghettoisation' of Baghdad into about thirty districts, according to Brigadier General John Campbell: 'Barrier walls will outline selected neighbourhoods around Baghdad in an attempt to help protect the Iraqi population from terrorists.'[66] This policy again highlighted the desperate plight of the capital's inhabitants, deprived of the basic amenities of life and unable to travel freely around their own city, and the growing tensions between the Iraqi government and the US military.

This brutalisation was manifest in the daily carnage. On 24 April nine American soldiers were killed and twenty injured when two lorries exploded in quick succession at an entrance to their base in Diyala, north of Baghdad. The first vehicles crashed into the concrete barriers surrounding the US outpost and exploded after the troops opened fire. Then a second lorry smashed into the wreckage, dragging it for 30 yards before the driver detonated his bomb. In Baqubah, gunmen dressed as police officers killed six people, and in a village south of Baghdad masked men slaughtered seven members of one family. The American troop surge had succeeded in temporarily reducing violence in some areas but – as acknowledged in an article by US senator Joseph Biden, chairman of the Senate Foreign Relations Committee – 'it [the violence] is up dramatically in the belt ringing Baghdad . . . The civilian death toll increased 15 per cent from February to March . . . When we squeeze the water balloon in one place, it bulges somewhere else.'[67]

On 25 April Sarah Leah Whitson, the Middle East director of Human Rights Watch, complained that the Iraqi government was no longer releasing figures for civilian deaths – implying that they would have been unhelpful to US propaganda about the success of the troop surge: 'The Iraqi government should make public its figures of civilian deaths even if the picture is bleak. Withholding the facts will not make the situation any safer.'[68] UN officials said that the Iraqi government had given no reason for withholding the data, encouraging speculation – according to Ivana Vuco, a UN human rights officer – that the situation was 'very grim'. The UN Assistance Mission in Iraq now estimated that the death toll was again rising, despite the initial impact of the troop surge, and found that the rate of sectarian cleansing was also mounting, with nearly three-quarters of a million people forced to flee their homes in the previous year. In response, the office of Prime Minister al-Maliki issued a statement calling the UN report 'inaccurate' and 'unbalanced', adding that it aggravated the humanitarian crisis in Iraq 'instead of solving it'.[69]

The United States itself was now being driven to acknowledge the failure of its Iraq policies, with even General David Petraeus giving a downbeat assessment – in sharp contrast to George Bush's perennially simplistic comments. On 26 April Petraeus admitted that the war would 'get harder before it gets easier', saying that the conflict was 'the most complex and challenging I have ever seen'. Moreover, he emphasised that any discernible achievements had 'not come without sacrifice', with the increasing use of car bombs and suicide attacks having 'led to greater US losses'.[70] When asked how long the US would have to remain in Iraq, Petraeus replied that he could not anticipate what the level 'might be some years down the road'. Nancy Pelosi, the Democrat speaker of the House, commented that the sacrifices borne by the US troops and their families 'demand more than the blank cheques the president is asking for, for a war without end'.[71] The Senate followed the House of Representatives in supporting legislation calling for most US troops to be out of Iraq by spring 2008, though a presidential veto was inevitable.

The American efforts in Iraq were being steadily eroded by the determination of the multiheaded monster of the insurgency, the endemic corruption in the country and the escalating sectarian war. With so few gains to show, and the US military seemingly unable to rely on the integrity of its own officers, it was inevitable that morale would suffer. Lieutenant Colonel William Steele, formerly head of the high-security Camp Cropper prison at Baghdad airport, had been arrested and charged with aiding the enemy – by providing them with unmonitored mobile phones –

and fraternising with the daughter of an inmate.[72] This was yet another blow to the US authorities already stained by the Abu Ghraib scandal.

In addition, morale was being drained by the steady increase in the number of American casualties, the inevitable consequence of an underresourced army fighting for years in a hostile environment it did not comprehend. By the end of April 2007 more than 3,300 American troops had been killed and 25,000 wounded in the Iraq War.[73] Most of the wounded were first transferred to a vast clinic compound near Landstuhl in Germany, close to the French border, in an area designed as a Hitler Youth campus. The *Times* journalists Roger Boyes and David Bebber reported the wounded being wheeled in – '23 on the first day that we were there, 39 the next' – and quoted Lieutenant Colonel Gary Southwell, chief psychologist at Landstuhl: 'Six hundred of the soldiers that came here from Iraq last year had mental health conditions, and 20 per cent of them were suffering from post-traumatic stress disorder [PTSD] – flashbacks, hypervigilance, memory loss. One of the major reasons people are being sent home is self-destructiveness, suicidal thoughts.'[74] A soldier in the intensive care unit told the chaplain that he had killed thirty-seven Iraqis, and then screamed: 'I'm going straight to Hell. They killed my buddies, I killed them and found joy in it. . . . I'm going to Hell!'[75]

British troops were affected in the same way: in late April a Ministry of Defence report revealed that the number of British troops in Iraq suffering from PTSD had doubled in a year, not least because of the deteriorating situation in southern Iraq.[76] Thus a returning soldier, Private Paul Barton, said on *Channel 4 News* that the situation in Basra was 'hopeless and lost', and accused the government of trying to save face by keeping troops in the region. The troops were 'sitting ducks' for the increasingly sophisticated insurgents who had taken control of the area.[77] Speaking to the *Daily Telegraph,* Barton declared:

> We have overstayed our welcome now. We should speed up the withdrawal. It's a lost battle, a hell hole that will not get any better. We should pull out and call it quits . . . We are meant to be there

peace-keeping . . . We are caught in the middle, coming under attack day and night.[78]

In 2006 the number of British troops reported to be suffering from PTSD increased from 208 to 363, but it was thought that the actual figure could be even higher.

The Americans were at that time reportedly building a three-mile 12ft-high wall, mostly at night, in Azamiyah in the centre of Baghdad to separate Sunni and Shi'ite communities – an unambiguous contribution to the wave of sectarian cleansing. Then Prime Minister al-Maliki objected to the construction of such a barrier around a Sunni community: 'This wall reminds us of other walls that we reject [around the Occupied Territories in Palestine], so I've ordered it to stop and to find other means of protection for the neighbourhoods.'

Hundreds of demonstrators had taken to the streets in protest, saying that the wall would jail them in their own communities and carrying banners with the slogans 'Separation wall is a big prison for Azamiyah citizens' and 'Azamiyah children want to see Baghdad without walls'. The US authorities, implying that al-Maliki had not been consulted before the building began, declared that they would 'respect the wishes' of the Iraqi government.[79] But then an Iraqi military spokesman, Brigadier General Qassim al-Moussawi, said that al-Maliki had been responding to exaggerated reports, and that the building of the 'security barriers' in the Azamiyah neighbourhood would continue. Al-Moussawi had expected this critical reaction from 'some weak-minded people'.[80]

The security situation continued to deteriorate. The bodies of victims were being stolen from the scenes of murders and car bombings by criminal gangs for ransom;[81] formerly harmonious mixed marriages between Sunnis and Shi'ites were under attack, splitting families and leading to more killings;[82] and as always the bloody attacks throughout the country were adding to the casualty toll. On 29 April another British soldier was shot dead in southern Iraq, the 146th member of the British armed forces to die in Iraq since the 2003 invasion; on the same day a suicide car bomber in Karbala killed sixty-eight people and wounded 178 more, with some body parts later found on the roofs of buildings.

The US troops surge was manifestly not working, and Washington and London seemed to have no other solution to the bloody chaos in Iraq. In the United Kingdom proposals were being compiled by Lord Ashdown, Lord King and Baroness Jay for a report that would be analogous to *The Iraq Study Group Report*, prepared – and largely ignored – in the United States. In the US the Republican hawks were beginning to trim their pro-war stance, and the residual support for the Bush administration seemed to be slipping away.[83] It remained to be seen how long George Bush could maintain his pro-war posture in the face of the growing congressional and public opposition to the Iraq conflict.

At the end of April a further congressional investigation revealed that six out of eight projects that the US government claimed to be a success were falling apart, throwing doubts over the viability of the entire reconstruction programme. Stuart Bowen, the special inspector general for Iraq reconstruction, said that 'concerns' about whether the Iraqis would sustain the project investments 'were valid'. Bowen's inspectors – including fifty-five auditors and inspectors in Iraq conducting no less than seventy-eight enquiries into fraud, waste and abuse of funds – had noted serious deterioration in the projects, and questioned whether they would even survive.[84] The inspectors expressed satisfaction with two projects, but said that a survey of thousands of others was impossible because of security problems.[85]

The Bush administration's troop surge was well under way, and the Iraq situation was not improving. The casualty toll in the US military continued to mount, with the Iraqi numbers of dead, injured, traumatised, bereaved and dispossessed running into the millions. The carnage and destruction rolled on with no end in sight.

5

Eroding the politics of denial

At the end of April 2007 Corporal Donald Payne – the first British soldier ever to be convicted of a war crime – was dismissed from the Army, lost £300,000 in pension and other benefits, and began a one-year jail sentence. Iraqi civilians held at a detention centre in Basra had been punched and kicked when hooded and handcuffed, with Payne conducting what he called 'the choir', striking the prisoners in sequence so that their groans and shrieks produced the 'music'. It had taken more than three and a half years to get the case to court, leading eventually to the absurd acquittal of Payne and six other soldiers of the manslaughter of the civilian Baha Mousa, found to have ninety-three injuries, including fractured ribs and a broken nose. Phil Shiner, Mousa's British lawyer, had called the trial a 'travesty', but Payne had admitted inhumanely treating the Iraqi civilians, which was a war crime under the International Criminal Court Act 2001. In sentencing Payne, Mr Justice McKinnon said that what Payne had done was 'particularly harmful' to the reputation of British troops, and he also criticised Payne's superiors for not supervising him.

At the final conclusion of the court findings General Sir Richard Dannatt, the Chief of the General Staff, said that the investigation into Mousa's death was not over: 'We need to know how Mr Baha Mousa died. We do not yet know who was responsible.'[1] It seemed unlikely that any other action would be taken: it was *already* known how Mousa had died, and no soldier was in the frame for further military or judicial action.

On 1 May Jonathan Holmes's play *Fallujah*, recalling the horrors of the US onslaughts on the city in 2004, opened at the Old Truman Brewery, London. This helped to remind us of the two vast sieges – Operation Vigilant Resolve in April of that year and Operation Phantom Fury in November – of one of Iraq's main population centres. Seventy articles of the Geneva Conventions were violated in the two separate months of siege warfare, not least the banning of chemical weapons. Holmes himself quotes Colonel Randolph Alles of Marine Air Group 11, interviewed by James Crawley of the *San Diego Union-Tribune*: 'Yeah, we napalmed those bridges. The generals love napalm.'[2]

In November 2004 Fallujah was facing a humanitarian crisis. Dardous al-Ubaidi, head of the Iraqi Red Crescent Society, said that her organisation had asked the Iraqi government for permission to deliver aid supplies but the request had been turned down: 'There is no water, no food, no medicine, no electricity and no fuel.' Ahmed al-Raqi, a Red Cross official, pointed out that movement was impossible in the city: 'The wounded find no help and bleed to death.' Of Fallujah's population, around 50,000 had remained in the city and were in dire straits; the majority, about 200,000 people, had fled to makeshift refugee camps in the desert lacking basic amenities. Hafid al-Dulaimi, head of the city's compensation committee, reported that 36,000 homes had been destroyed in the American onslaught, along with 8,400 shops, sixty nurseries and schools and sixty-five mosques and religious sanctuaries.[3] Two British journalists, Jonathan Steele and Dahr Jamail, wrote that Fallujah was 'this decade's unforgettable monument to brutality and overkill . . . a reminder that unpopular occupations will always degenerate into desperation and atrocity'.[4] Tony Lagouranis, a self-confessed US interrogator/torturer, described in graphic terms something of what it was like searching for intelligence in Fallujah:

> The dead man's skin was black, crawling with maggots, and wet with slime. Half his face was gone, and I peered into his skull . . . A team of marines had no trouble finding bodies . . . We tagged and bagged over five hundred over the course of four weeks . . . The sight of women and children blown apart was heart wrenching . . . When I unzipped the bag, I never knew what was going to be inside. If the bag felt light, it could be a partial torso, or it could be a kid.[5]

In Iraq the slaughter and destruction continued through 2007, widely predicted in much commentary before the invasion occurred. In early May it was reported that 'every British ambassador in the Middle East' had warned that invading Iraq would be a 'nightmare' and that popular opinion would be turned against the West.[6] Sir Ivor Richards, later the president of Trinity College, Oxford, saw telegrams sent by Britain's Middle East envoys when he served as ambassador to Ireland before the 2003 invasion. He subsequently recalled that the assessments were unanimous: 'Every ambassador in a Middle East post accurately predicted what a nightmare invading Iraq would be. The telegrams I saw were full of doom and gloom about the consequences'; every ambassador 'from the Arab world or the Muslim world was predicting how disastrously it would play in their countries at both public and government levels'.[7] And Richards hoped that 'how we landed up in this mess' would be the subject of a long inquiry.[8]

There was daily evidence of the failure of British and American policy in Iraq. On 1 May gunmen began attacks at 6.45 a.m., when a minibus was targeted as it passed by Iskandariya, killing eleven Shi'ites and wounding three more. Less than an hour later a group of gunmen standing on the road near Latifiya opened fire at civilian cars, killing three people and wounding five. Then, significantly enough, the Green Zone again came under fire, with six mortar rounds exploding in an area near Prime Minister Nouri al-Maliki's office. On 3 May, a rocket attack on the Green Zone killed four Filipino contractors working for the US government – yet again bringing into question the security of the fortified heart of the Iraqi government and the American presence. The Pentagon had already disclosed that documents captured in recent fighting in Baghdad had included two identity cards for access to the Green Zone and one for access to the US embassy. Already there was widespread speculation that the war would eventually descend on the Green Zone as it had on the US embassy in Saigon. Outside the gates of the fortified compound was 'hell', according to Haider Hassan, a store clerk at the Rashid Hotel inside the zone – but hell was 'starting to feel a lot closer'.[9] American soldiers had even been ordered not to travel through the Green Zone alone for fear of kidnapping, making it harder to maintain the propaganda illusions that had been fostered in the fortified bubble.

On 4 May a summit in Sharm al-Sheikh, Egypt, designed to bring stability to Iraq, ended in acrimony when Manouchehr Mottaki, the Foreign Minister of Iran, denounced American policy.[10] He blamed the United States for the violence in Iraq and demanded a timetable for the withdrawal of foreign forces: 'In our view, the continuation of occupation lies at the origin of the crisis. The United States must accept the responsibility arising from the occupation of Iraq and should not finger-point or put the blame on others.' At a later press conference Mottaki declared: 'These countries think they own the world. They think everyone has to listen to them and comply with their conditions.'[11] The conference in Sharm el-Sheikh did not lead to any discussions between the United States and Iran: The US Secretary of State, Condoleezza Rice, said that she had been willing to meet her Iranian counterpart but that the 'opportunity simply didn't arise'.

By now President George Bush had vetoed the congressional attempt to set a timetable for troop withdrawal from Iraq: 'Our troops and their families deserve better.'[12] In a televised statement he repeated the familiar denunciation of what he called a 'rigid and artificial' requirement that US troops withdraw by a certain time, saying that such a plan would allow the insurgents to take over the country. And he objected also to what many people might see as a primary condition of democratic government, that the military be controlled by an accountable civilian administration. It would place the US forces in an impossible position, Bush declared, if 'American commanders in the middle of a conflict zone' had 'to take orders from politicians 6,000 miles away in Washington DC'.[13] Leading Democrats were then scheduled to meet the President in the White House to discuss the terms of a possible compromise, but if Bush thought that wielding the veto would bring immediate and unanimous praise from the US military he was mistaken. Thus a number of top retired military figures expressed outrage at the President's veto of the act.[14]

In immediate response to the veto Lieutenant General Robert Gard (US Army, retired) declared that Bush had doomed the

United States to 'repeating a terrible history', his action being 'hauntingly reminiscent' of what had transpired in March 1968 in Vietnam. At that time both the Secretary of Defense and the President had recognised – just as military leaders in Iraq were recognising – that the conflict could not be won militarily alone. President Lyndon Johnson, dreading the prospect of being seen to lose a war, had authorised a surge of 25,000 extra troops to Vietnam. The American fatalities had already reached 24,000 soldiers killed in action; five years later another 34,000 combat deaths had occurred.[15]

Brigadier General John Johns (US Army, retired) asserted that, five years before, Congress had trusted the president 'to transform Iraq', but Bush had violated that trust and deceived the American people with a misuse of force: 'Today, the president violated the trust of the American people, our troops and their families by vetoing this bill and not choosing to do what is right. He has let us down.'[16] And Major General Mel Montano (US Army National Guard, retired) commented that Bush's rhetoric about Congress 'not supporting our troops' was pure 'hogwash'. The real 'non support of our troops' was the veto – which sent a message that the President would fund the troops to fight but was not concerned about returning them to their families.[17]

These were the latest in a long list of military leaders who had expressed dissatisfaction with Bush's handling of the war.[18] But it was obvious that the administration, seemingly oblivious to the military chorus of dissent, was impervious to such mounting criticism. Moira Whelan, communication director of the National Security Network, declared that 'daily' the views of 'disappointed and outraged' military leaders were being heard: 'Clearly, the commander-in-chief [Bush] is not listening to the generals. His veto is simply the latest blatant disregard for the American people, the Iraq Study Group, and the men and women who command our military forces. President Bush is marching in the wrong direction.'[19]

The body of military dissent even included two retired officers who had commanded troops in Iraq. Major General John Batiste (US Army, retired) asserted that the President's 'stubborn commitment to a failed strategy is incomprehensible'; the failed

strategy was 'in violation of basic principles of war'; and his failure
'to mobilize the nation to defeat worldwide Islamic extremism is
tragic'. The American people deserved 'more from the
commander-in-chief and his administration.'[20] In the same vein
Major General Paul Eaton (US Army, retired) declared that Bush
was holding the US troops 'hostage to his ego'; the army and the
marine corps were at war – 'alone, without their president's
support'.[21] Again the facts were plain: the Iraq War was being
prosecuted by an isolated President in the teeth of congressional,
military and public opinion.

In the United Kingdom, Prime Minister Tony Blair seemed
totally oblivious to the sheer weight of American opinion against
the war; and the British parliament, unlike Congress, was given no
opportunity to discuss and vote on a timetable for the withdrawal
of troops. Moreover, reflecting US military opinion, there were
also British military voices being raised against a continuation of
the occupation. On 3 May a retired British army officer, General
Sir Michael Rose,[22] told the BBC *Newsnight* programme that the
US and its allies should admit defeat and leave Iraq before more
soldiers were killed:

> It is the soldiers who have been telling me that the war they have been
> fighting is a hopeless war, that they cannot possibly win it and the
> sooner we start talking politics and not military solutions, the sooner
> they will come home and their lives will be preserved . . . Of course
> we have to admit defeat. The British admitted defeat in North
> America and the catastrophes that were predicted at the time never
> happened. The catastrophes that were predicted after Vietnam never
> happened. The same thing will occur after we leave Iraq.[23]

Rose also said that, while not excusing the Iraqi insurgents for 'some
of the terrible things they do', he could understand their feelings. If
he had been an American under British occupation of American
native soil he would 'never, never' have laid down his arms: 'I do
understand why they [the insurgents] are resisting the Americans.'[24]

On 10 May 2007 President Bush was told by eleven 'centrist'
Republican allies during a ninety-minute meeting that the party

would be likely to desert him if the situation in Iraq did not improve dramatically and he continued to keep American troops in the country. In this vein Representative Ray LaHood of Illinois said that the American people were 'war fatigued' and wanted to know that there was 'a way out'. Bush had been, in LaHood's words, if not surprised then 'maybe sobered', perhaps hearing such 'frank and no-holds-barred' opinion from his nominal allies for the first time.[25] Representative Tom Davis told Bush, 'in a very remarkable, candid conversation', that his approval rating was just 5 per cent in parts of his northern Virginia district: 'People are always saying that President Bush is in a bubble. Well, this was our chance and we took it.'[26]

At the same time a majority of Iraq's MPs pledged their support for a bill that would impose a deadline for foreign troops to leave the country. The draft legislation would oblige the Iraqi government to seek parliamentary approval for any extension of the United Nations mandate for foreign troops, due to expire at the end of 2007. Nasser al-Rubaie, a parliamentary supporter of Muqtada al-Sadr and sponsor of the measure, emphasised that the legislation would both cap the number of troops in the US-led coalition – to prevent further escalation of the war – and impose a withdrawal date.[27] Al-Rubaie claimed to have gathered signatures from 144 members of the 275-member parliament – the first time that such a majority had been achieved – before submitting the draft, but the Maliki administration was not about to upset the American occupiers. A government spokesman called for the proposal to be rejected, saying that the Iraqi security forces were too weak to impose order.

A situation had developed in which the US and UK governments, and their Maliki allies, were maintaining policies against majority opinion in the United States, Britain and Iraq. The rhetoric of George Bush and Tony Blair had constantly urged support for the 'burgeoning democracy' in Iraq, and yet their commitment to democracy did not extend to heeding majority opinion not only in the US and the UK but also in Iraq, whose parliamentary decisions Washington and London were explicitly pledged to support. In this context it was easy to understand the view – in America, in Britain and throughout the world – that democracy was far removed from the actual Bush–Blair realpolitik agenda. It was not difficult to imagine what that might be – a permanent strategic presence in Iraq and control of the country's resources, primarily oil.

On 10 May the US House of Representatives voted by 221 to 205, largely along party lines, to pay for the military operations by instalments, defying Bush's threat of a second presidential veto. The first portion of the bill would cover costs until 1 August, allowing $42.8 billion to buy equipment and to train Iraqi and Afghan security forces; the bill would also have necessitated a late July/early August Congress vote to free an additional $52.8 billion to cover war costs through to the 30 September end of the financial year. Bush immediately declared that such legislation 'would not work', but already he was being forced to compromise by agreeing to include achievement benchmarks for the Iraqi government, where he had previously demanded a 'clean' war-funding bill (i.e. legislation without 'time-wasting' conditions). It remained to be seen how the Senate would respond to the House vote.

In Iraq there seemed no escape from the continuing misery and mayhem, as revealed on an almost daily basis in the Western press. Thus, for example, the London-based Iraq Occupation Focus was regularly detailing in its newsletter the suffering of ordinary families under the occupation: one typical issue, citing sources in every case, recorded the killing of Iraqi children in a Diyala primary school by a US helicopter; dozens of families fleeing their homes after American attacks on Sadr City; an Iraqi contractor paying bribes to a police officer not to torture his imprisoned brother and business partner; an increase in the number of tortured bodies, often still in handcuffs; the murdering of eighty-two patients in hospital; the murder of a fifteen-year-old because he had the Sunni name Omar; the arrest and torture of a gay activist; a Pentagon survey that one in ten of US soldiers in Iraq mistreats civilians or damages their property, and that nearly half of US troops and marines in Iraq believed that torture should be used in some circumstances; and a US marine testifying in court that he had 'pissed' on the head of an Iraqi detainee, and also watched a superior officer kill five Iraqis as they tried to surrender.[28]

The Pentagon survey, based on interviews with 1,300 soldiers and 450 marines, revealed the strains that the war was imposing on the US military (and the consequent suffering inflicted on Iraqi civilians): 'Soldiers that have high levels of anger, experienced high levels of combat, or screened positive for a mental health problem were nearly twice as likely to mistreat [Iraqi] non-combatants as those who had low levels of anger or combat or who screened negative for a mental health problem.'[29] In short, psychologically damaged US troops were mistreating Iraqi civilians. The report also found that fewer than half of all soldiers and marines would report a team member for unethical behaviour.

The Pentagon was now imposing restrictions on internet postings from war zones, claiming that this was for fear of providing sensitive information to the enemy, but in fact it was because so many of the emails and blogs had been complaining about President Bush's decision to extend deployment from one year to fifteen months as part of the attempt to pacify Baghdad and Anbar province. Some soldiers said that the real reason for the curb was their negative comments about the war, including scepticism about the President's claims of progress. Matthew Burden, editor of *The Blog of War*, pulling together accounts from the field,[30] said that the Pentagon decision had silenced the military's 'most honest voice' out of the war zone.[31]

In Samarra, Iraqi civilians had had no running water for several days, were receiving only sporadic electricity, and had been banned from driving cars. The US-appointed mayor of the town was living in Tikrit because of the sectarian violence, and remained unwilling to visit the town he was supposed to be administering. Adnan al-Dulaimi, a senior member of the Concord Front, a Sunni voting bloc which had threatened to withdraw from Iraq's ruling coalition, said: 'Samarra suffers an inhumane and sectarian siege. People are not allowed to reach main streets, the power is off and taps are dry for the seventh day successively.'[32] The US military had completed the construction of the concrete wall around the Baghdad district of Adhamiya, despite protests from Prime Minister al-Maliki and local residents; an Iraqi soldier manning a checkpoint said that the region inside the wall was now more dangerous, and that the Americans 'do not listen to us'.[33]

*

In the sense that no part of the country – schools, hospitals, homes, prisons, roads etc. – was being spared the consequences of civil violence, the whole of Iraq had become a battlefield, afflicted by coalition onslaught, insurgent response, sectarian strife and criminal activity. No one was safe. On 4 May spokesman Major General William Caldwell claimed that insurgents had reportedly rigged the partially constructed Huda Girls' School in Tarmiyah, north of Baghdad, with explosives by building artillery shells into the walls, floors and ceilings: 'We found artillery shells that were literally being built into the ceiling. We found artillery shells, again all hooked up with wires, being built into the floors. We found propane tanks – two very large propane tanks – built into the floors under the stairwells.'[34] The explosives were discovered when American troops noticed a detonation wire across the street and followed it into the school, so foiling a plot that would have killed dozens of children. The insurgents had long incorporated explosives into paving stones to ambush security patrols but the character of the Tarmiyah scheme was unprecedented.

The conflict was also impacting on the lives of women and children in countless other ways, as bodies were dumped on the highways and families were driven from their homes for sectarian or other reasons. The Iraqi government was now executing women, as well as men, as alleged terrorists after brief trials and with a disregard of normal judicial process. On 10 May Amnesty International protested at the imminent execution of two women – Samar Sa'ad Abdullah and Wassan Talib – held at Baghdad's al-Kadhimiya prison: 'The death sentence is always wrong but Iraq's shaky and unfair legal system should never be imposing capital punishment.'[35]

Many children had stopped going to school for fear of bombs on the roads, exploding artillery shells or kidnap for ransom or sex trafficking. Where children did venture forth they were compelled to pass decomposing bodies outside their homes and were exposed to sudden bouts of sectarian intimidation and killing. And minority religious groups were being targeted by the extremists. The country's Christian communities were close to extinction as families were forced – under an al-Qaeda threat 'to convert [to Islam] or be killed' – to flee their traditional strongholds in Baghdad. Symbolically enough, heads had been cut off statues outside Christian churches, and people were being killed because of their faith. Many Christians had fled to the Kurdish village of Ankawa, an overcrowded 'city of Christ', while thousands more had managed to reach Syria and Jordan. Estimates suggested that half Baghdad's pre-2003 Christian population of hundreds of thousands had fled or been killed. Thus Father Bashar Warda of the St Peter Major Seminary said that the Iraqi government had a common understanding with the Islamic terrorists that Christians had no future in the country.[36]

Criminal gangs were preying on women and children to feed the trafficking market or to try and secure a large ransom for their release; and underworld financial exploitation extended to such criminal activities as protection rackets, the acquisition of abandoned homes and smuggling. For example, the Ashur family on the banks of the Shatt al-Arab had begun smuggling oil after the 2003 invasion, making about $5 million a week from their activities. When another tribe attempted to take over their business they were forced to hire gunmen from outside Basra to defend the fiefdom – according to one family member, paying $250,000 every week to gunmen 'to make sure we keep our terminals and preserve our rights'. This demonstrated that the Iraqi government had no control over such activities, that much of the country's economy was being run by the criminal underworld, and that any talk of post-invasion Iraq developing as a liberal free-market economy was farcical.[37]

The morale in the US military and their families was continuing to deteriorate. The tours of duty in Iraq and Afghanistan were being extended and the deployments to the battle zones were becoming more frequent. One divorced woman, Lieutenant Eva Crouch, even lost custody of her daughter after being called up for eighteen months' service in Iraq. She arrived home and phoned her ex-husband to collect her daughter, whereupon he replied: 'Not without a court order'; and it took a series of legal battles before she regained custody. This event led to a change in Kentucky state law to ensure that military personnel do not lose custody of their children by prolonged periods of absence, but such protection does not yet exist at federal level. Crouch was not the only parent to suffer the loss of a child in such a fashion: following the publicity surrounding her case, other soldiers contacted her to relate similar experiences. And since the divorce rate among soldiers and marines was increasing, the problem was becoming more prevalent. More than 74,000 regular US troops were single parents, and about a third of the US military personnel in Iraq were women.

The prolonged periods of service and the more frequent deployments were also affecting the employment prospects of returning soldiers. Supposedly protected jobs in the civilian sector were disappearing as employers refused to tolerate the lengthy absences, and this in turn was affecting the Pentagon's deployment policies: troops facing subsequent unemployment in the civilian sector were less willing to serve. The Pentagon had been forced to increase pay and to offer bonuses to attract recruits, but still the required troop levels had not been reached – despite the efforts of a thousand extra recruiters. George Bush's troop surge, putting further demands on an already stretched US military, had not helped. The recruiters were now targeting seventeen-year-olds as possible military candidates, a policy also adopted in the United Kingdom.

The British military was recruiting sixteen- and seventeen-year-olds and sending them to fight – and die – in Iraq. Karen Lincoln recalled the passing-out parade of her then seventeen-year-old son Aaron in Catterick, eight months before he died, aged eighteen, in Iraq. On 3 May the body of another teenager, Rifleman Paul Donnachie, was flown back to Britain from the Gulf: he too had enlisted aged seventeen, and had been killed a few months later.[38] The British government, following its 2003 ratification of the UN Convention of the Rights of the Child, had in fact frequently broken its pledge not to send under-eighteens to fight in Iraq. In a written answer to a parliamentary question the then defence minister, Adam Ingram, admitted that fifteen soldiers were 'inadvertently deployed to Iraq before their eighteenth birthday' between June 2003 and July 2005.

★

The Bush administration, sensitive to military criticism, was now trying to rejuvenate the senior defence staff by making a significant new appointment. The Defense Secretary, Robert Gates, declared that he had decided to replace General Peter Pace as chairman of the Joint Chiefs of Staff to avoid a 'divisive ordeal' in the Senate which would have had to approve an extension of the general's term. The then chief of naval operations, Admiral Michael Mullen, was nominated for the post, which invited further speculation that Iran – a significant naval power in the Gulf – was in the frame. Admiral Edmund Gambastiani, the vice-chairman of the Joint Chiefs of Staff, announced that he was retiring.

The decision not to fight for Pace – who had been a key architect of the 2003 invasion – suggested that George Bush was keen to garner support for the surge policy and so to open a new chapter on the Iraq War. Gates declared he had not lost faith in Pace but said that the 'circumstances' made the decision necessary. It was announced that leading Republican and Democrat figures were unanimous in respecting Pace – and equally unanimous in wanting a change for the Pentagon leadership. The decision invited further speculation about the reluctance of the administration to invite the sort of discussion of the Iraq policy that Senate hearings on Pace's record would have made inevitable. The last thing Bush wanted was a spotlight on the failing troop surge.

The US military was struggling to quell the violence in Baghdad while efforts persisted to resurrect Iraq's collapsed economy. On 9 May Paul Brinkley, the US deputy undersecretary of defence for business transformation, said that international retailers were interested in the products made in Iraq, that Iraqi-made leather and clothing would soon appear in Western retail outlets, and that he hoped to announce a substantial order for hand-made carpets produced by workshops in and around Baghdad. A task force of American business consultants was reportedly touring some of Iraq's most dangerous areas, visiting moribund ceramic works, cement factories, engineering plants and shopping centres, to see what could be salvaged. Paul Bremer, the early US administrator, had deliberately starved such enterprises of capital, believing that they would all soon be privatised, but the result had been soaring unemployment – 300,000 workers losing their jobs – and total industrial collapse.

Saddam Hussein had run the vast swathe of nationalised industries as a *de facto* social welfare programme, subsidising production – largely from oil revenues – to provide employment for the people. Now the decaying production apparatus was apparent everywhere, as was the appalling security situation. It had taken five armoured Humvees and a detachment of US troops to protect three of Paul Brinkley's consultants when they visited a dairy in the Abu Ghraib region. The Pentagon had now accepted that the state-owned firms would have to contribute to the rebuilding of the country's economy: 'The good thing is very few of these businesses completely disappeared [despite Bremer]. The majority still exist at some level. We want to work with those that are left to stimulate potentially profitable parts of the business . . . These idle plants are the engine of the Iraqi economy.'.[39]

The commentators and pundits continued to speculate about the impact of the surge. Some said that, by sheer weight of numbers, it had achieved greater stability – but at what cost in US and Iraqi deaths, and could it be sustained? American morale remained low, and few observers thought that the Iraqi forces would be able to control the 'cleared' areas. It was inevitable that the local populations would see the US troops as an intimidating, or murderous, presence. The only contact between the two cultural worlds was in conflict situations and when American soldiers were rampaging through Iraqi homes in search of weapons and suspect insurgents. They would use interpreters but often their English was poor, and communication was simple: 'Are there any bad guys in the area?' – to which the locals would shrug, not wanting to get involved. And it was usually difficult to know what was happening. One photographer, Sean Smith of *The Guardian*, admitted that 'by being embedded, I am seeing the country through the eyes of the occupiers'; and that there was no way he could tell 'the whole story'. But he could show the gap between the rhetoric of the Iraqi government and the reality on the ground: 'There is no effective administration here and the Iraqi army is a fiction. There are Iraqi soldiers alongside the Americans

. . . They are small gangs or bands of soldiers, not a national force.'[40] The Americans were 'good soldiers, sent to do an impossible political job . . . This isn't about governing Iraq; it's just trying to demonstrate nowhere is out of bounds.'[41]

On 11 May Major General Benjamin Mixon, the commander of US forces in northern Iraq, said that he did not have enough troops to bring stability since the region was now a haven for insurgents fleeing the American crackdown in Baghdad. There were already 3,500 US soldiers in the region but Mixon declared that he would need additional forces in Diyala province to bring the situation 'to an acceptable level'. This appeal was already sharpening the debate in the United States about the effectiveness of the troop surge, amid 'multiplying signs of disillusion' about the plan.[42]

In this context Vice-President Dick Cheney felt it necessary to go to Iraq to make the case for continuing the war: 'I want you to know that the American people do not support a policy of retreat. We want to complete the mission, get it done right and return with honour.'[43] He made no attempt to define the mission or to address the various opinion polls showing a growing number of Americans opposed to the war. However, the Bush administration could rely on Iraq's President, Jalal Talabani, who was now suggesting that US troops should remain in his country for up to two more years.

The Bush and Blair administrations were now plainly on the defensive. In the United States the House of Representatives Oversight Committee under Henry Waxman was probing the circumstances that led to war, saying: 'I voted to authorise President Bush to go to war in Iraq, based on claims that Saddam Hussein was developing nuclear weapons. We found out that, before the war began, the CIA knew the claim to be based on forgeries.'[44] In the United Kingdom the government was expecting to be questioned in Parliament by former defence minister Peter Kilfoyle about what discussions Tony Blair had with Bush to bomb the television satellite station Al Jazeera during the war – an act that would have constituted a violation of international law. Bush and Blair were still trying to win the propaganda war, but it was obvious that they were now principally occupied on a damage limitation exercise.

*

There were now also signs of tension between the various factions in Iraq ranged against the American occupation. Here relatively moderate Sunni groups were in conflict with the self-styled Islamic State of Iraq (ISI), set up by al-Qaeda as a prelude to the creation of a militant Islamic state within the Sunni heartland of Iraq. The Islamists were battling for control of the central and western areas, which they believed could attain independence from Kurdish and Shi'ite control once the US military had been forced to withdraw. The aim, according to an analysis by US intelligence agencies, was to create an enclave in the Iraqi provinces of Baghdad, Anbar, Diyala, Salah al-Din, Nineveh and parts of Babil. Thus an unnamed American official said that al-Qaeda was on the way to creating its first stronghold in the Middle East, which would be a 'catastrophe and an imminent danger to Saudi Arabia and Jordan'.[45]

In October 2006 al-Qaeda had adopted a draft constitution, *Notifying Mankind of the Birth of the Islamic State*, which was posted on a website based in Britain and which included the names of ten ministers under an emir, Abu Amer Al-Baghdad. This all signalled al-Qaeda's obvious political ambitions and reinforced the scope of its militant activities in Iraq and elsewhere. In early May 2007 the ISI released a video showing the execution of five Iraqi army soldiers and four police officers, and claiming that an Iraqi army colonel and two of his bodyguards had also been captured. The group also threatened to kill the colonel within twenty-four hours unless its demands for the release of al-Qaeda sympathisers were met.

The ISI was already established as one of the main insurgent groups fighting the Americans, and was supposedly responsible for many of the roadside bombs that had proved so effective against US patrols. On 13 May it posted a statement on the website carrying the al-Qaeda draft constitution, in which it claimed to have carried out a dawn attack on an American patrol south of Baghdad and to have captured three 'crusader soldiers'. The attack, al-Qaeda claimed, was retribution for the rape and murder of a fourteen-year-old Iraqi girl in 2006: 'You should remember what you have done to our sister Abeer.'[46]

The eight-member patrol – seven US soldiers and one Iraqi interpreter travelling in two Humvees – was ambushed 12 miles west of Mahmoudiyah, the aftermath witnessed by a farmer: 'We saw smoke rise from the area. Three vehicles were on fire and a fourth one had fallen into a canal.'[47] Other witnesses said that the patrol had been hit by a roadside bomb before coming under attack from small-arms fire. An unmanned US spotter drone flying over the area fifteen minutes later saw the burning vehicles but it took an hour for an American 'quick reaction force' to reach the area. The US military confirmed that three of its soldiers were missing and then launched a search-and-rescue mission involving helicopters, jets, spotter drones and 4,000 US troops across the Sunni belt. In Baghdad Lieutenant Colonel Christopher Garver admitted that the attack had 'al-Qaedaesque elements' and Major General William Caldwell emphasised the Soldier's Creed that a 'fallen comrade' would never be abandoned: 'every effort available' would be made to find the missing soldiers. The Iraqi deputy Prime Minister, Barham Salih, acknowledged that al-Qaeda had abducted the soldiers, and President Bush was reportedly receiving regular updates on the progress of the mission.

On 14 May the ISI issued a website statement demanding that the US military abandon its efforts to rescue the captured men: 'Four soldiers are in our grip. If you want the safety of your soldiers then do not search for them.' But by now thousands of US and Iraqi troops were searching palm groves, cars and houses, going from door to door looking for the missing men, though with no evident success. In June 2006 al-Qaeda abducted two American soldiers in the area where the ambush had taken place; a few days later, after a search by 8,000 US and Iraqi troops, their badly mutilated bodies were found.

The new ambush provided yet more evidence that the US troop surge was failing to quell the violence in Baghdad and the surrounding region. On the previous Sunday alone, 13 May, some 126 people had been killed throughout the country, and twenty or more bodies were still being found on the streets of the capital every day. It was plain that the US military had completely failed to break the back of the insurgency, to quell the sectarian war or to crush the criminal elements that continued to operate freely in Baghdad and other towns and cities. And it also seemed increasingly clear that the Americans and their Iraqi allies were reluctant to permit reports of their failure to reach the outside world. On 15 May Iraqi police, implementing a new policy to restrict media access, fired shots into the air to remove photographers from the scene of bomb blasts that had killed at least seven people in central Baghdad. But the Iraqi authorities were keen to emphasise the freedom of the press. Brigadier General Abdel-Karim Khalaf insisted that the new regulation was not intended to hamper the work of journalists and that other countries around the world operated similar restrictions; but Reporters without Borders, the media watchdog, warned of a total news blackout: 'It is vital that journalists can report on the security situation throughout the country without it being seen as incitement to violence. When the streets become impassable and the authorities provide no information . . . the role of the reporter becomes essential.'[48] Already more than 200 journalists and media workers had died in Iraq since the 2003 invasion, with suggestions that some had been deliberately targeted by the US military; Al Jazeera was facing legal action for 'insulting' the Shi'ite Grand Ayatollah Ali al-Sistani; in November 2006 the Iraqi parliament prevented journalists from reporting contradictory statements made by politicians; and in December the Interior Ministry announced the formation of a special unit to monitor journalistic coverage in order to correct 'fabricated and false news'.[49] The United States and Britain were keen to advertise the massive increase in the number of publications available in Iraq since the invasion; there was less enthusiasm for giving publicity to the fact of censorship and other restrictions on media freedom.

There was of course much to report on a daily basis – and little of this was congenial to the occupying forces. On 16 May a chlorine bomb, a horror weapon pioneered by Sunni insurgents in Ramada weeks before, killed forty-five people and wounded sixty others in the Abu Sayda market in Diyala. Whatever claims the US military was making about a decrease in violence in some Baghdad districts, it had dramatically increased in Diyala and elsewhere. Chlorine canisters had been loaded onto a small van and then exploded to achieve maximum effect, causing severe burns and affecting breathing and vision. At the same time mortar bombs were again landing on the Green Zone, killing two Iraqis and wounding ten other people.

In the Basra region the British forces were impotent in struggling to counter the growing power of the militias under Iranian control. The streets of the city were effectively under the control of the rival factions, battling to extend their territory, to gain access to local resources and to make money through arms smuggling. For most of the time the British troops were little more than bystanders, being attacked by all the militias and struggling to survive.[50] One Iraqi law professor commented: 'If the Prophet Mohammed would come to Basra today he would be killed because he doesn't have a militia. There is no state of law, the only law is the militia law.'[51] Abu Ammar, a former politician too scared to talk in a hotel lobby, said that when the religious parties declared that Basra was calm it was because they controlled the city and were looting it: 'All the militias have interests and they want to maintain the status quo. The moment their interests are under threat the whole city can burn.'[52] And he stressed, as others had done, that the functioning state was largely an illusion. The security forces themselves, hyped by the British as a success story, were riven with corruption and sectarian division: 'In any confrontation between political parties, the police force will splinter according to party line and fight each other.'[53]

Hence the British claim that power was being peacefully handed over to Iraqi forces meant in reality that the militias and the tribes were taking power themselves, forcing the foreign troops to cede more and more territory. The Iraqis *were* controlling the Basra region, but the Iraqis in question were not subject to the Iraqi government. The British must have known that the writ of the Maliki administration did not even run in Baghdad, much less in southern Iraq; but if British troops were ever to leave Basra it was essential to maintain the pretence. In addition, Western commentary included mounting criticism of the US troop surge in Baghdad.

On 19 May Alastair Campbell, the outgoing defence attaché at the British embassy, said that the surge was not working, that the extra US troops were not achieving the desired reduction in violence. Thus, speaking at Chatham House, the London-based foreign policy research institute, Campbell asserted that the surge policy was failing, if falling casualty numbers – demanded by US commanders – were the criterion of success: 'The figures in April [when 1,500 civilians were killed] were not encouraging.'[54] The United States was continuing to argue that the impact of the surge could not be properly assessed until September, when General David Petraeus was due to report, but even he had claimed that by then there might be no 'definitive' conclusions. However, the troop surge still had enthusiastic military supporters. Jack Keane, a retired general who had helped shape the surge blueprint, insisted that the policy was making steady progress, as shown by a drop in sectarian violence.

In Baghdad, insurgents fired mortars into the Green Zone, just as Tony Blair was making his seventh and final visit to the country as Prime Minister. Then he travelled to meet British troops at an army headquarters in Basra, and two more mortars exploded nearby. The troops, Blair declared, were doing a 'remarkable' job, and he dismissed the mortar explosions as something, like terrorist attacks, that happened every day: 'The question is, what are we going to do? . . . We don't give in to them.' And he refused to apologise for the decision to invade, because 'Iraq was liberated from a terrible dictatorship'. Blair's pro-US posture was never in doubt, but Washington was reportedly concerned that Gordon Brown might not be equally stalwart.[55] The divisions in the United States were becoming increasingly plain.

On 20 May former US President Jimmy Carter, citing the Iraq War and other issues, accused the Bush presidency of being the 'worst in history' and denounced Blair's supportive role. In a newspaper interview Carter said: 'I think as far as the adverse impact on the nation around the world, this administration has been the worst in history'; and speaking on BBC Radio 4, he criticised the British Prime Minister's relationship with George Bush: 'Abominable, loyal, blind, apparently subservient . . . I think that the almost undeviating support by Great Britain for the ill-advised policies of President Bush in Iraq have [sic] been a major tragedy for the world.'[56] If Blair had opposed the invasion it would have been much harder for Bush to ignore domestic criticism.

★

It was now widely known that the billions of dollars allocated to reconstruction in Iraq had largely been squandered through corruption, poor financial management and the diversion of funds to security. There was some debate as to whether it was the Iraqi authorities or the American occupying forces that were primarily responsible for this fiasco, but successive US audit reports revealed the scale of the many associated problems. The need for reconstruction was self-evident – in many aspects of performance the Iraqi civil infrastructure had not reached pre-occupation levels – and it was constantly advertised as a precondition of social regeneration, an attack on high unemployment and gradual movement towards a stable society.

The failure of the US authorities to achieve effective reconstruction was in marked contrast to their determination to build and consolidate their own fortified headquarters on Iraqi territory. In May 2007 pictures appeared of the American embassy, built in the Green Zone on the bank of the Tigris.[57] Occupying 104 acres of land and costing $592 million, the embassy complex was designed to comprise twenty-seven separate buildings and house more than sixty people behind bomb-proof walls. The high-security home assigned to the US ambassador was reported to occupy 16,000 square feet, with his deputy having to make do with 9,500 square feet. The embassy facilities included a swimming pool, a gymnasium, communal living areas and power and water supplies. The Iraqis living under US occupation were denied adequate electricity supplies and clean water, but there seemed to be no problem in supplying these benefits to American embassy staff.

Now doubts were being raised about building the world's largest American embassy in such a hazardous environment. Edward Peck, a former US diplomat in Iraq, commented to Associated Press: 'What kind of embassy is it when everyone lives inside and it's blast-proof, and people are running around with helmets and crouching behind sandbags?'[58] In the same vein Joost Hilderman, an Iraqi analyst with the International Crisis Group, said that the new embassy sent a 'really poor signal' to the Iraqis that the Americans could build such a huge compound in

Baghdad while maintaining the hated occupation. The United States expected to open the embassy in September and to have it fully staffed by the end of the year – and again some observers recalled US experience in Saigon. Toby Dodge, of the University of London, having just returned from the Green Zone, said that the fortress-style embassy would remain in Baghdad 'until helicopters come to airlift the last man and woman from the roof'; and he offered advice to the architects – 'include a large roof'.[59]

Outside the relatively calm Green Zone the violence on the streets continued unabated. On 21 May a cheering crowd in Basra celebrated the killing of a British serviceman, hastily taken to hospital, and the civilian driver who was dragged from a burning fuel lorry. Militants, said to be from the Mahdi Army, were shown cheering, brandishing AK-47s and rocket-propelled grenades as thick smoke from burning vehicles filled the air around them. Gunfire and grenade blasts were heard only a few hundred yards from the governor's office in the centre of the city. In Baghdad there were few signs that the troop surge was having the desired effect, with President Bush reportedly planning a further escalation of the war.[60]

The Bush administration planned to achieve a little-noticed 'second surge' by deploying yet more combat brigades and again extending the tours of duty for troops already in Iraq. This meant that by the end of 2007 the total number of troops in the country could be increased from 162,000 – the figure at the end of May – to more than 200,000, a total estimated by Hearst Newspapers on the basis of Pentagon deployment orders.[61] In response, a US Army spokesman, Lieutenant Colonel Carl S. Ey, denied any Pentagon intention to carry out a second surge, but William Nash, a retired major general and a former NATO commander in Bosnia, commented: 'It doesn't surprise me that they're not talking about it. I think they would be very happy not to have any more attention paid to this.'[62]

There were also reports that Bush, seemingly able to contemplate the failure of his war escalation policy, was about to turn to the UN in a search for a solution. This followed recommendations by the Iraq Study Group (ISG) that the issue be 'internationalised' and that UN help be sought.[63] It now seemed that the disillusionment with the Bush policy was increasingly pervasive outside the White House. Thus a former unnamed senior administration official, while acknowledging the 'brilliance' of General Petraeus, asserted that he was the 'captain of a sinking ship': 'Iraq's government is a mobile phone number that doesn't answer. Iraq probably can't be fixed.'[64] Bush, while not publicly admitting any doubts about the escalation policy, was expected to demand a continuation of the troop surge beyond September, when Petraeus was due to report. By now no one could imagine that Bush, trapped in a deepening well of political denial, would be able to signal an American failure in Iraq; but it seemed increasingly likely that in desperation he would call for international assistance. The new US plan would reportedly comprise:

- requesting UN involvement in Iraq's transition to a normal democratic state, including such elements as an enhanced role for UN humanitarian agencies, the creation of a UN command and possibly a Muslim-led peacekeeping force;
- increased involvement of the UN Security Council permanent members, Japan and the EU countries;
- a bigger support role for regional countries, notably the Sunni Arab Gulf states, and international institutions such as the IMF and the World Bank;
- renewed efforts to promote Iraqi government self-reliance, including national reconciliation benchmarks;
- the accelerated removal of US troops from front-line combat duties, as the handover to the Iraqi security forces, backed by an increased number of US advisors, proceeded.[65]

The messages, as so often, were confusing. While some commentaries and analyses suggested the likelihood of a 'second surge', other reports predicted that Bush, bowing to mounting congressional and public pressures, would agree an 'accelerated removal of US troops' from some areas of Iraq. In some commentaries it seemed likely that American combat forces could be cut in half in 2008 as the US military switched to a 'post-surge' strategy that would concentrate on training the Iraqi army, hunting down al-Qaeda terrorists and guarding the country's borders. In this context an unnamed Pentagon source said: 'As long as we don't leave Iraq, we haven't lost. It's that simple. We can keep our forces indefinitely out of harm's way, with enough teeth to stop a full-scale civil war and keep up the hunt for al-Qaeda.'[66]

So what new plan would emerge from the Petraeus report and other inputs to the US policy-making process? Would it be an abandonment of the surge effort and a total US withdrawal, a 'second surge' that would entail further escalation of the war or a 'post-surge' strategy where US troops would remain in Iraq but in a much reduced role? It seemed plain that Bush, instinctively stubborn and belligerent, was being forced to acknowledge the circumstances of the real world and admit that fundamental policy changes were essential. Perhaps the growing weight of facts was beginning to erode the politics of denial.

At such a time it might have seemed unlikely that the Democrats would reduce the pressure they were exerting on the Bush administration, but on 23 May 2007 the Democrats abandoned their demand that the war funding bill contain a withdrawal date for US troops in Iraq. Bush had secured the almost $90 billion he had demanded in February as essential to continuing the war, with the Democrats saying no more than that in the summer they would renew calls for a troop withdrawal. The media spoke of the Democrats 'backing down', a 'capitulation' that had given Bush a 'victory'.[67] The President had demonstrated that, despite his dismal poll ratings and the Democrat congressional majority, he was able to prosecute the war without interference. John Boehner, the Republican leader in the House, commented that the Democrats had 'finally conceded defeat in their effort to include mandatory surrender dates' in the funding bill, but some Democrats were suggesting that the battle was not over, arguing that the wars in Iraq and Afghanistan would only be adequately funded until the time of General Petraeus's report. Bush had allowed the inclusion of eighteen political and legislative benchmarks for the Iraqi government – and funds for farm and hurricane victims, veterans and health care for poor children.

(Little publicity was given to the character of the benchmarks, one of which demanded the privatisation of Iraqi oil – put simply, 'privatise your oil or you will receive no reconstruction funds'. The privatisation law, written by American oil company consultants hired by the Bush administration, would leave the Iraq National Oil Company controlling only seventeen of the eighty known oilfields, and all yet undiscovered fields would be up for grabs by private, mainly American, oil companies.)[68] However, the only way that Washington could respond to failures in these benchmark areas would be to cut off reconstruction aid and other funding – which would yet again focus attention on the Democratic will to confront the administration.[69]

On 24 May the US military confirmed that the half-naked body of one of the three soldiers abducted on 12 May, Private First Class Joseph Anzack Jr, had been found in the Euphrates south of Baghdad. A commanding officer identified the remains but army officials, while confirming the identification, told Private Anzack's family that DNA tests were still pending ('We're sorry to inform you that the body we found has been identified as Joe').[70] On the same day a car bomb exploded in Fallujah as a funeral procession for sixty-year-old Alaa Zuwaid, a man who had fought against al-Qaeda, passed by, killing twenty-six people and wounding forty-five others. He had formed an alliance with other tribal leaders to combat al-Qaeda, which had led to his death by shooting in front of his house; his 25-year-old son had been killed by militants a month before as he walked down the street. On 24 May, a typical day in Iraq, at least 104 people were killed in sectarian violence or from other causes, including thirty-two who died in suicide bombings.

On the following day Abu Mujtaba, a commander in the Mahdi Army, vowed to conduct revenge attacks on British soldiers in southern Iraq after Wissam Abu Qader, an alleged militant, was shot dead by Iraqi special forces working alongside British troops as he was travelling in his car with two other men: 'The Mahdi Army will attack any British unit they will see to avenge his killing. Our men are moving all over Basra now in civilian cars carrying RPGs and weapons. *We have the full cooperation of the police who will inform us on any moving British vehicles* [emphasis added].'[71] This followed a statement from Muqtada al-Sadr, whose whereabouts remained uncertain, demanding that the foreign forces leave Iraq or draw up a timetable for withdrawal: 'I ask the government not to let the occupiers extend their occupation even for one day.' Muqtada al-Sadr was now approaching the armed Sunni resistance in order to build a united national opposition to foreign troops in Iraq.[72] In Washington, Hillary Clinton and Barack Obama, the leading Democrat candidates in the presidential race, voted in the Senate against the bill to fund the war. Senator John McCain, a Republican candidate, said that this was 'the equivalent of waving a white flag to al-Qaeda'.[73]

However, it now seemed clear that the coalition forces would not be able to achieve a military victory, and that accommodations with the insurgents would have to be made. In the Basra region the British were simply withdrawing to fewer protected enclaves, effectively surrendering territory to the militias and the tribes, while talks were reportedly being initiated with militant groups. In late May 2007 Lieutenant General Graeme Lamb, Britain's top commander in Iraq and a former special forces officer, was leading negotiations in the Green Zone for an insurgent ceasefire under which Sunni fighters would abandon their armed struggle in return for an amnesty and senior posts in the national security services. In addition, the Sunnis were demanding an end to the ban on Ba'athists holding government jobs, and payment of pensions and other benefits to those who had held government and security jobs before the 2003 invasion. Lamb was also understood to be talking to some of the Shi'ite militias, whose death squads were formed partly as a response to al-Qaeda's sectarian campaign. A senior advisor to the US military, closely involved in the surge strategy, commented that the talks [between Lamb and the militant groups] were 'very informal' and normally took place in the Green Zone: 'Al-Qaeda are not there, but other Sunni insurgents are, as well as tribal leaders who have been supporting the fight [against al-Qaeda].'[74]

On 28 May Ryan Crocker, the US ambassador to Iraq, began talks in Baghdad with his Iranian counterpart, Hassan Kazemi-

Qomi, on the subject of stabilising Iraq. 'I wouldn't expect a breakthrough,' Crocker said. Nor, presumably, did Iran. Before the talks began, an official in Tehran, Ahmad Sobhani, formally complained via the Swiss ambassador about alleged US and British 'espionage networks' operating in Iran. According to Iranian state television, Sobhani demanded an explanation for groups he claimed were carrying out 'infiltration and sabotage in western, central and south-western areas of the country'. Such charges were not new. Iran had long complained of Western attempts to arouse its ethnic minorities to put pressure on the regime, and now there was a fresh opportunity for Tehran to air its grievances. And in fact there was some justification for the Iranian posture.[75] The Baghdad talks were supposed to focus solely on the Iraq issue but observers suggested that other matters might be raised.

In the event the discussion focused solely on Iraq. Crocker presented evidence that Iran was supplying C4 plastic explosives to Shi'ite insurgents in the country, posing a particular threat to US forces. He also suggested that Iran should stop funding and training the Shi'ite militias, whereupon Kazemi-Qomi declared that the United States should not be in Iraq at all. Crocker later commented that the talks had been 'positive and businesslike'; and Kazemi-Qomi, having suggested a three-way security mechanism involving also the Iraqi government, told Iranian television that the discussions had been 'frank and clear'. Nothing substantial had been accomplished. Both sides had agreed, without indicating any specific measures, to 'support and strengthen' the Iraqi government but the policies of the two parties were unlikely to change. Tehran was not about to abandon its Shi'ite brothers across the border, and the US military was not about to leave Iraq.[76]

There were now Sunni concerns that the US–Iranian talks would in fact boost Tehran's influence over Iraq's Shi'ite factions. Thus Ahmad bin Heli, the Arab League's deputy secretary general, commented that Iraq 'should not be stripped of its Arab identity, especially as it is one of the outstanding members and founders of the Arab League'; but the league's chief, Amr Moussa, told Associated Press that the group had always called for US–Iranian dialogue and described the Baghdad talks as a 'reassuring and positive step towards diplomatic dialogue instead of military confrontation'. However, the United States and Iran were 'not the only sides . . . concerned with the situation in Iraq . . . The developments in Iraq should not be conducted away from the Arabs' interests.' Sheikh Khalaf al-Alyan, the leader of the Iraqi National Dialogue Council, a small Sunni party in the ruling coalition, condemned the US–Iranian talks as an affront to Iraqi sovereignty:

> For Iran and America to meet on Iraq is neither a desirable nor an acceptable thing. They brought the problems to Iraq and they are trying to solve these problems by themselves in a way that serves their interests. America is the main reason for the problems in Iraq as an occupier. Iran also has interests in Iraq and is running terror.[77]

The Bush administration was doing what it could to keep the American people ignorant of the character of the war. Already, with US approval, the Iraqi government was restricting the work of reporters in the field, and some of the official hostility to news reporting resulted in journalists being shot dead in the street. Few journalists, particularly from the West, were able to travel in Iraq without being incorporated, 'embedded', in a US military unit – which inevitably meant that they saw the conflict through American eyes: they were able to lament over US casualties but rarely witnessed the effects of American bombing or artillery attacks on Iraqi communities. Moreover, the convention of embedding meant that journalists were permanently subject to US official surveillance and control: for example, since 2006 the military's embedding rules required journalists to obtain signed consent from a wounded soldier before his or her image could be published.[78] Such a regulation meant that a seemingly proper concern for a soldier's privacy could be used to establish broader constraints on information. Who could say, during or after a firefight in the streets of Sadr City, that one or more US soldiers had not been wounded? Would the publication of any photographs of such an event be banned until the results had been fully ascertained? And would soldiers facing amputation, permanent paralysis or brain damage be primarily concerned with providing written consent to journalists?

Ashley Gilbertson, a veteran freelance photographer who had worked for the *New York Times*, *Time* and *Newsweek*, said that the policy was coercive and unworkable: 'They are not letting us cover the realities of war. I think that this has little to do with the families or the soldiers and everything to do with politics.'[79] One wounded correspondent, Kimberly Dozier of CBS, at first thought that the regulation was a good idea, that soldiers should not sacrifice their right to privacy because they were in a combat zone and wounded – but then she changed her mind: 'The tough pictures, some pictures, need to get out. But choosing which ones is a very touchy matter.' It did seem likely that the US authorities had an interest in suppressing information about the war. Thus James Glanz, a Baghdad correspondent expected to become the *New York Times* bureau chief, commented that some military leaders were determined to protect something besides the privacy of their troops. The number of reporters in Iraq, under ever mounting pressure, was continuing to dwindle and in consequence their work was becoming increasingly important: 'This tiny remaining corps of reporters becomes a greater and greater problem for the military brass because we are the only people preventing them from telling the story the way they want it told.'[80]

On the United States' Memorial Day, 28 May, President Bush led tributes to fallen troops as it emerged that 103 US soldiers had died in Iraq that month. Again there was speculation that the number of American troops in the country would be reduced following the Petraeus report in September, leaving a residual force to fight al-Qaeda and to train the Iraqi security forces. Perhaps time really was running out before the Bush administration would be forced to face a definitive congressional and public revolt over the war. The Republican Jeff Sessions, a member of the Senate Armed Services Committee, said that the Petraeus report would provide an opportunity to scale back the US presence in Iraq: 'I think most people in Congress believe, unless something extraordinary occurs, that we should be on a move to draw those surge numbers down.'[81]

Nothing 'extraordinary' seemed likely to occur. On 29 May five British personnel – four security guards, working for the Canadian-based GardaWorld firm, and a finance expert, employed by the US management consultancy BearingPoint, who had been advising the Iraqi government – were kidnapped by men wearing police uniforms from the Finance Ministry in what appeared to be a carefully planned assault.[82] The US military and Iraqi troops responded by imposing a lockdown on parts of Baghdad and stormed Sadr City,[83] amid speculation that Muqtada al-Sadr might be involved in the kidnapping, as the search for the missing men began, while Tony Blair spoke of 'dangers and challenges . . . We shouldn't let those who are prepared to use kidnapping and terrorism succeed.'[84]

At least forty more people had been killed by bombs in Baghdad, while the US military announced that ten more American soldiers had been killed on Memorial Day, making May 2007 the deadliest month for US troops for more than two years. In addition, the ISI, linked to al-Qaeda, claimed on its website that it had shot down a helicopter in Diyala province, killing two US soldiers: 'God enabled the soldiers of the Islamic State in Iraq to down a Super Cobra aircraft . . . in Diyala and kill the two Crusader pilots aboard. It was attacked with air defence weapons and destroyed in the air, catching fire and exploding, its pieces flying in the sky over the area.'[85]

There were no signs that the troop surge and the associated security plan were working. As the US military ravaged various areas of Baghdad and elsewhere the sectarian and insurgency violence shifted from one region to another. The *New York Times* had reported that American and British aircraft were continuing to bomb Baghdad and Basra[86] – with the inevitable consequences for the civilian population. Thousands of Iraqis were fleeing their homes in Diyala province to escape the major offensive by US and Iraqi troops, and according to the Iraq Red Crescent Society, local people were facing a humanitarian tragedy.[87] A curfew – an effective siege – imposed on Samarra was pushing hundreds of families to desperation as the supplies of food, water, medicines and fuel dwindled alarmingly. Vehicles had been banned from entering or leaving the city, and ambulances had not been allowed to reach people. On 22 May a schoolteacher told the Inter Press Service news agency that the people were 'being butchered here

by the Americans'; the US military and the Iraqi forces, despite
desperate pleas from residents, were preventing aid from reaching
the stricken communities. An IRCS worker reported that people
were running out of food and that hospitals, lacking power and
medicines, had closed. A dozen people, including seven children,
had already died because life-saving machinery could no longer be
operated.[88]

Elsewhere the American and Iraqi forces were continuing to
attack civilian areas. In Shata' al-Tajiyat, Thera'a Digla and the
areas that surrounded a US base in Taji, houses and orchards were
being targeted; residents in the villages of Arab Jboor, north of
Muqdadiyah, claimed that the US military had razed dozens
of acres of groves and orchards, and imposed a ban on vehicles
which had made it impossible for the villagers to travel to their
workplaces. In addition, the Americans had cut off electricity and
drinking water.[89]

There were further reports that the British forces were involved
in forced disappearances, hostage-taking and torture of civilians.
The former chairman of the Red Crescent in Basra claimed that
he had been beaten unconscious by British soldiers; another Iraqi
civilian, kidnapped by the British, was later found shot dead, still
handcuffed, and wearing a UK prisoner name tag.[90] Mazin
Younis, the chairman of the UK-based Iraqi League, a human
rights group, said that such cases 'may only be the tip of an iceberg
of systematic abuse procedures devised high up the command
chain in the Army'.[91] The Parliamentary Joint Committee on
Human Rights had reportedly written to the Ministry of Defence
asking it to reconcile what appeared to be 'glaring differences'
between the MoD's official line on interrogation techniques and
the evidence of torture – in particular, the beating to death of
Baha Mousa (see Chapter 3) – that had emerged in the recent
court martial of seven British soldiers.[92]

As such information and much else reached the mainstream media
in the West, despite official efforts at containment, public opinion
continued to move inexorably against the war. A majority of
Americans were now sceptical of government reasons for the war
and were unsympathetic to how it was being run by the Bush

administration. In late May 2007 an Ipsos MORI poll in Britain revealed that only 17 per cent of respondents approved of how Tony Blair was handling the current situation in Iraq, with a mere 9 per cent approving of George Bush's Iraq policies.[93] American morale in Iraq was now poor. Thus Hussein al-Falluji, an MP from the largest Sunni bloc, said: 'When I sit with the Americans, I feel a kind of weakness [from them]. When I look in their eyes I feel that they are not the same as in 2003. From the inside they feel like they re failing here.'[94] The stakes were high but no-one was predicting significant progress. Increasingly the entire American venture in Iraq was being seen as a costly mistake, based on a failure 'to understand life in the real Iraq and irrelevant to it'.[95] By June 2007 the US and British governments, facing mounting public and political opposition to their Iraq policies, were being driven to admit the shape of the endgame. The task now was to search for a withdrawal strategy that, by means of lies and misinformation, would enable two fully discredited governments to escape from their reckless enterprise with something resembling dignity and honour.

6

Coalition 'making things worse'

There was now mounting speculation about what the end of Tony Blair's premiership would mean for Britain's Iraq policy. Some observers were suggesting that, since Gordon Brown had kept a relatively low profile on the issue during the Blair years, there was scope for a shift in policy; but no one imagined that the new Prime Minister, determined to maintain the so-called special relationship, would be prepared to upset Washington by resorting to 'cut and run'. Moreover, Brown, as Chancellor, had been the most weighty political figure after Blair in a Cabinet that had decided on war; he had been the paymaster for the British involvement in the invasion and occupation of Iraq. On 28 March *The Guardian* carried a judgement by Richard Horton, editor of *The Lancet*: 'This Labour government, which includes Gordon Brown as much as it does Tony Blair, is party to a war crime [in Iraq] of monstrous proportions . . . [It is] continuing to commit one of the worst international abuses of human rights in the past half-century.' It was scarcely credible that the new British Prime Minister was about to say it had all been a bad idea.[1]

In early June military chiefs were reportedly devising plans – to be presented to Brown within weeks – to withdraw the remaining British troops from Iraq within twelve months.[2] The new Prime Minister was to be told by defence chiefs that Britain should withdraw from Iraq in 'quick order' and concentrate on the war effort in Afghanistan.[3] Some senior officers disagreed with this plan, with one official arguing that Iraq was 'strategically far more important' than Afghanistan.[4]

On 6 June Hoshyar Zebari, the Iraqi Foreign Minister, said that the stakes were too high for Brown to make a hasty and dramatic change to Britain's military strategy, that any sign of weakness would fuel the insurgency, and that the new Prime Minister should 'stay the course'.[5] This was the time, Zebari claimed, 'to strengthen the international coalition . . . We hope the new Prime Minister Brown is also a friend of Iraq, of the Iraqi people, and will not make major or dramatic decisions . . . This is a time that we expect our friends . . . to stand by us.'[6] But he hardly inspired confidence in whatever progress he claimed was being achieved in the Basra region: 'The police force there is weak, the military is weak, the city council is not united.'[7] At the same time Zebari acknowledged that a growing number of Iraqi MPs wanted a timetable for withdrawal, and said that the government was planning a two-month summer recess to discuss constitutional reform and the new oil law. Christopher Meyer, former British ambassador to Washington, was saying that the UK and US military presence in Iraq was worsening security across the region and should be ended quickly. The process would be 'painful', but the mission was not worth the death of one more serviceman: 'I personally believe that the presence of . . . coalition forces is making things worse, not only inside Iraq but the wider region around Iraq. The arguments against staying for any greater length of time themselves strengthen with every day that passes.'[8]

In Baghdad the search for five British citizens – four security guards and a financial consultant – abducted on 29 May when visiting the Iraqi Finance Ministry was achieving nothing, despite the efforts of US soldiers, Iraqi special forces and Western diplomats. Senior Iraqi officials said that they were working on the theory that the group behind the kidnapping was a faction of the Mahdi Army, possibly operating under the influence of Iranian intelligence. The militia, nominally controlled by Muqtada al-Sadr, was in fact poorly organised and lacked discipline – which had allowed the Iranians to move in and take control of some Mahdi fighters. Now British officials were suggesting that some rogue cells in the militia had links with Iran's Revolutionary Guard but could also operate separately. Al-Sadr himself had denied any involvement: 'To do such a provocative act . . . would be counter-productive'. In this context there was speculation that an approach might be made to Tehran to assist in finding the missing men. An MI5 intelligence officer had reportedly flown to Baghdad and an SAS team was ready to take action if the location of the British citizens was discovered.[9] On 6 December 2007 the kidnappers released a video believed to show one of the men being held. Identifying himself as Jason, he said: 'I have been here now held for 173 days and I feel we have been forgotten.' The kidnappers accused Britain of plundering Iraq's wealth and demanded that UK troops pull out of the country within ten days.

On 2 June representatives of the Mahdi Army demanded an immediate end to British patrols in Basra and attempts to kill its leaders,[10] and sought the release of nine Mahdi officials, including their chief spokesman, Sheikh Abdul al-Hadi Darraji, held in British and American custody. One unnamed source said that the five British men would not be released until the Mahdi demands were met – which suggested al-Sadr's involvement in the abductions.[11]

Then the al-Qaeda-linked Islamic State of Iraq issued a statement on the internet that it had executed a man and a woman who had held 'important positions in the American embassy building'. The US State Department confirmed that two Iraqi employees of the American embassy in Baghdad had disappeared. In addition, an Islamic State video, showing the identity cards of two US soldiers held hostage, claimed that the men had been killed and buried. The video was released to bring an end to US operations to find the hostages, which were harming the Islamic State's 'Muslim brothers'. It remained to be seen whether the five abducted British citizens would meet a similar fate.[12]

The security situation continued to deteriorate throughout Iraq, exacerbating the refugee crisis. Turkey was continuing to build up its forces – tanks and troops preparing for 'spring manoeuvres' – on the Iraqi border, and clashes with Kurdish fighters had broken out, with Turkish troops shelling suspected rebel positions across the border. This was a further scene of mounting instability, likely to exacerbate the refugee problem. Syria and Jordan, already together hosting around two million dispossessed Iraqis, were starting to tighten the border controls to stem the flood of desperate families seeking sanctuary, while the United States announced in June 2007 that it was ready to accept up to 7,000 Iraqi refugees after months of delays and growing worldwide condemnation for its refusal to grant asylum to Iraqis fleeing the US-orchestrated war. By January 2007 the United States had admitted only 466 Iraqis, a figure that even by June stood at under 800, including former US government employees; according to Home Office figures, Britain had granted only 115 Iraqis asylum since 2003, out of 8,075 applications.

The American troop surge was now faltering in Baghdad. Four months into a security crackdown involving thousands of extra troops, the US-led forces controlled fewer than one-third of the capital's neighbourhoods. The *New York Times* reported that in only 146 of Baghdad's 457 neighbourhoods were the US military able to 'protect the population' and 'maintain physical influence over' the districts. Spokesman Lieutenant Colonel Christopher Garver stressed that the plan was 'just in its beginning phases'; and Scott Bleichwehl, another spokesman, emphasised that some of the extra US troops had yet to start operations: 'No one expects all 457 [neighbourhoods] to be under control at this time.'[13] Officials had warned that the fight would not be easy, and American casualties were continuing to rise. Little reliable support, it seemed, could be offered by the Iraqi forces. American Major General Joseph F. Fil Jr, heading the security operation in Baghdad, had expressed disappointment with the Iraqi police performance: 'The [Iraqi] army is coming along pretty well, but the police really need some work. You'll have to be very careful with them [since they were heavily infiltrated by Shi'ite militiamen].'[14] In fact the US military had frequently complained that the Iraqi police and army units that were sent to Baghdad for the security operation were often at only 60 per cent full strength, at best.

During a three-day period at the end of May fourteen American soldiers were killed, bringing the total number of fatalities among the US military since the invasion of March 2003 to 3,493. May 2007, with 127 American deaths reported, had been the bloodiest month for the United States since the war began. Iraqi casualties, escalating month by month, were numbered in the hundreds of thousands. On 3 June Iraqi

President Jalal Talabani, speaking on ABC's *This Week* programme, said that US troops would need to be in Iraq until the end of 2008.

In the United States seven Democrat presidential candidates, conscious of Iraq's central importance, were jostling for position. On 4 June they appeared at Saint Anselm College in Manchester, New Hampshire, and variously suggested how the war might be ended. Hillary Clinton, widely hailed as the winner in the debate, repeatedly played down any divisions between the candidates and tried to distance the Democrats from the Iraq conflict: 'I think it's important to remember this is George Bush's war. He started the war, he mismanaged the war and he refused to end the war . . . and each of us are [*sic*] trying to end the war.'[15]

It had already emerged that Clinton had not read the full pre-war intelligence assessment before she voted to support an invasion of Iraq, but she claimed to have consulted 'many sources' and to have been 'fully briefed'.[16] John Edwards, running third in the polls, pointed out that neither Clinton nor the second-placed Barack Obama had spoken on the funding legislation and had voted to oppose it at the last minute. He declared that the war on terror was little more than a 'bumper sticker' which George Bush 'used to justify everything he does . . . Iraq, Guantanamo, Abu Ghraib, spying on Americans, torture . . . They are not the United States of America.'[17] Edwards, like Clinton, had voted for the war; Obama against. (At Saint Anselm Obama said to Edwards: 'I agree it's important to lead. I was opposed to the war from the start. So you are 4½ years too late.')

On 4 June a car bomb killed at least fifteen people near Fallujah, reminding observers that the US troop surge was largely irrelevant outside Baghdad. The Iraqi government was making efforts to uphold the new security plan, though its measures sometimes seemed to be directed against ordinary Iraqis rather than violent insurgents. On 5 June the Iraqi authorities issued arrest warrants, based on a charge of 'sabotaging the economy', for the leaders of Iraq's 26,000-strong Federation of Oil Unions, which was on strike in protest at the government's failure to meet any of the promises made by Prime Minister Nouri al-Maliki on 16 May.

The union concerns had focused on wages, working and living conditions, and the character of the proposed oil law. Now al-Maliki, issuing the arrest warrants, was saying that he would meet threats to oil production 'with an iron fist'. The strike, headed by Hassan Juma'a Awad, was entering its 'second phase', which included the closure of the main distribution pipelines, used in part to supply oil to Baghdad. Sami Ramadani, from the union's UK-based support committee Naftana, commented that the warrants were 'an outrageous attack on trade unions and democratic freedoms'. Here a principal aim was to oppose the privatisation of the Iraqi oil industry, designed to hand over the country's main resource to foreign corporations. Now the Iraqi government was sending in troops to crush the strike, leading the TUC's general secretary, Brendan Barber, to urge negotiation rather than military intervention, while Ramadani said that British troops might have been involved in the action.

The industrial dispute was one of many signs of the deteriorating situation throughout Iraq. The US military and Iraqi forces had imposed a fresh curfew on parts of Baghdad, adding to the problems of communities struggling to survive. In Amiriyah, shops had been closed for a week and families were running out of basic essentials; one resident, Faiz Mohammed al-Janabi, said that his nine-year-old son had diarrhoea through drinking dirty water and it was impossible to seek medical help. In Doura, another Baghdad district, a two-week siege had crippled the supply of basic items and amenities, and the quarter had been turned into a massive prison. Four churches and three monasteries had been evacuated, and US troops had turned one of them into a barracks while US snipers on rooftops were preventing people from leaving their homes. Thousands of people were fleeing Baqubah in anticipation of an imminent American assault on the city, and a curfew had been extended in Fallujah as the US military extended the concrete walls to divide the city into small sections in an effort to facilitate control of the residents.[18]

The United States was stepping up every aspect of the war. The troop build-up was continuing and US warplanes were dropping bombs at more than twice the rate of the year before – which suggested a repeat of the 'shock and awe' campaign that had characterised the start of the 2003 invasion.[19] In the first 4½ months of 2007 American aircraft dropped 237 bombs and missiles in support of ground forces in Iraq, already surpassing the 229 expended in all of 2006.[20] In consequence, civilian casualties were continuing to mount. Thus according to Iraq Body Count, the most conservative of estimates, about forty civilians were being killed by bombs every month at the end of 2006, rising to more than fifty a month through 2007.[21] A Reuters reporter witnessed at least one air-to-ground missile streaking through the air before exploding in a Baghdad district; and US warplanes pounded an area in Mosul, wounding a woman and three men.[22] On 5 June the Iraqi parliament, demonstrating the growing opposition to the Maliki regime, passed a resolution requiring the government to seek parliamentary permission before asking the United Nations to extend the mandate for US-led forces in Iraq.

On 6 June it emerged that Lieutenant General Douglas Lute, newly appointed by George Bush as his war advisor, had expressed scepticism about the surge policy. In a written response to questions by the Senate Armed Services Committee, Lute confirmed news reports about his doubts: 'During the review [prior to Bush's surge announcement on 10 January], I registered concerns that a military "surge" would likely have only temporary and localized effects unless it were accompanied by counterpart "surges" by the Iraq government and the other, nonmilitary agencies of the US government.'[23] He had also commented that America's enemies in Iraq had in effect a 'vote' and should be expected to adopt specific measures to counter the new policy. At his confirmation hearing Lute said that the early results of the troop build-up had been mixed: 'No one is satisfied with the status quo: not the Iraqis, not key regional partners, not the US government, and not the American government . . . Conditions on the ground are deeply complex and we are likely to continue to evolve, meaning that we must constantly adapt.'[24] He urged a 'sober view of where we are now', suggesting that the outcome of the surge was far from certain and that policy changes would have to be made.

Again it seemed plain that the security plan was not working. In Baghdad the incidence of violence had shifted from one district to another, and the insurgents remained capable of avoiding the heavy American incursions into their familiar territory and able to select their targets. On 7 June the head of Iraq's antiquities board, Abbas al-Hussainy, speaking at the British Museum, said that the militants were attacking the country's archaeological heritage by bombing holy shrines; in the provinces of Diyala and Kirkuk about a dozen shrines had been hit in the previous two weeks. The US military was now causing inestimable damage to Iraq's heritage by siting bases on archaeological sites, by failing to control looting, and by launching military strikes with total indifference to environmental and other factors. Al-Hussainy was denied access by the Americans to the Great Ziggurat of Ur, now pockmarked with wartime shrapnel, and he indicated in his speech at the British Museum that countless other archaeological sites had been damaged or lost in the four-year 'looting frenzy'. The journalist Simon Jenkins, writing in *The Guardian*, commented that the allies (principally the US and Britain) had 'become the vandals'.[25]

The people of Iraq were being 'murdered in droves for want of order . . . If this is Tony Blair's "values war", then language has lost all meaning.'[26] On 8 June carloads of gunmen in Baqubah descended on the house of police chief Colonel Ali Dilayan al-Jorani, killing his wife, two brothers and eleven guards; the bodies of some of the guards were later found on the road. Soon after the raid, with al-Jorani not at home, a suicide bomber was seen driving towards a mosque; police officers fired at him, causing an explosion. In the southern town of Qurnah a parked minibus exploded at a bus terminal, killing at least sixteen people and wounding thirty-two more. Another US soldier was killed in a roadside bombing in Baghdad, bringing the American death toll in the country to more than 3,500.

In the midst of this continuing carnage there were signs of fresh instability in the Iraqi government. On 8 June Prime Minister al-Maliki declared that foreign intelligence agencies were behind attempts to overthrow his regime and to install Iyad Allawi, a US favourite and former Ba'athist, in power. The Allawi National Front coalition, al-Maliki claimed, was a vehicle for the Egyptian, Saudi and Turkish intelligence agencies – none of which could act in Baghdad without American approval: 'I feel astonished when I hear some politicians, under the shadow of democracy, saying that there is nothing wrong with Arab and Islamic countries interfering in Iraq's affairs.'[27]

The Saudi Arabian government had already signalled its dissatisfaction with the Iraqi regime. In May King Abdullah told US Vice-President Dick Cheney that he could no longer work with al-Maliki, and in a subsequent visit to Baghdad Cheney emphasised to the Iraqi government that US support was not indefinite. In addition, Iraqi Vice-President Tariq al-Hashemi, known to have a poor relationship with al-Maliki, was visiting Cairo to urge regional leaders to depose the Iraqi government: 'There should be an Arab stance before it's too late.'[28] It was obvious that the Iraqi regime was a government only in name. It was powerless to quell the violence in Baghdad and throughout Iraq; legislation was either delayed or ineffectual; and it had no control over Iraq's borders.

On the Iranian border the Iraqi guards were short of supplies and funds; while the Iranians manned a fort, bristling with radio antennae, overlooking the Qalalan plain, Iraq struggled to maintain a team of ten uniformed officers at the inaptly named Qalalan Castle. Some 370 Iraqi border guards were expected to patrol the 50-mile stretch of border in the central eastern Diyala province, and shortages of fuel meant that they could rarely patrol the road effectively and pursue suspect vehicles. Everyone assumed the border was porous and that Iran was continuing to train and supply the Shi'ite militias in southern Iraq, as US Sergeant Marty Cole observed: 'The locals have a long tradition of smuggling and can pretty much cross the border whenever they like . . . They [the Iranians] are building up over there. I'm sure it's for no good.' Moreover, Iraq's problems over its border with Turkey were not abating. On 8 June the Iraqi deputy Foreign Minister, Mohammed al-Haj Mahmoud, summoned the Turkish chargé d'affaires and called for an immediate halt to the shelling of northern Iraq, saying that such actions 'undermine confidence between the two nations and negatively affect their friendship'.[29] Iraq was quite prepared to denounce the separatist Kurdistan Workers' Party (PKK) but insisted on 'dialogue and positive cooperation' rather than a Turkish military response.

*

There was now mounting controversy over the building of the US embassy in the Green Zone, with investigations by the US Department of Justice into whether forced labour had been used. Employees' complaints had been rejected by a subsequent State Department inquiry but partially upheld by Defense Department auditors. Some workers from Asia and west Africa were claiming that they had been deceived in Kuwait into flying to Iraq when their boarding passes said Dubai. Once on the ground, the workers had their passports seized, forcing them to remain in Iraq and work for the Americans for a prolonged period. John Owens, an American who worked on the embassy project, told the *Wall Street Journal* that he had been handed a boarding card for Dubai along with dozens of workers from Third World countries who were unaware that they would be travelling to Iraq: 'I felt bad for those folks every day that I was in Iraq, and the feelings just built and built. They were basically being treated like slaves.'[30] The conditions were bad, forcing workers to the brink of rioting, after which they were menaced by armed security guards. There were reports of unsanitary conditions, cramped accommodation and employees forced to drink water from the heavily polluted Tigris when supplies ran low.[31]

There was now growing speculation that the building of the massive embassy and hardened military sites meant that Washington intended to maintain a permanent presence in the country. On 31 May Defense Secretary Robert Gates, speaking in Honolulu, said that the United States was looking for a 'long and enduring presence' in Iraq under an arrangement with the Iraqi government: 'The Korea model is one, the security relationship we have with Japan is another.' In early June the White House spokesman Tony Snow confirmed that President Bush wanted a lengthy American troop presence in Iraq: 'The situation in Iraq, and indeed, the larger war on terror, are things that are going to take a long time.'[32] Such remarks underlined an observation made months before by Jimmy Carter, speaking of 'people in Washington . . . who never intend to withdraw military forces from Iraq'; the 2003 invasion was intended 'to establish a permanent military base in the Gulf region'.[33] The building of fourteen 'enduring bases' in Iraq, at a cost of around $1 billion a year, did not suggest that Washington was about to agree an early withdrawal from the country. And there was discussion also about what the US forces would actually do in their bases, and in what circumstances they would venture forth. And the same question, writ small, was being asked about the future British role in southern Iraq.

On 9 June Sir Jeremy Greenstock, Britain's former representative in Baghdad, now giving evidence before the independent Iraq Commission (see Chapter 7), commented that troops should only leave their bases to deal with serious threats of instability: 'British forces shouldn't come out if there's an equal battle between political militias in the southern provinces. They should only come out if there's a legitimate request by the local governor.'[34] This recommendation raised many questions that were not addressed. How would an 'equal battle' be recognised, and what would happen when one side prevailed? What would constitute a 'legitimate' request from the local governor? Since local politicians, along with the local security forces, were in the pockets of the militias, any request for British assistance would inevitably have a partisan element. Why did Greenstock assume that a local governor would not have his own sectarian agenda? And what would the entrenched British forces do if no 'requests' were made? Would they just sit there waiting to be mortared?

The status of the occupation forces remained not only militarily uncertain but legally questionable: the issue of the legality of the 2003 invasion and the subsequent occupation was still generating discussion and speculation. On 11 June 2007 it emerged that Admiral Sir Alan West, the First Sea Lord, apparently unconvinced by government assurances, had sought his own private legal advice on the justification for the war.[35] He raised the question whether personnel under his command might eventually face war crimes charges in relation to their duties in Iraq. In his book *Soldier* General Sir Mike Jackson said: 'I spent a good deal of time recently in the Balkans making sure that Milošević was put behind bars. I have no intention of ending up in the cell next to him in The Hague';[36] and Lord Boyce, Chief of the Defence Staff, sought similar assurances about the legality of the planned invasion.[37] And through 2007 there was continuing speculation about the vulnerability of American and British leaders to arraignment for war crimes.

In the United States the question of impeachment of both Bush and Cheney remained a significant issue, and in Britain the possibility of extraditing Tony Blair to face war crimes and other charges was far from being a closed matter. It was being seriously suggested that a prosecution of Blair, after he left office, might arise out of the 2003 invasion of Iraq, out of torture allegations related to Guantanamo Bay, or out of British complicity in the US practice of 'extraordinary rendition', where prisoners were transported around the world into a gulag of secret prisons for likely torture.[38] On 11 June the UK government, via the mechanism of a fresh Commons debate, came under increased pressure as the Tories demanded a Privy Council inquiry into the causes of the war. Blair, never keen to become involved in Commons discussions on Iraq, left the chamber before the debate began. Sir Malcolm Rifkind, a former Conservative Foreign Secretary, commented that Iraq was worse than Vietnam, accused Blair of 'incompetence' and 'poor judgement' in deciding to go to war, and said that an inquiry was 'absolutely essential'.[39] In the final vote the government majority was halved.

In Iraq the random sectarian massacres, coalition depredations, kidnappings, torture and targeted assassinations continued to bring immeasurable suffering to a national people. The Iraqi journalist Sahar al-Haideri, after receiving a dozen death threats ('We know we will be killed soon'), was murdered in Mosul, bringing to 106 with thirty-nine support staff the number of journalists killed in Iraq since the 2003 invasion. Hundreds of unnamed Iraqis were being killed every week, and the mounting toll of American and British dead was having a profound impact on morale. By mid-June 2007 more than 11,000 cases of British soldiers going absent without leave (AWOL) had been recorded by the Ministry of Defence, with about a thousand remaining on the run; figures released under the Freedom of Information Act suggested that the military authorities had had only limited success in locating the deserters – and the problem was growing: 135 soldiers remained

AWOL from 2004, 157 from 2005, 279 from 2006 and 283 for the first half of 2007. Liam Fox, the shadow Defence Secretary, acknowledged in the Commons that the problem was 'continuous and possibly worsening': 'At a time of [army] overstretch we cannot have vital troops going AWOL.'[40] British troops then faced a year in prison for every day they remained absent without leave.

It is hard to imagine that the declining morale in coalition forces was not one of the factors influencing US and UK pressures for a military withdrawal. Now there was mounting speculation over the report to be presented to Congress by General Petraeus in mid-September, about the full range of military options in Iraq, including a full or partial withdrawal. If it were concluded that Iraq had become a failed state under the pressures of conflict and social collapse, then a continued American presence could only be seen as an unambiguous military occupation, where Washington explicitly rather than implicitly ran the country, and where there was no pretence at Iraqi sovereignty. Such a conclusion would demonstrate beyond all argument that the troop surge had failed.

The Bush administration was continuing to shuffle senior military staff in the hope that personnel irrevocably associated with the failures in Iraq could be marginalised. Thus General Peter Pace, who had wanted a second term as chairman of the Joint Chiefs of Staff, was jettisoned in favour of the current chief of naval operations, Admiral Michael Mullen since, according to Defense Secretary Gates, 'a divisive ordeal [in the Senate]' would not serve him (Pace) well.[41] It was essential to appoint new military leaders who were not compromised by past mistakes. In Baghdad also there were staff difficulties. On 11 June the Iraqi parliament voted to replace the Sunni speaker Mahmoud al-Mashhadani because of his 'rude behaviour' towards deputies. In fact, despite his sometimes abrasive manner, he was considered to be a moderate politician who had urged Sunni insurgents to begin a dialogue with the government, and encouraged the parties in the fractious Shi'ite ruling coalition to 'start talking the same language'.[42] Iraqi officials announced that al-Mashhadani's Shi'ite deputy would be acting speaker until a successor was found.

There were signs also that Gordon Brown, not yet Prime Minister, was beginning to distance himself, albeit slightly, from the Blair attitude to Iraq. In a surprise visit to Baghdad on 11 June he admitted that mistakes had been made and pledged to 'learn the lessons' of the run-up to the conflict. At the Labour Party conference of 2006 he had emphasised the element of conventional wisdom that was fast becoming a mantra: 'The lesson of Iraq is that we didn't prepare enough for the transition . . . the decisions that were made in the early days could and perhaps should have been different.' However, in June 2007, during his Baghdad visit, he still stood by the decision to go to war ('We made the decision. I take responsibility for that decision'), and he gave no promise of an early British withdrawal: 'This is not the right time to talk about [troop] numbers. I don't want to get into talking about timetables or numbers.'[43] Again some observers noted that Brown was still the paymaster for the war and recalled a comment by the late Robin Cook that the Chancellor had 'launched a long and passionate statement of support for Tony's strategy' at a Cabinet meeting ten days before the invasion.[44] Speaking to *The Times*, Prime Minister al-Maliki said he felt that Brown's visit to Iraq had been intended 'to ensure a positive British commitment . . . I feel he will follow the policy of Tony Blair . . . we agreed to make contact on all the important issues.'[45] At the same time it emerged that more than a thousand British servicemen had been treated at Priory Group health clinics for mental health problems since the start of the war at a cost of around £12.5 million, and that doctors were being urged to look out for suicidal tendencies among former soldiers who had served in Iraq.

On 12 June Defence Secretary Des Browne announced that from the following month British troops in southern Iraq would be confined to a single base at Basra airport, and that 500 British troops would be withdrawn from Iraq by the end of 2007. Britain was 'on course' to hand Basra Palace over to Iraqi forces, when the UK's military presence would be cut to about 5,000 troops. This, suggested Browne, was a 'probability' rather than a certainty, and he said that 'well over 80 per cent' of attacks in Basra were now aimed at the British forces, suggesting that UK troops were becoming increasingly vulnerable.[46]

★

In the United States the court hearing on the Haditha case, where some twenty-four Iraqis were murdered by American troops – another tip of the US atrocity iceberg – was running on. On 12 June prosecutors and defence attorneys presented their final arguments in the preliminary hearing for Lieutenant Colonel Jeffrey Chessani, charged with failing to investigate the killings by marines under his command. Here defence attorney Robert Muise, appealing to the hearing officer, Colonel Christopher Conlin, said: 'The reality is – you know, sir, you served in Iraq – that civilian deaths are a regrettable consequence of this war.' In the same vein Lieutenant Colonel Eric Smith, called as an expert witness, said that he did not suspect 'for a nanosecond' that Chessani had reason to believe that a war crime had been committed by his troops. And First Lieutenant Adam Mathes judged that the lesson of Haditha was that the troops looking for insurgents had two choices: let insurgents hiding behind civilians get away, or fight back and 'risk being part of an investigation for the next year and a half'.[47] Put simply, US troops should be free to kill civilians.

It was clear that the murder of innocent families signalled the growing desperation of the US military, increasingly frustrated at its seeming inability to crush a resilient insurgent movement. This desperation was shown in many other ways, not least the decision to arm Sunni dissidents in the hope that they would use their American weapons to attack only al-Qaeda fighters. The US high command had given permission for its officers to negotiate with local Sunni leaders and to hand over arms, ammunition, body armour, cash, fuel, pick-up trucks and other equipment in exchange for an agreement that such support would not be used against American troops. The new policy seemed absurd. What guarantees were there that the arms supplied to the Sunni factions would not be used against the occupying forces? Major General Rick Lynch attempted an explanation. No weapons would be given to militants who had attacked Americans – a condition that would evidently be satisfied by the use of fingerprinting, retinal scans and other tests to establish the innocence of the insurgents in question. One witness to the handing over of ammunition to a Sunni group suggested that the American soldiers saw the move as a stunt, suggesting it would accomplish nothing.[48] A more likely scenario was that the new policy, approved by General Petraeus, would increase the flood of American casualties back to the United States.

On 12 June a packed truck bomb blew apart a bridge in Baqubah that carried traffic over the Diyala River, forcing motorists and truckers to take a detour that ran through al-Qaeda-controlled territory. This followed a suicide blast that shut a superhighway east of Mahmoudiyah, south of Baghdad, in which a flyover collapsed, killing three US soldiers and wounding others guarding the span. American forces then used bulldozers to clear the rubble of the flyover, which had crashed onto Iraq's main north–south highway.

Such incidents were continuing to add to the US casualty toll. By 12 June some 3,512 Americans had been killed in Iraq, with another 25,950 wounded in combat. Furthermore, in order to minimise the escalating figures the Pentagon was ignoring the 27,022 military victims who had suffered 'non-hostile' injuries and illness. Many of the victims were not defined as 'casualties' since they had been discharged from active duty. By the beginning of 2007 some 180,000 US military veterans of Iraq and Afghanistan had filed disability claims. Another group of unreported casualties were the more than 12,971 dead and injured 'contractors' of American companies. Here 156 of the 971 dead were reported as Americans, which suggested the rest were foreign nationals – including everyone from food service workers to military mercenaries.[49]

On 13 June the UN Security Council, seemingly cowed into acquiescence, agreed to an Iraqi request to extend the mandate of the US-led multinational force after Foreign Minister Hoshyar Zebari declared that the foreign troops were 'vitally necessary'. The request was predictable and unsurprising: the US military was the only protective force preventing the Maliki regime from being swept into history. This meant also that the grim catalogue of brutality and abuse perpetrated by one of the main elements in the war would continue.

The US military had already fired more than twenty satellite-guided rockets into western Baqubah, with other attacks launched by Apache helicopters. American tanks moved through the narrow city lanes and shelled the mosque, killing five civilians, including two women; a further eleven people were wounded when a US warplane mistakenly bombed a civilian area in the Khatoon area of the city. Then it was announced that the American forces intended to take fingerprints and other biometric data from every resident in Baqubah who might be a potential fighter. British aircraft were now shelling the Majar and Qalat districts of the city of Amarah, resulting in strikes on houses while locals were sleeping on the roof (a common practice to remain cool), killing and injuring forty-five residents. Witnesses said that anti-personnel cluster bombs were used to destroy some neighbourhoods. Latif al-Tamimi, chief of the security committee of the council in Maysan province, of which Amarah is the capital, accused British troops of firing 'randomly' and called the operation a 'catastrophe'. Many women and children were among the fatalities.[50]

A virtual US-orchestrated siege of Fallujah was preventing aid workers entering the city to help displaced families. One resident, Muhammad Aydan, commented: 'We are living like prisoners, lacking assistance at all levels.' And Fatah Ahmed, a spokesman for the Iraqi Aid Association, commented:

> We have supplies but it is impossible to reach the families. They are afraid to leave their homes to look for food, and children are getting sick with diarrhoea caused by the dirty water they are drinking . . . pregnant women are delivering their babies at home as the curfew is preventing them from reaching hospital. It is a crime against the right to live . . . innocent civilians are the only ones who are paying.[51]

Many incidents were being reported in which US troops fired randomly into Iraqi civilian crowds.[52]

In mid-June 2007 one Iraqi civilian, a furniture maker called Maitham Mohammed al-Waz, described how he was treated at the British Temporary Detention Facility in Basra:

> I saw six or seven civilian men . . . all had their hands cuffed to the front and were hooded. They were groaning in pain. I was forced to

wear a hood, stand up, bend my knees and keep my arms stretched out in front. After five to ten minutes they dropped. I was hit with a bar across my back and on to my arms. I was also hit very forcibly on my left knee.[53]

Al-Waz was denied sleep for two nights – a recognised form of torture; meanwhile another civilian, Mohand Dhahir Abdullah, described similar experiences. He was beaten, urinated on, deprived of sleep, forced to kneel on sharp stones in 45°C heat, and made to drink urine when he begged for water.[54]

The prestigious journalist Robert Fisk went to see Kifah Taha, who had terrible wounds in his groin caused by beatings by British soldiers. They would call their prisoners by the names of football stars – Beckham was one – before kicking them around the detention headquarters in Basra. Again Iraqi detainees were forced to kneel on sharp stones, were forced to sit with their heads down lavatory bowls, and were kicked and punched in the groin, kidneys, back and shoulders.[55] All these details were among the evidence being taken to the High Court by ex-prisoners after Baha Mousa had been beaten to death by British soldiers.[56] On 13 June 2007 the House of Lords ruled that the Human Rights Act did apply to British soldiers operating in war zones abroad, a ruling that seemingly opened the way for civilian victims of military actions to sue the MoD.[57]

On 13 June al-Qaeda terrorists carried out a second devastating attack on Samarra's sacred al-Askari shrine, destroying the remaining minarets and reviving the sectarian hatreds that flared when the shrine was attacked in 2006. The first attack had reduced the shrine's golden dome to rubble and triggered a massive wave of sectarian cleansing as hundreds of thousands of Sunnis were driven from their homes. Now it seemed that the sectarian war would gain a new impetus. In a joint statement ambassador Ryan Crocker and General David Petraeus condemned the attack: 'We share the outrage of the Iraqi people against this crime, and we call on all Iraqis to reject this call to violence.'[58] More significantly, Iran's President Mahmoud Ahmadinejad blamed the continued American presence in Iraq for the bombing.

Despite the US statement and similar appeals by Prime Minister al-Maliki and Grand Ayatollah Ali al-Sistani, Iraq's most senior Shi'ite cleric, a wave of revenge attacks on Sunni mosques hit Baghdad. On 14 June a powerful explosion reduced a large Sunni mosque in Basra to rubble. Again the bombing of the shrine, then protected mainly by Iraqi forces – and the aftermath – showed the impotence of the Maliki government in the face of continuing sectarian violence. In particular it demonstrated the failure of the Baghdad security plan, now fully staffed with 28,500 extra US troops on the ground – a point partially conceded by Robert Gates, speaking to the AFP news agency in the Iraqi capital: 'Frankly we're disappointed with the progress so far and hope that this most recent bombing by Al-Qaeda won't further disrupt or delay the process.'[59] The Iraqi government immediately imposed a curfew on Baghdad and Samarra, which brought relative calm to the streets, possibly a lull before the next sectarian storm. Assad Mohammed, a Sunni technician, said: 'We hope it will stay quiet, but we are afraid that the Shi'ite militias will attack when the curfew is removed.'[60]

The Petraeus progress report was still being portrayed as a 'deadline' for President Bush, though the White House insisted that it would not represent 'a pivotal moment'. And General Petraeus himself would soon be setting the scene for further delays, declaring that he needed more time to make an assessment of the surge (see Chapter 7). Observers suggested that Petraeus would paint a mixed picture. It was unthinkable that he would signal his own incompetence by calling the troop surge a failure – so the report, whenever it appeared, would be mixed. In any event it was already plain that the Bush policy was not achieving its basic aims. Thus an advisor to Petraeus, Stephen Biddle, a senior fellow at the Council of Foreign Relations, commented that having only one-third of Baghdad under control 'is not as good as we had hoped for'. It was difficult to see how the situation on the ground would change over a month or two, or even over the extra few weeks that Petraeus would later demand.

On 14 June a US Air Force F-16 fighter jet crashed during a close air-support mission for ground forces – an uncommon loss that suggested the insurgents had gained a ground-to-air strike capacity beyond the usual small-arms fire and rocket-propelled grenades. This was yet another sign that the US military was increasingly vulnerable in the war and that more casualties could be expected. Robert Gates, speaking to reporters on a flight to Baghdad, admitted that the situation in Iraq 'was a very mixed picture'.[61] Leading Democrats were continuing to express their opposition to US policy on the war, even to the point of criticising General Petraeus for a lack of candour about conditions on the ground. On 15 June Senate leader Harry Reid was quoted as accusing America's top military commander of not being entirely candid about the war; moreover, he branded General Peter Pace, chairman of the Joint Chiefs of Staff as incompetent.[62] In response, the White House press secretary, Tony Snow, said that Reid had no right to insult the military leadership: 'At a time of war, for the leader of a party that says it supports the military, it seems outrageous to be issuing slanders toward the Chairman of the Joint Chiefs and also the man who is responsible for the bulk of military operations in Iraq.'[63] Snow added that Reid had already declared the war lost and the troop surge a failure, and that he should apologise.

The occupation being protected by Petraeus, Pace, Snow and the rest was presiding over a collapse of civic society and ever-escalating violence. The multifaceted conflict was stimulating a growing brutalisation of all the parties, and the 'democratically elected' government was no exception. For example, the Iraqi authorities were determined to sustain their country's reputation as one of the world's leading hanging states. Thus in prison cells inside a broad bend of the Tigris dozens of men and women – accused of attacking the US occupation in various ways – were waiting to be hanged. The trials had been perfunctory, causing human rights advocates to denounce the judicial processes and to urge change. Amnesty International has commented that the judicial practice is deeply flawed, beginning with Iraq's Anti-Terrorism Law, which defines the crime in 'broad and vague terms' as a criminal act against individuals or property designed to 'instill fear, terror and panic'. Moreover, 'the right to fair trial and

other basic safeguards are absent'.[64] The United Nations
Assistance Mission for Iraq reports had frequently emphasised that
there are too few judges in the juryless Central Criminal Court
(CCC) of Iraq to handle a huge caseload and to ensure fair trials.
Qais Salman, a defence lawyer representing two women facing
the death penalty, commented: 'The trials aren't fair because the
judge doesn't have enough time to read or think about each case.
The judge announces the verdict in haste, without thinking,
because he has to finish 10 to 20 cases a day.'[65] Some of the capital
cases involved ordinary murders and criminal kidnappings, but
death sentences were frequently handed down by the CCC for
anti-US attacks or planned attacks.[66]

On 16 June the remains – mostly skulls and bones entangled in
tattered sports uniforms – of thirteen members of an Iraqi tae
kwon do team, kidnapped the previous year, were found in
western Iraq. On the same day another Sunni mosque was
destroyed in the Basra area, signalling a continuation of the
sectarian war. Now the plight of Iraqi refugees was worsening as
Syria and Jordan, reeling under the pressure of hundreds of
thousands of new immigrants, imposed fresh restrictions. Hala
Numan Jabre, throwing her bags onto a bus destined for Syria,
said that staying in Iraq was 'like committing suicide'. Another
refugee, Hala, commented: 'There is no safe life in Iraq. It's like a
jungle. There are no public services, there is no rule of law, and
everywhere there is killing and kidnapping. That is why we have
decided to take our daughters away until things get better.'[67] The
UN High Commissioner for Refugees had acknowledged on 5
June that the situation in Iraq 'continues to worsen'.

By 17 June 2007 the US toll of dead in Iraq, according to an
Associated Press count, had reached 3,526, with at least 2,885
dying as a result of hostile action. The British military had
reported 150 deaths, with relatively few deaths reported by other
current or former coalition members. The death toll among
contractors, journalists and Iraqi civilians continued to mount. At
least 106 journalists, 84 of them Iraqis, had been killed since the
start of the war; and a dozen other Iraqi media employees had
disappeared, apparent victims of kidnap gangs or sectarian death
squads. The endless carnage, despite every fresh American attempt

to impose stability, created the impression that the Iraqi regime
was living on borrowed time, that even George Bush's stubborn
resolve would prove insufficient to prevent implicit deadlines
from shaping the course of events.

On 17 June General Petraeus said in a news conference that the
US military had begun a wide offensive outside Baghdad against
al-Qaeda forces, with Robert Gates emphasising that the
operation was intended to take the fight to al-Qaeda hideouts in
order to reduce the spate of car bombings. Here the new
emphasis on attacking insurgents' cells and bomb-making
factories was expected to be prolonged and wide-ranging; in
the past, similar operations had done no more than displace the
insurgents from one region to another. Thus, four months after
the beginning of the surge, the American military leaders were
acknowledging that more had to be done if the new security
policy was to be judged a success, and admitting that a sustained
lengthy campaign was essential. Petraeus said: 'In fact, typically, I
think historically, counter-insurgency operations have gone at
least nine or ten years. The question is, of course, at what level.
The fact is that, as we go on the offensive, the enemy is going to
respond. That is what has happened.' Ryan Crocker commented
that the situation in Iraq was 'a mixed picture, but certainly not
a hopeless one'. There were frustrations among the signs of
progress, but he stressed that the US forces should not be
withdrawn too soon, and again there was emphasis on the need
for the Iraqi government to increase its efforts to stem the
violence. Thus Senator Mitch McConnell of Kentucky said:
'The Iraqis will have to step up, not only on the political side, but
on the military side to a greater extent. We're not there
forever.'[68] And speaking on Fox News Petraeus emphasised that
the surge was only just beginning, implying that it was too early
to expect significant results.[69]

General Jay Garner, who had led the initial phase of the
occupation after the 2003 invasion, commented that Iraq was on
the brink of a genocidal civil war and that the Maliki government
would fall apart unless the United States allowed the emergence
of a three-way federal structure. He declared that he had been

shocked by the Pentagon's decision to reduce US troop levels and disband the Iraqi army:

> The problem from my standpoint within the United States was that there had been a lot of planning done by each element . . . by the CIA, the State Department, the Treasury Department, Defense Department . . . but the problem with that planning is that it had been done in the vertical stovepipe of that agency and the horizontal connection of those plans did not occur.[70]

Andrew Bearpark, the subsequent British director of operations for the Coalition Provisional Authority, which took over from Garner, had already revealed to *The Guardian* that the US plan to boost Iraq's post-invasion electricity production ran to one page and that those who had failed to plan for the aftermath were guilty of 'criminal irresponsibility'. According to Sir Jeremy Greenstock, Tony Blair was tearing his hair out, asking: 'What are the Americans up to?'[71]

The results of the lack of planning were plain to see. No one doubted that the collapse of the civil infrastructure and the resulting social chaos were fuelling the insurgency, and that the US surge would fail unless the basic needs of the Iraq people were met. In circumstances of deprivation, misery and bitter hatred there would always be recruits for the anti-occupation struggle. And again there were mounting problems with Iraq's porous borders. Iran was continuing to expand its influence in southern Iraq, and Turkey was massing its troops and tanks amid growing concern of a possible invasion in the north. On 17 June Cemil Bayik, a powerful figure in the PKK, said that the Turkish army would face 'a political and military disaster' if it began a cross-border offensive. The PKK, regarded as a terrorist organisation by the US, the EU and Turkey, did not seek a fight but would defend itself if attacked. Already Turkish forces had shelled northern Iran and launched a few minor incursions, but now Turkish chief of staff General Yaşar Büyükanıt was pressing the reluctant Ankara government to grant permission for a full-scale invasion of Iraq.

★

In the United States the scandal over the treatment of Iraq veterans was continuing to run. One mentally ill soldier, Private First Class Joshua Calloway, was flown out of Iraq and found himself in the locked-down psychiatric ward at the Walter Reed Army Medical Center. After witnessing his sergeant, Matthew Vosbein, step on a pressure-plate bomb in the road, the young soldier's knees buckled and he had vomited before being ordered to collect body parts. Then he had been sent to the combat-stress trailers and given antidepressants, but after a week he was still twitching and sleepless, and the army decided to fly him home. Young Private Calloway was put in robes that first night – forcing him to resemble 'a freakin' Haj' – and shoelaces and belts were prohibited. His dreams were full of corpses, he could taste blood and he was tormented by images of Sergeant Vosbein stepping on the bomb. He was soon 'stabilised' but continued to suffer disturbing compulsions, wanting to hatchet someone in the back of the neck: 'I want to see people that I hate die. I want to blow their heads off. I wish I didn't, but I do.'[72] On occasions he would continue to sweat and shake, and imagine he was back in the heat and sand of Iraq, and he was still having nightmares. He confessed to a doctor: 'I want to kill Arabs'; and on the phone to his mother he said that he was not getting any better.[73]

Every month up to forty soldiers were being evacuated because of mental health problems, and sufferers from post-traumatic stress disorder (PTSD) were outnumbering amputees by forty-three to one. In the Walter Reed hospital, lacking enough psychiatrists and clinicians to treat the growing number of war patients, soldiers with combat-stress disorders were mixed in with psychiatric patients suffering from every condition from marital strife to schizophrenia. Individual therapy for PTSD patients was infrequent. It was plain that Calloway and tens of thousands of other young Americans were victims in a bloody and seemingly endless conflict – and there were other US victims, not least those courageous and rare individuals prepared to expose gross American abuses in Iraq.

On 25 June 2007 Seymour Hersh, writing in the *New Yorker*, described the treatment afforded to Major General Antonio Taguba, who had reported on the Abu Ghraib abuses perpetrated by American personnel.[74] In a meeting with Donald Rumsfeld, the then Defense Secretary addressed him mockingly: 'Here . . . comes . . . that famous General Taguba . . . of the Taguba report.'[75] Early on in his inquiry, Taguba had been warned by a senior US general that his investigation could damage his career: the abused detainees were 'only Iraqis'.[76]

Rumsfeld complained he had not been given the report ('Here I am, just a Secretary of Defense, and we have not seen a copy of your report . . . and I have to testify to Congress tomorrow and talk about this'). Taguba commented that Rumsfeld was 'in denial' – more than a dozen copies of the report had been sent to the Pentagon and to the Central Command headquarters in Tampa, Florida; but by the time Taguba walked into Rumsfeld's conference room he (Taguba) had received no indication that any senior military leaders had read the report. One lieutenant general said: 'I don't want to get involved by looking.'[77] Rumsfeld, in his appearances before the Senate and the House Armed Services Committee on 7 May 2004, claimed to have had no idea of the extensive abuse – despite evidence to the contrary.[78] In June 2007 Taguba accused senior US Army commanders of involvement in torture at Abu Ghraib; and was convinced that Rumsfeld had lied under oath to the congressional committee about when and how much he knew of the scandal.[79] If true, this was a serious legal abrogation, as was the entire Iraq enterprise. In the United States the possibility of impeaching George Bush, Dick Cheney and other war leaders was still being discussed; and in Britain the Law Lords had agreed to hold an independent inquiry into how the Attorney General came to judge that the war was legal.[80]

On 18 June a joint American–British force launched a raid into southern Iraq to stop arms being smuggled from Iran across the border. The insurgents fought back and the large coalition force was forced to call in air strikes, later reporting that twenty militants had been killed; whereas a local hospital claimed that thirty-six Iraqis had been killed and 100 wounded, some of whom were civilians. Latif al-Tamini, a local provincial councillor, said: 'Most of the dead were killed in bombings as they were sleeping on roofs of their homes. Those killed were residents and not linked to any political party.'[81] The local council was sufficiently outraged by the operation to demand an apology from the British military and to suspend work for three days in protest at the action. At the same time a force of 10,000 American troops launched Operation Arrowhead Ripper against what they claimed were al-Qaeda hideouts across Diyala province and inside its capital, Baqubah. A military spokesman, Brigadier General Mick Bednarek, said that twenty-two suspected al-Qaeda militants had been killed: 'The end state is to destroy the al-Qaeda influences in this province and eliminate their threat against the people. That is the number one, bottom-line, up-front, in-your-face, task and purpose.'[82] On 19 June a lorry bomb struck the Shi'ite al-Khilani mosque in Baghdad, killing at least seventy-eight people and wounding 218 others.

There were now signs that the US embassy in Baghdad, the largest and most expensive diplomatic mission in the world, was poorly run and inadequately staffed. On 19 June it was revealed that Ryan Crocker had written a highly critical memorandum to Secretary of State Condoleezza Rice on 31 May:

> Several of the recommendations [of an internal report] are critical to our mission, and I hope that they will have your personal support . . . Simply put, we cannot do the nation's most important work if we do not have the department's best people. HR [human resources] has made heroic efforts to staff the embassy, but to a large extent HR has been working alone.[83]

He emphasised that 'staffing Iraq is an imperative', stressing the importance of a diplomatic surge to match the US military surge then under way. Already the American embassy employed 1,000 American officials and around 4,000 foreign citizens, to a budget of more than $1 billion.

On 20 June General Petraeus told *The Times* that the five kidnapped British citizens were being held by a group – a secret cell of the Mahdi Army – funded, trained and armed by Iran. He insisted that the United States did not have the option of walking away from Iraq after more than four years of war:

They [al-Qaeda] have a global war of terror, and Iraq is the central front, whether you like it or not. That is something that the leaders of the intelligence community in the West and our joint special operations commander agree on. It is certainly one very important consideration in looking at Iraq.

Petraeus stressed that it would be impossible to eliminate 'sensational attacks' and that the 'measure of success' would be reducing their number and their impact. Anticipating the report he was to deliver in September, he emphasised that he would describe what had been achieved and what had not: 'Neither of us [Petraeus and Crocker] is under any illusion.'[84] On 21 June the US military announced that fourteen more American soldiers had been killed, five by a single roadside bomb in north-east Baghdad; a US air strike aimed at what was thought to be a booby-trapped house in Baqubah missed its target and 'accidentally hit' another structure, wounding eleven Iraqi civilians; hospitals reported ambulances bringing in the bodies of dozens of people killed in American air strikes; and a series of mortars and rockets slammed into the Green Zone. Already, according to Associated Press, the US military had suffered fifty-nine fatalities in June. No reliable figures for the number of Iraqi deaths were available.

In the United States the political tensions were continuing to mount. The Democrats' presidential candidates were struggling to signal their opposition to the war without being seen as undermining the US soldiers 'in harm's way'. On 21 June Hillary Clinton, still the likely Democrat nominee, was faced with anti-war slogans – LEAD US OUT OF IRAQ NOW – when she gave a speech in Washington. The protesters, from Code Pink, a feminist anti-war group, booed but were countered by Clinton supporters who 'vocalised' to balance them out. Soon Clinton was blaming the Iraqis for the chaos in Iraq: 'It is the Iraqi government which has failed to make the tough decisions that are important to their own people.' She said that she saw the signs and commented that that was what 'we are trying to do'.[85]

In reality there was a growing possibility that combat tours for American troops would be extended – said by Robert Gates to be a worst-case scenario, despite expectations that the surge would extend into 2008. In addition, Gates was responding to a Pentagon report showing a rising incidence of psychological trauma among US forces,[86] poor mental health care, lack of trained staff and entrenched prejudices against what was called shell shock in the First World War and combat fatigue in the Second. He said: 'This is something that we can, must and will get fixed.'[87] It was now clear that tens of thousands of Iraq veterans were suffering from various psychological conditions, and that the number would increase over the coming months.

It was equally clear that Iraqis suffering trauma and other psychological diseases were numbered in the hundreds of thousands. Many had lost relatives and been forced to flee their homes; some struggled to live normal lives in conditions of violence and chaos, though having little optimism for the future. The journalist Richard Beeston, writing for *The Times*, described the case of Linda Hayali, who took her final Baghdad University examination on 23 June 2007. She had stayed with the course because she 'had no choice': 'Once I graduate I will just stay at home. There are no prospects for young people in this country, however educated they are . . . Believe me, if I could escape I would. But I am stuck here.'[88] The twenty-one universities in Iraq had been caught up in the general violence and chaos throughout the country, and in addition targeted by various Islamist groups determined to destroy any manifestations of Western culture and secular education.

The deepening chaos and social collapse were encouraging speculation that a partition of Iraq, acknowledging the *de facto* cantonisation between Sunnis and Shi'ites, was the only solution.[89] It was certainly true that the discourse focusing on the Iraq question constantly depicted the conflict as including the Sunni–Shi'ite divide, the role of the sectarian militias, the sectarian loyalties of parliamentary factions, the impact of the new constitution on regional powers and the degree of political autonomy being claimed by the Kurds.[90] Increasingly there was a sense that events were moving under their own momentum. The US political and military leaders ensconced in the Green Zone had displayed little awareness of the ethnic and sectarian realities on the ground, habitually criticising those who offered an unfamiliar expertise,[91] and allowing cultural differences to impair efforts to train local Iraqi forces to take care of security.[92] Lieutenant General Jack Stultz, head of the US Army Reserve, commented:

> There hasn't been a civil affairs surge [to accompany the military surge] . . . Before you go in and use the hard [military] effect, there's the opportunity to go in with the civil affairs and talk to the local community . . . The first reaction working with the Iraqi soldiers from the active army was the traditional drill sergeant approach: just yell at the guy . . . Just scream at him. The Iraqi soldier wasn't used to that. In some cases they would be offended or indignant.[93]

On 24 June Ali Hassan al-Majid, known as 'Chemical Ali' for his use of chemical weapons against the Kurds, was sentenced to death by Iraq's special tribunal. In particular, he was convicted of masterminding the genocidal Anfal campaign during the late 1980s, which in some estimates led to the deaths of 180,000 Kurds. Two other former senior regime members, former Defence Minister Sultan Hashim Ahmad al-Tai and former army chief of staff Hussein Rashid, were jailed for life for their complicity in the campaign. Few observers of the trial proceedings doubted that natural justice had been served but, as with the trial of Saddam Hussein,[94] there were questions about the court proceedings.

Richard Dicker, international director of Human Rights Watch, said that the impact of the genocide conviction would inevitably be 'hobbled' by the problems – including political interference – that the tribunal 'faced and failed to fix'. Dicker concluded: 'If the tribunal had more credibility or had it been a joint international-Iraqi tribunal, the verdict would have had more moral authority and legitimacy, and the Kurds' wretched experience would have seen proper redress.'[95] The town of Halabja, where 5,000 Kurds had been poisoned to death – an atrocity first blamed by the Pentagon on Iran at a time when Saddam was a US ally – predictably celebrated, but there were concerns that justice had not been fully realised.[96]

*

There were few signs that the new security crackdown was having much effect, apart from creating more carnage and destruction. Iraqi and American spokesmen were claiming to have shut down dozens of 'bomb factories', arrested nearly 18,000 insurgents and killed more than 3,000 others.[97] Such figures were difficult to verify and, even if true, indicated the scale of the resistance to the US-led occupation. A further sign of the task facing the US military was the policy of trying to split the resistance by encouraging Sunni groups to turn against their erstwhile al-Qaeda allies. This, as noted, involved supplying arms to Sunni insurgent groups in the hope that they would be used to combat al-Qaeda infiltration of Iraqi communities.

However, the insurgents were responding to the new security policy with a surge of their own, with a flurry of new tactics and fresh innovations. An unnamed Western official in Baghdad said: 'These [targeting US helicopters, bridges etc.] were all new kinds of attacks, and there were so many of them, it was hard to keep track. The message from al-Qaeda was, "You do your surge, we'll do ours."'[98] Massive IEDs were being manufactured and buried in roads likely to be used by American troops, or hidden nearby in sewers and irrigation culverts. The Islamic State of Iraq had already posted videos on the internet showing 'mine-protected' RG-31 troop carriers being blown up by such devices. In addition, al-Qaeda was striking back against tribal sheikhs that tried to switch their allegiance. On 25 June a suicide bomber caused devastation, killing a dozen people, at the heavily defended al-Mansour Melia Hotel in central Baghdad, where tribal leaders were gathered for an informal meeting.[99] Sheikh Mahmoud Daham, a tribal leader who survived the attack, said that the bomber had 'targeted the tribes that are fighting terrorism', but Iraq would 'stay standing, whatever you do'.[100]

In Britain there were signs that Gordon Brown would make some efforts, however desultory, to distance himself from the Iraq policies of the Blair years, in which of course he had been deeply complicit. Apart from plans to make some controversial appointments that would disturb the Americans, Brown apparently intended to allow anti-war protesters to demonstrate and march outside Parliament – a practice banned under Tony Blair. And the shifting mood of the Labour Party was demonstrated by the anti-war postures adopted by some of the candidates for the deputy leadership of the party. This led to the first gaffe from Harriet Harman, later to be elected deputy Labour leader, who declared on television that Britain should apologise for its support for the US-led invasion and later denied that she believed in any such thing.

Thus on 29 May, interviewed by Jeremy Paxman on *Newsnight*, deputy leadership candidate Jon Cruddas said: 'I do actually [believe that the party should apologise], as part of the general reconciliation with the British people over what has been a disaster in Iraq.' Harman interjected to say: 'Yup, I agree with that.' However, on 25 June, interviewed by Ed Stourton on BBC Radio 4's *Today* programme, she commented: 'I've never said the government should apologise. How many times can I say it? I haven't asked anybody else to do anything.' This seemingly trivial inconsistency revealed above all the simmering tensions within the Labour Party.[101] The leadership was sensitive to a powerful sector of opinion within the party, but Brown had implicitly and explicitly approved the Prime Minister's support for the US-led invasion and now was not about to shift ground in ways that would deeply alienate Washington. Minor gestures to win some party support were one thing, fundamental changes in Britain's Iraq policy quite another.

On 24 June Pope Benedict XVI reportedly rebuked Blair over the war in Iraq and other matters at odds with orthodox Roman Catholic doctrine. The Vatican said that there had been a 'frank exchange' on 'delicate subjects' when the Pope met Blair, who at the time was thought to have intentions of becoming a Catholic; while Vatican sources admitted that the verbal formula used was 'the nearest the Vatican comes to referring to a row without using the word'.[102] The Pope wished Blair well in his forthcoming role as a Middle East peace envoy, but by now it was plain that the pontiff had profound disagreements over an aspect of British foreign policy that had produced such disastrous results for a national people.

*

The Iraqi people as a whole were suffering but women had been largely left out of the picture. Now they were being terrorised by the pressures of war and sectarian cleansing, and also by the resurgent Islamists, who were hostile to any manifestations of female independence. Despite all this, a network of more than 150 women's organisations across Iraq was fighting to preserve their rights in the process of revising the constitution. As part of the campaign, the Iraqi Women's Movement sent a letter to Nancy Pelosi, speaker of the US House of Representatives, and another to UN secretary general Ban Ki-Moon, expressing concern over the constitutional review process and calling for international support:

> As women face escalating violence and exclusion in Iraq, they have been marginalised in reconciliation initiatives and negotiations for government positions. Even with the shy and insignificant pressure exerted by the UN and other international donors/players on the Iraqi government and politicians to fulfill minimum obligations of Security Council Resolution 1325, the action taken has been a sequence of disappointments.[103]

The adoption of Resolution 1325 by the Security Council on 31 October 2000 was of the utmost importance. Here was a comprehensive legal and ethical document affirming the rights of women throughout the world and requiring the secretary general to call for 'an increase in the participation of women at decision-making levels in conflict resolution and peace processes'.[104] Equally importantly, the adoption of a further Security Council resolution, 1483, on 22 May 2003 encouraged 'efforts by the people of Iraq to form a representative government based on the rule of law that affords equal rights and justice to all Iraqi citizens without regard to ethnicity, religion, or gender, and, in this connection, recalls resolution 1325 (2000) of 31 October 2000'. In short, all Islamist efforts to marginalise and exclude women, denying them an effective role in government and abusing their human rights, were illegal in international law. It was clear that the token allocation of seats in the Iraqi parliament to women, often selected by Islamist male campaigners with their own sexist agendas, did nothing to guarantee the female rights defined in law.[105]

In June 2007 Hanaa Edwar, leader of the Iraqi Women's Movement and founder of the Iraqi Al-Amal Association, a national civil group based in Baghdad, was campaigning against Article 41 of the draft constitution, which placed personal status laws under the influence of religion, sect or belief. The issue did not only bear on the position of women but also related to sectarian and other divisions in Iraqi society – a situation that was rooted in history but which had assumed new and frightening proportions since the 2003 invasion. The researcher Nadje Sadig al-Ali, having visited a conference, 'Gender and Empire', in Cairo in June 2006, surveyed the plight of Iraqi women:

> In Iraq, all political actors have been guilty of instrumentalizing women and women's issues: the USA and UK to legitimize their invasion and ongoing occupation; Islamist political parties and militias to signal a break with the past regime of Saddam Hussein, generally associated with secular policies; and Islamist militias and insurgents using women's dress, movement and wider gender ideologies and relations to resist American and British occupation and the imposition of Western values and norms.[106]

The course of events in Iraq through 2007–8, in conditions of continuing conflict, did not suggest that these concerns were being adequately addressed.

By the end of June 2007 the American troop surge had reached its full potential, and was seemingly doing little to establish stability in Baghdad and elsewhere. Throughout Iraq the carnage and destruction continued, and the rate of US casualties was running at an all-time high. Nothing had been achieved to diminish Iranian influence in Iraq, despite the US–Iran talks, and the US military seemed powerless to quell the Iranian support for Iraqi insurgents. Thus army spokesman Brigadier General Kevin Bergner said:

> There absolutely is evidence of Iranian operatives holding weapons, training fighters, providing resources, helping plan operations,

resourcing secret cells that is [*sic*] destabilising Iraq. We would like very much to see some action on [the Iranians'] part to reduce the level of effort and to help contribute to Iraq's security. We have not seen it yet.[107]

On 28 June a massive car bomb exploded in a bus depot during Baghdad's rush-hour, killing at least twenty-two people and wounding more than forty others in the predominantly Shi'ite Bayaa neighbourhood; this was the third time that the station had been targeted by bombers. Muqtada al-Sadr was calling for thousands of Iraqis to march in unity to the al-Askari shrine in Samarra, arousing fears that another bloodbath would ensue.

The violence was continuing to spread, with the insurgents now resorting to a range of new devices, including the types of gas cylinder bomb that had been used by guerrillas in Indian-ruled Kashmir and separatists in the north-eastern Indian state of Assam. Al-Qaeda had already used a gas cylinder bomb in an attack on Western oil workers in Algeria. In addition, Turkey had reportedly prepared plans for an invasion of northern Iraq if the US and Iraqi forces failed to dislodge the PKK fighters. Thus Turkey's Foreign Minister, Abdullah Gül, said: 'The military plans have been worked out in the finest detail. The government knows these plans and agrees with them.'[108]

Some Iraqis, contemplating the total collapse of the social infrastructure and fearful of bomb attacks, were now talking of the 'good days' under Saddam Hussein.[109] Life in Baghdad was continuing to get worse. Many residents were prisoners in their own homes,

dreaming of escape or watching the death and destruction on the new Arabic 24-hour news channels . . . The promises of democracy seem like a lost dream. The government remains weak and divided along sectarian lines . . . The police force is blamed for kidnappings and sectarian killings . . . The terror is gnawing away at the very fabric of Baghdad's diverse society.[110]

One man, close to tears, said: 'I don't care where I go. You choose. Anywhere but here. The farther away the better. We are dying.' Another Iraqi, a doctor, had on one day witnessed twenty Shi'ites beheaded and dumped on a river bank, and another twenty-one killed by a car bomb. His family had already fled to Syria: 'My wife told me to sell what I can and leave the house. The only thing she wants me to bring are our family photo albums. We want to be able to remember happier times and to forget this hell. Once we leave we will never come back.'[111]

On 27 June 2007 Tony Blair, one of the two principal architects of the 2003 invasion and subsequent occupation, having tendered his resignation as Prime Minister to the Queen, flew to his Sedgefield constituency to resign from Parliament with immediate effect. Gordon Brown, with no democratic mandate from the Labour Party or the British people, entered Downing Street and became Prime Minister. It remained to be seen whether the Brown government would go beyond a few cosmetic gestures and change Britain's Iraq policy or whether 'staying the course' mantras would be the order of the day. On the previous day the outgoing and controversial Attorney General, Lord Goldsmith, called for an investigation into how illegal torture techniques had come to be used by British soldiers in Iraq – 'a grave concern'. The irony that British troops would never have been in Iraq but for Goldsmith's bending the legal case for war clearly escaped him.

Brown began by appointing a number of Cabinet ministers who were discernibly unsympathetic to the war fever of the Blair years: David Miliband, who had at times criticised Blair's Middle East policies; Jack Straw, who had wanted a ceasefire when Israel bombed Lebanon in 2006; Sir Mark Malloch Brown (later Lord Malloch-Brown), who had been a fierce critic of the Iraq War; and John Denham, who had quit the Blair government in protest at the Iraq invasion. Some US observers were watching the new appointments with alarm, wondering whether Gordon Brown's attempts to 'rebalance' the government after the Blair years would yield a shift in British foreign policy. But the White House was focusing on its own domestic problems.

American casualties had reached 57,017 dead and wounded;[112] and senior Republicans were increasingly critical of American policy. Thus Richard Lugar, speaking from the Senate floor, declared that the troop surge was not working: 'We have overestimated what the military can achieve, we have set goals that are unrealistic, and we have inadequately factored in the broader regional consequences of our actions.' In the same vein Senator George Voinovich of Ohio, a Republican, had sent President Bush a letter insisting that he must develop 'a comprehensive plan for a gradual disengagement from Iraq', and in an interview with National Public Radio he said: 'My fear is that at some point we will have a withdrawal from Iraq that is very disorderly and not very well planned. That would be a tragedy for the troops, a tragedy for Iraq, a tragedy for us.' Harry Reid, the senior Democrat leader, seized on Lugar's remarks, saying that when the history books came to be written Senator Lugar's words would be remembered 'as a turning point'.[113]

7
Judging a 'bankrupt' policy

In early July, following the killing of twenty-six alleged insurgents and the detention of seventeen others in Sadr City by American troops, there were more angry accusations that the US forces were firing blindly on civilians as a matter of normal practice. The Americans said that pre-dawn raids had been conducted against terrorists who had attacked them with small-arms fire, rocket-propelled grenades and roadside bombs, but Iraqi police and hospital officials claimed that the dead were civilians who had been killed in their own homes, and Lieutenant Colonel Mahmoud Shakarchi admitted that women and children were among the dead and injured.[1] In addition, Fatah Ahmed, a spokesman for the Iraqi Aid Association, commented: 'People are scared to leave their homes to buy petrol for their generators or to fetch water. Many families will soon start to run out of food and many shops are closed. Locals are desperate and prefer to stay inside their homes rather than get killed while walking on the streets.'[2] In response Prime Minister Nouri al-Maliki issued a statement criticising the American actions: 'The Iraqi government totally rejects US military operations . . . conducted without pre-approval from the Iraqi military command.'[3]

It was now clear that the raids were part of conventional US policy that was inevitably producing many 'unintended' casualties. Thus American claims that an air attack on the village of al-Khalis, north of Baqubah, had targeted al-Qaeda gunmen were disputed by local residents, who said that those who died were local guards trying to protect the township from exactly the kind of attack that the US military said it foiled. According to villagers, some eleven guards were killed and five others injured when US helicopters fired rockets at them and then strafed them with heavy machine gun fire.[4] In the same vein the Americans were saying that many suspected terrorists had been eliminated in Diyala during Operation Arrowhead Ripper, while residents reported houses destroyed and many civilians killed. Salman Shakir from the Gatoon district of Baqubah told the Inter Press Service that many of his relatives and neighbours had been killed by the US military while attempting to flee the area: 'I cannot tell you how many people were killed, because bodies of civilians were left in the streets.'[5] Other reports cited the killing of a pregnant woman, the slaughter of Iraqi civilians leaving the Ahmad al-Moukhtar mosque in Doura and the killing of many Iraqis at checkpoints – all by US troops.[6] An American raid on the village of al-Qadiriyah resulted in a baby losing its left leg and the deaths of its mother and uncle and one of their neighbours. Again local villagers claimed that the US forces had fired randomly at civilians.[7]

Such events were seemingly having little impact on the political decision makers in Washington and London. Gordon Brown had appointed a few ministers known to have voiced anti-war sentiments in the past but there was no discernible shift in the Labour government's Iraq policy and he was emphasising that all ministers would have to follow government policy on Iraq and everything else. Nonetheless the Brown appointments had already triggered concern in Washington, with one unnamed Pentagon source complaining about 'some conflicting signals' coming from London: 'eyebrows had been raised' over the decision to appoint Lord Malloch-Brown, who had attacked George Bush's 'megaphone diplomacy', to a senior job in the Foreign Office.[8] There was much commentary about Prime Minister Brown 'distancing himself' from President Bush – speculation that would be reinforced by his subsequent trip to Camp David – but there was no prospect that the remaining British troops would soon be withdrawn from Basra province against the wishes of the US government. As the journalist Simon Jenkins observed, the policy of the Bush–Blair administration had 'caused the deaths of 156 British soldiers for fear of upsetting Washington . . . Brown appears manacled to the policy of his predecessor'.[9] In fact, Chancellor Brown had been deeply complicit in every aspect of Blair's Iraq policy. Without his support, Blair could never have launched British forces against Iraq or carried out the subsequent disastrous occupation.

In the United States the Democrats, after six months in control of Congress, were mired in low approval ratings. They had been defeated on the war funding bill and had hoped to focus on key domestic issues, such as homeland security and immigration, but had little to show for their efforts. Nancy Pelosi, the House of Representatives speaker, noted the 'obstructionism' of the Republicans in the Senate and declared herself 'not happy with Congress'. In the Senate, Harry Reid was still calling on Republicans to support legislation that would force the withdrawal of troops from Iraq ('Too many times, Republicans have stood in the way of progress instead of helping us lead the way'), and there was talk of weekly votes on the issue. Some Republicans were, as Reid put it, 'saying the right things on Iraq' but 'we will need far more Republicans to put partisan politics aside and work with us for the American people'. Steny Hoyer, the House majority leader, commented that the Democrat efforts would not stop 'until a change of policy' was achieved. In early July, according to a CNN poll, half the respondents disapproved of what the Democrats had accomplished but 57 per cent said that Democratic control of Congress was good for the country.

On 2 July a US Army spokesman, Brigadier General Kevin Bergner, publicly accused Iran of intervening in the Iraq conflict, saying that the covert Quds force of the Revolutionary Guard had been involved in an attack in Karbala that had led to the deaths of five Americans: 'The Quds force had developed detailed information regarding our soldiers' activities, shift changes and defences, and this information was shared with the attackers.' He also claimed, citing the testimony of Hezbollah veteran Ali Mussa Daqduq, captured in March, that the Quds force and Lebanese Shi'ites from Hezbollah were training Iraqi insurgents at a camp near Tehran. Now Joseph Lieberman, a former presidential candidate, was calling for air strikes against Iran in retaliation for its alleged role in Iraq: 'I think we've got to be prepared to take aggressive military action against the Iranians to stop them from killing Americans in Iraq.'[10]

The US military was now facing further pressures, in addition
to constant insurgent attacks and waning domestic support. The
lengthy deployments in Iraq and Afghanistan were drastically
affecting recruitment and causing many service personnel to leave
the armed forces. In Britain, according to the Commons Public
Accounts Committee, the number of people leaving the Army
and the RAF was at a ten-year high – again because of the
protracted Iraq and Afghanistan conflicts: 'The impact of
continuous downsizing [manpower cuts], pressures and overstretch is affecting the [MoD's] ability to retain and provide a
satisfactory life for Armed Forces personnel.'[11] It was expected
that these pressures would increase over the coming months.

In early July 2007 the number of US-paid private contractors in
Iraq exceeded that of US combat troops, raising further questions
about the privatisation of the war effort and Washington's ability
to carry out reconstruction and military campaigns. It was well
known that most of the contractors, effective mercenaries,
operated independently of US military discipline and outside any
realistic accountability structure. Put simply, the rules of war, such
as they were, did not apply to them. Scores of US troops had been
prosecuted for serious crimes in Iraq, though rarely attracting
significant penalties, but very few private security contractors had
faced legal charges. It was significant also that some British and
American military leaders were talking about contractors 'filling
the gap' as coalition forces were reduced – thus contradicting any
notion that a drawdown of overall force levels would help to end
the conflict.

More than 180,000 civilians – Americans, Iraqis and
'foreigners' – were working in Iraq under US contracts, compared
with the 160,000 American soldiers and a few thousand civilian
government employees working in the country.[12] There were
signs also that the actual number of civilians funded by the
American taxpayer was greater than that claimed by the State and
Defense departments, since not all the private security personnel
hired to protect government staff and buildings were included in
the figures. Moreover, the role of *de facto* mercenaries[13] was
causing inevitable problems. Thus William Nash, a retired army

general, commented: 'We don't have control of all the coalition guns in Iraq. That's dangerous for our country. The Pentagon is hiring guns. You can rationalize it all you want, but that's obscene.'[14]

Private contractors had always played a part in America's wars but in Iraq their role was more prominent than ever – a development officially justified, according to the Pentagon's Gary Motsek, who was overseeing the contractors, as cutting costs and allowing combat troops to focus on fighting rather than other tasks. In addition, there were concerns that non-military personnel may be unwilling to take risks in areas of conflict. Thus on one occasion in 2004 American troops were put on food rations when contractors baulked at taking supplies into a combat zone.[15]

In Iraq there were few signs that the troop surge was having its intended effects. The US military was continuing to attack 'suspected terrorist' positions, with all the devastation to local communities that this policy entailed, and the sectarian war was producing its daily toll of victims. In Kurdistan, according to a Human Rights Watch (HRW) report based on interviews in 2006, the US-backed security forces were routinely torturing detainees in overcrowded concentration camps. As with the detainees held elsewhere in Iraq, the vast majority had not been charged with a crime, allowed access to a lawyer or provided with a means of appeal. Sarah Leah Whitson, HRW's Middle East director, noted the irony of Kurds practising such violations when they themselves were victims of abuse under Saddam Hussein.[16] In Baghdad the Iraqi Cabinet, eager to satisfy their US protectors, unanimously passed the draft hydrocarbon law that had largely been written by Western oil consultants and approved by Washington and London.

Such events were doing nothing to disguise the evident collapse of US policy in Iraq. The military surge had 'already been written off as a failure, or not nearly successful enough, by many in Congress and beyond',[17] with the real debate focusing on how the inevitable American withdrawal was to be achieved ('whether a residual force should be left there, and which American objectives can be salvaged').[18] The policy, mainly associated with George Bush and his coterie, had manifestly achieved a terrible fiasco, and now the task was one of damage limitation. How was the US military to withdraw from the carnage and destruction with something approaching dignity and honour? How could some good be wrested from the chaos and suffering? According to Senator Richard Lugar the domestic divisions in the United States, having created a 'strident, polarised' debate, had already fatally undermined the surge and the likelihood of an orderly withdrawal. Some members of both parties were calling for a revival of the Iraq Study Group, its 2006 report already cherry-picked by Bush to no effect. Others awaited General David Petraeus's assessment, due in mid-September, though the Bush administration was already playing this down. The military report, according to the White House and some Bush supporters, would be nothing more than a snapshot of 'work in progress', with the surge likely to continue until the following spring or even longer. Would a deeply troubled Congress tolerate this, with all the further costs in troops and treasure that such a programme would entail? The veteran commentator David Broder, saying that a 'desperate' Bush was 'running out of time' at home and in Iraq,[19] was voicing a common sentiment in the United States and elsewhere.

In the United Kingdom, since the British involvement was less substantial than the American, the discernible agonising over Iraq policy was a more muted affair. The British parliament was largely derelict in failing to address the enormity of what war-making had done to the Iraqi people, and street protest was a pale shadow of the million-plus anti-war demonstration in London before the 2003 invasion of Iraq. One little-publicised and relatively inconsequential initiative, the Iraq Commission, modelled on the Iraq Study Group in the United States, had been set up by the Foreign Policy Centre in partnership with Channel 4 Television. The commission was intended to be an independent cross-party body charged with the task of producing recommendations on the future of Britain's role in Iraq.[20] It was jointly chaired by Lord Ashdown of Norton-sub-Hamdon,[21] Baroness Jay of Paddington[22] and Lord King of Bridgwater,[23] with support provided by nine commissioners.[24] In the event around fifty witnesses, drawing on a wide range of expertise and experience, gave evidence to the commission.

The results, bearing in mind the shape of the Iraq Commission, were largely predictable. The witnesses, properly representing many divergent opinions, inevitably focused on their own views and agendas – which left the commission to make sense of presentations that were often mutually incompatible. This meant that the findings were filtered through the attitudes and prejudices of the commissioners, in particular Ashdown, Jay and King. Little of the witness commentary added to what could already be found in quality reportage, but there were occasional details that gave the commissioners pause; for example, that Western companies wanting to do business in southern Iraq had first to make representations to Tehran. There were few signs that the new Brown administration paid much attention to the Iraq Commission report.

There was now a growing recognition that terrorist incidents in the United Kingdom were linked to the Iraq War, a consequence that had been widely predicted before the 2003 invasion. In 2005, immediately after the devastating 7/7 suicide bombings, Tony Blair and the pro-war press insisted that they had nothing to do with government foreign policy, despite much evidence to the contrary. The 'martyrdom videos' made by the London bombers spelt out that they saw their actions as revenge for British support for Israel, illegally occupying Arab land, and the occupations of Iraq and Afghanistan. One of the bombers, Mohammad Sidique Khan, declared: 'Until you stop the bombing, gassing, imprisonment and torture of my people we will not stop this fight.' The later bungled bombings in London, the alleged transatlantic airline plot of 2006 and the botched airport attack on 30 June 2007 provided further evidence of links between Islamic radicalism and Britain's Iraq policy.

The car bomb suspect Dr Bilal Abdulla, arrested at Glasgow airport, had been outraged by the suffering of Iraqis, the destruction of his country and the deaths of some of his friends in the Iraqi 'resistance'. According to his former tutor at Baghdad University, Professor Ahmed Ali, Abdulla's behaviour had often been criticised:

> We sent for his father many times . . . but the father supported his son.
> Once he verbally attacked the US Army . . . An officer was making a
> speech for the doctors about the future of Iraq. But Bilal stood up
> suddenly and said: 'You are a "kafir [unbeliever]" and all of you
> should die.'

He reportedly told one student, who complained to the
authorities many times, that she was beautiful but would burn in
hell for wearing revealing clothes.[25] Abdulla had later lived
in Cambridge, England; he was remembered as a 'confident and
educated' worshipper at the city's Abu Bakr mosque and was
known to hold grievances about events in Iraq. Now MI5 and
MI6 were investigating the role of al-Qaeda cells in Iraq to build
up a picture of the foreign contacts of the would-be suicide
bombers in London and Glasgow.[26] To many observers it was
'delusional and dangerous'[27] to deny the links between Islamic
terrorism in Britain and the government's Iraq policy.[28]

In the United States the extensive anti-war movement was taking
on various forms that were not evident in the many other protests
around the world. For example, on 4 July 2007, Independence
Day, the nation's first 'impeachment headquarters' opened its
doors in a storefront near the Beverly Center in Los Angeles.
Byron De Lear, a Green Party activist, commented: 'This is an
impeachment 4th of July,' adding that the removal of George
Bush and his Vice-President, Dick Cheney, was 'a patriotic duty
to restore the integrity of the United States.'[29] In this context it
was an easy matter to cite various actions and policies, 'lies', of the
Bush administration that had led the country into an illegal war;
and in addition to instance various Bush–Cheney policies that had
precipitated torture, illegal spying on American citizens and the
curtailment of privacy and civil rights in the name of fighting
terrorism. Representative Maxine Waters (Democrat) dubbed this
fresh impeachment initiative, allied to further planned street
protests, 'one of the most important efforts this country has ever
seen . . . We can make changes through organizing. If the
numbers are in the streets, Congress will listen.'[30] The
impeachment centre was sponsored by Progressive Democrats of

Los Angeles, Westside Greens, Santa Monica Democratic Club and Los Angeles Greens. Volunteers were planning to meet every Saturday to stuff envelopes, circulate petitions and lobby elected officials. Already they were emphasising that seventy-nine municipalities and townships nationwide had passed impeachment resolutions.

But no one was underestimating the difficulties facing the impeachment initiative. Any impeachment motion was required to pass through the House Judiciary Committee before being voted on by the House of Representatives – and Waters seemed to be the only pro-impeachment member of the committee. In the House it was possible to identify a total of fourteen lawmakers who were in favour of impeachment proceedings against Bush and Cheney, most of whom had signed the articles of impeachment against Cheney introduced by Representative Dennis Kucinich. Moreover, removing Bush or Cheney from office would need a two-thirds vote by the Senate, with Waters unable to cite a single senator who might support an impeachment motion. It was hard to avoid the conclusion that impeachment was an unrealistic option, even a distraction from Democrat efforts to secure legislation that would bring an end to the war.

Opposition to the Iraq policies of the Bush administration was now also coming from unexpected sources. Also on Independence Day a McClatchy newspaper, the *Olympian*, from Olympia, Washington, with a heavy military presence in its circulation area, declared in favour of an American withdrawal from Iraq. The paper carried the headline 'Bring home US troops' and concluded that the war 'isn't worth a single more American life'. The editor and publisher, John Winn Miller, commented:

The Fourth of July is a time when Americans celebrate the values that have made us a great nation. So it seems like an appropriate time to editorialize on what has become a national disgrace. It is a particularly important and local issue for us because we are in a military community with Fort Lewis and McCord Air Force Base in our area. We have seen too many of them killed, so many that Fort Lewis considered stopping individual memorials. Our men and women have done their duty with honor. It is time to honor their sacrifices by

ending this ill-conceived mission. A total of 134 service members
assigned to Fort Lewis have died in Iraq. A total of 208 service
members with ties to Washington State have died in the war.[31]

It was plain that a shadow hung over Independence Day 2007. At
a time when the American people would normally be waving the
flag with honour and respect, there was a growing disgust 'with
the trillion-dollar war being waged in their name with their tax
dollars'.[32] According to a CNN poll only 30 per cent of the
American people were now supporting the Iraq War, with Bush's
popularity running at the same level. A paltry 17 per cent thought
that the situation was improving, and even 42 per cent of
Republicans now believed that the United States should be withdrawing its troops from Iraq. In addition, publicity was being
given to signs of disaffection in Congress, with attention to a
comment by Republican senator Richard Lugar that the Iraq War
was a failure ('the costs and risk of continuing down the current
path outweigh the potential benefits') and to remarks on the
following day by Senator George Voinovich (Republican),
speaking to CNN, that a plan must be developed for a military
disengagement ('I think everybody knows that we fumbled the
ball right from the beginning on this').

It was also becoming more and more obvious that many of
Washington's problems stemmed from the unusual personality of
George Bush, increasingly remarked on by media observers and
others (see also Chapter 11). Thus an unnamed senior House
Republican, quoted in the *Washington Post*, commented: 'Our
members just wish this thing would be over. People are tired of
him . . . There's no adult supervision. It's like he's oblivious.
Maybe that's a defence mechanism.'[33] Lord Owen, a former
neurologist and British Foreign Secretary, noted that question
marks about Bush have related to 'his inattention, his incurious
nature and inarticulacy, signs that his brain functions in an unusual
way'.[34] And Dr Justin Frank, offering a psychological analysis of
the President's personality, suggested that 'a megalomaniac
solution' might have been an attractive way for Bush to cope with
early childhood troubles: 'Both megalomania and mania exhibit

three overtly similar defensive characteristics: control, contempt and triumph . . . The megalomaniac is indifferent to any damage he caused, because he had a reason for his actions; he is without guilt or compassion, and incapable of even thinking about making reparation.'[35]

The concerns and divisions over the Iraq War that were afflicting Britain and the United States were now also evident among the leaders of another of Bush's coalition partners, namely Australia. In early July 2007 the Howard government descended into confusion over conflicting statements on whether oil had played a part in Australia's support for the invasion and occupation. Thus on 5 July a front-page report in the newspaper *The Age* fore-shadowed a speech by John Howard in which he linked the Iraq War to world energy supplies. Immediately prior to the speech, Defence Minister Brendan Nelson declared on morning radio that Iraq was 'an important supplier of energy, oil in particular, to the rest of the world, and Australians and all of us' should consider what would happen if the coalition forces left Iraq before stability had been established. In his subsequent speech, delivered at an Australian Strategic Policy Institute conference, the Prime Minister, agreeing with Nelson, cited 'energy demand' as one of a number of reasons why it was important that the US-led forces succeed in Iraq: 'Many of the key strategic trends I have mentioned, including terrorism and extremism, challenging demographics, WMD aspirations, energy demand and great power competition, converge in the Middle East.'[36] But by the afternoon, for undisclosed reasons, Howard had accomplished a spectacular *volte-face*: speaking to Sydney's 2GB radio station he said: 'We are not there because of oil and we didn't go there because of oil, and we don't remain there because of oil. The reason we remain there is that we want to give the people of Iraq a possibility of embracing democracy.' And Treasurer Peter Costello moved quickly to deny Nelson's statement and Howard's initial observation that there was a link between oil and the occupation: 'This is about democracy and freedom in the Middle East.'[37] Professor Hugh White, a former senior defence official, commented that there had been a 'kind of washing machine of different arguments that have been tossing around' and 'the oil has come to the surface, so to speak, accidentally'. To have raised the oil issue now was 'simply a mistake'.[38]

In Iraq trade unionists and others, in no doubt that the 2003 invasion and subsequent occupation were primarily about oil, were continuing to fight against the hydrocarbon law, which favoured the multinational corporations. On 3 July George Bush had phoned Prime Minister al-Maliki to urge him and other Iraqi leaders to move 'aggressively forward' on the new legislation, even though it faced strong opposition from Iraqi oil workers. Faleh Abood Umara, general secretary of the Basra-based Southern Oil Company Union and the Federation of Oil Unions in Iraq, had recently toured the United States advocating both national control of Iraqi oil assets and immediate withdrawal of American troops from the country: the law, 'written in the United States . . . doesn't serve the interests of the Iraqi people . . . We would like to be sole owner of our wealth and use it to develop our country and cities.'[39] In fact, as noted, the legislation would allow foreign companies to export oil and profits from many Iraqi oilfields for up to thirty-five years under the production-sharing agreements.

The situation showed no signs of stabilising. American casualties were continuing to drain domestic support and to feed the growing divisions in the political establishment. In Basra the British forces were increasingly descending into a mere survival posture where hopes of achieving any useful purpose were rapidly dwindling. On 7 July two British soldiers were killed and three more injured during a night of heavy fighting, and the troops faced the prospect of a retreat from Basra Palace to the airport, leaving them with little more than a toehold in the country. The palace was coming under mortar and rocket attack several times every day and many of the roads within the city were now regarded as too dangerous to travel along. By now the British fatalities had reached 158, a toll that was set to increase in August, stimulating widespread talk of a final British withdrawal from the country.

The parlous state of Iraq's institutions was further exposed by revelations that Iraqi pupils were being failed in their exam-inations by examiners of different sectarian groups. Thus answers on exam papers from both Shi'ite and Sunni pupils were being erased to give marks below the 50 per cent pass level required to qualify for higher education. With six of the fourteen marking centres under exclusive sectarian control and marking abuses also affecting the other centres, a number of teachers had been sacked after the scandal was uncovered and many more were under investigation. Amir al-Khafaji, a spokesman for the Education Ministry, said that teachers had been able to identify pupils from rival sectarian groups by their names: 'We feel shame because these educated people have become some sort of terrorists. Next year, we will make all the teachers swear not to differentiate between Sunnis and Shias.'[40] One eighteen-year-old Shi'ite pupil, Haider Abed, said: 'If I found I was one of the victims of these [Sunni] teachers, then I'd do all that I can to cut off their heads.' A Sunni pupil, Doraid Kasim, was equally unforgiving: 'I studied very hard for a long year and I got excellent marks before the final test. I swear to kill all the Shia teachers if I get bad marks.'[41]

Prime Minister al-Maliki was now facing a no-confidence vote in Parliament, following news that 150 people may have been killed and twenty buildings destroyed in a truck bomb attack in the town of Amirli in northern Iraq. He called the bombing a 'heinous crime' but seemed powerless to prevent further atrocities in the mixed town of Arab Sunnis and Shias and the Turkmen ethnic minority, which had become a classic target for insurgents displaced from Baghdad by the US troops surge. A group of Sunni politicians headed by Vice-President Tariq al-Hashemi, the 'Iraq Group', was thought to be behind the likely no-confidence vote, which would further destabilise the government. And it was even suggested that al-Hashimi had discussed his plans with Dick Cheney on his recent visit to Baghdad,[42] perhaps indicating the growing American impatience with the ineffectual Maliki regime.

By now the crisis of confidence in George Bush's Iraq policy was being publicised throughout the American media, to the point that Defense Secretary Robert Gates suddenly postponed a long-planned trip to Latin America to focus on meetings about Iraq. On 9 July the *New York Times* ran a lead story, headed 'White House debate rises on Iraq pullback', which included the words: 'White House officials fear that the last pillars of political support among Senate Republicans for President Bush's Iraq strategy are collapsing around them, according to several administration officials.' Elsewhere David Kilcullen, a senior counter-insurgency advisor to General Petraeus, was quoted: 'We haven't turned the tide. We haven't turned the corner. There isn't light at the end of the tunnel.'[43] And in the same vein Christopher Fettweis, a national security professor at the Naval War College, the site of Bush's most recent 'rally around the surge' speech, discussed the crisis in a commentary entitled 'Post-Traumatic Iraq Syndrome': 'The endgame is now clear, in outline if not detail . . . There is no example of a modern democracy having changed its mind once it turned against a war. So we ought to come to grips with the meaning of losing in Iraq.'[44]

The US Marines company involved in the massacre of twenty-four Iraqi civilians in Haditha was now the focus of another war crimes investigation into the killing of eight unarmed Iraqis in Fallujah. Following an admission by Corporal Ryan Weemer, a former member of the company, that he had participated in an unlawful killing, the Naval Criminal Investigation Service was investigating claims that a dozen marines were involved in the murder of unarmed prisoners captured in Fallujah in November 2004.[45] When a marine radioed headquarters on what to do with prisoners he reportedly received the reply 'They're still alive?' – which the US soldiers interpreted as an order to kill the captives: 'That was taken to mean "whack those dudes". So they whacked them and moved on.' Weemer was being depicted by his lawyer, Paul Hackett, as an American hero, again raising the question of how seriously the Geneva Conventions were being taken by the US military in Iraq.

In Baghdad the Maliki regime, fearful that a US withdrawal would mean the immediate collapse of the government, was continuing to insist that the United States had an obligation to remain in the country. On 9 July Hoshyar Zebari, Iraq's Foreign Minister, responding to reports that Washington was discussing the possibility of a gradual troop withdrawal, predicted that Iraq would splinter into warring factions and that the conflict would spread into neighbouring countries if the Americans withdrew:

'The dangers could be civil war, dividing the country, regional wars and the collapse of the state.' With the Iraqi security forces not yet fully trained, the United States had a responsibility 'to stand with the Iraqi government as the forces are being built'. And he made reference to the reported attempts of Sunni lawmakers to orchestrate a no-confidence vote in the Shi'ite-led administration: 'There is rising speculation about the stability of the government. These speculations are exaggerated.'[46]

In fact two important political blocs, one Sunni and one Shi'ite, were maintaining their boycott of the government, making it impossible for parliamentarians to enact any legislation that would carry any sense of legitimacy. Salim Abdullah Jabouri, the spokesman for the 44-member Sunni bloc, said that it had no plans to end a boycott begun in protest at attempts to oust the Sunni Parliament speaker, but if a no-confidence vote was called the legislators would return to Parliament 'to oust' Prime Minister al-Maliki. In the same way the 32-member Shi'ite bloc loyal to Muqtada al-Sadr intended to continue its protest against the government's failure to provide adequate security. In this context an official in Najaf commented that it was 'very clear that the government is ending'.[47] In addition, the two blocs were also angry that the hydrocarbon legislation was being pushed through Parliament before various constitutional reforms, defining regional powers over national resources, had been finalised. Many al-Sadr supporters were now saying what was an increasingly common belief – that the bill was being promoted by the United States because it would allow foreign corporations, predominantly American, into the country to gain control of Iraqi oil.

Tony Snow, the White House press secretary, was now insisting that talk of a troop withdrawal was premature, that the surge was still at 'a very early stage'. Similarly, spokesman Tony Fratto commented: 'It shouldn't come as any surprise that we here in the Administration . . . are thinking what happens after a surge. A surge, by definition, is temporary in nature . . . We want to get us to a place after the surge where we can think about how we can draw down troops going forward.'[48] On 10 July retired US Army general Jack Keane, who had helped to develop the surge strategy, denounced the idea of a 'precipitous' withdrawal:

We have obligations to the Iraqi people to not let the thugs and killers have their way with them. We changed the Iraqi regime and we bear responsibility. It seems to me that if we let our adversaries push these people off the cliff – and tens of thousands would be killed – it would show a lack of character . . . If we are going to let suicide bombers drive us out of Iraq, we have got real problems as a country in this world.'[49]

He added that the fear in Washington 'is palpable in terms of what this [war] means to specific political careers'.[50]

In some American media reports the White House was in 'panic mode' over Iraq,[51] with administration officials repeating their denial that George Bush was considering a troop withdrawal. In response, *ABC World News* said that White House officials were 'extremely worried', with one unnamed spokesman also referring to 'panic mode'. Senior Pentagon officials were reportedly trying to determine what conditions must exist in Iraq short of outright victory to begin pulling troops out of Iraq without signalling that the US military had been effectively defeated. The White House continued to deny that such a debate was taking place but there was no doubt that support in the administration for the war was weakening. According to the *Washington Post* the President had rejected calls to change course but would soon announce plans to draw down troops in 2008 'and move towards a more limited mission if security conditions improve'.[52] In the same vein *NBC Nightly News* reported: 'There are signs and signals and indications that a turning point may be nearing on US involvement in the Iraq War,' but the White House was denying that anything had changed. In Baghdad the US ambassador, Ryan Crocker, echoing Zebari, was saying that the departure of American troops could lead to sharply increased violence, the deaths of thousands and a regional conflict that could draw in neighbouring countries.

It was predicted that a progress report soon to be delivered in Congress would conclude that the Iraqi government had not met any of its targets for political, economic and other reforms. As a result, on 15 July the *Washington Times* claimed that the 'pivot point' for addressing the administration's Iraq policy would no longer be mid-September but would come 'this week' as the soaring costs of the Afghanistan and Iraq conflicts became increasingly apparent. According to an Associated Press report citing congressional analysts, the wars were costing $12 billion a month, with the total for Iraq alone nearing $0.5 trillion. Since 9/11 Congress had appropriated $610 billion in war-related funds, roughly the same as the treasure expended on the Vietnam War.

On 9 July, quoting Senator Olympia Snowe ('the tide has turned and the President needs to understand that'), *ABC World News* said that a growing number of Republicans were now declaring that they wanted a new strategy for the war, indicating yet again that the problems for the President were rising while his support was falling, and the *Washington Post* reported that support for Bush was 'cracking'. The White House was reportedly being forced to debate whether to change its Iraq policy, whether in fact the surge was working.[53] Columnist Charles Krauthammer, appearing on Fox News's *Special Report*, said, seemingly in an attempt to boost Bush's new strategy:

> It looks as if there is a collapse on the part of Republicans. There certainly isn't on the part of the President. There are some murmurings in the White House, but he doesn't want to lose this war, and he thinks it can be won. What is really tragic about all of this is that after three years of searching for a policy that would work, we have a general and a policy that appears to be helping.

An umbrella organisation of anti-war groups, Americans Against Escalation in Iraq, was running an extensive 'robocalling project' to encourage constituents of twelve senators and fifty-two House members to press them into voting for the expected anti-war amendments. The calls included a pre-recorded message from Sergeant John Bruhns, an Iraq War veteran, insisting that it was time 'to get our troops out of this endless war'. But even now it seemed unlikely that enough Republicans would vote with the Democrats to force a withdrawal of American troops in the near future – a judgement that was widely reflected in the US media. Thus the *Weekly Standard*'s Fred Barnes, reflecting widespread opinion, said on Fox News said that even though many Republican senators were 'panicky', only 'three or four' would vote with the Democrats on a withdrawal timetable for US troops. The House Democrats were still planning to force a series of votes on Iraq that would increase the pressure on the White House and congressional Republicans to force a policy change, but it seemed unlikely that an increasingly isolated Bush and his policy advisors would respond.

The public support for the Iraq War was at a record low, according to a *USA Today*/Gallup poll, with Bush's approval rating having sunk to 29 per cent. One-fifth of Americans said that the troop surge had improved the situation in Iraq; half said it hadn't made any difference; and more than seven in ten favoured removing nearly all US troops by April 2008. However, 55 per cent said that Congress should wait until General Petraeus delivered his progress report in September before developing a new policy; 40 per cent judged that Congress should act immediately, without waiting for the September report.

On 10 July Bush, speaking in Ohio, rejected a call from Republicans for an immediate shift in policy but insisted that troops would be withdrawn when the security situation improved. More time had to be given for the surge to work but the reduction of US troops was a 'near-term' goal; 'Congress should wait for General Petraeus to give his assessment . . . Then we can work together on a way forward. I believe we can be in a different place in a while.' He suggested that American troops might be limited to securing Iraq's borders, hunting al-Qaeda and training the Iraqi forces – as the Iraq Study Group and the recent Republican defectors had demanded.[54] To add further complications, Recep Tayyip Erdoğan, the Turkish Prime Minister, was again threatening to send troops into northern Iraq to attack separatist Kurdish rebels ('We will not hesitate to take any required steps. We can take care of our own business'), and the US congressional turmoil was feeding into debate in Australia, one of Washington's main policy allies.

Thus Australia's Robert McClelland, the Labor opposition spokesman on foreign affairs, raised the possibility that Australian troops could be left 'holding the baby' in Iraq if the government failed to outline a withdrawal strategy. There were signs that congressional pressure would force Bush to withdraw some US

troops from the country and that a British government, now
headed by Gordon Brown, would be keen to accelerate its own
withdrawal agenda. McClelland also suggested that the United
Nations could be given a larger role in Iraq, a proposal denounced
by Foreign Minister Alexander Downer as contradictory to the
Labor policy that all international forces should be out of Iraq.[55]
As in Britain and the United States, a majority of the Australian
people wanted troops to be withdrawn from Iraq at once or to an
agreed timetable: recent Newspoll research revealed that more
than 60 per cent wanted the troops home either immediately, by
mid-2008 or by a date set for their withdrawal. Kevin Rudd, the
Labor leader, told reporters:

> Mr Howard [the Australian Prime Minister] has one responsibility
> today and that is to level with the Australian people as to what his exit
> strategy is from Iraq. My challenge is to all those Liberal and National
> Party backbenchers out there: what's their attitude in their
> communities to whether or not Australia needs a staged withdrawal
> strategy from Iraq?[56]

On 11 July Thomas L. Friedman, writing in the *New York Times*,
reported that the Democrats and a growing number of
Republicans were determined not to wait for the Petraeus report
for Bush to assess whether the surge was working: 'The American
people have had enough. They want out. As we move into the
endgame, though, the public needs to understand that neither
Republicans nor Democrats are presenting them with a realities
strategy.' It was obvious that Bush's policy was 'bankrupt', but a
partial withdrawal plan would not accommodate the demands for
a radical shift in course.

It would not be sustainable to leave half the troops in place –
'look at the British in Basra'. The British were slowly withdrawing
into a single base at Basra airport, leaving the void to be filled by
Shi'ite warlords, tribal clans and criminal gangs. Whenever British
troops ventured out they were being attacked, and the casualties
were mounting. Is this what a partial withdrawal would mean for
the American forces? 'Our real choices are either all in or all out',
and there were various advantages in getting out. No more

Americans would be dying; the threat of a full civil war might force the Iraqis into a political agreement; as the sectarian conflict played out it could painfully force a realignment of communities that would bring stability on a federal basis; and perhaps Washington would then be able to 'restore its deterrence with Iran'. ('We will be much freer to hit Iran – should we need to.') For these reasons Friedman declared himself in favour of setting a withdrawal plan, but accompanying it with a final UN-led diplomatic effort to get the Iraqis to reach a political settlement.[57]

At the same time Stephen Hadley, the US National Security Advisor, was being given a rough ride on Capitol Hill by several Republican senators insisting that American troops be brought home by 2008. The senators, most of whom were facing re-election, rejected the President's contention that the surge had not yet had time to work. Thomas Gingar, the chairman of the US National Intelligence Council, reported to Congress that even if the violence diminished, the Iraqi leaders would be hard pressed to achieve a sustained political reconciliation between the various warring factions: 'The struggle among and within Iraqi communities over national identity and the distribution of power has eclipsed attacks by Iraqis against the coalition forces as the greatest impediment to Iraq's future as a peaceful, democratic and unified state.'[58] Senator Snowe judged that Congress had reached 'the crossroads of hope and reality' and that a strong message should be sent on behalf of the American people that the current strategy was 'unacceptable and that we must move in a different course'; Senator Peter Dominici, another Republican defector, expressed the hope that the President would change his mind but had been given no indication that a policy shift was imminent.

On 12 July the White House, under pressure from mounting congressional criticism, released a 25-page report detailing the military and political progress in Iraq. In particular, the report found satisfactory progress in only eight of eighteen crucial benchmarks set by Congress for gauging the success of the surge strategy, and it was an easy matter to challenge the report's assessment in these areas.[59] There was little or no progress on political goals, a finding that seemed certain to increase the pressure on the Bush administration to change strategy and to start

withdrawing American troops. The Iraqi government had failed
to remove some of the restrictions on former members of the
Ba'ath Party, to enact a fair revenue-sharing formula for Iraq's oil
revenues or to prepare the ground for local elections. The report
acknowledged the levels of sectarian violence as a main reason for
lack of political progress: 'The levels of violence in 2006
undermined efforts to achieve political reconciliation by fuelling
sectarian tensions, emboldening extremists and discrediting the
coalition and Iraqi government.' It was expected that violence
would rise further over the next few months.

In response, Bush insisted that he had a winning strategy and
was sending Robert Gates and Condoleezza Rice to the region
early in August, but such moves were doing little to assuage the
anger of congressional opponents. Senator Joseph Biden, the
Democrat chairman of the Foreign Relations Committee, told
reporters that the progress report was like 'the guy who's falling
from a 100-storey building and says halfway down that
everything's fine. If we continue the way we're going . . . we're
headed for a crash landing.'[60] By now even Bush was adopting a
conciliatory tone, though not yet hinting at any change of policy:
speaking to reporters, he called the Republican dissidents 'friends
of mine' and acknowledged that the American people were war
weary: 'There is a war fatigue in America. It is affecting our
psychology. It's an ugly war.'[61] But then he commented that
Congress should not be 'running the war': any attempt 'to run a
war through resolution was a prescription for failure'.[62]

The dismal findings of the report were reinforced by other
commentary that Bush was being forced to address. According to
Bob Woodward of the *Washington Post*, the CIA director, Michael
Hayden, had told the Iraq Study Group in November that 'the
inability of the [Iraqi] government to govern seems irreversible' –
a judgement that July 2007 seemed to confirm. In addition a secret
Department of National Intelligence (DNI) assessment, *Al-Qaeda
Better Positioned to Strike the West*, concluded that al-Qaeda had
regrouped and was stronger than it had been at any time since the
9/11 attacks. According to a leak from this assessment, al-Qaeda
was stepping up its efforts to infiltrate operatives into the United
States and had rebuilt most of the capabilities needed to launch an

attack.[63] Critics were quick to point out that such developments said little for Bush's massively expensive years-long 'war on terror', and found it difficult to square his optimism with the actual situation in Iraq.

There was a growing sense, even among Iraqi politicians in Baghdad, that the Bush administration was playing its last cards. Mahmoud Othman, a veteran Iraqi legislator, commented: 'I assume that the US is going to start pulling out because 70 per cent of Americans and Congress want the troops to come home. The Americans are defeated. They haven't achieved any of their aims.'[64] On 12 July the US House of Representatives voted 223 to 201 to bring combat troops out of Iraq by 1 April 2008, despite the threat of a presidential veto. Such 'running the war' by resolution lacked the power to force a change of course but was designed to ratchet up the pressure on the White House. Rice commented that she understood people's 'concern' and 'impatience', but insisted that 'we ought to stick' to the surge strategy and wait for the September report by General Petraeus and Ambassador Crocker.

The DNI assessment report, noting that reconciliation in Iraq was being hampered by 'increasing concern among Iraqi political leaders that the United States may not have a long-term commitment', had acknowledged a sense in Iraq that the United States was on its way out. In some commentary on the report, 'vitally important failures' were being set against 'almost ludicrously trivial or meaningless successes' – a failure to reflect what ordinary Iraqis were being forced to endure every day on the street:

> The real and appalling situation on the ground . . . has been all too evident this week. Thirty bodies, the harvest of the death squads, were found on the streets of Baghdad on Wednesday . . . in addition, 20 rockets and mortar bombs were fired into the Green Zone, killing three people . . . US and British claims of success in Iraq over the past four years have a grim record of being entirely sculpted to political needs at home . . . Overall the 'surge' has already failed. It was never necessary to wait for yesterday's report or a further assessment in September . . . The occupation is unpopular and always has been . . . economic and social conditions are becoming more and more desperate . . . Oil pipelines are sabotaged by insurgents and punctured

by thieves . . . clerics have issued a fatwa against eating river fish – because the fish gorge on dead bodies floating in the Tigris.[65]

In a vain attempt to deflect some of the impact of the dismal assessment report Prime Minister al-Maliki insisted that Iraq's forces were getting ready to take over full security responsibility in the country but needed more training and equipment ('We are fully confident that we are able to take full responsibility for security any time the international forces wish to withdraw').[66] He applauded the 'positive' elements of the report but complained that it was not entirely fair:

> This [the period covered by the report] heralds a new phase in which [the Iraqi security forces] can take over the security responsibility in its entirety but they need more equipment and training. This [the failure of the report to treat all the issues in Iraq with accuracy] is normal for a complicated situation like Iraq. We cannot say that the political situation in Iraq is easy because it is the first time in our history that we have a national unity government.[67]

The Bush administration was coming under continuous pressure from a few dissident Republicans, perhaps feeding al-Maliki's doubts about America's long-term commitment to his regime. On 14 July 2007 Senators Richard Lugar and John Warner said that sectarian violence in Iraq could not be stopped 'any time soon' and probably 'cannot be controlled from the top'. In one sense this was an entirely unremarkable judgement: the White House, compelled to support the Maliki government, had long doubted its effectiveness. Lugar and Warner were now proposing that the President submit 'transition' plans by 16 October.

Already the two senior Republicans, anticipating the Petraeus report, were urging the government to prepare for change, suggesting that a troop withdrawal could begin by the end of the year. In this judgement a plan was needed for the 'transition of US combat forces from policing the civil strife or sectarian violence in Iraq' to the more narrowly defined goals of tackling terrorism, guarding borders and protecting assets and US troops. However, the Senate majority leader, Democrat Harry Reid, rejected the plan, saying that it did not insist on any implementation and recommending legislation that would require the American forces to leave by spring 2008: 'If you give this President a choice, he will stay hunkered down in Iraq for years to come'[68] – perhaps forgetting that the Bush term would expire in eighteen months. Tony Fratto, a White House spokesman, said that the new proposal would be considered but emphasised that the surge should be allowed time to succeed.

Douglas Alexander, the British International Development Secretary, used a speech in Washington to implicitly rebuke the Bush administration, saying that a country's might was 'too often measured in what [it] could destroy' and that 'in the twenty-first century, strength should be measured by what we can build together'.[69] It was hard to imagine that the tone of the speech was not approved by Prime Minister Gordon Brown, signalling a shift from the cosy Bush–Blair relationship that had so dismayed a majority of Labour voters. Some Bush administration officials were still smarting at the appointment of Lord Malloch-Brown – a former critic of President Bush – and Brown himself had used a recent radio interview to admit 'the failures at the beginning of the [Iraq] war'. Philip Gordon, of the Brookings Institution in Washington, said that the nuances of the Prime Minister's recent statements suggested 'that he is distancing himself from Mr Bush'.[70] In the same vein, Brown, in talks with UN Secretary General Ban Ki-Moon in London, assured him that though he did not rule out military action without UN approval as a last resort, he remained committed to multilateralism and working through the UN.

On 14 July Malloch-Brown, interviewed in the *Daily Telegraph*, declared that the Prime Minister and George Bush would no longer 'be joined at the hip' and that it was time for a more 'impartial' foreign policy, marking yet another criticism of the Blair years and a further distancing of the new Labour administration from the Bush regime.[71] Already officials were handling a 'heavy traffic' of calls from worried counterparts in Washington, following the Alexander speech; and it seemed that perhaps the current phase of 'distancing' had gone too far. An unnamed senior British source admitted that the speech had 'severely irritated the [Bush] administration', and Gordon Brown then asked Tom Scholar, his chief of staff, to write to all Cabinet members, emphasising the importance of the link with America and telling them that 'we will not allow people to separate us from the United States in dealing with the common challenges we face'. But no one doubted that the tone had changed: the Blair years were truly over.

The report of the independent Iraq Commission – chaired by Lord Ashdown, Baroness Jay and Lord King – recommended that British troops be withdrawn as soon as the Iraqi security forces could take over the security role in the Basra area, that the UK forces should only remain 'as long as they have a job to do'. This banal conclusion, revealed on 14 July, did no more than repeat established government policy, but the report did at least highlight the increasingly desperate plight of the British troops: 'The security situation is not improving in Basra, and UK forces on the streets are often a target for insurgents.' The current policy had 'stalled', 'has no clear end point' and 'effectively cedes decision-making to the insurgents'. The commission had concluded that there were 'no easy options left in Iraq, only painful ones', and urged the Prime Minister to launch a new diplomatic offensive, involving the UN, to restart the political process in Iraq. As far as British policy was concerned, an exit strategy was needed. There was nothing new or radical in any of the report's conclusions. The commissioners, including the three co-chairs, had simply cherry-picked from a wide range of conflicting testimonies to deliver recommendations that accorded with both government policy and their own political views. As with the congressionally approved Iraq Study Group in the US, the British Iraq Commission had produced a non-binding report that the government was free to ignore. In fact British policy was largely in line with what the commissioners had concluded.

Already the British forces in Iraq were planning to withdraw their remaining troops to the airport base in Basra in August, handing over the running of the last province they nominally controlled to an Iraqi military riddled with incompetence, corruption and sectarian allegiances. The British forces were to be cut by 500 to 5,000 from September – with the released troops scheduled for action in Afghanistan. In short the Shi'ite militias, completely outside the control of the Baghdad authorities, were taking over the Basra region: the British forces were in effect defeated.[72]

The media were constantly advertising the fact that the situation in Baghdad was quite different to that in Basra, and it was certainly true that in mid-July 2007 there were no plans for the US military that were akin to those for the British forces in southern Iraq. But if it was possible to argue that the UK troops had been defeated, there were now media observers prepared to suggest that the United States was facing a comprehensive policy failure that also amounted to defeat.

It was now being widely recognised that the White House assessment report contained several grim judgements 'that contrasted with the more upbeat public statements of President Bush, his top aides and public White House briefing materials in the past few weeks'.[73] Already Bush had been driven to admit that his earlier policy had been unsuccessful: 'It became clear that our approach in Iraq was not working. So . . . in January I announced a new way forward.'[74] But there were growing doubts that the new policy – amounting to no more than military escalation – would be any more successful. By mid-July it could be argued that the United States was 'staring at failure in Iraq'.[75] Many observers were suggesting that Bush was trapped in the politics of denial, determined to maintain his failed Iraq policies for the remainder of his term and to let his successor carry the odium of defeat. But it would be tens of thousands of Iraqis and US service personnel, not George Bush, who would pay the ultimate price.

On 12 July the Iraqi photographer Namir Noor-Eldeen and his driver, Saeed Chmagh, were killed in eastern Baghdad by a 'random American bombardment' that killed nine other people. A report issued by the al-Rashaad police station was based on witness accounts of the incident and was signed by the head of the station. One witness, Karim Shindakh, said: 'The aircraft [a US helicopter] began striking randomly and people were wounded. A Kia (minivan) arrived to take them away. They [the Americans] hit the Kia and killed . . . the two journalists.'[76] Two days later, eight people were killed in car bombings in Shi'ite districts of Baghdad, while another eight were shot dead in their beds. One survey of fifty combat veterans of the Iraq War, many bearing deep emotional and physical scars, revealed something of the impact of the conflict on Iraqi civilians.[77] A general conclusion was that the killing of Iraqi civilians was more common than the US authorities were admitting.

One American witness, medical specialist Michael Harmon, told of seeing a two-year-old child with a bullet through her leg. An IED (improvised explosive device) had gone off and 'gun-happy soldiers just started shooting anywhere . . . It might sound crazy, but she [the child] was asking me "Why?". You know, "Why do I have a bullet in my leg?".' The veterans described reckless firing when they went out on patrol. Some, for no reason, shot holes in cans of petrol being sold along the roadside and then tossed grenades into pools of gas to set them ablaze. Specialist Philip Chrystal recalled raiding between twenty and thirty homes during an eleven-month tour in Kirkuk and Hawija. In one a US soldier shot the family dog through the jaw and it was running round 'spraying blood all over the place': 'The family is sitting there, with three little children and a mom and a dad, horrified.'[78] Chrystal, in remorse, handed the family twenty dollars, but the shooting was never reported: such incidents were 'very common'.

Sergeant John Bruhns estimated he had taken part in raids of nearly a thousand Iraqi homes in the cities of Baghdad and Abu Ghraib. Typically, the soldiers would smash their way into a house at night, 'rip [the man of the house] out of bed in front of his wife . . . Then you go into a room and tear the room to shreds'; they would 'dump' sofa cushions and turn the couch upside down; 'if he has a fridge . . . you'll throw everything on the floor, and you'll take his drawers and you'll dump them . . . You'll open up his closet and you'll throw all the clothes on the floor and basically leave the house looking like a hurricane just hit it.' When, as was 'normally' the case, the soldiers found no evidence of links to the insurgency, they said: 'Sorry to disturb you. Have a nice evening.' The family had been humiliated and terrorised and their home had been destroyed. 'And then you go right next door and you do the same thing in a hundred homes.'[79] Detainees – most of whom were innocent or guilty of only minor infractions, according to the veterans – would be bound with plastic handcuffs and their heads hooded before being taken away in the night, despite the official banning of such practices after the Abu Ghraib scandal.

Specialist Josh Middleton testified that 'a lot of guys' supported the concept that, if the Iraqis did not speak English and had a darker skin, 'they're not as human as us, so we can do what we want'. A dozen soldiers and marines interviewed admitted that Iraqi culture, identity and customs were openly ridiculed in racist terms, with 'haji' used in the same derogatory way that 'gook' was used in Vietnam or 'raghead' in Afghanistan. Specialist Jeff Englehart said that Iraqis, 'or even Arabs in general', were dehumanised: 'Like it was very common for US soldiers to call them derogatory terms, like "camel jockey" or "jihad Johnny" or, you know, "sand nigger".'[80]

When columns of vehicles left their heavily fortified compounds they typically crashed through the central reservations in traffic jams, ignored traffic signals, rammed civilian vehicles off the road and swerved onto pavements, scattering pedestrians: 'Iraqi civilians, including children, were frequently run over and killed.'[81] Drivers of civilian cars were sometimes shot as a warning to other drivers to get out of the way, and soldiers often fired indiscriminately to suppress possible attacks, leaving many civilians dead and wounded. Specialist Ben Schrader, who had served in Baqubah, said he had seen this sort of behaviour 'on numerous occasions'.[82] Several veterans testified that US troops often fired into civilian crowds, planting AK-47s next to the bodies to make it seem as if the civilian dead were combatants. Thus Cavalry Scout Joe Hatcher said that 'every good cop carries a throwaway [AK-47]', ready to plant on unarmed victims ('you just drop one on 'em'). Nine of the veterans testified that they had seen civilians shot dead at checkpoints: 'Most of the time, it's a family' (Sergeant Larry Cannon). On one occasion US troops shot a woman driver in the face, killing her instantly; three little girls in the back seat were crying.

In response to a detailed list of questions submitted by Chris Hedges and Laila al-Arian, the journalists who carried out the interviews for the survey, the Pentagon referred the matter to the Multinational Force Iraq Combined Press Information Centre in Baghdad:

> Our service members are trained to protect themselves at all times . . . We adapt our TTPs [tactics, techniques or procedures] to ensure maximum combat effectiveness and safety of our troops. Hostile forces hide among the civilian populace and attack civilians and coalition forces. Coalition forces take great care to protect and minimise risks to civilians in this complex combat environment, and we investigate cases where our actions may have resulted in the injury of innocents . . . We hold our soldiers and marines to a high standard and we investigate reported improper use of force in Iraq.[83]

In this context the inevitable brutalisation of the US military was obvious: 'Instead of blaming your own command for putting you there in that situation, you start blaming the Iraqi people . . . So it's a constant psychological battle to try to, you know, keep . . . to stay humane' (Specialist Garett Reppenhagen); 'I felt there was this enormous reduction in my compassion for people. The only thing that wound up mattering is myself and the guys that I was with. And everybody else be damned' (Sergeant Ben Flanders).[84] Any idea that US policy included attempts 'to win hearts and minds' seemed more an empty slogan than any realistic process.[85]

Fortified military outposts, joint security stations, as noted, had been established in various places, including the lawless Arab Jabour region, where four such camps functioned as part of the surge strategy. Captain Dave Underwood, the senior officer at Patrol Base Whiskey One, told *The Times* that the level of resistance had been greater than expected but suggested that this was good news, showing that 'we are getting in their [al-Qaeda's] way'.[86] The theory was that such outposts would give US troops a presence in the local communities, instead of being confined to remote fortified bases, so helping them to win hearts and minds, but many soldiers were now suggesting that the mission was doomed. The American forces were being increasingly put in harm's way and this was being reflected in casualty figures. 'Surge me home,' said one soldier at Whiskey One.

★

The British forces in southern Iraq, trying to maintain the illusion
that they were not in retreat, were now suffering proportionately
greater fatalities than the US military – for the first time since the
start of the war.[87] This led the Tory MP Patrick Mercer, a former
infantry commander, to comment that this 'watershed' would
exert further pressure on politicians 'to decide just how quickly
our troops are withdrawn'.[88] In addition, large numbers of
wounded British soldiers, maimed and shell-shocked, were
returning home to a military medical system that could not cope,
had too few military surgeons and provided inadequate long-term
health care.[89]

There was growing anger in the British service community that
the Military Covenant – which pledges fair treatment for soldiers
in return for the rights they forgo – was being broken, and this led
to the foundation of the British Armed Forces Federation,
designed to campaign for an improvement in the treatment of
wounded veterans (see Chapter 8). There was now mounting
pressure on Prime Minister Brown to plan for a final troop
withdrawal from southern Iraq. Lord Ashdown had warned that
the coalition mission had been undermined by 'ridiculously'
overoptimistic aims; and Field Marshal Lord Inge, a former Chief
of the Defence Staff, had judged that both Iraq and Afghanistan
had become a 'strategic failure'. In response, Foreign Secretary
David Miliband said that he refused to 'get into the prediction
game' about when British troops would be withdrawn.[90]

In the United States an editorial in the *Pittsburgh Tribune-
Review*, owned by the billionaire Richard Mellon Scaife, called
the Bush administration's plans to stay the course in Iraq a
'prescription for American suicide':

And quite frankly, during last Thursday's news conference, when
George Bush started blathering about 'sometimes the decisions you
make and the consequences don't enable you to be loved', we had to
question his mental stability. President Bush warns that US
withdrawal would risk 'mass killings on a horrific scale'. What do we
have today, sir? If the president won't do the right thing and end this
war, then the people must. The House has voted to withdraw combat

troops from Iraq by April [2008]. *The Senate must follow suit.* Our brave
troops should take great pride that they rid Iraq of Saddam Hussein . . .
It will not be, in any way, an exercise in tail-tucking and running
[emphasis in original].[91]

On 15 July Senators John Warner and Richard Lugar demanded
that George Bush start planning for a change of course, requiring
the President to submit a plan to Congress by 16 October to begin
withdrawing combat troops early in 2008. As yet another signal of
worsening military morale, Jonathan Aponte, an American soldier
who had spent ten months in Iraq, admitted that he had paid
somebody $500 to shoot him in the leg rather than return for
another tour. In mid-July it was hard to find media comment,
even from those who had supported the 2003 invasion, that the
US/UK embroilment in Iraq was not a catastrophe; and some
pundits were worried that the disastrous invasion and occupation
would discredit the possibility of military intervention which in
other circumstances 'can be a very good thing'.[92]

The bunkered Bush and his coterie persisted in the belief that
conditions were improving in Iraq, and some American military
leaders, perhaps predictably, were keen to reject the idea of
withdrawal. Thus on 16 July Major General Rick Lynch,
launching an 8,000-troop offensive in southern Baghdad, said that
the Americans would remain in Iraq but, from his perspective, not
for political reasons: 'What they [Iraqi civilians] are worried about
is our leaving. And our answer is: "We're staying," because those
are my orders.' On the same day, coordinated bomb attacks in
Kirkuk killed more then eighty people and wounded 180 more.
In the words of one commentator, 'from Baghdad to Kirkuk, the
dead bodies show failure of the "surge"'.[93] The troop surge was
'bloodily failing across northern Iraq'; the United States was
'caught in a quagmire of its own making'.[94] Casualties were
mounting on all sides, and by now there was little doubt that US
policies had given a boost to terrorism in Iraq and elsewhere. On
17 July a declassified National Intelligence Estimate, representing
the views of sixteen US intelligence agencies, declared that the
Iraq War had helped al-Qaeda to 'raise resources and to recruit
and indoctrinate operatives, including for homeland attacks'.[95] In

the same vein Senator George Voinovich, nominally a close ally
of President Bush, bluntly expressed a widespread view that the
Bush administration had 'fucked up the war', and went on: 'The
President is a young man and should think about his legacy. He
should know that history will not be kind unless he can come up
with a plan that protects the troops and stabilises the region. I have
every reason to believe that the fur is going to start to fly, perhaps
sooner than what they may have wanted.'[96]

On the night of 17–18 July Senate Democrats staged a debate
on the Iraq War in an attempt to wear down Republicans who
refused to vote to begin bringing troops home by the autumn –
and, falling short by eight votes of the sixty needed to overcome
the filibuster, achieved nothing. Republican senator Tom Coburn
said: 'I bet I can stay up longer than they can,' and majority leader
Harry Reid retired after midnight to a camp bed set up in a room
adjacent to his office. It all meant that Bush, hanging onto
virtually all the Senate Republicans, had won the extra time he
wanted to demonstrate that the surge was succeeding. Again the
political establishment had managed to thwart the wishes of –
according to a recent Gallup poll – 71 per cent of the American
people wanting to remove 'all US troops from Iraq by April 1
[2008], except for a limited number that would be involved in
counter-terrorism efforts'.[97] It was obvious that a 'stubborn'
President, despite growing opposition from a majority of
Congress and the American people, was able to continue with his
deeply unpopular Iraq policies.[98] Already Ambassador Crocker
and various top commanders in Iraq were saying that General
Petraeus's anticipated report, scheduled for mid-September,
might have to be delayed,[99] and before long there would even be
suggestions that it was not Petraeus and Crocker who would write
the report but the White House (see Chapter 8).

In Baghdad the 32-member bloc of Iraqi MPs loyal to Muqtada
al-Sadr called off their five-week boycott of Parliament after the
government agreed to rebuild the Samarra mosque, which had
been demolished by two bombings. But the Sadrist bloc was still
maintaining its opposition to the hydrocarbon bill, perceived as
handing over Iraq's oil reserves to global corporations,[100] and the

Iraqi Accordance Front was still maintaining its boycott of the 275-member assembly. It was plain that a discordant parliament and an impotent administration were doing little to address the Iraqi people's needs for security and reconstruction.

On 18 July hundreds of protesters assembled in Baghdad's Firdos Square to press the government to improve the basic infrastructure and public services. Here Sunni, Shi'ite and secular Iraqis marched arm in arm, waving Iraqi national flags and banners urging the authorities to 'stop mocking us' and to make their key goal 'the protection of all Iraqis'. Sheikh Nihad al-Sharqawi expressed the common mood: 'Our demands are modest – we need security, electricity and water. The government has to provide these basic amenities so as to ensure the happiness of all Iraqi citizens. Otherwise, it must step down.'[101] But there seemed little reason for optimism. Ambassador Crocker was warning that the Iraqi government was unlikely to meet the benchmarks specified in the American surge plan by September; Turkish forces had begun bombing targets in northern Iraq; and seven of the most important Sunni-led insurgent organisations in Iraq were reportedly forming a public political alliance to begin negotiations in advance of an American withdrawal.[102] As one piece of positive news, some members of the lower al-Qaeda ranks, horrified at some of the atrocities being committed in their name, were reportedly becoming informants for the US military;[103] but the American casualties were continuing to mount, and more fatalities in Basra were signalling the increasing vulnerability of the British forces in southern Iraq.[104] According to Labour MPs on the Commons Defence Committee, British soldiers were going on 'nightly suicide missions', being attacked every night as they delivered supplies to the main British garrison. Kevan Jones MP said: 'We have a force surrounded like cowboys and Indians,' and the British troops were only staying in southern Iraq 'because of our relations with the US'.[105] Was this 'a price worth paying'?

On 22 July Iraqi MPs urged Parliament to take action against a US military assault on Husseiniyah, a Baghdad residential district, after air strikes had left two dozen dead, forty wounded and five houses destroyed: 'We ask the parliament to intervene to stop the military operation immediately and to ask the government to present the real reasons behind this operation and to offer rescue services and compensation for those who suffered losses.' Sheikh Waleed Kremawi, a spokesman for al-Sadr, said that the US forces were attacking civilians to force them to expel the Mahdi Army, and a Najaf Sadrist spokesman, Salah al-Obeidi, denounced US bombing that had mostly killed women and children. On 23 July a coalition of injured American war veterans filed a class-action lawsuit against the US government, charging that the Department of Veterans' Affairs (VA) had failed to provide disability benefits. The complaint stated that, unless drastic measures were instituted immediately, the results would be 'broken families, a new generation of unemployed and homeless veterans, increases in drug abuse and alcoholism and crushing burdens on the health-care delivery system'.[106]

On 23 July the Democrat presidential candidates attempted to answer a wide range of questions during a CNN/YouTube debate. The political hopefuls 'skirmished over the Iraq war', as they had done on previous occasions. Representative Dennis Kucinich of Ohio admitted that the Democrats 'had failed the people' in not being sufficiently robust in their opposition to the policies of the Bush administration; former Alaska Senator Mike Gravel said that US soldiers were dying in vain, but no other candidate would go that far; Barack Obama commented, implicitly criticising his rivals Hillary Clinton and John Edwards, who voted to give President Bush the power to make war, that 'the time to ask how we're going to get out of Iraq was before we got in'; Clinton, committing herself to nothing, said that US troops must be removed from Iraq 'safely and orderly [sic] and carefully'; and Governor Bill Richardson of New Mexico pointed out that he was the only candidate pledging to remove American forces within six months ('Our troops have become targets'), judged to be unrealistic by Senator Joseph Biden of Delaware.[107]

The same day twenty-two people were killed and dozens wounded by a suicide bomber in a market near to a children's hospital in the centre of the southern Iraqi city of al-Hilla. Most of the casualties were women and children, and the blast destroyed fifteen buildings and about twenty nearby shops. Hours later,

US–Iranian talks began in the Green Zone, involving Ambassador Ryan Crocker, the Iranian Foreign Minister, Hoshyar Zebari, and the Iranian ambassador, Hassan Kazemi-Qomi. The aim was to focus solely on the issue of Iraq's security and not on the matters of four American-Iranians currently detained in Iran or the five Iranian diplomats in custody in Iraq. Earlier talks on 28 May had made little progress and now a similar result was expected.

The *New York Times* reported that the troop surge would continue for at least another two years, but under a new strategy, the 'Joint Campaign Plan' (JCP), prepared by General Petraeus and Crocker and already given to Defense Secretary Robert Gates.[108] This was, according to US officials in Baghdad, a significant departure from expecting the Iraqis to take responsibility for their own security. Colonel Steve Boylan, the top US spokesman for Petraeus, told Al Pessin of Voice of America that he expected the new classified document, 'five months in the making and several centimetres thick', to be finalised that week: 'It doesn't really address troop levels or troop strength. This is more a conditions-based type of document, type of planning. This is the strategic, big-picture kind of planning that has to take place to give everyone else the direction they need to continue forward.'[109] According to the JCP, security would be achieved in Iraqi cities by June 2008 and throughout Iraq by a year later. Little attention was given to the mounting American fatalities in the war: by 24 July 2007 the toll of US dead and wounded had reached nearly 58,000, including nearly 30,000 killed or wounded by what the Pentagon called 'hostile' actions and more than 27,000 by 'non-hostile' causes (illness, suicide and accidents).

Gates, despite the JCP, was 'actively involved' in drawing up 'priority' contingency preparations for an American withdrawal from Iraq – as revealed in a letter to Hillary Clinton:

> You may rest assured that such planning is indeed taking place with my active involvement as well as that of senior military and civilian officials and our commanders in the field. I agree with you that planning concerning the future of US forces in Iraq – including the drawdown of those forces at the right time – is not only appropriate but essential.[110]

It seemed that, despite Bush's obduracy and the reluctance of US military commanders in the field to admit defeat, the United States was bracing itself for an early withdrawal from Iraq. Major Daniel Morgan, at Fort Leavenworth, Kansas, was reportedly analysing the lessons of the chaotic Soviet exit from Afghanistan in the late 1980s – and inevitably there were memories of the humiliating US withdrawal from Saigon. In Afghanistan the roads were choked with heavy equipment, making the demoralised Soviet troops an easy target for insurgents: 'The Soviet Army actually had to fight out of certain areas.'[111] Gary Anderson, a retired marine colonel who had conducted 'war games' prior to the 2003 invasion, had been invited back to the Pentagon to role-play US withdrawal strategies: 'They are starting to think in that direction. The Soviet scenario could certainly happen but what really worries me is the example of Vietnam.'[112]

The political and military tensions were mounting. It was easy to argue from the evidence – not least the regional strategic significance of hardened US bases throughout Iraq – that the United States intended to stay in the country for years, if not permanently. But the political pressure for a full withdrawal was swelling, and the Pentagon was clearly considering the real practicalities of an early pull-out of US troops. Admiral William Fallon, the US Middle East commander, had already commented: 'We have some really big decisions ahead of us. We have to ask ourselves if the surge is really working and what do we want to do afterward.'[113] Some 300 American towns, cities and states had now passed resolutions against the occupation of Iraq. Alderman Joe Moore, who had led the passage of anti-war resolutions in Chicago, said of the resolutions: 'We are the elected officials closest to the American people. This demand [for an end to the war] represents the will of the American people . . . Let's bring our brave men and women home.'[114]

There was ample evidence that the surge was not working. On 25 July two suicide bombers, in Mansour and Ghadeer, struck football fans in Baghdad as they were celebrating Iraq's victory in the Asian Cup semi-final (knocking out South Korea 4-3 on penalties), killing at least fifty people and wounding 136 more. On the same day the Iraq Accordance Front (IAF), which had six

Cabinet members and forty-four parliamentarians, suspended its membership of the Maliki government, again emphasising the fragility of the regime. The IAF leadership indicated that it would give Prime Minister al-Maliki a week to meet specific demands – including a security assessment for detainees who had not been charged, a commitment to human rights, disbanding the militias and the inclusion of all parties in the government – or the group would quit the Cabinet altogether. A week later the IAF said that the Maliki administration had slammed its door to reform, whereupon the government charged that the demands had amounted to blackmail and that the Sunni bloc had contributed to the situation. On 27 July American warplanes attacked targets in Karbala, killing nine people and wounding two dozen more, after US troops had been ambushed.

The Iraqi people were now facing a worsening humanitarian crisis, 'a nationwide catastrophe', according to a report jointly produced by Oxfam and a network of about eighty other aid agencies, the NGO Coordination Committee of Iraq (NCCI).[115] It was estimated that around eight million Iraqis – almost a third of the population – was in need of emergency aid. The bloody process of sectarian cleansing, displacing thousands of families, had forced many people out of the food rationing system; the social infrastructure of basic services had collapsed through conflict and deliberate sabotage; and the deteriorating security situation had heavily curtailed the efforts of the aid agencies, many of which had left the country.

Nearly half of all Iraqis were now living in 'absolute poverty'; the number of people without access to clear water had risen from 50 per cent in 2003 to 70 per cent in July 2007; more than three-quarters of the population lacked effective sanitation, causing an increase in diarrhoeal diseases; and most homes in Baghdad and other cities had only two hours of electricity a day. The report declared that children were suffering the worst, with 92 per cent showing learning difficulties because of the all-pervasive climate of fear. More than 800,000 had dropped out of school, because they had fled to refugee camps or because the schools had been bombed or were now being used to shelter the homeless.

It was estimated that around 40 per cent of Iraq's teachers, water engineers, medical staff and other professionals had left the country since the 2003 invasion. Amnesty International was now calling on the United States, Britain and other wealthy states to provide resettlement programmes for the more than two million Iraqis who had fled their homeland: the US was allowing a mere 7,000 Iraqis into their country,[116] as against the figure of more than a million Iraqi refugees in Syria and a similar number in Jordan, both relatively poor countries.

The conflict was continuing to have a catastrophic impact on coalition forces, with an escalating fatality rate and thousands of wounded being returned home from Iraq and Afghanistan to the United States and Britain to be given often inadequate treatment. Over the previous year, up to the end of July 2007, the number of British troops suffering psychiatric disorders – including post-traumatic stress, mood swings, and drink and drug problems – had doubled. Every month more than 150 members of the British armed forces who had served in Iraq were being diagnosed with mental health problems.

On 30 July Prime Minister Gordon Brown, at his first summit with George Bush at Camp David, emphasised the shared UK–US goals in Iraq (there were 'duties to discharge' and 'battles of ideas' in Iraq and Afghanistan to win) but he retained Britain's right to withdraw troops from Iraq more quickly than the Americans. He celebrated the bilateral relationship but declined to offer reciprocal personal praise to the American President, and stressed that 'whatever happens, we will make a full statement to Parliament when it returns'.[117] The message was clear. There would be no fawning public obeisance to George Bush. Perhaps the poodle years were over.

8

Rebirth of the Vietnam syndrome

By August fresh US estimates of war expenditure were gaining publicity. According to the non-partisan Congressional Budget Office (CBO) the war in Iraq could ultimately cost well over a trillion dollars, although this was less than some other estimates. It had already been estimated by Nobel laureate Joseph Stiglitz that total expenditure, including 'run-on' costs, would reach $2.3 trillion. The new figure, despite being only half the Stiglitz estimate, was at least double what had already been spent: the United States had already allocated more than $500 billion on day-to-day combat operations in Iraq, and even in the event of an immediate withdrawal of troops the American people would feel the financial impact of the war for at least a decade. Robert A. Sunshine, the budget office's assistant director for budget analysis, emphasised that the country was spending more than 10 per cent of all the government's annually appropriated funds on military activities.[1]

The CBO report considered two scenarios: one in which most US troops were withdrawn, and another in which a large contingent remained for several years. Even with the cheaper option the costs were considerable. If the United States were to reduce its troop level in Iraq to 30,000 by 2010 the government would still have to provide an extra $500 billion to sustain the military effort. Hence the anti-war protesters could legitimately ask not only what the war had cost so far but what it would inevitably cost in the years to come. Gordon England, the deputy Secretary of Defense, invited to comment on the budget office figures, replied that 'we don't have that degree of certainty' about the future costs of the war. This seemed disingenuous. Representative John Spratt, the Democrat chairman of the CBO

Committee on the Budget, said: 'The estimate was an extra-
polation from existing costs. And we've got five years of
experience, so they're . . . not building an assumption out of the
air. They're extrapolating from known costs to what future costs
are likely to be at certain force levels.'[2] In one sense the competing
estimates were a secondary matter: no one disputed that the Iraq
War and other military activities involved massive expenditure of
capital – and lives.

On 5 August the US House of Representatives voted 395-13 to
approve military expenditure of $459.6 billion in the 2008 fiscal
year, but postponed debate on items relating to the Iraq War until
later in the year. The Democrats decided not to press for amendments on the Iraq War or to limit funds for the Guantanamo prison
until September, when they expected to debate a further $140
billion of war expenditure. But the House vote had also allocated
$139 million less than George Bush had requested for building
missile defence sites in Poland and the Czech Republic, a reflection
of Democrat initiatives in the House Appropriations Committee.
There were already various signs that Bush was having to trim his
military expenditure, and that he would come under further
pressure when General David Petraeus and Ryan Crocker, the US
ambassador, delivered their September progress report.

The military expenditure of the United States included
allocations for various mercenary forces in Iraq, despite the 1989
United Nations convention comprehensively banning all
mercenary activity. Jeremy Scahill, in his book *Blackwater*,[3]
exposes the scale of US-funded mercenary activity, the extent to
which mercenary forces operate outside the law, and the role of
Christian devotion in the creation of a vast private army (Erik
Prince, Blackwater's founder, is as much a religious fundamentalist as Osama bin Laden). The war on terror and the Iraq
War have given birth to scores of American companies eagerly
seeking government contracts, but Blackwater – seeing itself as the
fifth arm of the US military (after the army, the navy, the air force
and the marine corps) – is the lead player. Already the company,
with a 7,000-acre headquarters in Moyock, North Carolina, the
largest private military facility in the world, deploys more than
2,300 private soldiers in nine countries, including the United

States; has a database of 21,000 former Special Forces troops, soldiers, and retired law enforcement agents on whom it can call at a moment's notice; and maintains a private fleet of more than twenty aircraft, including helicopter gunships and a surveillance blimp division. The company trains tens of thousands of federal and law enforcement agents a year and troops from 'friendly' foreign nations.[4]

Today Blackwater, seen by Scahill as 'a sort of Praetorian Guard' for the Bush administration's war on terror, is deeply enmeshed in the Iraq War, the source of massively lucrative contracts; and this development raises many questions – not least regarding the accountability of mercenary forces operating outside the conventional military structure, the propriety of funding groups that are banned in international law, and the reliability of 'drawdown' statistics (nominal troop reductions may disguise the 'outsourcing' of military effort to private companies, leaving the military and quasi-military presence in Iraq and elsewhere unchanged or even expanded). The White House remained determined to continue the war, despite mounting congressional and public opposition, and the reliable availability of mercenary forces made it easier for the Bush administration to hide the extent of the government war effort. But even with official and unofficial attempts to muzzle the media – for example, there were no regular broadcasts of Vietnam-type atrocities – graphic information was reaching the American people and helping to build opposition to the war.

One harrowing case concerned Joyce and Kevin Lucey, who claimed that their son Jeffrey, having served in Iraq, hanged himself after the US military refused to deal with his post-traumatic stress disorder. In May 2004 his parents committed him to a Veterans Association hospital, but he was discharged after a few days and two weeks later hanged himself from a hose in the cellar. Lying on his bed were the dog tags of two unarmed Iraqi prisoners he had said he was forced to kill. In early August 2007 two major lawsuits were filed, one of which, a class-action suit on behalf of hundreds of thousands of soldiers, accuses the Department of Veterans' Affairs (VA) of ignoring veterans' health needs and too readily denying medical care and benefits. The suit accuses the VA of conspiring with the Pentagon to avoid making payments by claiming that instances of post-traumatic stress disorder existed before service in Iraq and Afghanistan and so did not qualify for war benefits. The long waiting process meant that there were some 600,000 pending claims.

The low morale among veterans was mirrored in the active military forces and in the political posture of the Bush administration. The United States had sought Arab help for the Iraqi government from a gathering of several countries listed as recipients of an expanded US aid and weapons package, but to no avail. Thus a statement from the nine-nation meeting promised only 'to continue to support Iraq' with increased financial and political help, and to continue the opposition to terrorism. No practical proposals had been agreed, and Washington was increasingly being confronted with the failure of its Iraq policies. Even Vice-President Dick Cheney was driven to admit that he had been wrong to insist in 2005 that the insurgency was in its 'last throes': speaking on CNN's *Larry King Live*, he said: 'I think that the insurgency turned out to be more robust.'[5]

In the week ending on 1 August there had been some 482 violent deaths across Iraq, a rise of seventy fatalities on the previous week's total, with Iraqi civilians suffering both the greatest percentage rise in the number killed and the greatest total number of deaths. Iraqi officials were now claiming that more than 1,600 civilians had been killed in July, significantly more than in February when the US surge began. To add to the all-pervasive atmosphere of failure and disillusionment the Iraqi Accordance Front, the main Sunni Arab political bloc in the country announced that it was withdrawing from the government, and fuel and electricity shortages were worsening (one typical family in a Shi'ite neighbourhood in the capital saw its access to power plunge from an hour a day to ten minutes, while another monitored family continued to receive thirty minutes a day, and a third received no power for an entire week).[6]

The people of the Adhamiya district of Baghdad were receiving no power at all, and petrol queues were lengthening: seven- and eight-hour waits were reported by some people, and day-long waits were experienced by others. The prices of petrol and gas cylinders were soaring, and in some areas people were short of food: in Adhamiya, for example, delays in deliveries were being caused by Iraqi army checks on all food trucks. Oxfam and Iraqi NGOs had estimated that nearly a third of Iraq's population needed emergency aid, while the US authorities declared that corruption throughout the country was so bad that it amounted to 'a second insurgency'.[7] In the previous seven days a physio-therapist working for the Iraqi Olympic committee was killed, and bodies were found throughout the capital. The al-Yarmouk hospital, as one example, received a large number of unidentified bodies, including thirty from al-Dura, eight from the Taji district, and seven from the Amil and Bayaa districts, as well as the bodies of nine policemen.[8] A young boy was found by police, crying but unharmed, next to the bodies of his five brothers after they had been kidnapped by gunmen on their way home to the Rashaad district, to the south-west of Kirkuk. Three vehicle bombs in Baghdad killed at least seventy people and injured ninety-five others, while a roadside bomb killed three more American soldiers.

On 4 August Sergeant Lawrence Hutchins, a US marine squad leader, was convicted of murdering an Iraqi civilian in al-Hamdania while searching for a suspected insurgent to kill: when the squad could not find the suspect they kidnapped a neighbour, dragged him to a hole, shot him, and then planted a shovel and an AK-47 by the man's body to make it look as if he was planting a bomb. The defence lawyer claimed that US officers had given approval for marines to use violence in capturing and interro-gating suspects.

There were now growing signs that the United States and Britain were turning to the international community to resolve some of Iraq's political problems. On 2 August a draft resolution was sent to the UN Security Council to expand the UN mandate to promote political reconciliation and a national dialogue between sectarian and ethnic groups, as well as settling boundary disputes. It was even being suggested that certain militant groups could be reintegrated into the political process – a measure of the failure of the coalition to crush the insurgency. Sir Emyr Jones Parry,

Britain's UN ambassador, predicted an early vote on the 'straightforward' draft resolution, with observers quick to point out that the move signalled a reversal of US policy.

Washington and London continued to insist that their troops would stay in Iraq 'until the job is done', that a 'cut and run' withdrawal was off the agenda; but there were many signs of poor morale among active military personnel and Iraq veterans. The lamentable treatment of veterans in the United States was mirrored in Britain, with reports that thousands of front-line veterans from Iraq and Afghanistan were facing escalating mental health problems, alcoholism and family breakdown.[9] The Ministry of Defence said it would study such findings, reported by researchers in the *British Medical Journal* online, to better understand the mental health problems in the military; but it was clear that 'overstretch', forcing military personnel into longer terms of duty, was an important factor. Nicola Fear of King's College London, one of the researchers, said: 'We asked about problems with partners, children, financial problems and whether their families were receiving enough support . . . It could be that people aren't home long enough to adjust from military to family life.' It was found that nearly one in four of those deployed for longer than thirteen months had 'severe' alcohol problems, compared to one in ten of those in the theatre for less than five months; and in the same vein long-term veterans suffered a higher incidence of post-traumatic stress disorder. In response, opposition spokesmen noted Britain's 'massive overseas commitments' and the government's failure to share the military burden with allies.

The developments in Baghdad were giving the United States cause for increased pessimism. On 4 August Defense Secretary Robert Gates, returning from a four-day trip to the Middle East, offered a highly critical view of Iraq's political progress:

I just think that in some ways we probably all underestimated the depth of the mistrust and how difficult it would be for these guys to come together on legislation which, let's face it, is not just some kind of secondary thing. The kinds of legislation they're talking about establish the framework of Iraq for the future, so it's almost like our constitutional convention.[10]

Gates noted the resignation of six Sunni ministers from the Iraqi Cabinet, which he found 'discouraging', and said that Prime Minister Nouri al-Maliki had done nothing to meet their demands, including the disbanding of the Shi'ite militias. In addition, it was reported also that Sunni Vice-President Tariq al-Hashemi, the only Iraqi Accordance Front member remaining in the government, was on the verge of resigning. He had already declared to Ryan Crocker that the Iraqi government needed a 'political shock' to stop it from continuing to marginalise the Sunnis: 'We need these major political moves to tell everyone that what is happening is in no way tolerable. Nobody on earth or in Iraq is happy with the performance of the government.'[11]

In Baghdad, with temperatures at around 48°C, large areas of the city had been without running water for six days because the inadequate electricity supply could not provide sufficient power to run water purification and pumping stations. This situation, the most extended and widespread in recent memory, represented a further deterioration of the capital's infrastructure. Jamil Hussein, a retired army officer in north-east Baghdad, said that for two weeks his house had been receiving no water, except for two hours at night, and that the water smelled and was unclean. Two of his children had severe diarrhoea, despite attempts to boil the water before it was drunk: 'We'll have to continue drinking it because we don't have money to buy bottled water.'

Adel al-Ardawi, a spokesman for the city government, said that even with sufficient electricity 'it would take twenty-four hours for the water mains to refill so we can begin pumping to residents. And even then the water won't be clean for a time. We just don't have the electricity or fuel for our generators to keep the system flowing.' One resident in eastern Baghdad, Um Zainab, thought about the poor who were unable to buy clean water: 'This shows the weakness and the inefficiency of the government, who are good at only one thing – blaming each other for the problems we face.'

The Iraqi parliament had gone into recess without passing the US-friendly hydrocarbon law – a continuing irritant to a Washington keen to secure a notionally legal grip on Iraqi energy reserves. The adoption of the oil law was regarded by the Bush administration as an important benchmark, an indication that the political process was yielding the required results and that the military surge was working. Vice-President Cheney and the oil lobby were reportedly 'enraged' that the oil law had not been passed, with suggestions that Iraqi legislators were beginning to see the proposed legislation as a threat to the country's interests.[12] The Iraqi oil unions had held strikes against the oil law, even though this made arrests of strikers almost inevitable, and oil experts and the media were beginning to stir on the energy issue. In early August John Sweeney, president of the American Federation of Labor and Congress of Industrial Organizations, sent a letter to Prime Minister al-Maliki condemning an order by the Iraqi Oil Minister to state-owned oil companies not to recognise or deal with the Federation of Oil Unions in Iraq, an organisation that represents 26,000 of the 36,000 oil sector workers in Iraq.[13] This was not the sort of political progress that the Bush administration intended.[14]

On 7 August the activist group Labour Friends of Iraq and Iraqi democrats joined the British Trades Union Congress in urging the Maliki regime to scrap anti-union laws and to promote social dialogue in the oil sector. In a formal complaint to al-Maliki, the TUC general secretary, Brendan Barber, urged the repeal of the Saddam-era anti-union laws and called for conformity to the International Labour Organization's conventions on industrial relations. Barber commented that these matters were 'of gravest concern' to the British and international trade union movement, and that the promotion of free and democratic trade unionism and effective social dialogue were 'essential prerequisites for reconstruction'.

Now a group of British and American NGOs were suggesting that most Iraqis opposed the plans of the Bush administration to open up the oilfields to foreign penetration, but already foreign companies were active in Iraqi Kurdistan with the prospect of more investment to come. One operation was being managed by TTOPCO (the Taq Taq Operating Company), a joint venture between Genel Enerji, a Turkish firm, and Addax Petroleum, an independent exploration and development company quoted on the London and Toronto stock exchanges. Valuable deposits of high-quality crude oil had been discovered following drilling that began in May 2006, with estimates suggesting a yield of 200,000 barrels per day within five years. But these developments were adding to the tensions in the country: the contracts had been negotiated and signed by the Kurdish authorities, independently of the Maliki regime. Bill Farren-Price, deputy editor of the *Middle East Economic Survey*, commented: 'One way or another, the government in Baghdad really wants to see a resumption of a centrally controlled system. But the Kurds are saying that the constitution specifically makes it clear that regions should be responsible for bringing in investment and developing new fields.'[15]

The Bush administration, determined to see the adoption of the hydrocarbon law, also clearly intended, specific detailed policies apart, to buy time by wearing away congressional opposition in order to achieve a bipartisan approach to America's strategic posture in the Middle East. Already the leading Democrat presidential candidates were seemingly ambivalent about the troop withdrawal plans favoured by Congress, and a defeat for the Republicans in November 2008 could not be guaranteed to bring about an American withdrawal from the hardened bases and the massive embassy complex in Baghdad. Hillary Clinton was reportedly in favour of keeping between 50,000 and 75,000 US troops in Iraq for the long term, and even Barack Obama, with his stronger anti-war posture, is known to have favoured military action against Iran and Pakistan.[16] In addition the Democrats, in trying to accommodate the handful of Republican dissenters on withdrawal, were being pressured into obvious compromises which were exasperating the growing body of anti-war activists in the country. It seemed increasingly unlikely that the congressional and public majorities against the war would translate into either a total US withdrawal during the Bush presidency or an early withdrawal after the 2008 presidential elections.

In Britain the MoD, keen to suppress factual reports from the front line, was organising a fresh propaganda offensive – against children. In early August the MoD was employing an agency, Kids Connections, to write lesson plans for use in UK schools in

September as part of the Defence Dynamic Project. The organisation School Students against the War, campaigning against army recruiters being given access to schools, branded the MoD initiative 'a blatant propaganda exercise justifying the invasion and occupation of Iraq'. The 'fact sheet' produced by Kids Connections claimed: 'Over 150 healthcare facilities completed and many more are in progress. Twenty hospitals rehabilitated. Seven hundred and fifty nurses trained in maternal and health services. Immunisation programme restored in 2003.'[17] Here there was no mention of the scale of civilian casualties, the collapse of the health infrastructure, the flight of countless professionals through sectarian cleansing, Islamist terror directed at employed women and all the rest. All media enquiries addressed to Kids Connections were being redirected to the MoD.

In the United States efforts to recruit young Americans were reportedly being hampered by foul-mouthed drill sergeants accustomed to addressing their charges as 'maggot', 'worm' and worse. Now, in a desperate bid to reduce the fall-out rate among the young recruits, the tyrants of the training camp were being urged to exude 'calm authority' rather than deriding the novices. One of the instructors, worried that they were being turned into 'babysitters', told a reporter: 'If you can't handle a little bit of stress from a drill sergeant, you sure can't handle a bunch of stress from reality in Iraq.'[18] Such an issue highlighted what had long become apparent, that the US Army was being forced to examine traditional practices in order to stem the seepage of young recruits confronted with the possibility of service in an unpopular war.

It was also emerging that a form of apartheid was being practised at a US Army base four miles west of Baqubah, the capital of Diyala province. Iraqis – including interpreters who walked the same foot patrols and slept in the same tents as US troops – were ordered to use segregated bathrooms. A sign, 'US MILITARY, CONTRACTORS, CIVILIANS, ONLY!!!', in both English and Arabic, was taped to the men's latrine, and another in a dining hall warned Iraqis and 'third-country nationals' that they were allowed just one hour for breakfast, lunch or dinner, compared with the three hours given to American troops. Major Raul Marquez, a US spokesman, commented on the latrine sign: 'We are at war, and operational security and force protection are critical in this environment. We screen all our local nationals working and living in the FOB [forward operating base] . . . you can never know what's in their mind.' One interpreter, Ahmed Mohammed, denounced the latrine policy as 'racist'.[19] It was inevitable that such cultural phenomena should fuel tensions between the American and Iraqi communities.

On 4 August suspected al-Qaeda terrorists exploded five car bombs in the Karrada neighbourhood of Baghdad, a mixed city centre district formerly regarded as a peaceful enclave where the Shi'ite majority lived alongside Kurdish, Christian and Sunni neighbours. More than eighty people were killed in the blasts and many more injured as large crowds continued to celebrate the victory of the Iraqi football team in the Asian Cup. One of the bombs tore a six-foot hole in the concrete and wrecked dozens of buildings. Hisham Fadal, a supermarket owner, said: 'The explosions happened here because it is a peaceful place where Sunnis and Shias have no difference. Here people stay out every night in the streets until 11 p.m., unlike anywhere else in Baghdad or Iraq, where they don't feel safe. The terrorists want to change that.'[20] Elsewhere the murders and bombings continued, with dozens of people being kidnapped, tortured and killed or ransomed for cash payments extorted from desperate relatives.[21] On 5 August Iraqi police found sixty decomposed bodies dumped in thick grass in Baqubah, where extra US troops had been sent in an attempt to quell the violence.

The national power grid was now on the brink of collapse because of insurgent action (fifteen of seventeen power lines running into the capital sabotaged), rising demand through the summer months, the usual fuel shortages and individual provinces unplugging local power stations from the national grid in order to safeguard their own supplies. The provinces claimed that they had no choice as they were receiving little power in return for what they generated since Baghdad was making such enormous demands. Many southern provinces – such as Basra, Diwaniyah,

Nasiriyah and Babil – and some northern provinces, such as Kurdistan, had already disconnected their power plants from the national grid. According to Aziz al-Shimari, an Electricity Ministry spokesman, national power generation was only reaching half the demand, and there had been four nationwide blackouts over the previous two days. Karbala province was without power, causing the water mains to run dry in the city of Karbala, and residents were forced to consume unclean water and bad food. Hazim Obeid, a market seller, said: 'We no longer need television documentaries about the Stone Age. We are actually living in it. We are in constant danger because of the filthy water and the rotten food we are having.' The power shortages were also affecting the capacity of towns to treat sewage. In Karbala, for example, sewage was seeping above ground across nearly half the city because the trucks used to clean the septic tanks could not operate owing to fuel shortages. Iraq, with the second largest oil reserves in the world, was faced with the paradox of having to import large amounts of kerosene and other oil products. Qassim Hussein, a labourer in Karbala, said: 'The people are fed up. There is no water, no electricity, there is nothing but death.'[22]

The American death toll, as well as the Iraqi, continued to rise. On 6 August four more US soldiers were killed by a car bomb in Baghdad, bringing to nineteen the number of Americans killed in the first week of August. A British soldier died after a gun battle in Basra, bringing to 165 the number of British armed forces personnel killed in Iraq since the 2003 invasion. American commanders were warning that the insurgents would try to upstage the anticipated Petraeus report by further acts of violence. Now the US military was deploying robots armed with automatic weapons as a way of reducing the American casualty rate. Thus a US division of the British defence company QinetiQ revealed that the 3rd Infantry Division, based in the south of Baghdad, had purchased three Talon Sword robots – equipped with M240 machine guns, operated by a soldier using a laptop computer, and costing 'only' £100,000 each – for use in Baghdad. John Saitta, a consultant on the project, said: 'Anytime you use technology to take a US service member out of harm's way, it is worth every penny. These armed robots can be used as a force multiplier to augment an already significant force in the field.'[23]

It was now emerging that the US military had been extraordinarily careless in losing track of about 190,000 weapons issued to the Iraqi security forces since the 2003 invasion, many of which had certainly ended up in the hands of the insurgents. A twenty-page report published by the US Government Accountability Office (GAO) revealed a 30 per cent gap between the number of weapons issued to the Iraqi forces and records held by the US military.[24] This meant that the multinational force in Iraq responsible for training (i.e. the US military) 'cannot fully account for about 110,000 AK-47 rifles, 80,000 pistols, 135,000 items of body armor, and 115,000 helmets reported as issued to Iraqi forces as of September 22, 2005'.[25] Moreover, the failure to account for weapons had not been rectified: a GAO review of the books in January 2007 'found continuing problems with missing and incomplete records'. Another congressional investigative body, reporting in 2006, put the number of missing weapons at around a mere 114,000, quite sufficient to significantly boost insurgent operations. Moreover, it could not be assumed that weapons supplied to Iraqi forces trained by the US military would not be used against American forces. One senior Pentagon official cited the case of an Iraqi brigade trained in Fallujah that had dissolved in September 2004 and then turned its weapons against US troops.[26]

On 6 August Britain was accused of abandoning nearly 100 Iraqi interpreters to possible insurgent reprisals, in plain contradiction of the government's familiar mantra that it would honour its obligations to the Iraqi people. The government had ignored personal appeals from senior army officers in Basra to relax asylum regulations and make special provision for Iraqis whose loyal service had put their lives at risk. Already hundreds of interpreters and other Iraqi personnel employed by UK forces had been kidnapped, tortured and murdered as 'collaborators', and there was mounting evidence of an insurgent campaign to target interpreters as the British troops prepared to leave Basra.[27] On 7 August Prime Minister Gordon Brown, professing to know nothing of the British asylum policy on Iraqi interpreters, ordered an urgent review.[28]

The interpreter issue was highlighted in the context of the expected British withdrawal from Basra Palace to the airport – a clear manifestation of the coalition's failure to impose an orderly political regime on the region and evidence that the UK forces were well placed to organise an eventual airlift out of Iraq. At the same time the United States was being driven to agree negotiations with Iran about security issues, as urged in *The Iraq Study Group Report*. On 8 August America and Iran began the first substantive talks on Iraq's security situation, though the abrasive tone of the meeting suggested that little would be accomplished. Lieutenant General Raymond Odierno, the operations commander of US forces in Iraq, began by saying that Iran was responsible for three-quarters of American troop casualties in the previous month, after which officials below the rank of ambassador held talks in Nouri al-Maliki's Baghdad office. Philip Reeker, the US embassy spokesman, described the discussions as 'frank and serious', diplomatic code for a confrontational exchange that stopped short of a complete breakdown: '[The Iranians] agreed to continue the discussions at a date to be established, through regular diplomatic channels.' Iran's deputy foreign minister, Labid Abawi, determined to paint an optimistic picture, said that the encounter had been 'positive and good'.[29]

It now seemed clear that, whatever Iran's involvement, the security situation in Iraq was not improving. The Baghdad government had agreed to take action against Kurdistan Workers' Party (PKK) activities in northern Iraq in an attempt to avoid further Turkish military incursions, but the Maliki regime had little control over events in Iraqi Kurdistan and the US military was unwilling to rein back a NATO ally. It also seemed clear that the surge, despite temporary local gains, had not been accompanied by political progress, and the American posture was not being helped by British plans for withdrawal in southern Iraq. On 7 August a senior US intelligence official, commenting in the *Washington Post*, said that British commanders had allowed the Shi'ite militias loyal to Muqtada al-Sadr to take control of Basra: 'The British have basically been defeated in the south.' In the same vein Kenneth Pollack, of the Washington-based Brookings Institution, commented:

> I am assuming that the British will no longer be there. They are not there now. We have a British battle group holed up in Basra airport. I do not see what good that does except for people flying in and out. It is the wild west. Basra is out of control.[30]

The *Washington Post* report said that the 500 British troops based at Basra Palace were 'surrounded like cowboys and Indians', implying that the UK forces were now solely engaged in defensive operations. About eighty British personnel had died in Basra city, and the lowest estimate suggested that nearly 2,000 Iraqi police and civilians had been killed, with a half of all Iraqis in the south having experienced the murder or kidnapping of friends. The British government was being forced to face the grim reality that the original goal of creating a stable region was not achievable by a foreign occupation. The British were manifestly 'under siege',[31] and no longer able to accomplish enough to justify the mounting casualty rate. Already there were signs that the Bush administration intended to reduce its forces in Iraq in 2008 but Washington was becoming increasingly concerned that the so-called 'coalition of the willing' was about to lose one of its staunchest American allies. Unnamed sources close to the White House were saying that the Bush administration was worried about the political consequences of losing British troops: 'If the difference is between the British leaving at the end of the year or staying through to next year or the year after, it is a safe assumption that President Bush would prefer them to stay as long as the Americans are there.'[32] Dick Cheney was predictably warning against any early withdrawal, saying that no one could 'plead ignorance' about the consequences of 'walking away from Iraq . . . before Iraqis can defend themselves'. It was obvious that a principal American concern was that US troops would have to be sent south to fill the gap left by the fleeing British forces, further hampering American military operations in Baghdad and elsewhere.

The Bush administration continued to be frustrated at the performance of the Maliki government, forced to acknowledge

that any gains achieved by the surge were useless without
accompanying political progress in Baghdad. Al-Maliki had lost
almost half his Cabinet to boycotts and resignations after a spate of
disputes, and now four secularist ministers loyal to Iyad Allawi
were announcing their withdrawal from the government. In
recent weeks seventeen ministers had walked out, tendering their
resignations or refusing to attend Cabinet meetings, making it
impossible for al-Maliki to demonstrate progress in reconciling
the sectarian divisions in the country. Speaking in Turkey, al-
Maliki denounced the withdrawals as 'irresponsible . . . a sign of
their lack of credibility and lack of sincerity in the political
process, or a sign of a different agenda which is contrary to the
political agenda that we currently have' – language that seemed
sure to consolidate the political divisions in the Baghdad regime.
This meant that the Maliki administration, lacking any ministers
with Sunni affiliations, could no longer pretend to be the national
unity government that was so essential to US propaganda. An
unnamed Western diplomat commented: 'It's a big challenge to
the [Iraqi] government . . . a moment of truth for how they might
handle this particular problem.' Kamsal al-Deen al-Qasem, a
professor of politics at Baghdad University, judged that Allawi's
political group and the Sunni Accordance Front were taking
advantage of the government's weakness to ensure the collapse of
the administration: the withdrawals were 'the standard means' of
achieving such an objective.

The Iraqi people, rarely mentioned in the deliberations of the
mighty, were continuing to suffer. On 5 August the Association
of Muslim Scholars in Iraq reported that the US military had
conducted early-morning ground attacks and air raids on districts
in Doluia, leaving women and children dead and thirty-five
people wounded; on 9 August the *Washington Post* reported that
the US military had launched a two-pronged attack on a Shi'ite
district, killing seventeen people including women and children;
and on 11 August Voices of Iraq reported that eight electricity
workers had been killed and two others wounded when a US
aircraft fired at their vehicle in the al-Jalisiya neighbourhood of
Samarra. Other items, listed with documentation by Iraq

Occupation Focus, included: an American soldier convicted of the rape and murder of an Iraqi teenager; a US officer telling a soldier to 'finish off' an injured man; an American soldier given a mere reprimand, with no reduction in rank, for beating up an Iraqi detainee with a baseball bat and then lying about it; thousands of rare books and manuscripts in peril after Iraq's national library and archive was occupied by the Iraqi security forces; Iraqi gays targeted by militias and police; the number of Iraqi detainees held in American facilities up to around 25,000 as a result of the surge; and record profits for such US arms manufacturers as Northrop Grumman, General Dynamics and Lockheed as a result of the Iraq War.[33]

On 8 August reports revealed that Total and Chevron, two of the world's largest oil companies, had signed an agreement to work together on projects in Iraq with particular focus on Majnoon, the fourth-biggest oilfield in the country. The deal made with Iraqi officials was judged to be less lucrative to the multinationals than the terms enshrined in the controversial hydrocarbon bill, but the agreement was designed to give the companies a foothold for other deals. Already such companies as BP, Shell and ExxonMobil had a presence in Iraq, with the imminent legislation likely to expand their activities despite mounting Iraqi opposition. A national poll had revealed that two-thirds of Iraqis, independent of ethnic or sectarian allegiance, opposed the plans to open the country's oilfields to foreign investment; and most Iraqis felt that they had been kept in the dark about the oil plans. Hussein Shahrastani, Iraq's oil minister, had banned Iraqi trade unions from participating in any official discussions about the oil law 'since these unions have no legal status to work in the state sector'.[34] Oil companies involved in shaping the hydrocarbon law, independent of any Iraqi parliamentary input, included Chevron, ExxonMobil, Conoco-Phillips, Marathon, BP and Shell.[35]

The United States and Britain were now moving to transfer some of their problems to the UN – a policy previously bitterly resisted by Washington but now adopted in desperation. Little publicity was given to a unanimous vote by the UN staff association, representing 6,000 people in New York and 18,000 personnel involved in peacekeeping and other operations overseas, that the UN should *not* expand its role in Iraq. The staff association even went further, demanding that existing staff in Iraq be removed because of the high risks.[36] On 8 August the UN insisted that it would be able to find enough people to fill the new posts despite the overwhelming staff opposition to what would become Resolution 1770. *Newsday* graphically summarised the obvious contradiction: while US ambassador Zalmay Khalilzad saw the resolution 'as an important new phase in the UN's role in Iraq . . . a springboard to greater international support for Iraq's government and people', the UN staffers were vowing 'hell, no, we won't go'.[37]

Resolution 1770 was adopted by the Security Council on 10 August 2007. Like other UN resolutions it reaffirmed 'the independence, sovereignty, unity and territorial integrity of Iraq', a manifest absurdity in view of the 2003 invasion by foreign powers and the continuing occupation. The fresh resolution acknowledged that 'a democratically elected' government was now in place, despite the fact that Article 7 of the new Iraqi constitution banned the Ba'athists and other parties from standing in the elections, and it expressed 'concern' for the humanitarian plight of the Iraqi people, which was doubtless comforting for the four million refugees and the millions of dead, injured, tortured and bereaved. Resolution 1770 authorised a special representative of the UN secretary general, Ashraf Jehangir Qazi of Pakistan (due to stand down in October), and the UN Assistance Mission for Iraq to assist the Iraqi government, at its request, in various ways. But since the Maliki administration was falling apart and in any case was completely impotent for various reasons, the resolution seemed little more than an impractical wish list and US–UK window-dressing.

The UN staff in Iraq would be increased from sixty-five to ninety-five, and the Security Council planned to spend $130 million on building a fortified compound in Baghdad. The United States had offered to help with the costs – which meant, in view of Secretary General Ban Ki-Moon's pliant subservience to Washington – that any new UN headquarters in Baghdad would be little more than an obedient adjunct to the US embassy.

★

The mounting pressures on Washington because of the Iraq involvement were now having many unintended consequences. One was a curtailment of financial support for Israel to bolster it against Iran – a significant diversion of funds that caused a budget shortfall of around $500 million in Israel, forcing Prime Minister Ehud Olmert to convene an emergency Cabinet meeting. As commentators predicted austerity measures, the delay in expected American funds was beginning to affect relations between Israel and the United States.[38] The US military surge was incurring massive extra costs, as well as devastating yet more communities in Iraq and worsening the nationwide humanitarian crisis.[39]

Washington and London were succeeding in preventing graphic details of the human consequences of the war reaching the public. There had always been restrictions on media reporting of events on the ground – returning coffins, depictions of limbless and brain-damaged soldiers and the dismembered bodies of children and adults on the streets of Iraq. It was virtually impossible for independent journalists to work in the country, and the reports of 'embedded' correspondents were tightly controlled to serve the coalition's propaganda agenda. This was in marked contrast to what had happened during the Vietnam War, when public awareness of the horrors of what was being perpetrated forced an end to the conflict.[40] On 9 August the British Ministry of Defence issued guidelines to all members of the armed forces, effectively gagging soldiers from relating their thoughts and experiences in internet blogs, chat rooms and other forms of communication with the public.[41]

The aim was to ensure that all service personnel obtained authorisation before talking to the outside world in ways that might be judged unhelpful to the military authorities. The human rights lawyer Geoffrey Robertson commented that the new guidelines would contravene the Human Rights Act: 'It's increasingly important, given Britain's escalating foreign troops engagements, often in conjunction with less-disciplined forces that soldiers, officers and officials can speak frankly to the media about their engagements without having their honest briefings subject to any spin.'[42] In short, free speech should not be suborned to the needs of propaganda.

The casualties among coalition service personnel were continuing to mount: by 12 August American fatalities had reached 3,689, and with four more British soldiers killed in a week the UK armed forces were set to have lost more troops during the occupation than during the 2003 invasion. At least one senior advisor to the White House, faced with the tens of thousands of US soldiers killed or wounded and poor recruitment figures, was reportedly considering conscription: Lieutenant General Douglas Lute, President Bush's deputy security advisor, said: 'I think it makes sense to certainly consider [conscription], and I can tell you, this has always been an option on the table.'[43] Bush had said he did not favour the idea, but the floating of the idea by a senior general was regarded as a significant contribution to the growing debate about how to expand the US armed forces.

Already the White House was signalling that the surge would continue well into 2008, and the US military was aware it would need to 'plug the hole' left by the withdrawal of British troops.[44] American opinion on the surge remained bitterly divided, and an inquiry by British MPs suggested that it was likely to fail. On 12 August a report from the Foreign Affairs Committee said: 'It is too early to provide a definitive assessment of the US "surge" but it does not look likely to succeed.' But such an assessment did nothing to constrain the frequent rampages of the American armed forces. As the US military began a major new offensive, Operation Lightning Hammer (part of the countrywide Operation Phantom Strike), with a late-night air assault the grim catalogue of carnage continued. A suicide bomb killed ten people and destroyed a bridge linking Baghdad to the north; fifteen corpses identified as Sunni Arabs were found dumped on a roadway; and Imam Ali Hospital in Sadr City said that it had received three more bodies, including that of a five-year-old girl and her father, shot dead during a US raid (a bloodstained mattress showed where the girl had been killed as she slept on the roof to keep cool). On 14 August at least 175 people from the minority Yezidi sect were killed and around 200 injured when suicide bombers detonated fuel tankers near the Syrian border, yet again demonstrating that the surge was powerless to prevent planned massacres.[45]

It was now also being revealed that Italian anti-Mafia investigators, during a probe called Operation Parabellum, had uncovered a shipment of 105,000 rifles to Iraq of which the American high command was unaware. The order had been made by the Iraqi Interior Ministry without informing the Americans, even though the US military expected to be told of any such shipment. In response, Lieutenant Colonel Daniel Williams of the Multi-National Security Transition Command – Iraq said that the ministry had not reported that they were making arms purchases. A spokesman for the Interior Ministry insisted that the weapons were intended mainly for the Iraqi police in Anbar province, but the irregular nature of the purchase indicated that the arms were intended for the militias.

Again there were signs that the burdens of the war were eroding morale in the coalition forces. The journalist Peter Beaumont described the state of American soldiers forced to endure an unwinnable conflict:

> The Americans he [Lieutenant Clay Hanna, looking 'sick and white'] commands, like the other men at Sullivan – a combat outpost in Zafraniya, south east Baghdad – hit their cots when they get in from operations. But even when they wake up there is something tired and groggy about them . . . It is an exhaustion that accumulates over the patrols and the rotations, over the multiple deployments, until it all joins up, wiping out any memory of leave or time at home . . . A whole army is exhausted and worn out . . . 'We are just keeping people in theatre who are exhausted,' says a soldier . . . They are not supposed to talk like this . . . Another . . . adds bitterly: 'We should just be allowed to tell the media what is happening here. Let them know that people are worn out . . . We've become no more than numbers now.'[46]

The wars in Iraq and Afghanistan had also led to the destruction or wearing out of 40 per cent of the US Army's equipment, totalling around $212 billion.[47] This was one of the factors that led Joseph Stiglitz to predict the total cost of the war, including replacing army equipment, at $2.3 trillion.

Morale was also being affected by the inadequate attention being given to US and UK war veterans, already noted. In mid-August 2007 there was growing anger in the British service community that the so-called Military Covenant, which says that soldiers should always be given fair treatment in return for their sacrifices, was not being upheld. Thus the newly founded British Armed Forces Federation declared that the covenant was 'now a dead letter'; and the British Legion, known for its welfare work for veterans, announced that it would launch a campaign to force the government to observe the covenant by providing the armed forces and their families with proper care, in return for asking them to make 'the ultimate sacrifice for their country'. According to the legion there was a 'growing sense of disillusionment among service personnel and veterans about their treatment by the state'.[48]

There was now growing speculation about the likely contents of the Petraeus report, and already some of his thoughts were being reported. On 15 August the general disclosed that he would recommend force reductions by the summer of 2008 but cautioned against a large troop withdrawal. The US footprint, he said, would have to be 'a good bit smaller by next summer' but the surge would continue in order to protect 'the gains we have fought so hard to achieve':

> We know that the surge has to come to an end, there's no question about that. I think that everyone understands that by about a year or so from now we've got to be a good bit smaller than we are right now. The question is how do you do that . . . We are not at all satisfied where we are right now. We have made some progress but again there's still a lot of hard work to be done against the different extremist elements that threaten the new Iraq.[49]

General Petraeus and his staff were 'trying to do the battlefield geometry right now' as he prepared his recommendations. He highlighted the 'very significant development' that the Sunni tribesmen of Anbar province had become involved in the battle against the al-Qaeda terrorists ('You have to pinch yourself to make sure this is real') – which had led the US military to begin arming some of the former insurgent factions. The American forces were now reportedly paying Sunni insurgents hundreds of thousands of dollars in cash to switch sides and help them fight al-Qaeda.[50] This in turn had alarmed the Shi'ite supporters of the Maliki regime, since they feared that the Sunni forces would now be equipped with American arms and cash to use against them in the continuing civil strife.

It now seemed clear that Petraeus, clearly aware of congressional and public opposition to the surge, quite apart from any incidental Iraqi opinions, was responding to the 'worn-out' state of the US military and the logistical difficulties of maintaining adequate equipment in the years-long war.[51] It seemed equally clear that Petraeus – in effect reporting on his own military competence – had an interest in demonstrating the success of the surge, with George Bush determined to prove to Congress and the American people that his policies were working. On 19 August the broadcaster John Simpson, speaking on BBC Radio 4's *Today* programme, suggested that in fact the White House would write the Petraeus report, a theme that was taken up in other commentary in the days that followed. On 16 August the White House was denying reports that the Bush administration intended to hear the Petraeus–Crocker testimonies in secret.

On the same day Peter Galbraith wrote in the *New York Review of Books* that the Iraq War was lost: 'Bush and his band of backers won't admit that – but their strategy is already defined by the specter of American defeat.' On the same day the Pentagon published a report showing that the number of suicides among US troops in Iraq and Afghanistan was at its highest level since the 1991 Gulf War.[52] The longer and more frequent deployments were adding to the strain on US forces, resulting in a jump of more than 30 per cent in the number of suicides in combat zones. Post-traumatic stress disorder was given as a principal reason, as well as the break-up of relationships and financial worries.

The possibility of an American defeat, however unlikely, was being mirrored in the predicament of the UK forces in southern Iraq. By mid-August 2007 more British troops (thirty-six) had died compared with the twenty-two killed in 2003, the year of the invasion, when there were nearly ten times as many British forces

in the country. General Sir Richard Dannatt, head of the British
Army, had said in 2006 that 'we should get ourselves out
sometime because our presence exacerbates the security problem';
and Clare Spencer, head of the Middle East programme at the
Chatham House think tank, voiced a common perception: 'There
is a head of steam building up [asking] what exactly are we in there
for.' Ninety per cent of the attacks in the Basra region were
targeted against British troops, and the Iraqi forces were unable to
prevent such insurgent activity. Brigadier Chris Hughes,
responsible for military commitments, had recently testified
before the Commons Defence Committee, quoting an Iraqi
general as saying that some police officers were 'totally
incompetent' and pointing out that it had been 'a long time since
anybody has talked about victory in Iraq'.[53] Hughes emphasised
that the army did not want to talk about 'defeat' or 'cut and run'.

The political posture of the British government rested on the
notion of a planned handover to Iraqi forces – despite their
incompetence, corruption and clear commitments to sectarian
factions. Three weeks before, Sir Jock Stirrup, Chief of the
Defence Staff, had commented on a BBC programme:

We are very close to being able to hand over Basra in my judgement.
Just when we will reach that point is at the moment uncertain but I
am fairly confident it'll be in the second half of the year [2007]. Our
mission was not to make the place look somewhere green and
peaceful.

Nor was there any prospect of a British 'surge', if only to cover a
withdrawal from Basra Palace. Colonel Christopher Langton of
the International Institute for Strategic Studies commented: 'We
don't have the troops to do that.'[54]

Already General Petraeus, scheduled with Ambassador Crocker to
report to Congress in September, was facing criticism in the
United States – to the point that some observers, including one
retired general, were privately calling him 'General Betraeus'.
Critics were suggesting that he was too ambitious to deliver a
balanced report, and in any case could hardly be expected to

question his own performance. Lawrence Korb, a former defence official under President Ronald Reagan and later a senior fellow at the Washington-based Center for American Progress, regarded Petraeus as 'the most political general since General [Douglas] MacArthur', who, despite his chequered military career, had been touted as a possible President. There were suggestions also that George Bush had been hiding behind Petraeus's reputation, even going so far as to suggest that the surge was a Petraeus idea. Frederick Kagan of the American Enterprise Institute, an advocate of the surge, believed that Petraeus would deliver an honest assessment 'even if it were true that he is too ambitious'.

A poll by CNN/Opinion Research Corporation revealed that 53 per cent of Americans believed that Petraeus would try to make the situation in Iraq seem more favourable than it was; only 43 per cent said that they trusted the US commander to give an objective picture.[55] And again suspicions were raised that, despite the testimonies of Petraeus and Crocker before Congress, the report would be written by White House staff.

It was also clear that the American predicament was not being helped by what was widely perceived as an effective British defeat in southern Iraq. A British presence in the country had always been important to the White House, keen to promote the occupation as an international enterprise, with the implied corollary that US pressure had served to extend the British activity in the Basra area.[56] Stephen Biddle, a military advisor to Petraeus, said that the Iranian-backed Shi'ite militias would want to create the impression that they were forcing the British to retreat: 'They want to make it clear that they have forced the British out. This means they'll use car bombs, ambushes, RPGs [rocket-propelled grenades] . . . and there will be a number of British casualties . . . It will be a hard withdrawal . . . It will be ugly and embarrassing.'[57] He added that it was quite clear the British did not have enough troops to 'stabilise' the area: 'The south is in badly declining shape and poses some serious dilemmas for the theatre command in Baghdad.'

The prospect of a total British withdrawal was clearly causing concern in the US military. Thus one unnamed American officer commented: 'We could not afford to see southern Iraq overrun by insurgents which would threaten any future use of our main supply route from Kuwait.'[58] And by now the British were being forced to concede that they had failed in Basra. One officer accepted that 'we haven't done the best job possible' and blamed underresourcing: 'Basra is a hellhole because we do not have enough troops there to control the city. We have been left to hold the flag while politicians enjoy their holidays and wait for Bush to make a decision.'[59] Again it was being suggested that the British posture was waiting on the Washington strategists to decide what to do.

A meeting between British and American commanders called by Petraeus only served to highlight the growing tensions on war policy between London and Washington. Major General Jonathan Shaw, keen to emphasise Britain's long counter-insurgency experience in Northern Ireland, took the opportunity to suggest how the US military might operate in Baghdad. A senior US strategist was quick to point out that few American officers were in the mood to be lectured by a British commander already involved in a military retreat:

> It's insufferable, for Christ's sake. He comes on and he lectures everybody in the room about how to do a counter-insurgency. The guys were just rolling their eyeballs . . . It's pretty frustrating. It would be okay if he was best in class, but now he's worst in class. Everybody else's area is getting better and his is getting worse.[60]

An American officer stressed that the US military, unlike the British, did not intend to 'cut and run'. And in the same vein Michael O'Hanlon of the Brookings Institution said: 'Basra is a mess . . . an example of what not to do.'[61] Now British officers were telling the Brown government that the UK forces could do 'nothing more' in southern Iraq and that the 5,500 British troops in the area should be withdrawn as soon as possible.[62]

On 16 August Nouri al-Maliki and President Jalal Talabani, speaking at a news conference, announced a fresh alliance of moderate Shi'ites and Kurds to try to save the crumbling government, but Sunni Vice-President Tariq al-Hashemi and his moderate Iraqi Islamic party refused to join the new grouping. Al-

Maliki and Talabani, joined by the Kurdish Massoud Barzani and the Shi'ite vice-president Adel Abdul-Mahdi, signed a three-page agreement to define the new accord. The Prime Minister, now leading an essentially Shi'ite administration, said the move was 'a first step. It is not final and the door is still open for all who agree with us on the need to push the political process forward.' Few observers were optimistic that the new alliance would make significant political progress.

The sectarian war was continuing and al-Qaeda attacks were undiminished. A *USA Today* report (13 August), possibly preparing the ground for the Petraeus report, said that al-Qaeda attacks had massively declined, but further scrutiny seemed to undermine this claim. The Brookings Institution's Iraq Index, which tracks military and political developments, provides a count of multiple fatality bombings and casualties from such attacks. This showed a slight decline in bombings, but nothing close to the 50 per cent being claimed by the US command, and July's total was slightly higher than the previous two months. There was a slight increase in the use of vehicle bombs from March to July; civilian deaths had declined slightly; and US and Iraqi forces fatalities had increased. Moreover, according to the Index, multiple fatality bombings targeting civilians were higher in July than in the previous two months.

As always, there were many different estimates of civilian deaths. The Associated Press reported at least 2,024 violent deaths in July,[63] while the Iraqi government reported 1,652 fatalities[64] – still a significant increase from the previous month. In addition, Leila Fadel of McClatchy Newspapers commented:

> US officials say the number of civilian casualties in the Iraqi capital is down 50 per cent. But US officials declined to provide specific numbers, and statistics gathered by McClatchy Newspapers don't support the claim . . . No pattern of improvement is discernible for violence during the five months of the surge. In January, the last full month before the surge began, 438 people were killed in the capital in bombings. In February, that number jumped to 520. It declined in March to 323, but jumped again in April, to 414.[65]

The US military had an obvious interest in indicating progress, but much of the available information seemed to contradict what everyone assumed would be a highly optimistic Petraeus report.

In addition, Pentagon auditors were struggling to get to grips with the scale of financial corruption in Iraq. The expenditure of $4 billion on reconstruction contracts was being scrutinised, and already more than two dozen people involved in illegal activities had been charged or convicted. Between September 2006 and February 2007 some $35 million worth of corruption had occurred within ministries headed by senior Iraqi Cabinet members, and over the same period almost fifty investigations and prosecutions had been cancelled by Iraq's Commission on Public Integrity.[66] It appeared that vast funds had disappeared in a black hole of carelessness, theft, bribery and corruption.

In Puerto Rico, where the United States disbursed $1.88 billion in education finance in 2007, all schools receiving American funding were required under the terms of the No Child Left Behind Act of 2001 to provide their students' names, addresses and phone numbers to the US Department of Defense (DOD), with the assumption that this would provide a reliable recruitment source. In response, political activists were handing out opt-out forms emblazoned with the slogan 'Our youth should not go to war'. Juan Dalmau, secretary general of the Puerto Rican Independence Party, considered that it was important to save the island's children from becoming 'colonial cannon meat'.[67]

We should not be surprised in this context that the DOD was trying to recruit in the poorest American communities. Thus the National Priorities Project, a Massachusetts research group, found that nearly two-thirds of all military recruits were from zip code areas with average household incomes below the US median.[68] The Pentagon was finding it fruitful to recruit the poor, who had fewer employment options, for service in Iraq, as had happened for the Vietnam War and many other conflicts.[69]

On 18 August the Republicans defeated a Democrat proposal in the Senate (by fifty-two votes to forty-seven) that would have required the United States to start bringing troops home within 120 days and to complete the pullout by June 2008. The bill would have allowed a small number of troops to remain in Iraq to conduct a narrow set of missions, but the senators had no stomach for setting a clear timeline. Opposition to the war was being maintained by various activist groups – for example, Americans against Escalation in Iraq (AAEI), a broad coalition of advocacy organisations and political action committees from across the political spectrum.[70]

In Iraq the grim catalogue of suffering continued unabated. Samarra was under curfew after the Iraqi police called in US air support to bomb suspected insurgents. Elsewhere, according to the Iraqi Interior Ministry, at least ten civilians, including women and children, were killed and fifteen wounded when US troops backed by helicopters tried to arrest 'several wanted persons'; Nasser al-Rubaie, head of a parliamentary bloc loyal to Muqtada al-Sadr, claimed that the US assault had killed 'twenty civilians, including women, children and elderly', and injured 'tens more, some in critical condition' (the bodies of women were among those delivered to the local morgue). Other civilians were killed by American forces in the town of al-Bu Abdi, 20 miles north of Baqubah city, and in the district of Khalis, also north of Baqubah. A witness told Voices of Iraq that US soldiers had opened fire on demonstrators, killing six and wounding five others, who were rushed to the local hospital. On 17 August 2007 American aircraft bombed the Muhammad al-Amin mosque in Tarimiyah district while US troops broke down doors and smashed furniture in the Anas bin Malek secondary school, at the time holding a social event.[71]

On 18 August *The Independent* reported a mounting humanitarian crisis in Iraq with the mass exodus of medical staff fleeing chronic violence; Oxfam reported that the lack of doctors and nurses had pushed the health system to the brink of collapse. Nearly a third of children were being born underweight, and nearly half of all Iraqis suffered 'absolute poverty' following the 2003 invasion. Of the four million dependent on food aid, only 60 per cent had access to the government-run distribution system – a dramatic decline from 96 per cent three years before. On 26 August IRIN reported that the power supply situation was steadily deteriorating and that millions of people were getting less than three hours of power a day, resulting in severe dehydration for many people in the intense summer heat. Price inflation on basic foodstuffs (baby formula, Vietnamese rice, vegetable ghee etc.) was rampant, further affecting nutrition and health.

On 24 August the *International Herald Tribune* reported that the number of Iraqi detainees held by the Americans had increased by 50 per cent during the period of the surge, with the inmate population swelling to 24,500; about 800 juveniles were being held in the American internment facilities. Six days later, a 55-year-old mother, Saadiya from the Abu Ghraib area of Baghdad told Inter Press Service (IPS): 'My three sons were selling vegetables in Baghdad when Americans took them away over a year ago. We learned three months ago that they were taken to Bucca prison. They were only farmers.' In the same vein Farhan Abbas told IPS that a force from the Interior Ministry had abducted forty-five men from their village and he did not know their whereabouts: 'When we went to the ministry to ask about them, they told us to get lost or else they would arrest us too.' In addition, Iranian forces had begun shelling mountain villages on the Iraqi side of the border as an attack on Kurdish guerrillas, adding to the all-pervasive sense of instability and tension.[72]

In the face of such conditions the Maliki regime seemed largely powerless, with the government struggling to address the basic security problems. On 19 August nearly 500 guards were removed from their posts at the Ministry of Culture in an attempt to purge sectarian influence. Most of the 170,000 gunmen, many of them with allegiances to the militias and death squads, hired to protect official buildings and installations, lacked training and had not been vetted for their loyalty to the Maliki regime. The Ministry of Health, dominated by Sadr loyalists, had been accused of hiring members of the Mahdi Army; and the Ministry of Culture, under the control of a Sunni minister, was suspected of hiring Sunni insurgents to work as security guards.

In southern Iraq the rocket attacks on the British troops sheltering at the Basra air base, many of them living under canvas, had increased considerably. One officer, aware that more than 450 rockets had rained down in the last three months, said that all people could do was to put on their body armour and helmets and 'pray' they were not hit. An RAF officer commented: 'The situation is far worse than is being portrayed back home. We have no hard cover in most accommodation so people are just relying on luck to stay alive.'[73] One military source said that the Mahdi Army, attempting to claim credit for 'drumming' the British out of the region, was intensifying the pressure on the UK forces. Three RAF regiment men were killed in July while off duty, and two RAF airmen were wounded when they were driving out in the open. Major Mike Shearer, the British military spokesman in Basra, tried to strike a comforting note: 'Accommodation protection is constantly being improved . . . However, it must be recognised that it is impossible to completely mitigate against all threats.'[74]

In early August Khalil Jalil Hamza, the governor of Qadissiyah province, and police chief Major General Khalid Hassan were killed in a roadside attack while returning to the provincial capital of Diwaniyah after attending a funeral for a tribal sheikh. On 19 August Mohammed Ali al-Hassani, the governor of Muthanna province, an area praised by George Bush in his weekly radio broadcast for its political progress, was blown up by a roadside bomb – the second southern governor to be killed in less than a fortnight. In Basra the various militias were vying for power, and certain areas had become no-go zones. The presence of the British troops was an irrelevance, except in so far as it exacerbated the levels of tension and violence in the region. On 20 August Muqtada al-Sadr commented:

> The British have given up and they know they will be leaving Iraq soon. They are retreating because of the resistance they have faced. Without that, they would have stayed much longer, there is no doubt. The British have realised this is not a war they should be fighting or one they can win.[75]

It was hard to avoid the conclusion that the British forces were in retreat. Lindsey German, of the London-based Stop the War Coalition, noted the 'truth' that the British troops in Iraq had been defeated, and said that they were only there to save face and to shore up the US occupation.

*

There was mounting criticism of Prime Minister al-Maliki in the United States – to the point that some senators were demanding his removal. On 20 August senators Carl Levin, the chairman of the Senate Armed Services Committee, and John Warner, a former Secretary of the Navy, completed a two-day tour of Iraq and then said that al-Maliki should be voted from office. In a joint statement they declared that in the view of politicians in Washington and the American people 'time has run out' on attempts to forge a political consensus in Baghdad, and that the stalemate could be blamed on al-Maliki and other officials who were unable to operate independently of religious and sectarian leaders. Levin said: 'I've concluded that this is a government which cannot . . . achieve a political settlement. It is too bound to its own sectarian roots, and it is too tied to forces in Iraq, which do not yield themselves to compromise.' The Iraqi government had 'totally and utterly failed' to produce a team able to forge national unity.

Warner, while not calling for the removal of al-Maliki, declared that they were not optimistic about whether the Iraqi government could make the necessary compromises to achieve political progress.[76] Other senators, including Hillary Clinton, were also demanding a change of leadership in Baghdad. And on 21 August Bush, speaking at a trade summit in Canada, conceded his dissatisfaction with the Maliki government: 'There's a certain level of frustration with the leadership in general. The fundamental question is, will the government respond to the demands of the people? And [if not], they will replace the government. That's up to the Iraqis to make that decision, not American politicians.'[77] Again it was being emphasised that al-Maliki was beholden to Shi'ite factions and unable to achieve any effective sectarian reconciliation and a national government.[78]

Al-Maliki, understandably alarmed at what seemed to be an ebbing of support in Washington, blamed the presidential election campaign for many of the 'discourteous' comments. Speaking at the end of a visit to Syria, he declared that Iraq would pay no attention to such criticisms and could rely on other friends: 'No one has the right to place timetables on the Iraq government. It was elected by its people. Those who make such statements are bothered by our visit to Syria. We will pay no attention. We care for our people and our constitution and can find friends elsewhere' – so seemingly confirming American suspicions that the Maliki regime was not taking the necessary steps to prevent terrorist infiltration from Syria and other states, and to pursue policies that were not being shaped in Tehran.[79]

Events on the ground were scarcely encouraging. Fourteen US soldiers had died when a Black Hawk helicopter in which they were travelling crashed in northern Iraq – caused, the US military claimed, not by enemy fire but by a mechanical fault. In the northern city of Baiji at least twenty people were killed and fifty injured when a suicide bomber rammed a fuel tanker into a police station. And there seemed little hope that the Iraqi forces would be able to assume responsibility for security in the near future. Thus the American intelligence agencies, providing an updated National Intelligence Estimate, concluded that Iraq's fractured military would be 'hard-pressed' over the next twelve to eighteen months to 'execute significantly increased security responsibilities, and particularly to operate independently against Shia militias with any success'.[80]

Some Western and Kurdish observers took comfort in the fact that Saddam Hussein's cousin, Ali Hassan al-Majid ('Chemical Ali'), and fourteen others were appearing before the Iraqi High Tribunal. But many Iraqis, by now regarding Saddam's erstwhile cronies as past history, regarded the fresh trial as largely irrelevant to the current plight of the country. Washington was also happy to see a significant shift in the political posture of the French government, following the election of President Nicolas Sarkozy; the Foreign Minister, Bernard Kouchner, visited Washington to pledge support, saying: 'We want to be at the side of this large and important country [Iraq] at the birth of its democracy.'[81] But the Iraqi government, perhaps weary of Western involvement, was more circumspect. A conference of Iraqi leaders outside the country, proposed by Kouchner, was not 'necessary' (President Talabani, in an interview in *Le Monde*) and Iraq was solving its own problems: 'In Iraq, we speak to each other and we meet each other every day. Each community participates in the dialogue. We will find a way out without a conference.'[82] A few days later, the French Foreign Minister had a telephone conversation with Condoleezza Rice in which he 'told her' that al-Maliki had to be replaced: 'I don't know if that will go through though . . . it seems that President Bush is attached to Mr Maliki [Bush had called al-Maliki 'a good man, a good man with a difficult job and I support him']. But the [Iraqi] government is not functioning.'[83]

There were now further signs that the United States was unhappy with the planned British withdrawal from southern Iraq. On 22 August General Jack Keane, an architect of the surge policy, told BBC radio that Britain's 'disengagement' was a source of frustration for US military commanders: Britain had never had enough forces to 'truly protect' civilians, who were increasingly becoming prey to 'gangland warfare'; if Britain were to withdraw its remaining 5,500 troops, the situation 'will continue to deteriorate', and the answer was more US and British troops on the ground. The United States, Keane maintained, was facing up to this 'fact': 'The British army needs to grow in size to help assist in maintaining security.'[84] In fact the British military was in the grip of a personnel 'crisis' as it emerged that a substantial number of troops had left over the previous three months – to the point that there were worries that the constant strain of overseas tours could 'break' the services. Liam Fox, the shadow Defence Secretary, said: 'The government must jolt itself out of its complacency and understand the effect a worsening crisis will have on national security. The overstretch we have seen so graphically in the Army now seems to be afflicting the other services.'[85] As with the United States, and in particular the imminent Petraeus report, it seemed that British policies would be shaped in large part not by 'commitments to the Iraqi people and the international community' but by a growing perception of the ravaged state of a weary army.

On 23 August George Bush, perhaps in desperation, used one of the most dreaded words in the American lexicon – *Vietnam*[86] – to argue that the chaos in south-east Asia after the US military withdrawal was one of the reasons why American troops should remain in Iraq:

Then, as now, people argued that the real problem was America's presence and that if we would just withdraw, the killing would end. The world would learn just how costly these misimpressions would be. In Cambodia, the Khmer Rouge began a murderous rule in which hundreds of thousands of Cambodians died by starvation, torture or execution. In Vietnam, former American allies, government workers, intellectuals and businessmen were sent off to prison camps, where tens of thousands perished.[87]

The 'unmistakable legacy of Vietnam', according to Bush, was that the price of an early American withdrawal was paid for by innocent citizens whose suffering added 'to our vocabulary new terms like "boat people", "re-education camps" and "killing fields".' No one was surprised that Bush did not mention such details as the American carpet bombing of Cambodia (the 'killing fields' began with B-52s), the lies told about it all by successive US administrations, or the role of the CIA in destabilising the Cambodian monarchy. The Khmer Rouge, later diplomatically recognised by the United States, was a direct consequence of the American intervention in south-east Asia. Nor was there mention of the millions of Asian dead, victims in their own countries of American arms: while the United States was fretting over 2,000 missing in action the Vietnamese MIAs numbered 300,000.

The Vietnam precedent had been cited many times before Bush decided to exploit that earlier catastrophic war – to the point that Donald Rumsfeld used to taunt journalists at press conferences with the words 'all together now… quagmire'. On 13 April 2004 Bush had argued that comparing the quagmire in Iraq with Vietnam would only be a disservice to the American troops. Three weeks later Lawrence Korb of the Center for American Progress cited Robert McNamara's book *In Retrospect*[88] in arguing that the Bush team was repeating the mistakes made in Vietnam (McNamara, the Secretary of Defense under Kennedy and Johnson, had helped lead the United States into the Vietnam War).[89] McNamara said that the decisions over Vietnam had been made in the tradition of the values of America: 'Yet we were wrong, terribly wrong. We owe it to future generations to explain why.'[90] Alas, future generations were not listening. A more recent book, comparing the Iraq and Vietnam situations, carries the subtitle 'How **Not** to Learn from the Past' (original emphasis).[91]

It is easy to chart the similarities between the two wars. Both were launched on a big lie – the fabricated Tonkin Bay incident (Vietnam) and the mythical weapons of mass destruction (Iraq); the total pulverisation of national infrastructures; the establishment of a comprehensive torture regime – Operation Phoenix (Vietnam) and Abu Ghraib and the associated nationwide interrogation system (Iraq); the creation of puppet regimes with some notionally 'democratic' credentials; the exploitation of ethnically different enemies for depersonalisation and racist stereotyping; and US generals begging Congress for extra time 'to get the job done' – Westmoreland (1967) and Petraeus (2007). Bush had no interest in such comparisons. His main concern throughout 2007 was to emphasise what had always been apparent: apart from a few cosmetic military adjustments, he intended no US withdrawal from Iraq while he was President – if only to provide strategy advantage in the growing confrontation with Iran. It remained to be seen whether an American army under mounting stress, and public opinion, would force a change of mind.

On 23 August 2007 Senator John Warner, an erstwhile Bush ally, urged the President to begin a troop withdrawal from Iraq by Christmas: '5,000 [troops] could begin to redeploy and be home to their loved ones and families no later than Christmas of this year' – and this at a time when the recent National Intelligence Estimate had predicted that the Maliki government 'will become more precarious over the next six to 12 months'.[92] America remained deeply divided, with even some leading Democrats uncertain what posture to adopt. Hillary Clinton, speaking to veterans in Kansas City, Missouri, declared that the Bush administration had begun to change tactics in Iraq – 'and in some areas . . . it's working'; and Barack Obama, though steadfastly opposed to the war, conceded that the surge had succeeded in quelling violence in and around Baghdad. In addition, two of the Democrats' most influential strategists, Michael O'Hanlon and Kenneth Pollack of the Brookings Institution, wrote an article, 'A war we might just win', in the *New York Times* – a godsend to the

Bush administration struggling with a Democratic-controlled Congress over withdrawal. Vice-President Cheney seized on the piece as vindication, and its authors became objects of hate for some Democrats and liberal activists. No one doubted that General Petraeus would tell Congress that the new policy was working, albeit slowly, and that more time was needed. And again there were suggestions that 'White House officials will actually be writing the report, though using evaluations and analysis from Petraeus and US Ambassador to Iran Ryan Crocker'.[93]

Now, in contrast to the earlier grandiose claims that Iraq would become a democratic beacon in the region, President Bush's senior advisors were contemplating a future without democracy. What mattered above all, including democratic legitimacy, was a government that could function and guarantee security.[94] Brigadier General John Bednarek, the commander of US forces in Diyala province, told CNN: 'Democratic institutions are not necessarily the way ahead in the long-term future.' Major General Benjamin Mixon, influential in the surge strategy, wondered what the Iraqi government would look like ('Will it be a democracy? Will it not?'). And even Petraeus was admitting that the US was pursuing 'less lofty and ambitious goals than was the case at the outset'.[95] In the sense of being forced to abandon a primary objective, the United States was already defeated.

To add to the irony – and tragedy – of the situation, Saddam Hussein's Ba'ath Party, banned from the electoral process and from holding government posts, had forged a list of preconditions for direct talks with the Americans to facilitate a US withdrawal from the country. Abu Mohammad, a Ba'athist leader living in Syria, commented on the rapidly evolving situation: 'Blair made Britain a satellite for the US. Bush humiliated America and Blair humiliated Britain. If they [Britain] pull out they will break one wing of the occupation.'[96] The Ba'athists were dismissing draft legislation to ease the ban on party members from holding government jobs, saying that they would not deal with the Iraqi leadership until all foreign occupation forces had left the country. This served to highlight a central problem facing the Maliki regime – what was the sovereign legitimacy of any regulations or legislation adopted under pressure from a foreign occupation?

★

On 28 August President Bush announced in a televised speech
that he had authorised US military commanders to 'confront
Tehran's murderous activities' in Iraq. The nature of the
confrontation was not revealed, but it was clear that US–Iranian
tensions were escalating. The US military had briefly detained
more Iranians in Baghdad and there were frequent American
claims that Tehran was training and arming insurgents in the
country. Moreover, Washington was persistently representing
Iranian nuclear technology as a hazard to the region and the
world. Bush said: 'Iran has long been a source of trouble in the
region. Iran's active pursuit of technology that could lead to
nuclear weapons threatens to put a region already known for
instability and violence under the shadow of a nuclear holocaust.'[97] The President frequently claimed that security was
improving in Iraq, despite Iranian depredations, but official US
reports told a different story. Thus the 69-page report (leaked to
the *Washington Post*) by the Government Accountability Office
(GAO), the investigative arm of Congress, declared that only
three of eighteen political and security benchmarks set by the
Bush administration had been met; the number of attacks on Iraqi
civilians had remained unchanged. In addition, there was failure
to have three Iraqi brigades battle ready to operate in Baghdad,
failure to tackle sectarianism, and failure to draft a law to establish
a militia disarmament programme. The White House predictably
rejected the findings of the GAO report,[98] but there was growing
talk about the possibility of US troop withdrawals from Iraq.
General Peter Pace, chairman of the Joint Chiefs of Staff, and
General George Casey, of army administration, were reported by
Pentagon officials to be considering recommending steep troop
reductions by the end of 2008, perhaps to half of the twenty
combat brigades then in the country.[99]

British troops were now on the verge of a pullout ('within
days') from Basra Palace, their last remaining base in the city. The
Mahdi Army had reportedly overrun a police station, looting the
former provisional joint command centre and driving away
vehicles donated by the British, after the station had been handed
over to the Iraqi government;[100] it seemed likely that the same

would happen to Basra Palace. On 28 August Foreign Secretary David Miliband declared that Britain's strategy in Basra would not take its lead from Washington but would be determined by the UK's national interest – further fuelling US suspicions that Britain was about to cut and run. Prime Minister Gordon Brown was still refusing to set 'a pre-determined exit' timetable for a full pullout from Iraq, but there was speculation in Washington and elsewhere that the British government was withdrawing to the Basra air base as a prelude to an early exit from the country.[101]

There was further speculation, following a six-month ceasefire announced by Muqtada al-Sadr (after inter-Shi'ite conflict in Karbala had left more than fifty dead), that the British had negotiated with the militias to allow a trouble-free evacuation of Basra Palace. The MoD denied the charge but rumours persisted. In any event the Shi'ite rivalries continued in southern Iraq, and the violence in Baghdad was undimmed. Prime Minister al-Maliki announced some moves towards sectarian reconciliation,[102] but few people expected any significant change in the security situation. The bare statistics revealed the extent of the catastrophe that had been visited on Iraq: by July 2007 there were 1.14 million internally displaced people in the country (compared with 447,000 on 1 January 2007); two million citizens had fled the country since the 2003 invasion; some 50,000 people were fleeing their homes every month.[103]

An engineer, who would not give his name, declared of life in the capital: 'It is unbearable. It is hell, a jail in hell.' Millions of Iraqis were receiving fewer than three hours of electricity a day; they had no power for fridges, fans or air conditioners – in temperatures regularly exceeding 52°C (126°F); most of the time there was no water in the taps; and people tried to escape the heat at night by sleeping on their roofs despite the constant roar of American helicopters overhead. The engineer expressed the common view: 'Every day is worse than the day before.'[104]

9

Withdrawal: UK now, US later?

The construction of one particular building complex, on the west bank of the Tigris in Baghdad, had proceeded at an impressive pace – namely, the American embassy, officially handed over to the US government on 1 September 2007. The new embassy, the only big new building project in the capital in the previous four years, was rendered almost invisible from ground level by towering reinforced walls. Viewed from the roof of the Babylon Hotel across the river, the embassy complex appeared as two dozen dun and grey blocks set in 104 acres, approximately the size of the Vatican, and built at a cost of around $600 million – a fortress within the larger fortress of the Green Zone. At a time when the citizens of Baghdad were often struggling without electricity or clean water, the US embassy was entirely self-sufficient with its own fresh water supply, electricity plant, sewage treatment facility, maintenance shops and warehouses. In addition, the 1,000 staff would have access to a school, shopping centre, food court, swimming pool, tennis courts, basketball courts, gymnasium, cinema, beauty salon and social club. One young Iraqi commented: 'People are very angry. It's for the Americans, not for the Iraqis.'[1]

An earlier controversy had focused on how the embassy had been built with imported Filipino construction workers – in effect, slave labour. A US congressional committee had already heard charges that the First Kuwaiti General Trading & Contracting Company had enticed workers onto a plane supposedly flying to Dubai, not to Baghdad. When they landed in the Iraqi capital they were forced to work on a vast building complex, surrounded by blast walls and cut off from the rest of Baghdad, that was likened to 'the crusader castles that once dominated the Middle East'.[2] The traditional role of embassies in foreign countries had been abandoned. Here there was no attempt to encourage interaction with the host community; the intention was to protect the Americans and US-friendly staff from attacks by the indigenous population and other elements. The US diplomats ensconced in the fortress were geographically in Iraq, but they may as well have been in Washington: 'Although the US Government regularly proclaims confidence in Iraq's democratic future . . . the US has built a fortress capable of sustaining a massive long-term presence in the face of continued violence.'[3] In the same vein Edward Peck, a former US ambassador to Iraq, commented: 'The embassy is going to have a thousand people bunkered behind sandbags. I don't know how you conduct diplomacy that way.'[4]

Outside the fortress walls the carnage and destruction continued, with underreported consequences for the civilian population. Casualty figures, for both combatants and others, were generally regarded as unreliable, though much had emerged about the character of the war. A US military court had been told by Lance Corporal Sanick Dela Cruz that a colleague, Sergeant Frank Wuterich, had opened fire on five unarmed Iraqis before asking for help in covering up the killings. The prosecutors were charging that Wuterich had led marines on a killing spree that had left twenty-four civilians dead in retaliation for a bomb attack that had killed a popular comrade. Dela Cruz testified that Wuterich had told his men to kill 'everyone in the area' if the Americans were hit by a bomb.[5] It was easy to speculate that such events, most of them unreported, were commonplace.

The United States was now coming under fresh criticism – this time from a senior British officer – for the way it had handled the post-war administration of the country. General Sir Mike Jackson, the head of the British Army during the invasion of Iraq, said in his autobiography, *Soldier*, that the approach taken by Donald Rumsfeld had been 'intellectually bankrupt', and he described his claim that US forces 'don't do nation-building' as 'nonsensical'.[6] He acknowledged that the US State Department had carried out planning for the war's aftermath but said that all this preliminary

work had 'gone to waste'. In addition, Jackson charged that the
US approach to tackling global terrorism was 'inadequate' because
it relied too heavily on military power at the expense of diplomacy
and nation-building. In the same vein, Tim Cross, a retired British
major general, commented that the preparation for a post-war
Iraq had been inadequate: 'Right from the beginning we were all
very concerned about the lack of detail that had gone into the
post-war plan, and there is no doubt that Rumsfeld was at the
heart of that process.'[7] Mary Dejevsky, writing in *The Independent*,
was not the only person to wonder why these senior military
figures had not thought to mention their reservations at the time.[8]

Such comments by senior British military figures again advertised
the growing tensions between London and Washington over the
handling of the occupation. It was manifestly obvious that the
invasion and its aftermath had done nothing to improve the lives of
most Iraqi citizens or to stabilise the region. Now it was impossible
to ignore the scale of the dislocation in Iraq and the fact that the two
million Iraqi refugees in Syria and Jordan were putting immense
pressures on social infrastructures, suggesting that two further
countries in the region might become chronically unstable.[9] The
aid agencies were now complaining that the international
community was failing to address the refugee issue – in particular,
that the required financial support was not forthcoming.

Funding problems were also at the heart of the frustration being
experienced by injured British soldiers and their families,
sometimes forced to wait years for compensation. There were
more than 1,500 injured soldiers entitled to payment under the
Armed Forces Compensation scheme, and it was reckoned that
some of them would have to wait four years until their claims
were met. Liam Fox, the shadow Defence Secretary, charged that
the Service Personnel and Veterans Agency, responsible for the
payouts, was toying with the lives of Britain's 'fallen heroes' by
taking months to respond to requests for help, then offering
'inadequate' sums: 'This failure to put sufficient resources in place
. . . is an indication of how low down Gordon Brown's agenda
the armed forces come.'[10]

Perhaps it was significant also that very little publicity was being
given to the nature of the soldiers' injuries, which were sometimes

horrific, and that in consequence the public were not being exposed to what the Iraq War had come to mean for thousands of serving men and women and their families.[11] It was in response to this shielding of the public from graphic material, particularly in the United States, that the film director Brian De Palma made *Redacted*, billed as a 'fictional story inspired by true events'.[12] The film follows a group of bored American soldiers in Iraq who rape and kill a teenage girl and then slaughter her family – all based on actual events in Mahmoudiyah, south of Baghdad, when US troops raped a fourteen-year-old girl before setting her body alight and shooting dead her parents and five-year-old sister. De Palma commented:

> Unlike Vietnam, when we saw the destruction and sorrow of the people we were maiming and killing, and soldiers coming home in body bags, we see none of that in this war . . . You can find it if you look for it, but it's not in the mainstream media. The terrible thing about this war is we don't see those images, we don't have those stories. I remember picking up *Life* magazine and seeing pictures that would horrify me about the Vietnam War. We don't have those pictures in America now. The pictures are what will stop the war. If we get those pictures and stories in front of a mass audience, maybe it will do something.[13]

He 'only hoped' that the film would 'get the public incensed enough to motivate their Congressmen [*sic*] to vote against this war', adding that if the images did not exist, 'how can you be incensed?'[14] At least the screening left the audience at the Venice Film Festival 'stunned, silent and in a few cases tearful. The combination of De Palma's visceral style and the horrifying subject matter left one reviewer 'reeling'.[15]

The US military and Bush supporters in Washington continued to insist that the surge was working, that violence in Baghdad and elsewhere had been reduced, and that this was no time to desert 'our boys in harm's way'. General David Petraeus was releasing statistics to show that American policy was at last succeeding and that with more patience 'the job would be done'. Again while it was argued that ethnic killings in Baghdad were down by 75 per cent, it was acknowledged that civilian deaths were continuing to increase (from 1,653 in July to 1,773 in August).[16] The first week of September 2007 saw the symbolic reopening of Abu Nawas Street in Baghdad, formerly a favourite place for night-time socialising, where the cooking of popular *masgouf* fish dinners had been ended by car bombs. Perhaps this was a sign that normal life might eventually be restored.

But other events told a different story. Armed gangs were continuing to roam freely in Baghdad, and hundreds of bodies showing signs of torture or execution were arriving at the Baghdad mortuary every month. The Shi'ite death squads were still feared, and the Iraqi security forces were heavily infiltrated by militiamen and criminal elements. The Maliki regime, struggling to stave off a complete political collapse, seemed powerless to control the continuing violence or to make significant progress on the 'benchmarks' defined by the increasingly frustrated Bush administration. In early September the Iraqi government announced that up to 6,000 Sunni insurgents were to be freed from Iraqi jails in a last-ditch attempt to survive the strains of sectarian divisions within the Cabinet and parliament.[17] Without specific information on most of the detainees, it seemed likely that the amnesty would result in a number of committed insurgents returning to the streets. Optimists saw the move as a sign of practical reconciliation, noting also that the five main Shi'ite, Sunni and Kurdish political blocs had agreed a key accord to aid the government after fifteen months of deadlock.

As the British forces prepared to withdraw from Basra, the United States announced that it would deploy troops to the region if necessary to fill the vacuum. Brigadier General Richard Sherlock, the Pentagon's deputy director for operational planning, insisted that the US military would not allow any security advances in Basra to be squandered: 'As the UK forces reposition [i.e. retreat to Basra airfield] . . . all that will be taken into account.'[18] Reports noted a 'simmering row' between London and Washington over the planned UK withdrawal,[19] which was serious enough to prompt Defence Secretary Des Browne and Foreign Secretary

David Miliband to write a rebuttal, published in the *Washington Post*, to accusations that the British forces had failed in Basra and were not 'cutting and running': 'Recent weeks have brought a lot of misplaced criticism. It is time to set the record straight.' Now the British government was talking about the 'overwatch' role of the British troops, a responsibility that would continue when they withdrew from Basra to the airport; they would continue to train Iraqi forces and would protect themselves, responding to threats only if attacked; and they would guard US supply routes from Kuwait. And there was talk of intervening on behalf of local officials if a crisis developed, but this option was never made clear. Local officials, inevitably linked to the militias, would face crises only through outbreaks of sectarian violence, tribal rivalries and the ubiquitous activities of criminal gangs. Did the British military forces really want to take sides in sectarian or tribal disputes, or to police anarchic communities determined to expel them from the country? The British posture had become incoherent.

On 2 September, under cover of darkness, some 500 UK troops from 4th Battalion The Rifles started pulling out of Basra Palace with a view to handing over the base to Iraqi forces. This was widely regarded as the final stage before a complete withdrawal of the 5,500 British troops still in Iraq. A Ministry of Defence statement, designed to quell talk of retreat, emphasised that the pullout from Basra to the airport was a long-planned redeployment showing the success of the British mission:

> The Iraqi security forces want to take full responsibility for their own security and the handover is a step towards that goal. The decision is an Iraqi-led initiative and is part of a coalition-endorsed process, developed in consultation with the Iraqi government, and follows the successful handover of several other bases within and around the city.[20]

A senior Iraqi commander, General Mohan al-Fireji, declared that Iraqi forces were already deployed in the palace and ready to assume security responsibility in Basra.[21] On 3 September a final column of British troops left Basra city 'with flags flying and heads held high'.[22] Sheikh Hazim al-Badhadi, one of Muqtada al-Sadr's Mahdi Army commanders, said: 'They ran away from us because we killed so many of them. They were tired. All they could do was to flee for their dignity.'[23] More than two-thirds of the British public thought that the UK forces were losing the war, and more than half believed that the war was already lost.[24]

In such reportage nothing emerged about the state of the Iraqi security forces, the levels of corruption and the extent to which they were controlled by the militias. It was clear that the British withdrawal to a relatively insecure base at the airport had angered much American opinion, reinforcing the view that the 'coalition of the willing' now comprised only the United States. While Washington was struggling to portray its own surge in Baghdad as a military success the British forces were withdrawing from Iraq's second city. Tim Ripley, an analyst with *Jane's Defence Weekly*, expressed the widespread opinion that the UK departure from the palace 'widens the differences in our [the British] approach from our American allies who are continuing with their surge operations. We are retreating, the Americans are on the offensive.'[25] The US strategists reportedly had real fears about the security of southern Iraq. Vital supplies were transported through Kuwait, the tribes were already contesting access to oil resources in the region, Shi'ite factions were involved in their own low-level civil war, and criminal gangs were continuing to act with impunity. This was the shape of the success being lauded by the British government.

President George Bush was now struggling to shore up his support in Congress, stressing that the surge was providing the necessary security for political progress. But there was no sign of any such development. Senator Joseph Biden commented: 'It doesn't matter how many troops we put there. Unless you have a political settlement, when we leave we're going to leave chaos behind. You'll find you have a regional war.' And even the claims being made about the surge seemed unreliable. For every month in 2007 there were more US military fatalities than the same month in 2006; and while the Pentagon claimed that civilian casualties were down, it was not prepared to release its numbers or to explain how they were compiled. In fact, according to the Government Accountability Office, US government agencies 'differed' on whether the sectarian violence had been reduced.[26] And independent attempts to estimate civilian deaths from news reports, hospital records and other sources had not found any significant decline. On 14 September the *Los Angeles Times* reported a new survey suggesting that the death toll from the war could be more than 1.2 million.[27] The figure was derived from the British polling agency Opinion Research Business (ORB), a company with experience in more than thirty-five countries, following a survey of 1,461 adults in Iraq who were asked the question: 'How many members of your household, if any, have died as a result of the conflict in Iraq since 2003?' Based on an estimate of 4,050,597 Iraqi households, ORB concluded that a death toll of 1.2 million was a reasonable estimate.

The Bush administration was under mounting pressure to show the sort of progress that would allow American soldiers to return home. If security was improving in Iraq, as he maintained, why was it not possible to have an immediate drawdown of troops? On 3 September, on a surprise six-hour visit to Anbar province, west of Baghdad, Bush announced that troop cuts would be possible if the security gains could be spread to other parts of the country, but no one imagined that the prevailing situation in Iraq heralded any significant American withdrawal.

Throughout Iraq the carnage continued but received little attention in the mainstream Western media. On 4 September the American Civil Liberties Union released documents totalling nearly 10,000 pages, revealing crimes of torture and killing (including a drowning and a suffocation) of Iraqi civilians by US troops. On 7 September US combat helicopters and tanks bombarded the Al-Washash neighbourhood of Baghdad, in predawn raids, destroying houses and killing fourteen sleeping civilians including women and children. A resident, Abu Ali Saad, said: 'The tanks started firing, then the helicopters came. Missiles were fired from the air. Houses were destroyed. A family of five was killed in this house [referring to a neighbour's home]. We are a peaceful neighbourhood. There were no exchanges of fire. We were all sleeping.' On 11 September a US patrol opened fire on civilians in the Sinak district of the capital, killing some and wounding others. A witness told how the soldiers had suddenly started firing in all directions: 'The random fire killed many Iraqis.'[28]

Baghdad itself had been converted into a city divided by high concrete walls, barbed wire and checkpoints, with armoured columns moving through deserted streets lit by the glow of searchlights and emptied by official curfews. The capital, like much of Iraq, had been turned into a prison. People had a growing sense of isolation and fear; the monthly food rationing system, on which millions of Iraqis depended, was not working properly, with insufficient food to meet people's needs and unreliable deliveries to distribution centres; armed groups levied unofficial 'taxes' on residents with impunity; more than 14,000 employees in the Interior Ministry had been sacked for human rights abuses; cholera was spreading in northern Iraq; more than 100,000 Iraqis, mostly without charge or trial, were in jail; and the bodies continued to pile up at the Baghdad morgue.

The British had left Basra but not yet the airport outside the city. Tony Blair had said that the troops would stay 'until the job is done', but by no reckoning had this been achieved – the British mission had ended as it began: in the words of the journalist Martin Bell, 'on the basis of a falsehood'.[29] And, as noted, the public was not being told about the horrendous human costs of the whole misguided enterprise: 'If the public had an idea of the scale of [the] injuries – the many hundreds disabled in body and mind – they would have risen up in anger long ago.'[30] Presumably, UK troops would soon no longer be required to pay Blair's 'blood price',[31] but the toll of Iraqis and Americans had no end in sight. Sixteen representatives from Shi'ite and Sunni groups in Iraq had agreed a twelve-point 'road map'[32] after four days of secret talks in Finland, convened by the John W. McCormack Graduate School of Policy Studies at the University of Massachusetts. But whether this would affect events on the ground remained to be seen.

The US military was still operating in a situation in which no useful Iraqi political progress could be discerned, and fresh constitutional issues were being raised in the United States. In one analysis Mario Cuomo, the governor of New York from 1983 to 1994 and now practising law, pointed out that George Bush had been able to go to war because Congress refused to insist on the constitutional requirement (Article 1, Section 8) that it was Congress, not the President, that shall have 'the power to declare war'. Cuomo has made the interesting point that even though this provision has been ignored by 'timid Congresses since World War II' (allowing wars in Vietnam and elsewhere), it retains its significance. The congressional resolutions of 2001 and 2002 (see Chapter 10) that nominally authorised the Iraq invasion were not 'adequate substitutes for the formal declaration of war demanded by the founding fathers'.[33] In short, Bush had violated the American constitution by evading Article 1, Section 8, just as President Lyndon Johnson had violated it in waging war against Vietnam. Arguably, such derelictions were grounds for impeachment. At the same time Representative Barbara Lee, co-chair of the Congressional Progressive Caucus and a co-founder of the Out of Iraq Caucus, was continuing to urge Congress to act to force an American withdrawal from Iraq: 'Congress has the power to bring a responsible end to the Bush administration's failed policy . . . The best way for us to do that is for members of Congress to commit to only providing funds for the safe, timely and responsible redeployment of our troops from Iraq.'[34] Such an approach would be immune to the President's veto powers: Congress could simply stop funding the war.

It was obvious that Bush, hiding behind the imminent report from General Petraeus and Ambassador Ryan Crocker, was relying on enough members of Congress *not* using their appropriations powers to reverse US policy. It seemed likely that the surge would continue into 2008 and that, if necessary, US forces would be deployed in southern Iraq to compensate for a British withdrawal.[35] Petraeus was continuing to signal, only days before his congressional appearance, that some nominal rollback might be possible the following year, if only to relieve the mounting strains on US forces: 'There are limits to what our military can provide, so, my recommendations have to be informed by, not driven by, . . . the strain we have put on our military services.'[36] Hence a defeat, of sorts, was being envisaged.

But the rollback, if it occurred, would only affect the 30,000 troops of the surge: a worn-out army, with severely depleted equipment, would still be expected to seek an ill-defined and impossible victory.

In the United States the Democrats were divided on how to proceed on the Iraq issue. The leadership appeared willing to seek a compromise ('beginning to sound like a dirty word') on a with-drawal timetable, but rank-and-file members in both chambers were concerned that a bipartisan consensus might leave Bush's policy largely intact. The House Speaker, Nancy Pelosi, and the Senate majority leader, Harry Reid, knowing that their efforts to win over enough Republicans to end the war had stalled, were reportedly working for a 'position of realism'; and two leading Democrats, Carl Levin and Jack Reed, both with military experience, were considering a mandated withdrawal that lacked a completion date. It was obvious that such an option did nothing to reflect majority public opinion, and presented no problem to the Bush administration.

On 7 September Representative Lynn Woolsey, one of the founding members of the Out of Iraq Caucus, commented: 'Anything that takes us back from where we were this spring [a firm withdrawal date] is unacceptable. Bipartisanship is great only if it puts together an orderly withdrawal of the troops.'[37] The activist group Americans Against Escalation in Iraq was running anti-war advertisements in New Mexico, Minnesota, Kentucky and Maine – all aimed at targeting incumbent Republican senators. Another, the National Security Network, backed by liberal groups such as the Center for American Progress, was questioning whether the imminent Petraeus report would be an accurate assessment of the Iraq situation – an important consid-eration because the 'compromise Democrats' were assuming that the report would be broadly supportive of government policies. Representative Maxine Waters, another founder of Out of Iraq, which had more than seventy members, pointed out that there would always be some Democrats 'who will lean over backwards to believe what they hear from generals on the ground', and added: 'We're prepared to do what we have to do to avoid accepting a report that does not truthfully represent the situation on the ground.'[38] But she declined to say how she would make such a judgement. How would she know that the report was untruthful? All this meant that the Democrats were on the defensive, stymied by the prospect of a presidential veto and lacking a unified strategy to win sufficient Republican support. The shadow of Petraeus, increasingly portrayed as a Bush ally, had fallen over Washington.

The British government, facing different problems, was making desultory efforts to free itself from the baleful residue of Tony Blair. The tone was different but the Iraq policy, shaped when Gordon Brown was Chancellor, was much the same: a steady withdrawal was under way, but no completion dates were given. The new government was on the defensive but was managing to keep the Iraq question largely off the agenda, not least because Parliament was still in recess. On 6 September a cross-party group of 118 MPs took the little-publicised step of calling on the government to 'come clean' over its part in the drafting of Iraq's controversial new oil law, designed to transfer most of the country's oil from the public sector to US and British trans-nationals such as Shell and BP. Thus an early day motion, tabled by Labour MP Katy Clark, insisted that 'decisions on the Iraqi oil industry should be made by the Iraqi people without outside interference', and she pointed out that the British government had sought the views of oil companies in deciding 'the possible types of contracts that the Iraq government should offer': 'There is widespread opposition to this proposed law from within Iraq itself from Iraqi MPs, trade unions and the general public. I hope the government will take stock and look at the concerns being caused.'[39] The Iraqi people were largely opposed to the hydrocarbon bill and concerned about much else.

Civilians were still dying in their hundreds every month, in part because of the bloody effects of the surge. The journalists Martin Fletcher and Richard Mills described the treatment of soldiers and 'enemy' side by side at the 28th Combat Support Hospital inside the Green Zone. One surviving nineteen-year-old American soldier had lost all four limbs and had 70 per cent burns to what was left of his body; he was bound for Germany and from there would fly to the Brooke Army Medical Center in Texas. The officer in charge, Lieutenant Colonel Bill Costello, spoke of such 'devastating injuries' of which he had 'seen so many'.[40]

Then a helicopter delivered a blindfolded, heavily sedated Iraqi detainee from Camp Bucca in southern Iraq. The medics removed the blindfold to find that both eyeballs had been gouged from their sockets and were hanging loose. His fellow prisoners had also cut off his tongue. All four limbs had to be slit to relieve the swelling caused by extensive beating. Major Won Kim, the ophthalmologist who removed the eyeballs, noted this 'stunning degree of cruelty'.[41] Why had the man been detained? Had he been charged and tried? Why had the prison guards not exercised duty of care? Other victims were a seven-year-old boy hit in the abdomen, a two-year-old girl with a bullet in her brain, an eight-year-old boy shot in the head by a US soldier, and a 62-year-old Sunni elder with at least five bullet holes in his back. Sometimes body parts of suicide bombers were found embedded in victims. And even with such reportage little was being reported of events on the street: 'For Western publics this is a sanitised war. Iraq is too dangerous for news teams to record properly the daily shootings, bombings and executions.'[42] The horrors of the war were being hidden from the people most likely to demand political change.

It was possible, likely even, that some of the atrocities were being perpetrated by gunmen armed by the US military. The Americans had recruited and trained some 20,000 Sunni men – many of whom had fought Shi'ites, US troops and the Iraqi security forces – to police their neighbourhoods in what had been dubbed 'concerned citizen' groups. After all of three days of training, one batch of fifty new Iraqi 'policemen' graduated and were treated to a speech by US Staff Sergeant Kason Fark in which he urged them not to abuse people or to do other 'wrong things': 'Today we give you your badges, but they don't let you enter people's homes. They don't let you mistreat anybody . . . We'll be very disappointed if we see you doing wrong things, and there will be punishments.' A senior unnamed Western diplomat commented to *The Times* that there were risks in arming groups that might have a 'short-term coincidence of views and objectives but where any sustainable control and loyalty is at best questionable'.[43] The US military was admitting that some of the recruits had shady pasts but argued that the risks were worth while if the Sunnis could be enlisted to fight al-Qaeda and other terrorist groups.

Many observers, including senior US military figures, were unimpressed with such a policy, and were continuing to urge withdrawal. On 7 September the Independent Commission on the Security Forces of Iraq, a twenty-member panel chaired by retired general James Jones and comprising other retired senior military and police officers, reported to Congress that the massive deployment of US troops in and around Baghdad had given Iraqis the impression that the US military was a permanent occupying force. The Iraqi forces should assume more control, allowing the Americans to step back – so reinforcing one element of what General Petraeus was saying: 'I expect to be able to recommend that some of our forces will be redeployed without replacement.' As the surge troops, comprising five additional brigades, ended their tours of duty over the spring and summer of 2008 they would not be replaced. This redeployment, amounting to about 30,000 troops, was far removed from what many in Congress had been hoping to achieve. It meant that the basic force would stay in Iraq, unaffected by the mood of the American public and political dissent. The report recommended that Iraq's national police force, riddled with sectarianism and corruption, be scrapped and rebuilt – a significant admission that an important plank of the US government policy had been an abject failure.

The Iraq issue continued to dominate the Washington political climate and was hovering also over international affairs. President Bush himself, on his way to the Asia-Pacific Economic Cooperation summit in Sydney, felt obliged to make his stopover visit in Anbar, and in speech after speech he attempted to justify the war as an ideological struggle against people who use murder as a weapon to achieve their vision. At a Sydney air base Bush declared: 'I believe the work you're doing alongside our forces is necessary for peace. I believe we are writing one of the great chapters in the history of liberty and peace.' The Australian Prime

Minister, John Howard, was happy to echo the mantra: his country's forces, such as they were, would remain in Iraq, 'not based on any calendar, but based on conditions on the ground'. Kevin Rudd, the Labor leader, captured the mood of a population that did not like Bush and was opposed to the war: if elected, he would bring the troops home almost immediately.[44] Bush and Howard liked the idea of a continuing war, and so did Osama bin Laden. In a video release on 7 September he mocked the United States as 'weak' and pledged to continue the struggle in Iraq.[45]

The speculation about the Petraeus report was mounting, in effect leaving little for the general to say. Asked whether he was doing a good job, what was he likely to say? The columnist Paul Krugman, writing about the anticipated appearance of Petraeus and Crocker before Congress the following week, had no doubt about what would transpire:

> Democrats will look at General Petraeus's uniform and medals and fall into their usual cringe. They won't ask hard questions out of fear that someone might accuse them of attacking the military. After the testimony, they'll desperately try to get Republicans to agree to a resolution that politely asks President Bush to maybe, possibly, withdraw some troops, if he feels like it.'[46]

The Bush–Petraeus case hinged on demonstrable military and political progress: military successes were irrelevant unless they 'created space' (in the jargon) for political advances that could be advertised in ways that were coherent and comprehensible. Again, the familiar question was being asked: is progress being made? The columnist Leila Fadel, writing for McClatchy Newspapers, was in no doubt that the setbacks had outweighed the successes since the surge began: Baghdad had become more segregated, with Sunni Muslims now living in ghettos encircled by concrete blast walls; the Shi'ite militias were pushing to control the last mixed neighbourhoods in the south-west by forcing Sunnis to flee and killing those who resisted; the basic services throughout Baghdad had not improved; tens of thousands more Iraqis were becoming refugees; the Iraqi security forces were run by the militias; and civilian deaths had not declined, despite unsupported claims by the US military.[47] Even Petraeus, forced to admit reality, occasionally hinted that the US policies were not working, suggesting, as noted, that a small redeployment might be possible in 2008. On 7 September, on the eve of his testimony to Congress, he conceded in a letter to his troops that the surge had not achieved the desired results: the situation was 'exceedingly complex' and progress had been uneven: 'It [the surge] has not worked out as we had hoped. Many of us had hoped this summer would be a time of tangible political progress at the national level. All participants, Iraqi and coalition alike, are dissatisfied by the halting progress on major legislative initiatives.'[48] This rare departure for Petraeus had been forced upon him by the difficulties being encountered by the US forces: 'We have to contend with the relentless pace of operations, the crushing heat, and the emotions that we all experience during long deployments and tough combat.'[49] In short, it was time to admit that there were limits to what an overstretched US military could achieve.

The British Army, by contrast, was embarking upon part of a 'reconciliation process', paving the way for a final withdrawal. More Iraqi detainees held by UK troops, including members of the Mahdi Army, were to be released – in part as a placatory gesture and in part to lighten the burden on the British forces. It was acknowledged that there was little evidence against most of the detainees (twenty-six had been released over the previous three months but seventy-seven were still in custody). Some were to be transferred to the Iraqi judicial authorities but most were to be freed without condition.

For the first time the MoD admitted that senior British officers had negotiated with the Mahdi Army and other militia groups, illegal bodies according to Article 9(B) of the Iraqi constitution.[50] The talks had already led to fewer attacks on British troops and in consequence to the withdrawal from Basra Palace being achieved without loss. The MoD insisted that there had been no 'deal', though events on the ground suggested otherwise. Some commentators, including the heads of America's armed forces, were continuing to insist that the UK forces were in retreat – a spate of public bickering that reportedly led to an unnamed 'very senior [American] defence figure' telling US generals to cease the 'sniping against Britain'.[51] Some observers thought it significant that Gordon Brown and George Bush had not spoken since they met at Camp David six weeks before, in contrast to the weekly Bush–Blair conversations. But possible tensions between London and Washington existed also among senior US military leaders. Admiral William Fallon, chief of the US central command in the region, was reportedly pressing for a significant withdrawal of troops, against General Petraeus's demands, so that there would be sufficient forces for purposes outside Iraq.[52] And the anti-war campaigners were maintaining their unremitting pressure for withdrawal. On 10 September an advertisement from MoveOn, an activist group, appeared in the *New York Times* under the familiar slogan 'General Petraeus or General Betray Us?'.

While the Washington chattering classes were busy 'agonising' over the Iraq War or discussing the presidential campaign, young Americans were having parts of their brains blasted away in a distant country. Brain damage, we learned, could happen in various ways. Assorted pieces of hot metal could penetrate helmets and skulls to wreak havoc without killing, or bullet impacts and nearby explosions could shake heads around until soft brain tissue was lacerated and bleeding. In one account, by Marilynn Marchione of Associated Press, one legacy of the war was that throughout America there was 'an epidemic of brain-damaged soldiers'.[53] Thousands of US troops had been diagnosed with traumatic brain injury (TBI), evidently much worse than the traumas suffered in falls and car crashes. Thus Sandy Schneider, director of Vanderbilt University's brain injury rehabilitation programme, commented: 'I've been in the field for 20-plus years dealing with TBI. I have a very experienced staff. And they're saying to me, "We're seeing things we've never seen before."'[54]

Such injuries were often accompanied by post-traumatic stress disorder, adding to the difficulties of treatment. At least one former Vanderbilt patient committed suicide, and it was likely that others would do so in the future. A fifth of troops with even 'mild' TBI were expected to have prolonged or lifelong symptoms, as would most of the moderate or severe cases. Already the US

Department of Veterans' Affairs was dealing with ageing veterans with diabetes, heart disease, lung disease and other problems. Now thousands of TBI sufferers – typically experiencing dizziness, depression, mental confusion, speech or vision impairments, mental confusion and other personality disorders – were being added to the lists.

It was now emerging that the United States had exerted pressure on the UK government to delay the withdrawal from Basra Palace, further inflaming the tensions between the two allies. Brigadier James Bashall, the commander of the British 1st Mechanised Brigade, said that UK troops could have pulled out of the palace and back to the airport five months before if America had not asked them to stay. He commented that 'politics prevented' such an earlier withdrawal – with the consequence that eleven more British troops were killed and sixty-two injured: 'In April we could have come out and done the transition completely and that would have been the right thing to do . . . The Americans asked us to stay for longer.' Hence the UK forces were compelled to remain in Basra because of a 'political strategy being played out at highest level'.[55] The US had no headquarters or consular activity at Basra airport, and the CIA was keen to monitor Iranian activities, making it reluctant to leave Basra city in Iraqi hands.

Clearly the politics in southern Iraq, for which the British had been responsible, was not congenial to the US strategists. The Iraqi authorities were deemed to be unreliable, and the UK withdrawal meant that there would be only a minimal coalition presence in the region. It was equally obvious that the Baghdad-focused surge was not achieving the intended results. An opinion poll, commissioned by the BBC, ABC News (US) and NHK of Japan, carried out by D3 Systems and KA Research Ltd and published on 10 September, recorded the experiences and views of 2,112 Iraqis in more than 450 neighbourhoods across all of the provinces of Iraq between 17 August and 24 August 2007.[56] The basic question was whether the surge had made things better or worse or had had no effect. In response, around 70 per cent of respondents thought that the surge had made matters worse in the areas it had affected, with less than 20 per cent judging that things had improved. There was growing disillusionment with the US occupation and a growing proportion (47 per cent, compared with 35 per cent in February) of respondents who thought that the foreign troops should leave Iraq immediately.[57]

The publication of this poll, highly significant for anyone bothered about what the Iraqi people might think, was over-shadowed by the appearance of General David Petraeus and Ambassador Ryan Crocker before Congress. On 10 September 2007 the commander of US forces in Iraq offered a presentation that in many respects, because of the plethora of leaks and speculation, was deeply anti-climactic. Put simply, *Are you doing a good job, General? – You bet I am.* Congress was treated to a sequence of impressive graphical displays intended to establish that the surge was achieving the desired results. As a prelude, Petraeus emphasised that data was collected from many sources and handled with sophisticated expertise, implying that any competing calculations that questioned his conclusions were mistaken. But despite the lengthy self-congratulatory commentary, Petraeus admitted that much work had yet to be done and there was no question of an early total withdrawal of US forces. He conceded, as expected, that 30,000 troops could be withdrawn by the summer of 2008, but this suggestion did no more than reduce the American forces to pre-surge levels.

In large part the Western media obligingly echoed the upbeat message, with at least one mainstream newspaper, *The Times*, prepared to proclaim on its front page a 'turning point for America in Iraq': 'The United States is winning the war in Iraq with the objectives of President Bush's military surge this year "largely met", General David Petraeus told Congress yesterday.'[58] Other reportage was more circumspect, duly conveying in detail the essence of the general's message but reminding people that the situation in Baghdad told a different story.[59] The *Washington Post* noted a significant shift in the Petraeus contribution to the debate: the question now was not if there would be a pullout but when.[60]

Inevitably, other commentary was mixed. Various contributors in *The Guardian* suggested that Petraeus had bought time for George Bush but would not change any minds in Washington.

Michael Clarke, Director of the Royal United Services Institute, London, saw Petraeus as 'holding off the Democrats and an increasing section of the public from boxing the president into a precipitate withdrawal from Iraq'; Toby Dodge, of the University of London, emphasised a 'profound doubt' that the United States had the capacity or staying power' to rebuild Iraq, a doubt which Petraeus 'had done little' to reduce; Rosemary Hollis, director of research at Chatham House, saw Petraeus as buying time for all the Iraqi factions and other players to continue consultations; Max Root, of Council on Foreign Relations, New York, suggested that the Petraeus–Crocker view that the American people should continue to support the US military in Iraq would probably prevail; and Major Matthew Burden, who served in the first Gulf War and now runs Blackfive, the largest US military blog, stressed that Petraeus had to succeed both militarily and politically ('only time will tell').[61]

Some commentators, unimpressed by uniforms and military decorations, were prepared to declare that elements of the Petraeus testimony amounted to clear absurdity. Thus Paul Krugman pointed out that once sectarian cleansing had evicted one sect or another the murder rate would fall, and that this was scant reason for the US military to congratulate itself: 'And guess what? When a Sunni enclave is eliminated and the death toll in that district falls because there's nobody left to kill, that counts as progress by the Pentagon's metric.'[62] The columnist Andrew Sullivan, writing in the *Sunday Times*, pointed out a significant Petraeus admission. When staunch Republican Jack Warner asked the general whether the Iraq War had made America safer Petraeus replied: 'I don't know, actually. I have not sat down and sorted in my own mind.'[63] In a flash one of the central elements in the Bush posture collapsed. After all the colossal American expenditure of blood and treasure Petraeus could not even say that the United States was a safer place. Perhaps a few other people should have sorted in their own minds before launching the whole grim enterprise.

Many Democrats, still seeing Petraeus as a Bush man, were furious at what they saw as a politically inspired whitewash of the situation in Iraq. Tom Landos, chairman of the House Foreign

Relations Committee, said: 'The administration has sent you here today to convince the members of . . . Congress that victory is at hand. I don't buy it.'[64] In the same vein Senator Lindsey Graham of South Carolina summarised Petraeus's responses to his questions:

> We're spending $9 billion a month to stay in Iraq . . . So you're saying to the Congress that you know that at least sixty soldiers, airmen and marines are likely to be killed every month from now to July [2008], that we're going to spend $9 billion a month of American taxpayer dollars, and when it's all said and done, we'll still have 100,000 people there.[65]

The principal Democrat contenders in the presidential race – Hillary Clinton ('You have been dealt a very hard hand and it's a hand that is unlikely to improve') and Barack Obama ('The question is, how long will this take and at what point do we say "enough"?') – seemed reluctant to offer strong criticism of the Petraeus posture for fear of inviting charges that they were betraying American soldiers in the field.

Crocker attempted to reinforce the Bush–Petraeus line, but with a much less assured address to Congress than the general's presentation. He declined to mention or glossed over some of the major difficulties of the previous nine months, failing to address the sectarian war, the internal wave of internal displacements and the failure of the Maliki regime to repair the collapsing infrastructure. He spoke of the growth of provincial power but ignored the extent to which some provinces were 'becoming rival power centres [which] could as easily contribute to the country's disintegration as to its stability'.[66] Crocker's task was more difficult than that of Petraeus, having to portray manifest political collapse as significant progress.

Many of the congressional opponents of the Bush administration were dismayed by the pro-government Petraeus–Crocker stance – as if they could have expected anything else. It was expected that the President, planning to address the nation on 13 September, would echo the Petraeus prediction of a 30,000-troop drawdown by August 2008 – too little too late, according to Democrats, anti-war activists, a majority of the American people and most world opinion.

★

The post-Petraeus world seemed little different to what had gone before: *more of the same* was the message. The British could do what they wanted in southern Iraq (they were currently being ordered to the Iranian border amid US charges that Tehran was fomenting a 'proxy war'), but President Bush and General Petraeus were in Iraq for the long haul – unless Congress decided to use its appropriation powers to end the war, or the US military collapsed through exhaustion. Even a change of President in January 2009 could not be guaranteed to bring a total American withdrawal, and the likely victory of the Democrats was no reason for optimism. Hillary Clinton had said she would contemplate a long-term US presence in Iraq, and even Barack Obama, despite his anti-war credentials and urging the steady withdrawal of combat brigades every month, was suggesting that a 'substantial presence of American forces' could remain in Iraq in 2009 for a 'limited humanitarian mission'.[67] Some of Obama's Democrat rivals and the anti-war activists thought that he was taking a step backwards by not specifying clear withdrawal dates. His ideas were, in the words of American columnist Jennifer Hunter, 'very safe'.[68] Here was yet another leading Democrat that seemingly had no heart for a serious confrontation with the Bush administration over the Iraq issue.

In Baghdad two American soldiers, Staff Sergeant Yance Gray and Sergeant Omar Mora, who with five others had written a devastating criticism of the Bush war policy that had been published in the *New York Times* the previous month,[69] were killed when their cargo truck rolled over. There had been speculation that the men would have been punished for being so openly critical, as had happened before. Private Scott Beauchamp, who had written a shocking article in *New Republic* magazine about a soldier keeping a child's skull as a souvenir,[70] had his mobile phone and laptop confiscated. American soldiers were not expected to advertise the realities on the ground, where an unpopular occupation had brought misery and terror to countless families.

Now a US body was recommending yet more ghettoisation for Baghdad. A report by the Independent Commission on the

Security Forces of Iraq urged the building of more 'peace walls' throughout the capital to reduce sectarian slaughter. One of the report's authors, Duncan McCausland, assistant chief constable in the Northern Ireland Police Service, recommended the creation of walls similar to the twenty-six barriers that have kept Protestant and Catholic communities apart in Belfast since 1969.[71] On 13 September 2007 hundreds of Iraqis, waving flags and chanting slogans ('No to the dividing wall', 'The wall is US terrorism'), staged a demonstration against the building of walls between Sunni and Shi'ite communities in Baghdad, and demanded that the Iraqi government intervene to stop the US military building a barrier between the Shula and Ghazaliya districts. Hassan al-Tai, a tribal leader, said: 'The wall is in accordance with al-Qaeda's plans . . . [It would] separate family from family.' He added that the Iraqi government should act against those 'planting division and sectarianism amongst Iraqis. The wall is dividing small neighbourhoods and will lead to the partitioning of Iraq.'[72]

This splintering of communities was taken as one of the US military's principal successes, seen as separating the warring factions and so reducing the violence. It rated with the Bush triumph of bribing Sunni insurgents to fight al-Qaeda, despite frequent criticisms that such mercenary and opportunistic allies could not be relied upon. When George Bush briefly visited Anbar province on 3 September he shook hands with one of his new Sunni comrades in arms, Sheikh Abdul-Sattar Abu Risha, celebrating a fresh situation in the province that would swing the course of the war.[73] Petraeus too, in his address to Congress, cited Anbar as one of America's most notable successes. On 13 September, hours before Bush offered an upbeat assessment of the war's progress, the sheikh and two of his bodyguards were blown up by insurgents or al-Qaeda. General Petraeus said: 'It shows al-Qaeda in Iraq remains a very dangerous and barbaric enemy.'[74] On 15 September the Islamic State of Iraq, an al-Qaeda front group, warned that it would kill any other Sunni tribal leaders who cooperated with the US military and its Iraqi partners, at the same time announcing a Ramadan offensive in honour of Abu Masab al-Zarqawi, the founder of al-Qaeda in Iraq who was killed by a US air strike in 2006.

This was further evidence that the security of collaborators could not be guaranteed. People who had worked with the Americans or the British had always been primary targets since the 2003 invasion, and the surge had done nothing to change this. Iraqi interpreters working for the British had long been advised to leave the country or be killed.[75] On 13 September Colonel Saleem Agaa al-Zabon, who leads Basra's special forces, said: 'All the interpreters have to leave Basra because these militia will never let them rest. They will kill everybody they know [who worked for the British]. The interpreters have to leave. They have no choice.'[76]

On one occasion nine or ten masked men went to the home of an interpreter, Moayed Ahmed Khalef, in the al-Hayaniah district of Basra, beat him in front of his wife and mother, dragged him away and shot him multiple times. His body was found on al-Qa'ed Street later the same night. Al-Zabon commented that the hunt for collaborators had accelerated since the British left Basra Palace, and Colonel Ali Manshed, commander of the Shatt al-Arab police station, confirmed what was now transpiring: 'All the people who worked for the British forces are not safe now. Even people who quit one or two years ago are in danger.'[77]

On 14 September a White House report to Congress (a follow-up to the July report) confirmed that the Iraqi government had made little political progress over the previous months. The eighteen 'benchmarks' originally set by the Bush administration had not been met or had only been met in part. In manifest desperation the White House was now suggesting, in a lengthy preamble to the report, that the benchmarks were an imperfect measure of progress and that they should be viewed 'in a larger context'. In short, *the Iraqi government had not met the political criteria we deemed to be essential; what other criteria can we dream up that might suggest some sort of progress?* Senator Robert Menendez, a New Jersey Democrat, commented: 'According to this latest report card, the President's war policy is still flunking. It's clear that Iraq is still light-years away from security or political stability.'[78] George Bush and Dick Cheney were busy visiting troops at army bases in an effort to shore up support, as the Democrats were reportedly agreeing a deal that would allow soldiers to spend more time at home. If the new measure were approved by Congress it would force US military commanders to withdraw troops from Iraq at a much faster rate than that suggested in the Bush–Petraeus policy.[79] Defense Secretary Robert Gates was now hinting that the present level of about 170,000 American troops in Iraq might be reduced to about 100,000 by the end of 2008: 'That would be the math.' But even this cautious suggestion had to be qualified. Gates quickly added that, because 'there is no script' in war, his hoped-for cuts could vanish.

It seemed that cuts in British forces were on track, with reports that the residual contingent at Basra airport might be halved by December as about 2,500 soldiers moved to Kuwait. A team of officers from Permanent Joint Headquarters (PJHQ) in Northwood had been reviewing the remaining deployment in southern Iraq and were expected to recommend that British troops transferred to Kuwait would be able to escort convoys and train Iraqi forces. The PJHQ group was expected to report to Gordon Brown before General Petraeus and Ambassador Crocker came to London the following week. Again there were signs that the Bush administration was not happy about the imminent drawdown of British troops, with speculation that Petraeus would press Brown to move troops to the Iranian border to cut off the smuggling of Iranian weapons to the Shi'ite militias.[80] (Many Americans, we may assume, felt encouraged by the policies of the British government. On 15 September thousands of anti-war protesters marched near the Capitol, where hundreds sprawled on the ground in a symbolic 'die-in'; the police arrested 189 people, including ten Iraq War veterans.)

There was no doubt that part of the purpose of the Petraeus visit was to halt the growing transatlantic tensions over the British troop withdrawal from Basra, signalled by accusations from several Republican and Democrat senators that Britain was abandoning southern Iraq to the Shi'ite death squads.[81] On 18 September Petraeus and Crocker, stopping over in London, stated that the Iraqi government still had to make meaningful progress on legislation and other acts to promote reconciliation. However, tangible progress had been made, which should not be put at risk by an early British withdrawal: there would be 'devastating consequences' if the UK forces were removed prematurely. Alex Bigham of the London-based Foreign Policy Centre acknowledged that the size of the British force in southern Iraq was of concern to the Americans because they felt that 'they might have to backfill with troops of their own and . . . because it would add to the political clamour that's going on in Washington, which says, if the British are prepared to withdraw, why don't we withdraw American troops?'[82] General Petraeus, speaking at the Royal United Services Institute, was keen to deny any rift between London and Washington and went out of his way to praise 'your troopers and your diplomats [who] have done magnificent work. All citizens of the United Kingdom should be proud of them . . . a credit to your great country.'[83] He acknowledged also that the British withdrawal from Basra Palace had reduced the level of violence in the province,[84] but with many fewer coalition personnel in the area this could not be known for certain. In public at least, the general did not object to the British drawdown, encouraging speculation that a scheduled statement by Gordon Brown to the Commons on 8 October might include details of troop withdrawals.

Petraeus had reportedly discussed the 'rotation' of British troops in southern Iraq with Defence Secretary Des Browne and British defence chiefs, with a change of brigades expected before December – which would provide an opportunity for a new round of cuts.[85] The general expected Britain to transfer the security responsibilities of Basra province to the Iraqis 'later this fall or in the winter', which suggested he knew of further imminent withdrawals. Petraeus had spoken at the institute, held talks with the British government and then attended a press conference – and had been variously quoted. So would an early British withdrawal bring 'devastating consequences', leaving US forces and a key north–south supply route open to attack, or was Petraeus happy to see further UK troop redeployments within a matter of weeks? It seemed that the Americans were making the best of an unwelcome situation, preferring to maintain the 'coalition of the willing' but seeing the writing on the wall. Whatever was happening in Baghdad, the British government was determined to maintain the drawdown of British troops in southern Iraq begun under Tony Blair. His successor was not about to be pressured by two high US officials who had proved themselves incapable of convincing a majority in Congress or the bulk of the American people.

The problems facing American policy in Iraq intensified when employees of the security firm Blackwater killed seventeen Iraqi civilians and a policeman, wounding thirteen more, when shots were fired from a US state department convoy. Prime Minister Nouri al-Maliki, noting that the incident had generated 'a lot of hatred' against Blackwater, said that the shooting was 'the seventh of its kind' involving the company. The Iraqi Ministry of the Interior immediately announced that Blackwater would have its licence revoked and would be expelled from the country – a bitter blow to the United States because many diplomats, engineers and other Westerners in Iraq relied heavily on armed protection provided by what was in essence, as noted, a mercenary organisation designed to complement the US armed forces.[86] As a preliminary response, the United States suspended all road journeys by its diplomats outside the Green Zone, so conceding that the US military was incapable of protecting its own officials. Condoleezza Rice hurried to apologise to the Iraqi government in the hope of keeping the mercenary personnel, prohibited in international law, on the American payroll. A later statement from al-Maliki's office noted that Rice had expressed her personal apologies and those of the United States, confirming that action would be taken to prevent such a thing happening again. Al-Maliki declared that the Iraqi government would initiate an inquiry into the role of security firms in Iraq, and Rice said that there would be a full US investigation into the incident.[87] On 19 September Muqtada al-Sadr called on the Iraqi government to expel all 48,000 foreign mercenaries, while one unnamed company employee suggested that Blackwater was 'at the aggressive end of the market'.[88] The US and Iraqi governments finally announced that they would hold a joint inquiry into the killings.

On 23 September al-Maliki, interviewed by Associated Press in New York, insisted that Blackwater posed 'a serious challenge to the sovereignty of Iraq and cannot be accepted';[89] action, he declared, must be taken against the company. In addition a draft law intended to place private security firms under Interior Ministry supervision was being submitted to a state legal committee, the State Shura Council, for review before being presented to Parliament.[90] However, an unnamed Iraqi official, doubtless influenced by Rice's blandishments, was now saying that Iraq would not rush to expel the firm because that would leave a 'security vacuum' in Baghdad. Then it was announced that an FBI team was being sent to Baghdad to collect evidence that might lead to a prosecution, and that Erik Prince, the chief executive of Blackwater, would be called to testify before Congress. Already employees of the company in Iraq had reportedly been involved in many incidents in which they 'fired first'.[91]

In his subsequent appearance before the House of Representatives Oversight Committee Prince disputed a congressional report that had charged Blackwater guards with being indifferent to Iraqi casualties and frequently opening fire first from moving cars without stopping to count the dead or treat the wounded. He claimed that there had been 'a rush to judgement based on inaccurate information and many public reports have wrongly pronounced Blackwater's guilt for the deaths of varying numbers of civilians'. However, 'to the extent' that there was loss of innocent life 'I consider that tragic . . . [but] the Blackwater team acted appropriately while operating in a very complex war zone'.[92]

A congressional memorandum claimed that Blackwater personnel had been involved in an average of 1.4 shootings a week, including an incident on 24 December 2006 when a Blackwater employee had killed a bodyguard to Adil Abdul-Mahdi, the Iraqi Shi'ite Vice-President; according to witnesses, the Blackwater contractor had been drunk after a party.[93] Other reports suggested that Blackwater staff had been involved in nearly 200 firing incidents over the previous two years, in 80 per cent of which they had fired first.[94]

The Blackwater links to President Bush's Republican Party had long been known: Prince and his first and second wives had donated $300,000 to Republican candidates and political action committees.[95] What was less well known was that the company and its subsidiaries also had links, albeit less mercenary, to Hillary Clinton. Mark Penn, her top strategist, had also taken on the public-relations task of improving Blackwater's tattered image. Clinton had been keen to criticise Blackwater's conduct in Iraq but Penn had never clarified his financial stake in the Blackwater group.[96]

On 8 October the Iraqi government announced that it would punish Blackwater after an inquiry had revealed that the security contractors had opened fire without provocation on Iraqi civilians: 'The investigation committee appointed by . . . Maliki . . . has found no evidence that the convoy of Blackwater came under fire either directly or indirectly. It was not touched even by a stone. [The Blackwater personnel] have committed a deliberate crime and should be punished under the law.'[97] The following day the Iraqi government demanded that Blackwater pay $100 million to the families of the victims, and called on Washington to sever all the company's contracts in Iraq within six months. The role of security contractors in general was now being scrutinised by the Iraqi authorities, and in the United States the House of Representatives overwhelmingly approved a bill that would bring all US government contractors in Iraq under the jurisdiction of US law.[98]

The United States was now advertising any seeming successes, such as the dubious 'turnaround' in Anbar province, to avoid charges of total policy failure. Another apparent 'breakthrough' was announced when some of the 7,000 Iraqi detainees in Camp Cropper prison handed over four forcibly shaven and blood-stained Islamic 'extremists', inviting claims that the jailed 'moderates' had regained control. Major General Douglas Stone declared: 'It's a breakthrough. The *takfiris* [extremists] terrorised the prison. This is the first time the moderates have felt empowered enough to identify them and take back control.' But he then commented: 'We were feeding and warehousing a 25,000-strong army [throughout the prison system] dedicated to the battle against us. We were breeding an insurgency in our internal facilities.'[99] So the brutalisation for unknown reasons of four unnamed detainees constituted a 'tide' of revolt against the tens of thousands of insurgents that US policy was generating. Stone, an evident radical among American camp commanders, had discovered that most of the detainees had no idea why they were imprisoned, nor did the American military court system.[100] For the first time probably innocent Iraqis who had been imprisoned for years were being questioned by panels about their alleged crimes. Another breakthrough?

Throughout Iraq the security situation remained grim. An ancient community, the Mandeans, deriving from the same roots as Judaism, Christianity and Islam, was facing extinction through kidnap, murder and attempts at forced conversion – treatment that was analogous to the abuse of the Yezidis.[101] The killing of two more of the aides of Grand Ayatollah Ali al-Sistani, the leading moderate cleric in Iraq, suggested a worsening Shi'ite power struggle in the oil-rich south of the country, inviting comments that the residual UK forces should intervene to help the police. Colonel Abdul Kareem el-Zaydee, the main police spokesman in Basra, said: 'The British military should support the Iraqi security forces and not just stay at their airport base.'[102] On 25 September a suicide bomb detonated in the Shifta Shi'ite mosque in Diyala province ripped through a 'reconciliation meeting' attended by Shi'ite and Sunni leaders, killing twenty-four and wounding thirty-seven more. And Sami Ramadani, of Iraqi Democrats against Occupation, spoke in London of the 'deep hatred' that Iraqis had of both the US-led occupiers and terrorists: 'People are overwhelmingly armed in Iraq and they take pot shots at occupation forces whenever they can.'[103]

A new report by the US embassy in Baghdad concluded that many Iraqi ministries were controlled by militias and death squads, with corruption and intimidation the norm. In addition, the Maliki office was criticised for 'open hostility' to efforts to establish an independent anti-corruption agency.[104] At the same time the United States was experimenting with its bombing of Iraq by using robot aircraft (Predators and Reapers), capable of carrying Hellfire missiles and 500-pound bombs. ('It is possible that in our lifetime we will be able to run a war without ever leaving the US,' said Lieutenant Colonel David Branham.)[105] And in Washington comfortable politicians endlessly debated whether 'progress' was being made in a foreign country thousands of miles away.

On 24 September 2007 Gordon Brown, speaking to the Labour conference for the first time as Prime Minister and leader of the party, spent a few seconds dismissing Iraq in an hour-plus speech. The next day David Miliband, speaking to the conference, admitted that the government bore the scars of its decision to invade Iraq: 'Whatever the rights and wrongs – and there have been both – we have got to focus on the future.' And he declared, in an unmistakable reference to Tony Blair: 'The lesson is that it is not good enough to have good intentions. To assert shared values is not enough.'[106] *Whatever the rights and wrongs.* The mantra was dismally familiar. The message was always the same: whatever crimes we have perpetrated we are not accountable. An unspoken statute of limitations abolishes all responsibility and all guilt. Just imagine how Blair, Brown, Miliband, Straw, Hoon, Bush, Rumsfeld, Cheney, Rice and all the rest would have responded if Hermann Goering, Slobodan Milošević and Saddam Hussein had said: 'We have no legal or ethical responsibility for the past. There is no accountability. The important thing, whatever the rights and wrongs, is to move on.'

A week later Brown made a surprise visit to Baghdad and Basra, and announced that another thousand British troops would be withdrawn by Christmas, bringing the military presence down to 4,500 – a superficially welcome statement that immediately attracted widespread criticism. The announcement had been made in Basra, not to the House of Commons, which would have been more appropriate; the timing, in the middle of the annual Conservative Party conference, was widely seen as a political ruse to upstage Tory publicity; and even the figure of 1,000 troops being withdrawn seemed highly dubious. Some 250 of the thousand had already returned to Britain, and a proportion of the total, due for deployment to Iraq from Germany, would not now be sent.[107] On 2 October Bob Ainsworth, the armed forces minister, was robustly quizzed by Jeremy Paxman on the BBC *Newsnight* programme – and seemed unable to clear up the manifest ambiguities.[108] At best the Prime Minister had been careless in presenting misleading statistics; at worst he had added yet another lie to the plethora of falsehoods that now littered the Iraq adventure.

In addition, Brown was being roundly criticised for seemingly using his Iraq visit and other government announcements to prepare the ground for an early general election – an option which, in the word of many commentators, he 'bottled' when opinion polls turned against him at the end of the Conservative conference. In a difficult press conference on 8 October 2007 he attempted to deflect the mounting criticism by resorting to generalities and repeatedly having 'visions'.

On the same day Brown addressed the House of Commons on Iraq. He spoke of an early planned reduction by Christmas in the number of UK troops in southern Iraq, and a later reduction to 2,500 troops in the spring of 2008, but indicated that a significant British presence would be maintained for a period in an 'overwatch' capacity. In addition, he presented a highly ambiguous and ill-defined package designed to protect Iraqi interpreters who had worked for the British forces. There was nothing in the statement that indicated a complete withdrawal of UK troops from southern Iraq. Indeed the contrary was the case. On 25 September Des Browne, speaking at the Labour Party conference, had already declared that Britain must be prepared for a commitment to Iraq and Afghanistan lasting decades – or even generations.[109]

Predictably, Gordon Brown ventured no criticism of the continuing American war, no comment on the extent to which US pressure was keeping British troops in Iraq, and no reference to the vast suffering of the Iraqi people. At one level his statement was an irrelevance. In a sense it did not matter how popular or well received was the emerging British policy, since one great and growing constituency was not able to express an opinion. The dead are disenfranchised.

10

A successful surge?

By the end of 2007 the character and consequences of the US-led war against Iraq were plain for all to see: an illegal unprovoked aggression had been launched against an accredited member state of the United Nations with devastating consequences for a national people. The scale of the catastrophe had been rehearsed many times. In less than five years more than a million Iraqis had been killed, according to some estimates; and, according to other estimates, more than five million had been driven from their homes[1] – out of a total population of around twenty-four million. This meant that millions more had been rendered victims in one way or another, variously wounded, traumatised or bereaved. Perhaps half the entire Iraqi people had died, been injured, lost family members or been dispossessed.

The civilian population was being targeted in various ways. Coalition forces were shelling and bombing urban areas thought to house 'suspected terrorists'. Whole communities, struggling to cope with a ravaged infrastructure, were being subjected to ethnic and sectarian cleansing. Many towns and cities had been fragmented by apartheid walls in a vain attempt to improve security. The militias were fighting turf wars among themselves in order to exploit the power vacuum, and criminal gangs were resorting to theft and kidnapping for ransom with impunity. At the same time fundamentalist factions were attacking women, minority religious groups, teachers and shopkeepers to enforce Islamist orthodoxy. In such circumstances the weakest members of society – the sick, the old, minorities lacking militia protection – were particularly vulnerable.

On 1 October Amnesty International issued a press release to launch a new report,[2] urging the Iraqi government and the US-led occupation forces to move to protect 'the increasingly beleaguered Palestinian refugee community', since thousands of stranded refugees, unable to flee, were being 'hunted down [by sectarian militiamen], abducted, tortured and, in some cases, killed without any effective steps being taken to protect them'.[3] Malcolm Smart of Amnesty emphasised that the Palestinians were facing great obstacles in seeking refuge 'as the authorities in both Syria and Jordan, the main countries hosting Iraqi refugees, remain extremely reluctant to allow Palestinian refugees to enter their territory'.[4] The Palestine Liberation Organisation in Lebanon had sent Amnesty a list of nearly 500 names of Palestinians murdered in Iraq, and the attacks and killings were continuing. On 5 October the Archbishop of Canterbury, Dr Rowan Williams, claimed that the Iraq conflict was wreaking more damage on the region that was being acknowledged, and that his meeting with Iraqi refugees in Syria had been 'heartbreaking and harrowing'.[5] The refugees, many of them Christians, had fled because their families had been kidnapped or executed.

It was by now equally clear that, despite official denials, the US military were often targeting unarmed Iraqis.[6] The reporter Chris Hedges, who talked with soldiers, officers and medical personnel in Iraq,

> revealed disturbing patterns of behaviour by American troops: innocents terrorized during midnight raids, civilian cars fired upon when they got too close to supply columns. The campaign against a mostly invisible enemy . . . has given rise to a culture of fear and even hatred among US forces, many of whom . . . have, in effect, declared war on all Iraqis.

One soldier interviewed by Hedges, Sergeant Camilio Mejia, said that the killing of innocent Iraqi civilians at checkpoints had 'long since ceased to arouse much interest or even comment'.[7] Sergeant Evan Vela, testifying at a trial concerning the killing of innocent Iraqis and the planting of weapons to cover up the deaths, claimed that he had been ordered to kill a wounded Iraqi.[8] At the same time it seemed unlikely that any US marines would face murder charges for the much-publicised massacre of seventeen Iraqi civilians, including five children and two women, in Haditha in November 2005.[9] On 7 October, according to Iraqi eye-witnesses, local residents in Diyala suffered sixty-five casualties when the US military targeted 'suspected terrorists'. Similarly, twenty-five civilians were killed and forty others injured when US planes bombed the Jezani al-Imam village in the Hibhib district, near Baqubah: 'The number of casualties is most likely to increase as many bodies are waiting to be recovered from under the destroyed houses. Locals [had so far] recovered dead bodies and scores of wounded from under the destroyed houses.'[10] The UN then urged the US military to mount a vigorous investigation into the air strikes and to make the findings public.[11] Such events were far from isolated.

On 13 October American soldiers killed an ambulance driver and a first aid worker in Mosul, which led to medical workers staging a sit-in to protest at the killing of their colleagues. At the same time two US Army subcontractors from Titan and CACI International who had worked in Abu Ghraib jail were being charged with abusing detainees. One former Iraqi prisoner who now lives in Sweden said that he had been sodomised, nearly strangled with a belt, given repeated electric shocks, and tied by his genitals to other detainees.[12] The US military was now holding around 25,000 Iraqi detainees, nearly a thousand of them under the age of sixteen, and thousands of them innocent women with contagious diseases held in overcrowded conditions without medical help, detained essentially to exert pressure on their husbands. There were also reports that children were being tortured during interrogation. Thus Khalid Rabia'a, a spokesman for the Prisoners' Association for Justice, commented:

> Children are being treated as adults in Iraqi prisons and our investigations have shown that they are being abused and tortured. Five children showed signs of torture all over their bodies. They had marks of cigarette burns over their legs and one couldn't speak as the shock sessions affected his conversation.[13]

On 9 October employees of the Australian-run Unity Resources Group shot dead an Iraqi woman taxi driver who was an Armenian

Christian, and a female civilian passenger; another woman passenger was shot in the shoulder and a child was injured by flying glass. After blazing away at the car the security guards sped off 'like gangsters', according to an Iraqi eyewitness.[14] On 11 October at least fifteen Iraqi civilians, including nine children, were killed in US air strikes against 'suspected militants' near Lake Tharthar, north of Baghdad. A military spokesman, Major Brad Leighton, told reporters: 'We regret that civilians are hurt or killed while coalition forces search to rid Iraq of terrorism.'[15] On 23 October another US spokesperson, Major Peggy Kageleiry, expressed regret at the deaths of civilians. Such expressions of regret followed complaints by Prime Minister Nouri al-Maliki that General David Petraeus, in seeking to ensure the success of the military surge, was inflicting a heavy toll on civilians.

The new three-monthly UN Assistance Mission for Iraq (UNAMI) report, covering the period ending 30 June 2007, noted the 'ever-deepening crisis' in Iraq, with thousands of people driven from their homes each month and suffering devastating consequences of violence across the country. The report documented more than 100 civilians killed by US raids and air strikes. Ivana Vuco, a UN human rights officer in Baghdad, said: 'The killings are still taking place, the torture is still being reported, the due process issues are still unresolved.'[16]

With the prevalence of violence throughout Iraq and the collapse of the social infrastructure it was impossible to guarantee adequate water supplies or sufficient food. In the Baghdad area hundreds of mothers were scavenging through other people's dustbins for leftovers on which to feed their children. Mayada Zuhair, a spokeswoman for the Baghdad-based Women's Rights Association, which had conducted a survey of families in twelve provinces, reported an increase of 25 per cent since December 2005 in the number of mothers who fed their children by becoming sex workers or by scavenging through rubbish.[17] It was hardly surprising that in such circumstances there was a significant increase in the incidence of psychiatric disorders among ordinary Iraqis. Acording to Shalan Aboudy, director of the Ibn-Rushd psychiatric hospital in Baghdad, about 100 patients ('the majority . . . women, fewer men . . . plenty of children') were visiting the hospital every day since it was the only such facility in the capital. At the same time it lacked supplies and medical staff. Before the 2003 invasion the hospital had fourteen psychiatric specialists but in October 2007 there were just four, the rest having fled the country.

There were no signs that the Iraqi government was attempting to address such matters, or that the US authorities were prepared to expose the extent of Iraqi incompetence and corruption. As one example, the Iraqi contractor Abu Ahmed told the Inter Press Service (IPS) news agency that the governor's office in Diyala was directly involved in corrupt practices: the official monitoring committee was being coerced into signing invoices, even when jobs were left unfinished.[18] Abu Qassim, a former police officer, said that people had to pay bribes to become a police officer: 'You bring your CV, with a few hundred dollars . . . Sometimes there are hundreds of false names whose salaries go to the senior officers . . . [An officer] may be told that he can have half of the salary without coming to the office [the other half going to a senior policeman].'[19] Following allegations that al-Maliki had blocked corruption investigations into his Cabinet and family members, Lawrence E. Butler, the US deputy assistant secretary of state for Near Eastern affairs, refused to divulge relevant information to congressional investigators, saying that such material was considered classified.[20] However, it was known that Judge Radhi Hamza al-Rahdi, Iraq's leading anti-corruption official, had been forced to flee to America because of death threats. According to al-Rahdi, al-Maliki had blocked investigations in a number of high-profile cases. Only 241 cases out of 3,000 had reached court, and al-Rahdi believed that corruption had cost Iraq more than $15 billion over the previous three years, with much of the money ending up in the hands of the sectarian militias.[21]

There was confusion also about casualty statistics intended to throw light on the progress of the surge. While the White House was proclaiming a massively reduced incidence of deaths and injuries, other reports suggested that casualties were continuing to rise. Thus in early November 2007 the news agency AFP reported that the number of Iraqis killed in insurgent and sectarian attacks, according to Iraqi government figures, had again risen in October:

at least 887 Iraqis had been killed that month, compared
September, with the dead overwhelmingly civilians.[22] In t.
week of November the death of six more American troops m
2007 the most deadly year for the US military in Iraq. So-calle
'friendly fire' incidents were continuing to account for a number
of the casualties. In mid-November Iraqi witnesses claimed that
American troops had killed forty Sunnis on a US-approved
mission against insurgents.[23] In late October and early November
the British security firm Erinys, which reportedly had close ties to
Ahmed Chalabi, was being sued for causing the death of an
American soldier.[24] At the same time a US convoy in Samawah,
the capital of Muthanna province, opened fire on Iraqi motorists
who were rushing to get out of the way, killing two men,
wounding four more and destroying a truckload of sheep.[25]

On 13 October Lieutenant General Ricardo Sanchez, who had
commanded US forces in Iraq for a year after the 2003 invasion,
declared that President Bush's government was 'incompetent' and
'negligent', presiding over 'a nightmare [in Iraq] with no end in
sight'. Sanchez denounced the Bush administration's 'catastro-
phically flawed, unrealistically optimistic war plan' and said that
there had been 'a glaring and unfortunate display of incompetent
strategic leadership within our national borders'.[26] By now few
observers could doubt that the strategic confusion was matched by
a host of tactical uncertainties and blunders.

The tactics of the surge were quelling violence in some areas but
at a horrendous cost to the civilian population. With US military
operations being given a primary role, reconstruction projects had
slowed or been abandoned; areas had been cleansed of 'suspected
terrorists', but overwhelming American firepower had caused
inevitable 'collateral' damage, devastating local communities and
adding to the toll of dead and wounded. The US authorities were
insisting that the private security firms were essential to their work
in Iraq, even though the Iraqi government was threatening to bring
them within the scope of national law. On 23 October a
congressional investigation found that the US State Department
could not account for most of the $1.2 billion allocated to DynCorp
to provide housing, food, security facilities and staff for police
training in Iraq and Afghanistan. The Bureau of International

Narcotics and Law Enforcements Affairs (INL), which had awarded the contract, was forced to admit that there had been problems with invoices and other paperwork. The report concluded: 'INL's prior lack of [financial] controls created an environment vulnerable to waste and fraud.'[27] The financial corruption and incompetence that had become so clear in Iraq was mirrored in the United States' control of its own contracting companies.

The patterns had become established over the period of the occupation: mounting Iraqi and US casualties, the bombing of urban areas, sieges and roadblocks, apartheid walls, and the destruction of a social infrastructure no longer able to meet the mounting needs of a national population. On 21 October US ground forces and helicopters attacked targets in Sadr City, killing 'an estimated 49 criminals' during a raid intended to capture a militia commander, but Iraqi police and hospital officials reported only thirteen fatalities, among them a woman and three children. The US military claimed to be unaware of any innocent civilians killed during the operation, but press photographs showed the bodies of two toddlers on the floor of the local morgue, said by relatives to have been killed when helicopter gunfire hit their house as they slept.[28]

None of this was helping the morale of the coalition troops, many of whom had been returned home after suffering traumatic experiences. In early November it emerged that more American military veterans had been committing suicide than had been dying in Iraq. In 2005 alone at least 6,256 US veterans took their lives, compared with a total of 3,863 military deaths in Iraq since the invasion.[29] The US Army was acknowledging that as many as 20 per cent of its soldiers and marines had suffered at least 'mild traumatic brain injury' from blows to the head or shockwaves caused by explosions, damage that often had psychological consequences. And in Britain there was now mounting concern that undiagnosed brain injuries after exposure to high-velocity explosions might be affecting up to 20,000 soldiers.[30] In calculating the costs of the Iraq War such matters were rarely given prominence, but few commentators were unaware of the mounting financial price of the conflict. In October the non-partisan Congressional Budget Office provided an estimate that the wars in Iraq and Afghanistan could cost as much as \$2.4 trillion through the next decade.[31]

Events in Iraq, not least the supposed impact of the surge, were encouraging speculation about troop withdrawals. The White House was suggesting that the surge quota would be drawn down in 2008, and Downing Street was indicating that phased withdrawals would begin in the near future. In early October 2007 it was proposed that the first stage of a British withdrawal, called 'tactical overwatch', would mean British troops ceasing to patrol and leaving such tasks to Iraqi officers and troops. The next phase, 'operation overwatch', would require British forces to be retained as a 'beyond-the-horizon reserve', at first in Iraqi bases and then in Kuwait or Cyprus, to be used in circumstances beyond the Iraqi army's control. The final phase, involving total withdrawal, would happen at some unspecified time in the future.

On 7 October, speaking in a BBC television interview, Prime Minister Gordon Brown heralded a Commons statement that would be 'far more comprehensive' than the comments that had been made so far. It was expected that British troops would be reduced to 4,500 by Christmas and that further cuts would leave a force of around 3,000 after May 2008.[32] The statement on 8 October encouraged further speculation that all British troops could be out of southern Iraq by the end of the following year, with an unnamed defence official quoted as saying that 'there is no guarantee' that British troops would remain in Iraq beyond 2008.[33] One seeming paradox was the declared plan to send nearly 1,000 extra troops to the region before Christmas to cover the British handover of Basra to the Iraqis, a temporary addition of 850 to the current force of 5,000 in the Basra area.[34]

It seemed clear that by now the British forces, despite constant political assertions of high morale, wanted to be out of a disastrous engagement. In early October Air Chief Marshal Sir Jock Stirrup, Chief of the Defence Staff, declared that the government was giving the public 'false and inflated expectations' of what could be achieved by British troops in Iraq, and that it would take many years for conditions in Basra to improve substantially.[35] A senior British officer in Iraq, speaking on condition of anonymity, told the *Sunday Telegraph* that 'we are tired of firing at people' and would 'prefer to find a political accommodation'.[36] Here there were suggestions also that deals had been done with the Shi'ite militias that dominated Basra city, reflected in fewer attacks on the British forces. Far from bringing peace and security to the region, the British army had been forced to allow death squads to operate with impunity in Basra.[37] The Iraqi army remained too weak to fight against the militias, and the supposed role of foreign forces seemed increasingly irrelevant. On 3 December the Commons Defence Committee suggested that the government's plan to cut the number of British troops in Iraq in half by the middle of 2008 would not work because the remaining contingent would be unable to do more than defend itself.

Brown had bowed to public pressure to increase financial compensation for troops suffering from the most serious injuries and a package had been introduced to help Iraqi interpreters at risk of reprisals. But the impression remained that the British forces were being given insufficient support, leaving soldiers feeling 'devalued, angry and suffering from Iraq fatigue'.[38] Here General Sir Richard Dannatt suggested, in a leaked commentary, that the military covenant under which service personnel were supposedly to be given decent homes, medical facilities and welfare benefits was 'clearly out of kilter'; the Iraq and Afghanistan operations were putting soldiers and their families under 'great pressure', and the long-term impact was 'mortgaging the goodwill of the people'.[39] Any US version of the military covenant was under even greater pressure: for example, veterans made up one in four homeless people in the United States, even though they compose only 11 per cent of the general adult population.[40]

Figures from the British Ministry of Defence showed that attempting to fight two counter-insurgency wars simultaneously was damaging the armed forces' ability to prepare for conventional military engagements. Since 2004 some 200 training exercises had been cancelled, most of them because of operational commitments and some of them to save money. Dannatt had recently declared: 'We cannot take our eye off the far future. There is still the potential for so-called "dark futures" and we would be foolish to rule out the possibility of some involvement in inter-state conflict. The role of the military is to be prepared for the unexpected.'[41]

In the United States leading Democrats, a few dissident Republicans and hundreds of thousands of protesters continued to campaign for a total withdrawal of US forces from Iraq and Afghanistan, but it seemed highly unlikely that this would be achieved. The White House was continuing to press for substantial war funding, and political opponents were never able to garner enough support to link the authorisation of funding to troop withdrawals. The threat of a presidential veto, even in the circumstances of a Democrat House and Senate, was always sufficient to block anti-war moves. For example, on 16 November 2007 the Senate defeated a Democrat proposal to link war funding to the start of troop withdrawals. The 53–45 vote was fifteen votes short of the sixty needed to advance the proposal.[42] At the same time the Bush administration and its supporters were working to exploit controversial news from Iraq to suggest that the surge was working, and so to throw the anti-war campaigners onto the defensive (see below). And there were now ample signs that the White House intended to maintain a permanent military presence in Iraq. It seemed that the only comfort for the anti-war movement was the defeat of Prime Minister John Howard in Australia. Kevin Rudd, the incoming Labor premier, stated that all Australian troops would be out of Iraq by mid-2008, so honouring a pledge made during the election campaign.[43]

In early October 2007 the White House was making much of claims that US military losses in Iraq were seventy for September, the lowest monthly figure since July 2006 and the fourth consecutive drop in the monthly death toll after a high of 121 in May 2007. In addition, the US government was claiming that the civilian deaths from violence were also dropping – from 1,773 in August to 884 in September, the lowest figure since the start of the surge. In early November the US military claimed that it had succeeded in expelling al-Qaeda from every neighbourhood in Baghdad, and had cut the number of murders by 80 per cent. Now it was being suggested that such developments, regarded as overoptimistic by some observers, would make it easier to reduce the American forces from early 2008. Major General Joseph F. Fil Jr, commander of the US forces in Baghdad, said that there was 'just no question' but that violence had declined since a rise in June: 'The Iraqi people have decided that they've had it up to here with violence.'[44] One European defence analyst, wanting to remain anonymous, described Major General Fil's assessment as 'wildly optimistic'.[45]

On 30 October Joe Christoff of the US Government Accountability Office said before the House Appropriations Committee that the reduction in violence should be taken with a grain of salt, as it coincided with increased sectarian cleansing and a massive refugee displacement ('there might be fewer attacks because you have ethnically cleansed neighbourhoods'). In the same vein Ali Fadhily, reporting for IPS (9 November), said that the relative calm was because many people had fled or been killed; and others blamed the media for lack of adequate reportage. Muhammad Younis, a businessman from Mosul visiting Baghdad, acknowledged that attacks on US forces had diminished but added that 'media coverage has almost disappeared'.[46] In Duluiya, 90 miles north of Baghdad, a US army unit raided a house and killed a young man inside, but Sunni witnesses complained that the media was not covering either the resistance activity or the regular 'crimes' committed by US and Iraqi government forces against innocent civilians.[47] Some observers noted that the US bombing of Iraq had increased five-fold in the first six months of 2007, suggesting that air strikes were increasingly replacing ground operations to avoid American military casualties.

The incidence of roadside bombs had reportedly diminished from 3,239 in March to 1,560 in October, perhaps statistically significant if the figures could be believed but saying nothing about the shifting US tactics adopted in desperation. The US military was doing deals with militiamen, Sunni insurgents and death squads in order to create the illusion that peace was returning to Iraq's towns and cities. Groups of 'concerned citizens', often erstwhile 'terrorists', were being armed and bribed by the Americans to confront al-Qaeda forces wherever possible. There was nothing here of lawful authority, of transferring power to a legitimate democratically elected government. The US had perceived that a military solution, on America's terms, was impossible – and so, as the British had done in Basra, urban Iraq was gradually being handed over to the thugs. The journalist Ghaith Abdul-Ahad has described how the *sakkaka*, or assassins, in Hayaniya Square in Basra were allowed to gather with impunity and awaited the opportunity to carry out lucrative kidnappings or murders, while a Mahdi Army commander celebrated having liberated the city from the British.[48]

In one ceremony nearly 6,000 Sunni Arabs were presided over by a dozen sheikhs draped in black robes trimmed with gold braiding who signed a contract on behalf of the tribesmen pledging support for the US military. The plan was for the Sunnis, some of them former insurgents, to be paid $275 a month each to man checkpoints north of Baghdad. According to one estimate around 77,000 Iraqis nationwide had resolved to cease their insurgent activities and to join the US-backed self-defence groups.[49] This meant that any attempt to rely solely on the Iraqi security forces, answerable to a democratically elected government, to guarantee security had been abandoned. The erstwhile Sunni insurgents, newly involved with US paymasters, had no well-defined rules of engagement and were in effect answerable only to local warlords. The journalist Hala Jaber has described the 'American-backed killer militias', belonging to such groups as the Knights of Amiriyah and the Guardians of Ghazaliya, strutting across Iraq and brandishing their new AK-47s.[50] Some of these Sunnis had been linked to al-Qaeda only weeks before. Who could say where, mercenary motives apart, their basic loyalties lay? In any event the Shi'ite communities, contemplating the sudden upsurge of US-funded masked killers, were wondering how their own security would be compromised. Another journalist, James Hider, has indicated how Abu Abed al-Obeidi, a former Iraqi military intelligence officer working as an American double agent, imposes order through force and dispenses advice on how the US-funded Sunnis should fight the Mahdi Army and other Shi'ite militias.[51] And there were signs that even the Sunni residents saw trouble ahead.

Some of the new enforcers were former members of the al-Qaeda-linked Islamic Army, deemed responsible for the murder of the Italian journalist Enzo Baldoni, and they still retained their fundamentalist beliefs. Thus in one Amiriyah school the 'knights' went from one class to another looking for mobile phones with 'un-Islamic' ringtones. One child with a pop music ringtone was slapped in the face and kicked as a warning to others. At the same time former insurgents now part of the pro-American 'Sunni Awakening' were continuing the campaign of sectarian cleansing.[52]

The US military had been driven to do deals with former 'terrorists', many of whom had killed American, British and Iraqi soldiers. And the British had followed the American example. Thus Major General Paul Newton, a senior British army commander in Iraq, revealed that discussions had taken place – often in hotels in neighbouring countries – with insurgent groups in an effort to reduce the levels of violence. ('Do we talk to people with blood on their hands? I certainly hope so. There is no point in talking to people who haven't.')[53]

The Bush administration was also applauding the numbers of Iraqi refugees returning home, though the motives of the returnees were mixed and the statistics were questionable.[54] Some cited messages from neighbours saying that 'the situation [in Iraq] is really good now'. Others said that it was financially impossible to continue living in Damascus and other parts of Syria: 'We had to go back to square one when we came here. Rents are high and I could only put my son into school. I couldn't pay for clothes or books for my daughters. It's impossible to live here. Once you leave your country, you have no dignity.'[55] Some refugees claimed that, though education in Damascus was free, head-teachers were demanding bribes or saying that there was no room for Iraqi children. In addition, the returns had been forced by Syria's decision to tighten visa rules from 1 October, making it harder for Iraqis to renew their permission to stay in the country – an understandable move when we consider the burdens imposed on Syria by the sudden influx of hundreds of thousands of immigrants. It did not help that UN appeals for refugee support had received such a dismal response from the United States, Britain and most other European countries.

Now the US military was beginning to realise that the return of Iraqi refugees, useful for propaganda purposes, carried its own potential problems. What would happen when the returnees found that their homes were occupied by other Iraqis of a different sect? There had been massive levels of ethnic cleansing in Baghdad and other urban centres, and by now the pattern was familiar. Individuals would be kidnapped, threatened or murdered and other family members would flee in terror, their homes then occupied to consolidate the sectarian purity of the neighbour-hood. Colonel William Rapp, a senior aide working for General Petraeus, commented at a two-day briefing for American reporters in Baghdad: 'All these guys coming back are probably going to find somebody else living in their house. We have been pleading with the government of Iraq to come up with a policy.'[56]

There was no mechanism to settle property disputes, and no plans for aid, shelter and other essential services for the thousands of Iraqis expected to return to the capital and other towns and cities. At one level it seemed unclear how there could be a property dispute. Formerly mixed areas had become predom-inantly Sunni or Shi'ite, with Sunnis moving into abandoned Shi'ite homes and vice versa. Did the original house occupiers no longer own their properties? Or was there something akin to squatters' rights in Iraqi law or natural justice? The obvious fear was that matters would be settled in the ways that had become the norm in Iraq since the 2003 invasion. Refugees unprotected by militias or death squads could expect to be consigned to pauperdom, torture or an early grave. The claimed security gains, if real, would quickly melt away in a new phase of sectarian bloodletting.

What the Bush administration advertised as the 'success' of the surge was throwing his domestic opponents onto the defensive, rendering the pro-war politicians jubilant. Thus Senator Joseph Lieberman, sitting as an independent, referred to the 'thrilling' progress in Iraq and declared that the Democrats were 'in deep denial, emotionally invested in a narrative of retreat and defeat'.[57] The opponents of the war, keen to acknowledge the 'magnificent' US troops in Iraq (Senator Barack Obama), were being forced to focus on the lack of political progress in the country.[58] In these circumstances the endless carnage was largely ignored in Washington, though there was ample available evidence of continuing attacks on US forces, the American bombing of urban areas, and the inevitable heavy toll of Iraqi civilians. Thus the US commander Colonel Don Farris expressed his concern about 'special groups', lethal Iran-backed Shi'ites maintaining their attacks on American troops, in part by planting high-powered bombs that were killing US soldiers.[59] In late November American troops killed at least five civilians, including women and a child, and dozens of people were dying elsewhere in the country.[60] There were signs that the Sunni-led resistance groups had scaled back their attacks on US forces in Baghdad, and were regrouping and retraining to wait out the surge.[61] Furthermore, it could not be assumed that the Mahdi Army would maintain its self-imposed ceasefire, particularly in view of the implications of the Sunni Awakening, where armed former insurgents were being invited by the Americans to act with impunity, Mafia style, to impose security.

On 29 November 2007 President Bush and Prime Minister al-Maliki signed an agreement to begin negotiations for a long-term American commitment to the puppet regime. Lieutenant General Douglas Lute, the administration's deputy National Security Advisor for Iraq and Afghanistan, signalled 'an enduring relation-ship based on mutual interests', with Iraq 'increasingly able to stand on its own . . . but it won't have to stand alone'. The agreement, it was emphasised, was not a treaty. Formal negotiations would begin early in 2008 and conclude by July, the time when the surge troops would begin withdrawing. Many aspects of the 'enduring relationship' would be discussed, including the question of permanent bases and foreign invest-ment, a potential bonanza for US oil companies.

The plans for a permanent American involvement in Iraqi affairs did not mean that the US–Iraqi relationship was one of concord and mutual respect. In fact opinion in Iraq on a continuing American presence was deeply divided. As far back as mid-2004 more than 90 per cent of Iraqis regarded the US-led forces as 'occupiers' rather than 'liberators', a situation that had deteriorated, from the US perspective, from that time. This meant that the UN mandate, conferring 'legitimacy' on the multi-national force in Iraq, had become increasingly problematic. Was the democratic will of the Iraqi people, not least as expressed through their notional parliament, to be totally ignored?

At the end of 2007 the mandate was coming up for renewal and, bearing in mind the US domination of the Security Council, few doubted that it would be secured. In 2006 al-Maliki requested the renewal of the mandate without consulting the legislature – a violation of Iraqi law, according to many parliamentarians.[62] In June 2007 the parliament passed a binding resolution to force al-Maliki to give parliamentarians the opportunity to block the UN mandate. Al-Maliki failed to exercise his veto in the allowed period (fifteen days) and the resolution became the law of the land in mid-June 2007. When he again sought to extend the UN mandate in October, wrongly regarding the resolution as 'non-binding', a protest letter signed by a majority (144) of Iraq's parliamentarians was received by UN special envoy Ashraf Qazi – but never distributed to Security Council members, as required by the Security Council resolution governing the mandate. The Iraqi parliament and the Iraqi people had been excised from the legislative process. These events clearly demonstrate, if any further demonstration were necessary, that Iraq is not governed by a parliamentary system but by a puppet regime under military occupation.

However, the puppet status of the Maliki administration did not mean that there were no tensions and difficulties between the Americans and the Iraqi regime. On such key issues as corruption, sectarian reconciliation and the regional sharing of oil revenues there were obvious tensions between the Bush administration and the Maliki government. Overall, the White House remained deeply ambivalent about the status and competence of a government it was seemingly committed to protect at all costs. Steps had been taken by the US military to involve compliant militia factions, criminal groups and local warlords in efforts to improve security, so sidelining the Iraqi authorities. In turn, the Maliki regime was beginning to look beyond the United States to meet some of its perceived survival needs, perhaps at last anticipating an eventual reduction in American forces that would leave the government exposed. Thus in October 2007, after revelations that Iraq had been ordering $100 million-worth of armaments from China, Iraq's President Jalal Talabani criticised the US for failing to deliver arms shipments in good time. In the same vein some Iraqi provinces were exacerbating sectarian tensions – contrary to American demands – by shutting out people fleeing conflict elsewhere in the country.

On 15 November US commanders were saying that the Iraqi government, by virtue of its political stagnation, posed a greater danger than al-Qaeda or anti-American insurgents.[63] General Raymond Odierno, responsible for day-to-day military operations, commented that there was a window of opportunity but it was 'unclear how long that window is going to be open'.[64] In the same vein the US did not believe that the Iraqi forces were meeting the security challenges: progress was being made but it was insufficient. Lieutenant General James Dubik, in charge of training Iraqi soldiers, said that progress had been good but mixed, and that there was no way that the Iraqis would be able to take over as many provinces by 2008 as the US authorities had intended: 'I don't think we'll make that [the original plan]. We're not on a timeline at all. The conditions in each province will dictate when we do that.'[65] The Iraqi authorities, even when backed by the US military, were unable to guarantee urban security or even to achieve agreement with the Iraqi Kurds on oil deals with foreign contractors. Nor could they secure their own borders. It was acknowledged that 'terrorists' were continuing to infiltrate from Syria, Iran and Saudi Arabia, and the mounting tensions between Turkey and the PKK were leading to Turkish military incursions and shelling of Iraqi sovereign territory.[66] At every level the American–British Iraq policy had been an unmitigated disaster.

On 16 December 2007 dozens of Turkish warplanes, accompanied by long-range artillery shelling, bombed suspected Kurdish insurgent positions inside Iraq up to 60 miles from the Turkish border. Kurdish officials claimed that villages rather than bases had been hit and reported civilian casualties, including one woman killed and two others injured. Recep Tayyip Erdoğan, the Turkish Prime Minister, promised more military action to come: 'Our struggle will continue inside and outside Turkey with the same determination.'[67] General Yaşar Büyükanıt, the head of the

Turkish military, was quoted by the Anatolian state news agency as saying that the US had opened Iraqi airspace to facilitate the Turkish bombing raids.[68] Two days later, hundreds of Turkish troops invaded Iraq in pursuit of PKK fighters. Massoud Barzani, president of the Kurdish region, cancelled talks in Baghdad with Condoleezza Rice in protest, and prime minister Nechirvan Barzani commented: 'It is unacceptable that the US, in charge of monitoring our airspace, authorised Turkey to bomb our villages.'[69] Again it was plain that the growing Kurdish appetite for autonomy caused by the Iraq War was exacerbating the confrontation between Turkey and northern Iraq.

At the same time Britain was continuing its withdrawal from the conflict. On 16 December Major General Graham Binns, commanding officer of the British forces in southern Iraq, and Mohammed al-Waili, the Basra governor, signed the legal documents confirming the handover of Basra province to the Iraqi security forces. This in effect ended the British military's combat role in the country. Commentators were quick to note the irony that the low-key ceremony was held in the departure lounge of Basra airport, miles from Basra city and one of the few places where the deal could be conducted in safety.

The British depiction of the event was predictable. Binns declared that he had come 'to rid Basra of its enemies and I now formally hand Basra back to its friends',[70] and Foreign Secretary David Miliband, while forced to admit that Iraq was 'not a land of milk and honey', described the handover of the strategically most important of the four provinces that had been under British control as an opportunity for Iraqis to show what they could do. The political spin suggested that the British withdrawal was not a defeat, that it had long been planned ('conditions-driven', in the jargon), and that the Iraqi security forces would be able to cope: 'The factors that contribute to the decision to transfer to provincial Iraqi control are partly the degree of threat, and partly the capability of the Iraqi security forces to take over. We consider that they are now capable to deal with the current situation [Binns].'[71]

In fact, the British had been driven out of the city by the Iraqi insurgents, not least by 'the increasing accuracy of the militias'

mortar crews'.[72] Security had not been established and Basra was
in the grip of feuding sectarian groups, criminal gangs and tribal
factions. Residents were quoted as saying that the British forces
had contributed to a 'Talibanisation'[73] under the control of
Islamist thugs and bigots. Major General Jalil Khalaf, Basra's police
chief, declared in an interview for Guardian Films and ITV that
the British forces had left chaos behind them: 'They left me
militia, they left me gangsters, and they left me all the troubles in
the world.'[74] And he listed specific failures: Basra had become so
lawless that in the last three months dozens of women had been
killed by the Islamists for being 'immoral'; the British had
unintentionally rearmed the Shi'ite militias by failing to recognise
the sectarian loyalties of Iraqi troops; and the Shi'ite militias were
now better armed than the Iraqi security forces and controlled
Iraq's main port.[75] Was all this what the British government had
worked to achieve?

The journalist Marie Colvin conveyed what the 'Talibanisation'
facilitated by the British forces had come to mean for women in
southern Iraq.[76] They were being killed for dressing wrongly or for
being 'immoral' in other ways. Thus the police held forty-eight
manila files containing photographs of discarded female corpses
and close-ups of their last expressions. The women were invariably
labelled 'female, unknown identity', and something of their
suffering was graphically recorded. In one picture a woman's eyes
are popping in terror, in another a woman's nose is crushed, lines
of blood trail from the eye of another; some of the women had
their faces slashed for wearing make-up, one has bullet wounds in
her hands and arms, and two of the women had been beheaded,
one with a saw.[77] The police were not investigating. No suspects
had been arrested. Everyone lived in fear of the militias.

And it was not only women who were being tortured and
murdered. Professionals such as engineers, doctors and scientists
were being dragged from their homes and killed. Khalaf,
struggling to impose order, commented that the militias were
winning:

'The problems are like an interlocking chain. The militias control the
ports, which earns them huge sums of money . . . Smugglers cross the

borders with guns and weapons and these go to the militias. We don't
have enough guards or the sophisticated equipment you need to stop
them. You could smuggle a tank across that border [the Iran–Iraq
border] if you wanted.'[78]

The British were largely to blame for allowing the political parties
to nominate people for positions in the police: 'Of course the
parties nominated their own [sectarian] members.'[79] Masses of
police communications equipment had been delivered from police
warehouses to the militias, and 1,000 cars bearing police insignia
had disappeared. Some 3,500 members of the police force were
being paid at great cost to the Iraqi treasury, but they were working
with the militias and not even bothering to turn up for work.

According to an opinion poll commissioned by the BBC just 2
per cent of people in Basra believed that the British presence had
had a positive effect on their province since 2003; some 86 per cent
saw the British forces as having had a negative impact.[80] And the
troops in Iraq, according to Brigadier Andrew Mackay, the
commander in Afghanistan, had themselves been demoralised by
the nature of the conflict, mired as it was in 'spin and dodgy dossiers'
and unable to escape the 'legality issue' of the 2003 invasion.[81]

The British government, despite everything, continued to insist
that its mission in Iraq had been a success. When Gordon Brown
was questioned in the Commons about the plight of Iraqi women
he refused to address the issue, saying instead that Iraq was a
democracy, people had voted, and 'Iraqis were taking control of
their own security'. This last was a lie, unless Brown was referring
to the Shi'ite militias. The British involvement in Iraq had begun
on a lie and it was ending on a lie – and such major lies had
spawned a plethora of falsehoods.

There was now speculation that US troops might have to be sent
to Basra once the British forces were further reduced in 2008.[82]
And there was continuing discussion in late 2007 and early 2008
about the alleged success of the American military surge in and
around Baghdad. Arguably, the US military had sold out by
arming and funding Sunni insurgents to combat al-Qaeda and to
impose order on their neighbourhoods by whatever brutal means

were necessary, just as the British forces, knowingly or unknow-
ingly, had armed and trained the Shi'ite militias in southern Iraq.
It was also possible that the claimed successes in the security
situation, in early 2008 massively under-reported by the few
independent journalists still able to operate, were no more than a
lull while the insurgents regrouped and retrained, waiting for the
predicted drawdown of surge troops in mid-2008. And how was
the US-imposed order, in so far as it existed, to be evaluated?
What methods had been used? We knew that bombing raids of
urban areas had intensified through 2007, the detainee population
had soared, and apartheid walls had been used to fragment Iraqi
towns and cities in prison ghettos. Are casualty statistics, even if
believable, the only criterion of political success? Were we
expected to rejoice at how the Nazis brought order to French and
Polish towns?

There is another consideration. Even accepting all the claims of
the Bush administration that security in Iraq is vastly improved, that
there is now 'space' for reconstruction and political progress, and
that the Iraqi civilian population is now better off then ever before
– and no one outside the White House bunker really believes
this – then there is still the history of what has been perpetrated over
the last five years. Events do not escape ethical and legal analysis
simply because they are of finite duration. Hiroshima stopped
burning, the Rwanda genocide came to an end, and the Auschwitz
extermination camp became a tourist attraction.

11

Psychology, lies and the wider world

There is a theory, to which I do not subscribe, that personalities can be ignored in analysing political developments. It is suggested that such things as the character, beliefs and charisma of national leaders are not relevant to political change: policies are what count. It seems to me that both personality and policies deeply affect the course of change in society; and that, in particular, the personalities of George Bush and Tony Blair have impinged directly on the course of US–UK policies on Iraq and the wider world. Bush and Blair, whatever the nature of global crises and whatever pressures were being exerted in Washington and London, did not have to go to war. There are reasons for thinking that other leaders, lacking their messianic zeal and an obsession with the 'broad picture', would have chosen differently.

President Bill Clinton was under constant pressure from the neoconservatives and other elements to force regime change in Iraq, if necessary by taking military action. On 26 January 1998 a group of influential Americans wrote an open letter to the Honorable William J. Clinton ('Dear Mr President') urging the adoption of a strategy that would aim 'above all, at the removal of Saddam Hussein's regime from power'. Here it was asserted that the United States could 'no longer depend on our partners in the Gulf war coalition to continue to uphold the sanctions or to punish Saddam when he blocks or evades UN inspectors', with the consequence that the US ability 'to ensure that Saddam is not producing weapons of mass destruction . . . has substantially diminished'. This meant that the President should show his willingness 'to undertake military action as diplomacy is clearly failing . . . it means removing Saddam and his regime from power'. That, declared the signatories to the letter, 'needs to become the aim of American foreign policy'.[1]

The letter is of particular interest because, written during the Clinton era, it prefigured the bellicosity of a new presidency. Many of the people who signed the letter were destined to become leading figures (Rumsfeld, Wolfowitz, Zoellick, Armitage, Bolton, Dobriansky, Rodman, Abrams, Khalilzad and Perle) in the Bush administration. The agitation for war, unsuccessful under Clinton,[2] gained immense impetus with the election, through questionable tactics,[3] of someone totally amenable to neocon and other belligerent pressures.

In the same way Tony Blair was eager to go to war in Iraq, whereas an earlier Labour Prime Minister, Harold Wilson, had resisted all American pressures to send British troops to Vietnam. President Lyndon Johnson was quick to point out that Britain had sent troops to Korea but was not prepared to support the US in Vietnam in the same way.[4] He did not mention that the Korean War, unlike Vietnam, had been authorised by the UN. When Wilson and Johnson met the following year (1966), the American President declared that a platoon of bagpipers would have been sufficient: 'It was the British flag that was needed' – to aid US propaganda that the anti-Vietnam coalition involved more countries than the United States, Australia and South Korea. In 1968 Secretary of State Dean Rusk told the British journalist Louis Heren: 'All we needed was one regiment. The Black Watch would have done. Just one regiment, but you wouldn't. Well, don't expect us to save you again. They [the Russians] can invade Sussex, and we wouldn't do a damned thing about it.'[5] And there were more immediate pressures.

Johnson was trying to exploit the chronic weakness of sterling to blackmail Wilson into sending a token ground force to Vietnam. Thus McGeorge Bundy, the US National Security Advisor, advised the President: 'It makes no sense for us to rescue the pound in a situation in which there is no British flag in Vietnam. A British brigade in Vietnam would be worth a billion dollars at the moment of truth for sterling.'[6] Is there a clue here why Blair, Brown, Howard and the rest of the British political establishment were so keen to go to war in Iraq?

Wilson, despite refusing to send even the Black Watch regiment to Vietnam, said: 'We fully support the action of the US in resisting aggression in Vietnam' – by which he meant the alleged communist aggression and not the American intervention. And he helped the US war effort in various overt and covert ways.[7] But the fact remains that he robustly refused to send British troops to die in Vietnam – an enduring irritation to Washington that led the earthy Johnson to respond with personal abuse.[8] In any event Blair was not about to face similar commentary. Both he and George Bush shared a similar messianic fervour which, in defiance of wiser counsels, plunged both countries – and the Iraqi people – into a hugely destructive war, one that was to have vast regional and global consequences.

An important feature, worth noting, in the peculiar Bush–Blair symbiosis is religiosity and faith, involving attitudes to belief and accountability that necessarily diminish loyalty to empirical facts and secular democratic structures. When George Bush was asked by the journalist Bob Woodward whether he ever asked his father for advice, the American President replied: 'He is the wrong father to appeal to for advice. The wrong father to go to, to appeal to in terms of strength. There's a higher Father that I appeal to.'[9] This reliance on a supernatural source of wisdom has sometimes yielded dramatic results. In a major BBC television production Abu Mazen, the then Palestinian Prime Minister, and Nabil Shaath, his Foreign Minister, described their first meeting with Bush: 'President Bush said to all of us: "I'm driven with a mission from God. God would tell me: 'George, go and fight those terrorists in Afghanistan.' And I did, and then God would tell me: 'George, go and end the tyranny in Iraq.' . . . And I did."'[10]

In addition, Bush has surrounded himself with evangelicals deeply hostile to many aspects of scientific thought and competing creeds. On 13 December 2003, when Saddam Hussein was captured, Bush phoned his father, Attorney General John Ashcroft and also three evangelicals – Rev. Billy Graham, Rev. Franklin Graham and his own preacher at the United Methodist Church, Highland Park, Texas. Then, with Ashcroft in the office and the preachers in teleconference, Bush again phoned his father and mother to link them by telephone. With Bush and Ashcroft on their knees in the Oval Office, Franklin Graham led the prayer:

Jesus, your fingerprints are on this mission, and it is because of you, O Lord, that the Evil that is Saddam Hussein has been brought to justice. In the name of Jesus Christ, we thank you for bearing this great gift to the good people of the blessed United States of America.[11]

In the same vein, General William Boykin, a fervent Bush supporter who had served in Somalia, publicly upheld the United States as a 'Christian nation' and derided Islam: 'I knew that my God was bigger than [my Islamic foe's], and I knew that my God was a real God and his was an idol . . . We are in an army of God for such a time as this [the war with Iraq].'[12] When Pastor Ron, preaching in Texas, asked his congregation two questions on behalf of the author Barbara Victor the response was unanimous. 'Who is the devil?'

'Muslims, Arabs, the terrorists who kill Americans.'

'Is George W. Bush a good President?'

'Blessed by God!'[13]

Such focused devotion has inevitable consequences for any attempt to understand the real world. It is no accident that fervent American Christians are the ones most likely to disparage the fact of biological evolution, preferring instead to contemplate an idyllic scene where children frolic with vegetarian dinosaurs. The American psychoanalyst Justin A. Frank, attempting a remote analysis of Bush, commented: 'The individual who clings tenaciously to unverified beliefs confuses his beliefs with fact, and often inflicts this confusion on others in his struggle to resolve it in his favour.'[14] The corollary is that the individual is often uncertain or ignorant about details of the real world, a circumstance that has been amply demonstrated in the case of George Bush.

On the eve of the invasion of Iraq in 2003 the American commander-in-chief was unfamiliar with the terms 'Sunni' and 'Shi'ite'.[15] Later he appeared to believe that Iraq shared a border with Palestine.[16] And in September 2007, attending the APEC (Asia-Pacific Economic Cooperation) summit in Australia, he seemed to think he was attending an OPEC (Organization of Petroleum Exporting Countries) summit in Austria[17] – a typical Bush 'misspeak'. Bush's childlike grasp of language ('Is our children learning') was further illustrated on 25 September 2007 by the leak on the United Nations website of a phonetic guide [sar–KO-zee, moo–GAH-bee etc.] provided by his staff to aid the President's speech to the UN General Assembly.

Robert Draper, interviewing Bush to write his profile of the President (*Dead Certain: The Presidency of George W. Bush*, 2007) asked him whether Paul Bremer had been allowed in May 2003 to disband the Iraqi army without pay – a foolish decision that had fuelled the insurgency. Bush was stumped by the question: 'Yeah, I can't remember: I'm sure I said, "This is the policy, what happened?" . . . Hadley [National Security Advisor Stephen Hadley] has got notes on all this stuff.'[18] This response provoked widespread outrage in America and elsewhere. James Fallows, of *Atlantic Monthly*, wrote:

> Think about this. The dissolution of the Iraq military is one of the six most criticised and most-often-discussed aspects of the Administration's entire approach to Iraq . . . and the President who has staked the fortunes of his Administration, his party, his place in history, and (come to think of it) his nation on the success of the Iraq policy cannot remember and even now cannot be bothered to find out how the decision was made.[19]

In the same vein Alastair Campbell's diaries revealed that Tony Blair, who has often proclaimed the importance of faith in his life, prayed to 'his maker' for guidance during the run-up to the Iraq invasion. Blair, silenced on one occasion by Campbell ('We don't do God'), also declared in an ITV interview with Michael Parkinson on 3 May 2003 that he would be judged by his maker (and by history) for his political decisions. These frequent admissions of reliance on a supernatural power coupled with Blair's messianic certainties encouraged some commentators to query, not entirely frivolously, his sanity.[20] David Owen, a politician and medical doctor, notes that the 'very experience of holding office seems to infect them [politicians] with something that causes them to behave in ways which, on the face of it at least, seem symptomatic of a sort of mental disease', and then he explores the 'hubristic syndrome' that both Bush and Blair developed while in power.[21]

Both Bush and Blair have used their religious beliefs to reinforce simplistic moral postures that in any other contexts would be generally regarded as immature and ill informed. Blair 'seemed wholly uninterested in Iraq as a complex and puzzling society, wanting confirmation merely that deposing Saddam would remove "evil" from the country',[22] just as Bush enjoys denouncing 'evil doers'.[23] It is possible also to detail the typical features of psychopathology and to see how particular individuals match the list. Thus Robert Hare, professor emeritus from the University of British Columbia, depicts psychopaths as typically glib, charming, manipulative, deceitful and ruthless. Moreover, they are not troubled by conscience, have a marked lack of empathy, and 'seduce victims with a hypnotic charm that masks their true nature as pathological liars, master con artists, and heartless manipulators'.[24] Many observers would suggest that Bush and Blair fit the bill.

There are many features that characterise the Bush–Blair symbiosis: in particular, the capacity to misread and misrepresent reality. In one interpretation they are foolish men, unable to address the complex information that is relevant to the political problems they encounter. Perhaps more plausibly, they are depicted as dissemblers, prepared to lie comprehensively in pursuit of messianic goals – to the point that 'Blair' was frequently transmuted into 'Bliar' for the posters and literature of activist opponents. It is likely that George Bush failed to fully grasp what was happening – and lacked empathy and a troubled conscience; and Tony Blair managed to convince himself that what he was saying was true, an ability that typifies the most effective type of con artist – and equally lacked empathy and a troubled conscience. This is a benevolent interpretation. Neither man was a liar in the strict sense of the word: one was an ignoramus and the other a self-delusionist. Both were helplessly enmeshed in the politics of denial, psychologically unable to comprehend what was patently obvious to the rest of the world. Alas, it is difficult to be so charitable. The panoply of deception became so vast and so multi-layered that we are hard pressed to believe that Bush and Blair did not know what it was all about.

At the simplest level it all began with weapons of mass destruction. The intelligence sources stated that the evidence was uncertain and partial: Bush and Blair said it was clear and comprehensive (see Introduction). But it did not end here. A plethora of falsehoods clustered around this central deception, eroding the integrity of governments and the faith of citizens in their democracies.[25] This is part of the dark and wider picture that developed around the decision to invade Iraq.

It was claimed that Iraq, along with Iran and North Korea (the three-member 'axis of evil'), was the worst potential nuclear proliferator, a danger to the region and the world. Had Saddam not already waged war on Iran (with the support of the US, the UK and others) and invaded Kuwait (with US encouragement)? The accusations against Saddam were made at a time when Israel was free to develop nuclear weapons to be launched from submarines, aircraft and missile bases; when Washington was rewarding a nuclear India with technology deals to facilitate further development; and when the United States, looking to its own interests, was aiding Pakistan's acquisition and proliferation of nuclear weapons.[26] In these circumstances, in all of which Washington was a key player, to focus on Iraq as the worst potential proliferator was a gross distortion of reality.

It was further claimed that since Iraq's Ba'athist regime was a tyranny it should be overthrown as a human rights issue. But the United States and Britain have worked hard to cultivate friendly tyrants – for example, Pakistan's Pervez Musharraf, Egypt's Hosni Mubarak and the Saudi royals – where perceived national interests were at stake. If Ba'athism needed to be overthrown there had to be another reason. That Iraq was an Islamic state was no problem. Saddam was a secular Sunni Muslim, and Islamic fundamentalists were among his victims. The Iraqi dictator would have been a staunch ally against al-Qaeda, just as today the US celebrates its alliance with Sunni tribes in Anbar fighting foreign terrorists. The reason for regime change had to lie in another direction.

In fact one of the principal motives of many for overthrowing the Iraqi government (see Introduction) was that Ba'athism was essentially socialist, insistent on maintaining a comprehensive state sector and hostile to foreign capital penetration. When Paul

Bremer was installed in a post-invasion Baghdad he soon set about dismantling Iraq's state sector and preparing the ground for a free-enterprise economy, just as had happened in the Balkans. The new Iraqi constitution, drafted with US involvement, stipulated that the new government 'guarantees the reform of the Iraqi economy' in accordance with 'the encouragement and the development of the private sector' (Article 25). The United States, it seems, is instinctively unable to tolerate the few residual outposts of socialism perched insecurely on a capitalist globe. (We may speculate that Iran and North Korea might have been allowed to proliferate happily if they had not enshrined significant state sectors hostile to American economic ambitions.)

Another vital US consideration is the enduring euro–dollar war, a global competition for economic power and influence that encourages Washington to achieve regime change wherever appropriate and possible. Some observers have suggested that a general migration from the dollar to the euro is slowly creating a new reserve currency for the world, and that the US financial structure will collapse unless the United States can destroy its enemies first.

It has been argued that it was Saddam's decision to support the euro, so helping to erode an American financial empire built on the dollar, that finally sealed his fate.[27] It is also significant that Iran, long vilified by the US and others, decided to set up an oil bourse based on the euro rather than the dollar. In 2005–6 Tehran developed a euro-dominated international oil trading mechanism to begin competing with the New York Mercantile Exchange and London's International Petroleum Exchange with respect to international oil trades. In addition, Venezuela's President Hugo Chávez took steps in 2003 to replace the dollar with the euro, causing further alarm in Washington.[28] Such developments meant that the amount of trade in dollars would reduce, so curtailing the 'transaction demand' for that currency, further weakening America's global posture.[29] It was clear that Washington had an interest in blocking this trend, suggesting that a vast deception had been propagated in disguising such powerful financial motives for war (in addition to funding the Bush-friendly corporations whose lobbyists clustered on Capitol Hill).

Other deceptions related to the impact of the war and occupation on Iraqi civilians. *Every care is taken to avoid civilian casualties. Smart weapons are used in order to minimise collateral damage. The mistreatment of detainees is not allowed and perpetrators will be punished. Torture has never been an official part of US policy. The Iraqi people are now better off living in a burgeoning democracy.* All these lies have been dealt with comprehensively elsewhere.[30] Here it is enough to indicate briefly some of the consequences of the 2003 invasion and the ensuing occupation.

The war was launched on a largely defenceless country with the tactic of shock and awe, a military doctrine that achieves such massive immediate destruction that the enemy is not only unable to respond in practical terms but is also so shattered psychologically that the will to resist is crushed. In one respect at least, the tactic failed: the war continued. In another respect it was grimly successful. Great buildings at the heart of Baghdad were consumed in fireballs, which surely should have evoked empathy in Americans grieving at the loss of two iconic structures in New York.

The writer Naomi Klein has described in graphic terms the American success in erasing Iraq: 'It's a tried-and-tested torture technique: strike fear into your victims, deprive them of cherished essentials and then eradicate their memories.'[31] And this was to be done to a nation. It began with the terror campaign ('showing the instruments'). There was media talk of shock and awe, the doctrine's author, Harlan Ullman, describing an effect 'rather like the nuclear weapons at Hiroshima, not taking days or weeks but in minutes', and of the 'moab' (massive ordnance bomb), weighing 21,000 pounds and able to create 'a 10,000ft-high mushroom cloud that looks and feels like a nuclear weapon' (Jamie McIntyre, CNN). The campaign was allowed months to sink in.[32]

Next, with the start of the onslaught, the city's sensory systems were eradicated – the ears first, with the destruction of the telephone exchanges and the communications ministry, and then the eyes, as the five million people of Baghdad were 'plunged into an awful endless night'. And then the stripping of the victim began, as the city's most important institutions were looted and the heart of the country was erased. McGuire Gibson, an archaeologist at the University of Chicago, called the desecration 'a lot like a lobotomy. The deep memory of an entire culture, a culture that has continued for thousands of years, has been removed.'[33]

The Americans made no attempt to indicate the likely number of civilian casualties, helpless in a city that was being consumed by fire. Estimates would be attempted later, but they would not be made public by the US authorities. Eventually we would learn that hundreds of thousands had died in the initial onslaught and the bloody years of carnage that followed. And something of the character of the US-led invasion would emerge. One witness, Sergeant Eric Olson in an American tank platoon, wrote in his diary:

> Behind the enemy truck was a blown up civilian car that had a family in it. The father was twitching on the ground with no skin on his body. The mother was sitting on the ground rocking back and forth, her body was smoking, and in her arms she cradled an infant . . . A boy about ten years old . . . had no hair and very little skin left. His eyes were fused shut as he walked round aimlessly, with layers of skin hanging off his body. I wanted to help them . . . We had to keep pushing forward.[34]

The civilians were killed both accidentally and deliberately: they were targeted by US troops[35] and denied the necessities of life until they agreed to cooperate with the occupation forces. The New York-based International Action Center described the fresh American strategy: 'deliberately preventing Iraqi civilians in Nasiriyah and other towns from receiving food and water unless they cooperate with the occupation forces'. A US Marines operations commander, Lieutenant Colonel Paul Roche, confirmed the policy: 'The US strategy towards the people of Nasiriyah included the use of food and water as a weapon to terrorise and break the will of the civilian population.'[36] He did not mention, and he probably did not know, that any such policy was a gross violation of international law: for example, Article 54 of the 1977 Protocol 1 Addition to the Geneva Conventions stipulates that 'starvation of civilians as a method of warfare is prohibited'.

★

The US forces also adopted the use of torture, despite its illegality in both domestic and international law.[37] Alfred W. McCoy, professor of history at the University of Wisconsin-Madison, commented: 'After the attacks on September 11, 2001, the White House made torture its secret weapon in the war on terror . . . soon [replicating] the same patterns first seen during [Washington's] "dirty war" in Vietnam . . . an uncontrolled proliferation of torture.'[38] US Major General Antonio Taguba, who comprehensively investigated the abuses at Abu Ghraib (and was ridiculed by Donald Rumsfeld for his efforts), concluded that 'sadistic, blatant and wanton criminal abuses' were common in the prison.[39] Here it is enough to give one quotation from Taguba's report:

> Punching, slapping and kicking detainees; videotaping and photographing naked male and female detainees; forcibly arranging detainees in various sexually explicit positions for photographing; forcing detainees to remove their clothing and keeping them naked for several days at a time; forcing groups of male detainees to masturbate themselves while being photographed and videotaped; a male Military Police guard having sex with a female detainee; breaking chemical lights and pouring the phosphoric liquid on detainees . . . sodomizing a detainee with a chemical light . . . using military dogs to frighten and intimidate . . . in one instance actually biting a detainee.[40]

It should not be thought that the abuse and torture of detainees was confined to Abu Ghraib. Such treatment characterised the entire detention system, whether or not the responsible authorities were American or Iraqi. One US interrogator/ torturer, Tony Lagouranis, described in detail the abusive activities in which he became involved: detainees had been beaten 'for days . . . I learned about using stress positions, loud music, lights, sleep "adjustment", sexual humiliation, and manipulation of diet and environment, which included using the cold weather to distress the detainee' (the Americans hoped for bad weather because it was no 'fun' leaving a naked detainee outside overnight in the mud if the weather was 'balmy').[41] Another US soldier,

Tomas, told Lagouranis that he had seen half a dozen prisoners chained to poles in different stress positions, 'sort of hanging there like overripe tomatoes on vines supported by stakes'. Most of the detainees had nothing to do with the insurgency or other forms of violence: in Abu Ghraib there were 'growing ranks of innocent detainees', and Lagouranis 'had a real problem with seeing them interrogated and tortured when they should have been put through a trial'.[42]

On one occasion, deeply frustrated by one detainee, he had the thought (quickly rejected) 'chop his fucking fingers off'; for a moment 'it made perfect sense to cut his fingers off'.[43] And he found himself abusing detainees 'for my own amusement' with no evidence that they were guilty of anything: 'I'd probably sent many innocent people to indefinite detention.' On 21 September 2006 Professor Manfred Nowak, the UN's special investigator on torture worldwide, said that torture in Iraq ('totally out of hand') was worse than under Saddam: 'The situation is so bad that many people say that it is worse than it had been in the time of Saddam Hussein. That means something because the torture methods applied under Saddam Hussein were the worst you could imagine.'[44]

It was inevitable that unnumbered Iraqis died under this sort of treatment (Lagouranis mentions a dozen): the corpse of Manadel al-Jamadi appeared in the Abu Ghraib photographs, with grinning US guards giving the thumbs-up sign. By 2008 it was common knowledge that the Bush regime had authorised torture, despite frequent denials – and all the prohibitions in domestic and international law.[45] Vice-President Dick Cheney, who had characteristically deployed euphemism to support the use of torture, declared: 'We have to sort of work the dark side, if you will. We have to spend time in the shadows.'[46]

The Iraqi forces, trained and protected by the US military, had also adopted torture as a routine practice. In an interview with the *Daily Telegraph* Iyad Allawi, the former Iraqi Prime Minister, claimed that the Maliki regime was using tactics that were 'even worse' than Saddam's reign of terror and intimidation.[47] One Briton, Mohammed Hussein, was among hundreds detained for membership of a Shi'ite cult, the Soldiers of Heaven, even though he denied any links to terrorism. He claimed to have been 'beaten badly for days and days' and they 'tried to take my nails out . . . They twisted both my arms. They are worse than Saddam, they do the same and even worse'. His wife Ebtihal claimed to have seen other women tortured: 'They beat up a woman in front of me, her legs were blue . . . They hanged her from the ceiling and beat her.'[48]

Officials of the Bush administration, still keen to deny such practices, have lied about torture as they have lied about so much else. One investigative journalist, the award-winning Stephen Grey, said in his impressively researched book *Ghost Plane*: 'America's senior politicians and CIA leadership insisted that the United States "does not do torture". Yet, as I show, such claims were falsehoods.'[49] America does 'do torture' – on US territory, at Guantanamo, in Iraq and Afghanistan – and, through 'rendition', the CIA knowingly transports detainees for torture abroad.[50] On 10 October 2007 Jimmy Carter, interviewed on CNN, declared that the United States was torturing people in violation of international law. George Bush, in an address to Congress, had already said: 'One by one, the terrorists are learning the meaning of American justice' – and so was the rest of the world.

It is scarcely necessary to refer again to the suffering of the Iraqi people through the grim years of war: some indication has been given already of the collapsed infrastructure, the shortage of clean water and electricity, and the enduring terror that forced more than four million citizens to flee their homes. Here we simply note the plight of more than half the Iraqi population – namely, the women. One feature of the vast change in society was the Islamist ascendancy, the growth of a mediaeval obscurantism no longer constrained by a secular Ba'athism. As the conflict and anarchy wore on the women in Iraq became increasingly repressed by a misogynistic creed, a doctrine born in the deserts of Arabia in the seventh century that proclaimed the inferiority of half the human race, the suppression of women by men. The Koran asserts that men are superior to women (Sura 4, verse 34), are a 'degree above women' (Sura 3, verse 28) and can beat their wives when they are disobedient (4, 34).[51] The consequences of this ascendant mediaevalism have been horrific throughout Iraq.

In April 2003 Christian girls wearing lipstick and no head-scarves voiced fears that their freedoms would end if hardline Shi'ite clerics turned the secular Iraq into an Islamic republic. After the 2003 invasion the female blogger 'Riverbend' recorded that it felt like women had been thrown back fifty years. She, a computer science graduate, used to dress the way she wanted. Now women and girls wearing jeans and Western tops risked being attacked, abducted and even killed by fundamentalists. And, like thousands of other Iraqi women, she was terrorised into unemployment: 'I cried bitterly all the way home – cried for my job, cried for my future and cried for the torn streets, damaged buildings and crumbling people.'

Women were being prevented from participating in public life, forced out of education and work. Dr Kafaya, determined to continue working in a women and children's hospital, was shot dead; one witness, Mrs Aziz, spoke of other murdered female friends. A female Iraqi film maker, trying to chart the plight of women, was forced to keep her identity secret: 'No one sees what we are going through.' A 26-year-old university lecturer, Noor, used to go out with her boyfriend until the 'men in black' arrived on her doorstep and told her to observe Islamic strictures. Other women have been dragged into buildings to have their heads shaved for dressing inappropriately. The clerics, both Shi'ite and Sunni, were issuing anti-feminist fatwas. Today Iraqi women are virtual prisoners in their own homes, subject to wide-ranging strictures that, while common in such countries as Iran and Saudi Arabia, did not exist under Saddam.[52]

On 18 September 2001, in the immediate flood of emotion after 9/11, Congress adopted a resolution entitling George Bush to make war.[53] This joint resolution authorised the use of the US armed forces 'against those responsible for the recent attacks launched against the United States', and in particular authorised the President 'to take action to deter and prevent acts of inter-national terrorism against the United States'. No reference was made in the resolution to Iraq or Afghanistan, and no limits were placed on the President's war-making powers (as required by the constitution – see Chapter 9).[54] Bush was given a 'blank cheque' to wage war against any nation whenever he felt like it, not just any nation that might have harboured the 9/11 terrorists (such as Saudi Arabia) but any nation that might be implicated in terrorist acts in the future. This reminded us of words written by Abraham Lincoln to his law associate William H. Herndon on 15 February 1848: 'Allow the president to invade a . . . nation whenever he shall deem it necessary to repel an invasion and you allow him to do so whenever he may choose to say he deems it necessary for such a purpose . . . and you allow him to make war at pleasure.'

The invasion and occupation of Iraq created waves for the region and the world, in part consolidating and reinforcing political trends that were already in train. Much of the Arab world was dismayed at what was widely perceived as a new colonialism, with one Arabic daily comparing the collapse of Iraqi resistance prior to the growth of the insurgency as a new *nakba* (catastrophe) akin to the creation of Israel on Arab land in 1948. Kuwait, already an American colony, celebrated the 'new liberation'. American troops had poured into Kuwait in preparation for the invasion, slicing the country in two and placing half of it off limits to its own people. The military occupation of Kuwait, little remarked on in the Western media, preceded the occupation of Iraq.

Saudi Arabia, unlike in 1991, was unwilling to allow an American invasion to be launched from its territory, but continued to host vast US air bases that were important to the war effort. Jordan, aware of its tactical blunder in supporting Iraq in the first Gulf War, was now determined to be on the 'right' (i.e. prudent) side. It emerged that King Abdullah was prepared to support the 2003 invasion in return for economic and security guarantees. In Qatar the Americans expanded their massive $1 billion al-Udeid air base, 20 miles from Doha, the capital, while the Qatari government struggled to placate the Arab world by issuing routine condemnations of the imminent war. By March 2003 al-Udeid was equipped to accommodate up to 10,000 American troops. President Mubarak's Egypt, as a 'moderate' state relying on police repression, torture and US aid to maintain the regime, valued its peace deal with Israel and American largesse too much to oppose the war, and set about blaming the victim. On 25 March 2003 Mubarak began a televised speech with the words 'I hope that the Iraqi government recognises the dangerous situation it has put itself and us in'. The Mubarak regime was smarting under US pressures for 'democratisation' and increasingly alarmed by the growth of the Muslim Brotherhood, which, with its candidates standing under other party banners, had made significant parliamentary gains (without seriously threatening the effective dictatorship).

The other Arab states – Ba'athist Syria, Bahrain, the United Arab Emirates, Oman and Lebanon – watched the unfolding events of 2003 and the subsequent 'crusader' occupation of a brother Muslim state with increasing alarm. The Palestinians, deprived of their sole robust Arab ally, viewed the future with mounting despair. Turkey, like Saudi Arabia a state with a largely Muslim population and unwilling to directly support a fresh invasion of Iraq, continued to host US air bases as part of its NATO membership. Syria, routinely denounced by Israel and the US for infiltrating terrorists into Iraq, was bombed in September 2007 for reasons that remain unclear but with some reports suggesting that a nuclear facility had been targeted. Hamas, duly observing Washington's enthusiasm for 'democracy', was legitimately elected in Palestine and then deposed by a US-orchestrated *coup d'état*, while Hezbollah, with politicians already elected to the Lebanese parliament, was expanding its popular support by supporting reconstruction after massive Israeli bombing. Saudi Arabia, run by the extremist Wahabists, yet another version of Sunni Islam (but in conflict with the Sunni al-Qaeda) was increasingly worried by the emergence of an Iranian-backed Shi'ite-run state on its borders. And on 16 October Turkey, long plagued by the separatist Kurdistan Workers' Party (PKK), delivered an overwhelming parliamentary vote to invade northern Iraq in pursuit of 'terrorists' – an option adopted, without decisive results, many times in the 1990s. The pro-US Iraqi puppet government declared, with unconscious irony, that any invasion of Iraq would be a violation of national sovereignty.

Through 2007 and early 2008 the prospect of an American bombing onslaught on Iran intensified, with US denunciations of Iran's alleged nuclear-weapons ambitions and Iranian support for the Iraqi insurgency ('the Iranians are killing American soldiers').

An assortment of Israeli and US officials had frequently recommended – and continued to do so – the bombing of Iran, some
even suggesting the use of nuclear weapons. On 16 September
2007 the *Sunday Telegraph* carried the headline, 'Bush setting
America on the road to war with Iran', suggesting a massive new
conflagration in the Middle East that would have devastating
consequences – and it seemed that already Gordon Brown was 'on
board'.[55] The threats and instability already inflicted on the region
by an American hegemony able to assume supine British
acquiescence was being expanded by the month. And throughout
the world al-Qaeda and other terrorist groups, boosted by US
policies, were recruiting, regrouping and planning fresh atrocities.

In summary, the US-led war and occupation of Iraq, exemplifying
the most belligerent and brutal aspects of American and British
foreign policy,

- destroyed a sovereign, accredited UN member state;
- produced millions of victims through violence and disease;
- drastically eroded the status of women under occupation;
- sanctioned state kidnapping, 'disappearances' and torture;
- contributed to regional and global destabilisation;
- eroded the authority of the UN and international law;
- damaged relationships with traditional allies;
- shattered the people's faith in democratic institutions;
- suborned the media through 'plants', law and intimidation;
- stimulated powerful states to increase arms expenditure;
- boosted domestic and international extremism;
- fed the worst elements of fundamentalist religion;
- fuelled native and imported terrorism throughout the world;
- encouraged many governments to attack human rights;
- helped prepare the ground for a vast new war.

The legacies of George Bush and Tony Blair have many aspects.

Notes

Introduction

1. Amin Maalouf, *The Crusades through Arab Eyes*, tr. Jon Rothschild (London: Al Saqi, 1984).

2. Joachim Kahl, *The Misery of Christianity; or, A Plea for Humanity without God*, tr. N. D. Smith (Harmondsworth: Penguin, 1971).

3. Quoted in Said Aburish, *A Brutal Friendship: The West and the Arab Elite* (London: Victor Gollancz, 1997).

4. In March 1988 around 5,000 people were gassed to death by Iraqi forces in the village of Halabja, near the Iranian border. This action, an event in the Iran–Iraq War (1980–8), was ordered by Ali Hassan al-Majid, otherwise known as 'Chemical Ali'. He was sentenced to death in June 2007, but the sentence was upheld in September that year and as late as December 2007 the execution was still being delayed for political reasons.

5. Quoted in Mark Danner, *The Secret Way to War: The Downing Street Memo and the Iraq War's Buried History* (New York: New York Review, 2006).

6. Ibid.

7. Hansard, HL Deb, 22 February 2007, vol. 689, col. 1169.

8. On 4 June this quotation, although correct, was misconstrued by *The Guardian* on its website. Two days later the paper apologised in 'Corrections and Clarifications' and withdrew the offending item.

9. Alan Greenspan, *The Age of Turbulence: Adventures in a New World* (New York: Penguin Press, 2007).

10. Jeff Gerth and Don Van Natta Jr, *Her Way: The Hopes and Ambitions of Hillary Rodham Clinton* (New York: Little, Brown, 2007).

11. Quoted in Jeffrey Jowell, 'Legality of war: "It raises concerns of the greatest constitutional significance"', *The Guardian*, 29 April 2005.

12. Tony Lagouranis, *Fear Up Harsh: An Army Interrogator's Dark Journey through Iraq* (New York: NAL Caliber, 2007).

13. Lawrence Anthony, *Babylon's Ark: The Incredible Wartime Rescue of the Baghdad Zoo* (New York: Thomas Dunne, 2007).

14. Jeremy Scahill, *Blackwater: The Rise of the World's Most Powerful Mercenary Army* (New York: Nation, 2007).

15. Michael Rose, *Washington's War: From Independence to Iraq* (London: Weidenfeld & Nicolson, 2007).

Chapter 1: Surge: a new way forward?

1. Among these was the oil strategy, meaning not only access to supplies but also control of production to avoid the United States being 'held to ransom' in the event of a political crisis. American strategists saw also the strategic advantages of maintaining a military presence at the heart of the Middle East, despite the inevitable Arab and Muslim hostility that such a policy would generate. It was also arguable that the United States would see benefit in an anarchic and fragmented Iraq, preventing the emergence of a strong Shi'ite nation likely to form an alliance with Iran that would be hostile to American interests. Such a policy also had advantages for US corporations intent on maximising their revenue from successive American administrations determined to spend well in excess of $400 billion a year on war and preparations for war.

2. Participants in the work of the Iraq Study Group included George W. Bush and members of his Cabinet; Bill Clinton; the Iraqi President, Jalal Talabani; Iraq's Prime Minister, Nouri Kamal al-Maliki; Generals John Abizaid, George Casey and Anthony Zinni; Colin Powell; Thomas Friedman; George Packer; and many others.

3. James A. Baker III and Lee H. Hamilton (co-chairs), *The Iraq Study Group Report* (New York: Vintage, 2006).

4. See, for example, the five elements of the report's Recommendation 63, designed to protect the American interest in Iraqi oil supplies.

5. Baker and Hamilton, *Iraq Study Group Report* , p. xiii.

6. Ibid., p. 1.

7. Ibid., p. 32.

8. Paragraph 7(b)(iii) of Resolution 1546 (2004) provides a mandate for UNAMI to 'promote the protection of human rights, national reconciliation, and judicial and legal reform in order to strengthen the rule of law in Iraq'. The status of Resolution 1546 is questionable. How legitimate is a Security Council resolution

designed to uphold an invasion declared illegal by the UN secretary general? The UNAMI posture, assuming the legitimacy of what many observers regarded as a 'puppet' Iraqi regime, was similarly questionable.

9. United Nations Assistance Mission for Iraq, *Human Rights Report 1 January–31 March 2007*, Paragraph 10.

10. Ibid., Paragraph 2.

11. See Chapter 2 of the present book.

12. *Human Rights Report 1 January–31 March 2007*, Paragraph 4.

13. Ibid., Paragraph 12.

14. Ibid., Paragraphs 15 and 16.

15. Ibid., Paragraph 19.

16. Ibid., Paragraph 23.

17. Ibid., Paragraph 25.

18. See examples given in Geoff Simons, *They Destroyed Iraq and Called It Freedom* (London: Legacy, 2008), Chapter 6.

19. In January 2007 the 30,622 detainees throughout Iraq were held by various bodies: the multinational force (14,534), the Ministry of Justice (9,263), the Ministry of the Interior (2,908), the Ministry of Defence (1,362), the Ministry of Labour and Social Affairs (456) and the Kurdistan regional government (2,099). Source: Iraqi Ministry of Human Rights, cited in United Nations Assistance Mission for Iraq, *Human Rights Report 1 January–31 March 2007*, Paragraph 66. Most of the detainees had not been charged or tried and few had access to adequate legal representation. Some, including women, faced indefinite incarceration or execution for alleged terrorist involvement or alleged non-terrorist criminal activities.

20. *Human Rights Report 1 January–31 March 2007*, Paragraph 77.

21. See also Chapter 2 of the present book.

22. The sequence of events through the trial of Saddam Hussein and some commentary are included in Simons, *They Destroyed Iraq and Called It Freedom*, Chapter 10.

23. Ewen MacAskill and Michael Howard, 'How Saddam died on the gallows', *The Guardian*, 1 January 2007.

24. The promise of an investigation proved to be empty. Some of the Iraqis involved in the execution were arrested, but on 6 January 2007 the Prime Minister, Nouri al-Maliki, insisted that the execution was an 'internal affair' and warned critical countries that the Iraqi government could review its relations with them.

25. Damien McElroy, 'They made Saddam a martyr, says Mubarak', *Daily Telegraph*, 6 January 2007.

26. James Bone, 'Bush sleeps through execution', *The Times*, 1 January 2007. An editorial, 'Milestone on the road to nowhere', in *The Guardian* on 1 January 2007, stated: 'Saddam Hussein's execution is likely to make little difference [to the fate of Iraq] . . . Neither [the Iraqi] judges nor [the Iraqi] lawyers showed an understanding of international criminal law . . . A UN or international tribunal would have been better. It bears repeating that the death penalty remains a cruel and unusual punishment.'

27. Brian Whitaker, 'Emotions in Arab world range from elation to outrage', *The Guardian*, 1 January 2007.

28. Ibid.

29. Graeme Wilson, 'Prescott attacks filming of Saddam's execution', *Daily Telegraph*, 3 January 2007.

30. David Cracknell, 'Brown attacks Saddam hanging', *Sunday Times*, 7 January 2007.

31. Wilson, 'Prescott attacks filming of Saddam's execution'.

32. Boris Johnson, 'Blair is strangely silent about the disgusting death of Saddam', *Daily Telegraph*, 4 January 2007.

33. David Hencke, 'Brown bounces No. 10 into Saddam comment', *The Guardian*, 8 January 2007.

34. Will Woodward and Ian Black, 'Blair breaks silence to condemn manner of Saddam hanging', *The Guardian*, 10 January 2007.

35. Ibid.

36. Ibid.

37. Ed Pilkington, 'US criticised for limiting Iraqi refugee intake to 500', *The Guardian*, 3 January 2007. The US, under pressure from humanitarian bodies and international opinion, later increased the quota.

38. Suzanne Goldenberg, 'Democrats to go on offensive as new Congress convenes', *The Guardian*, 3 January 2007.

39. Ibid.

40. Quoted in 'Iraqi PM Nouri al-Maliki rules out second term in newspaper interview', Fox News online, 3 January 2007.

41. Ned Parker, 'To troops on the ground, it's an ugly job that must be done', *The Times*, 2 January 2007.

42. Baker and Hamilton, *Iraq Study Group Report*, p. 40.

43. Ibid., p. 38.

44. Ibid., p. 39.

45. Ibid., pp. 70–7.

46. Bob Herbert, 'Another thousand lives', *New York Times*, 4 January 2007.

47. Quoted ibid.
48. Quoted ibid.
49. Ibid.
50. Ibid.
51. Tim Reid, 'Bush surrounds himself with war supporters', *The Times*, 6 January 2007.
52. Petraeus holds a doctorate from Princeton University, and is a skilled communicator and an athlete. He was shot in the chest in a training accident in 1991, and later broke his pelvis in a parachute landing. He recuperated to run a 10-mile race in under 64 minutes. When he was active in Mosul, some tribal leaders called him 'King David' as he played the role of a viceroy, dispensing largesse. NBC News called him 'the pied piper of northern Iraq'.
53. Michael R. Gordon and Thom Shanker, 'US team in charge of Iraq is reshuffled', *International Herald Tribune*, 5 January 2007.
54. The Democrats held the House of Representatives by 233 seats to 202, and had a slim majority in the Senate, 51 to 49.
55. Geoff Elliott, 'Pelosi takes gavel amid Iraq split', *Australian*, 6 January 2007.
56. Sarah Baxter, 'Bush's final gamble on victory in Iraq', *Sunday Times*, 7 January 2007.
57. Ibid.
58. Ibid.
59. Ibid.
60. The suggestion of a more equitable distribution of oil revenues was clearly a piece of propaganda window-dressing: the US corporations had their own plans for exploiting Iraq's energy resources.
61. Ed Pilkington, 'Bush $1bn jobs plan to draw Iraqis into fold', *The Guardian*, 9 January 2007.
62. Tom Baldwin, 'Bush's Iraq strategy in danger as Congress rules out blank cheque', *The Times*, 8 January 2007.
63. Ewen MacAskill, 'Rising Iraqi deaths loom over Bush announcement', *The Guardian*, 9 January 2007.
64. Quoted in Anne Flaherty, 'Democrats to challenge Bush's Iraq plan', *The Guardian*, 9 January 2007.
65. Quoted ibid.
66. MacAskill, 'Rising Iraqi deaths loom over Bush announcement'.
67. 'Bush acknowledges Iraq "mistakes"', *Morning Star*, 11 January 2007.
68. Toby Harnden, 'Bush gambles on his Iraq "surge"', *Daily Telegraph*, 11 January 2007.

69. Ibid.

70. Simon Jenkins, 'One last push and that's you finished in Iraq, Mr President', *Sunday Times*, 7 January 2007.

71. Harnden, 'Bush gambles on his Iraq "surge"'.

72. Ewen MacAskill, Julian Borger and Richard Norton-Taylor, 'The new plan: Fight the Mahdi army toe to toe, hope Iraqi army holds', *The Guardian*, 12 January 2007.

73. Thomas Harding, 'Commanders draw up plans for handing over bases in Basra', *Daily Telegraph*, 11 January 2007.

74. MacAskill *et al.*, 'New plan'.

75. In 2005 Colonel H. R. McMaster had cut off Tal Afar to deny access to outside fighters, and then worked through district after district, leaving troops in control of each area to prevent the return of insurgent factions. It seemed unlikely that a relatively small US troop increase would be able to treat Baghdad in the same way.

76. MacAskill *et al.*, 'New plan'.

77. Ewen MacAskill and Julian Borger, 'Isolated Bush faces rebellion over Iraq', *The Guardian*, 12 January 2007.

78. MacAskill *et al.*, 'New plan'.

79. Stephen Farrell, 'We will send them home in body bags: Insurgents respond to the Bush "surge"', *The Times*, 12 January 2007.

80. Ibid.

81. Ibid.

82. Ibid.

83. Bronwen Maddox, 'US has ignored seven clear pointers to failure', *The Times*, 12 January 2007.

84. Quoted in Toby Harnden, 'Under-fire Bush tries to rally the troops', *Daily Telegraph*, 12 January 2007.

85. Ibid.

86. 'World reaction', *Daily Telegraph*, 12 January 2007.

87. Quoted Damien McElroy, 'Iraqi leader faces his last chance', *Daily Telegraph*, 13 January 2007.

88. Quoted ibid.

89. Quoted in Philip Sherwell, 'US diluting surge, general says', *Sunday Telegraph*, 14 January 2007.

90. By tradition the head of the World Bank is nominated by the US President, which guarantees that bank policies always support American corporate interests.

91. Baker and Hamilton, *Iraq Study Group Report*, Recommendations 62 & 63, pp. 83–6.

92. See also Simons, *They Destroyed Iraq and Called It Freedom*, Chapter 3.

93. Quoted in Raymond Whitaker, Danny Fortson, Andrew Murray-Watson, Geoffrey Lean and Tim Webb, 'Blood and oil: How the West will profit from Iraq's most precious commodity', *Independent on Sunday*, 7 January 2007.

94. Kamil Mahdi, 'Iraqis will never accept this sellout to the oil corporations', *The Guardian*, 16 January 2007.

95. Philip Sherwell, 'Bush gave secret order to hunt down and destroy Iranian networks in Iraq', *Sunday Times*, 14 January 2007.

96. Ibid.

97. Ibid.

98. Quoted in Robert Tait and Julian Borger, 'Bush admits past mistakes as row with Tehran grows over arrest of "diplomats"', *The Guardian*, 15 January 2007.

99. Quoted in Julian Borger, Ian Traynor and Ewen MacAskill, 'We are not leaving, Gates warns Iran as troop surge begins', *The Guardian*, 16 January 2007.

100. Quoted ibid.

101. Thomas Harding, 'Iran "taking control of Basra by stealth"', *Daily Telegraph*, 16 January 2007.

102. Damien McElroy, 'Saudis back US Iraq strategy as fears grow over Iran's influence', *Daily Telegraph*, 17 January 2007.

103. Tim Reid, 'Iraq is much less stable now than before we invaded, admits Bush', *The Times*, 15 January 2007.

104. Graeme Baker and Malcolm Moore, 'Bush says death of Saddam like a revenge killing', *Daily Telegraph*, 17 January 2007.

105. Quoted in 'Nadler introduces bill to protect the troops and bring them home', press release, Representative Jerrold Nadler, 12 January 2007.

106. Quoted in 'Farr introduces bill to force withdrawal from Iraq', press release, Representative Sam Farr, 11 January 2007.

107. Jon Swain and Sarah Baxter, 'Iraqis get all-firing foretaste of Bush's final Baghdad gamble', *Sunday Times*, 14 January 2007.

108. Ibid.

109. The Iraqi government claimed that 12,357 Iraqi civilians had been killed in 2006, the *Washington Post* 22,950, Iraq Body Count 24,000, and the United Nations (UNAMI) 34,452. It was possible to argue that all the estimates were conservative: many bodies were not being delivered to hospitals and morgues, and many war-related fatalities were not recorded as deaths caused through violence.

110. United Nations Assistance Mission for Iraq, *Human Rights Report 1 November–31 December 2006*, Paragraph 4.

111. Stephen Farrell, '65 students die in university blasts', *The Times*, 17 January 2007.

112. Colin Brown, 'The battle to save Iraq's children: Doctors issue plea to Tony Blair to end the scandal of shortages in the war zone', *The Independent*, 19 January 2007.

113. Ibid.

114. Ibid.

115. Colin Brown, 'Benn aims to stamp out corruption', *The Independent*, 20 January 2007.

116. Stephen Farrell, 'Give us guns – and troops can go, says Iraqi leader', *The Times*, 18 January 2007.

117. Ibid.

118. Ned Parker, 'How ghost soldiers are bleeding Iraqi army of guns and money', *The Times*, 19 January 2007.

119. Aqeel Hussein and Gethin Chamberlain, 'Shias order Palestinians to leave Iraq or "prepare to die"', *Sunday Telegraph*, 21 January 2007.

120. Suzanne Goldenberg, 'Republican rebels defy Bush line', *The Guardian*, 19 January 2007.

121. Toby Harnden, 'Bush Iraq policy too timid, says general', *Daily Telegraph*, 20 January 2007.

122. Tim Reid, 'No guarantees for Iraq plan, says general in charge', *Daily Telegraph*, 24 January 2007.

123. The American media never attempt to catalogue the horrors that the Iraqi people are forced to endure. However, details can be obtained from other sources; for example, from *Iraq Occupation Focus Newsletter*, no. 62, 7 February 2007, which lists events that occurred in January. These include: the struggle of a 32-year-old widow, Lina Massufi, to survive with her two children after her husband was accidentally killed by US troops; Shi'ite Iraqi soldiers delivering a 'brutal beating' to several local Sunnis, as US soldiers looked on and then attempted to 'seize the [video] footage' of the Channel 4 journalists recording the event; the stranding of Palestinian refugees at a desolate camp at the al-Tanf border crossing into Syria; the deteriorating petrol situation, with police no longer able to prevent chaos at filling stations; UN confirmation of 'violent campaigns' against Iraqi gays and 'the assassination of homosexuals in Iraq'; asthmatic children dying through lack of medicines in Baghdad's Children Teaching Hospital; and 60 per cent of 2,000 people interviewed in all eighteen Iraqi provinces having panic attacks through fear of explosions. The newsletter also recorded that 100,000 anti-war protesters marched against the surge

policy in Washington on 27 January; and that tens of thousands
more marched in Salt Lake City, San Francisco and Los Angeles.

124. Quoted in Max Elbaum, 'Washington's wars and occupations:
Month in review', *War Times/Tempo de Guerras*, 29 January 2007.

Chapter 2: One million deaths and counting

1. In American propaganda the troop surge was an Iraqi-led security
plan (*Khittat Fardh al-Qamun*), though no one doubted that the
United States was dictating every aspect of the new policy to the
completely ineffectual Maliki administration.

2. Hala Jaber and Sarah Baxter, 'Death squad chieftains flee to beat
Baghdad surge', *Sunday Times*, 28 January 2007.

3. Ibid.

4. In November 2006, according to some estimates, there were at
least 100,000 Iraqis in Egypt; up to 40,000 in Lebanon; 700,000 in
Jordan; 600,000 in Syria; and 54,000 in Iran. Unofficial estimates
put the figures much higher. Thus Kasaram Mufarah, executive
coordinator of 300 non-governmental aid agencies involved with
alleviating Iraq's humanitarian situation, commented: 'It is a critical
situation. We are talking of between 1.5 million to 2 million
displaced inside Iraq, and 4 million outside.' (Quoted in John
Swain, 'The hunted: Iraq's forgotten refugees', *Sunday Times*, 28
January 2007.)

5. Jon Swain, 'The hunted: Iraq's forgotten refugees', *Sunday Times*,
28 January 2007.

6. Ibid.

7. United Nations Assistance Mission for Iraq, *Human Rights Report
1 January–31 March 2007*, Paragraph 18.

8. Ibid., Paragraph 12.

9. Ibid., Paragraph 6.

10. Ibid., Paragraph 16.

11. The deliberate killing of journalists has often been put down to
'crossfire'.

12. United Nations Assistance Mission for Iraq, *Human Rights Report
1 January–31 March 2007*, Paragraph 29.

13. Ibid., Paragraph 17.

14. Ibid., Paragraph 39.

15. In February 2007 the 34,992 detainees were held by various bodies:
Multinational Force (16,931); Ministry of Justice (9,116); Ministry
of Interior (4,692); Ministry of Defence (1,606); Ministry of

Labour and Social Affairs (503); Kurdistan Regional Government (2,144). Source: Iraqi Ministry of Human Rights, cited ibid., Paragraph 66.

16. Ibid., Paragraph 68.
17. Ibid., Paragraph 69.
18. Ibid., Paragraph 70.
19. Ibid., Paragraph 71.
20. Ewen MacAskill, 'Millions wasted in Iraq reconstruction, report concludes', *The Guardian*, 1 February 2007.
21. Ibid.
22. Toby Harnden, 'Iraq chaos like a civil war, say US spies', *Daily Telegraph*, 3 February 2007.
23. Tom Baldwin, 'Bush bids for bigger war chest as "no-confidence" vote looms', *The Times*, 5 February 2007.
24. Ed Pilkington, 'Iraqi insurgents may have anti-aircraft missile', *The Guardian*, 5 February 2007. The helicopter crashes 'raised concerns that the insurgents . . . have acquired new weaponry'. This affected not only US military operations but the activities of the civilian security firms who had become increasingly dependent on the use of helicopters to move and protect employees.
25. Ibid.
26. Martin Fletcher, 'Last bid to save Baghdad at the Alamo', *The Times*, 5 February 2007.
27. Ibid. 'Humvee' derives from the initials HMMWV, standing for High Mobility Multipurpose Wheeled Vehicle.
28. Ibid.
29. Ibid.
30. Damien McElroy, 'Syria is haven for bombers, says Iraq', *Daily Telegraph*, 5 February 2007.
31. Tim Reid and Stephen Farrell, 'Bush seeks billions for war as his "surge" plan threatens to split party', *The Times*, 6 February 2007.
32. On 5 February 2007 publicity was given in the British media to the 100th British soldier to die in action in Iraq, one of the 131 service personnel to have died in the country since the 2003 invasion.
33. Michael Howard, 'Children of war: The generation traumatised by violence in Iraq', *The Guardian*, 6 February 2007.
34. Ibid.
35. Ibid.
36. Ibid.
37. Ewen MacAskill, 'Bush slashes aid to poor to boost Iraq war chest', *The Guardian*, 6 February 2007.

38. Ibid.

39. In October 2006 an estimate of '655,000 post-invasion excess deaths in occupied Iraq as of July 2006' was produced by an epidemiology research team in the Bloomberg School of Public Health at Johns Hopkins University, and was peer-reviewed in the *Lancet* and endorsed by twenty-seven top Australian medical experts in the area. On 5 March 2007 *The Times* published an analysis by Anjana Ahuja ('Could 650,000 Iraqis really have died because of the invasion?'), questioning the methodology that formed the basis of the Johns Hopkins estimate. Here it was suggested that independent academics had raised questions that had not been satisfactorily answered, that 'the figures arrived at were likely to exceed the true number', and that the paper was 'poorly reviewed'. Dr Richard Horton, editor of the *Lancet*, refuted the charges.

40. Gideon Polya, 'US Iraqi Holocaust And One Million Excess Deaths', Countercurrents.org, 7 February 2007. Dr Polya has published some 130 works in a four-decade scientific career, most recently a massive pharmacological text. He is currently editing a completed book on global avoidable mortality.

41. The $2.3 trillion estimate was provided by Professor Joseph Stiglitz of Columbia University, a Nobel laureate in economics, and his Harvard colleague Professor Linda Bilmes.

42. The estimate comprises two million refugees outside Iraq and 1.7 million inside the country. The UNHCR estimated that there would be 2.3 million internally displaced people within Iraq by the end of 2007.

43. According to UN Population Division data.

44. Polya, 'US Iraqi Holocaust And One Million Excess Deaths'.

45. Ibid.

46. An objection to Polya's calculations might be raised on the ground that he overestimates the Iraqi population. If the normal figure of 24 million is used then the (b) calculation is $9.3 \times 2,400 \times 4 = 894,800$ deaths, less than a million but significantly more than the *Lancet* figure of 655,000.

47. The International Court of Justice famously claimed jurisdiction over the United States in 1984 and delivered a multifaceted verdict in 1986 that the US was guilty of terrorist acts against Nicaragua. Thus it would be a suitable candidate for trying Bush and Blair. The International Criminal Court might also claim jurisdiction, even though the US has not recognised it, on the ground that the

US has not been willing to try Bush at home, despite various attempts to bring impeachment actions. Another alternative would be a special court set up by the UN Security Council, as with the special courts established for Rwanda and the Balkans. However, here Washington and London would be sure to use their permanent-member vetos.

48. Suzanne Goldenberg, 'First US officer since Vietnam goes on trial for speaking out', *The Guardian*, 3 February 2007.

49. Damien McElroy and Alex Massie, '"Take back Baghdad" surge begins', *The Guardian*, 6 February 2007.

50. On 9 February 2007 US helicopters accidentally killed at least five Kurdish troops in Mosul, an event that was given little publicity in the Western media.

51. 'Malaysia puts Bush and Blair in the dock over Iraq war crimes', *Morning Star*, 7 February 2007.

52. Robert Tait and Reuters, 'Iranian diplomat is kidnapped in Baghdad', *The Guardian*, 7 February 2007.

53. Jonathan Steel, 'Minister loyal to Sadr arrested in Baghdad raid', *The Guardian*, 9 February 2007.

54. Stephen Farrell and Ali Hamdani, 'Bribes and boldness fuel a daring flight from murder and madness', *The Times*, 9 February 2007.

55. Ibid.

56. Ibid.

57. Michael Evans, 'Gated communities will add to Baghdad security', *The Guardian*, 10 February 2007.

58. Jonathan Steele and Dahr Jamail, 'This is our Guernica', *The Guardian*, 27 April 2005.

59. Evans, 'Gated communities will add to Baghdad security'.

60. Leon Panetta, a member of the ISG, commented that Gates was 'very concerned about what to do if the Iraqis couldn't get their act together'. Gates was being a 'good soldier and implementing what the President wants', but he had not forgotten the recommendations of the ISG to which he, along with Panetta, had also contributed.

61. Sarah Baxter and Hamoudi Saffar, 'US "prepares for failure" in Iraq surge', *Sunday Times*, 11 February 2007.

62. Ibid.

63. Ibid.

64. Stephen Farrell and Richard Beeston, 'US blames Tehran agents for troop deaths', *The Times*, 12 February 2007; David Blair and Ben Rooney, 'US puts weapons on show to "prove" Iran is arming insurgents', *Daily Telegraph*, 12 February 2007.

65. Stephen Farrell, 'Suicide bombers shatter anniversary', *The Times*, 13 February 2007.

66. Michael Howard, 'Cleric Sadr "in Iran" ahead of Iraq crackdown', *The Guardian*, 14 February 2007; Stephen Farrell, 'US says that Shia leader has fled to Iran as Baghdad crackdown looms', *The Times*, 15 February 2007.

67. Michael Howard, 'Mahdi army commanders withdraw to Iran to lie low during security crackdown', *The Guardian*, 15 February 2007.

68. Ibid.

69. 'US citizens want out: Six in ten oppose Bush "surge"', *Morning Star*, 15 February 2007.

70. Richard Norton-Taylor, 'Troops close Iranian border and crack down on insurgents', *The Guardian*, 16 February 2007.

71. UNHCR statistics showed that 20,000 Iraqis had applied for asylum in the EU in 2006, with well under 10 per cent of those applying being granted refugee status.

72. Vivienne Walt, 'Comfort in a cold place', *Time*, 19 February 2007.

73. 'UN urges EU help for Iraqi refugees: US plan to take just 7,000 asylum-seekers', *Morning Star*, 16 February 2007; David Gowe, 'EU braces itself for influx of Iraqi refugees', *The Guardian*, 16 February 2007.

74. Suzanne Goldenberg and Duncan Campbell, 'By 246 votes to 182, Congress sends rebuke to Bush over Iraq troops surge', *The Guardian*, 17 February 2007.

75. Ibid.

76. Dana Priest and Anne Hall, 'Soldiers face neglect, frustration at army's top medical facility', *Washington Post*, 18 February 2007; other articles would follow.

77. Ibid.

78. Ibid.

79. Ibid.

80. Ibid.

81. Damien McElroy, 'Baghdad car bombs kill 60 as sectarian violence resumes', *Daily Telegraph*, 19 February 2007.

82. Stephen Farrell, Ned Parker and Richard Beeston, 'Mixture of fear and celebration in Basra over Army's pullout', *The Times*, 22 February 2007.

83. Sarah Baxter, Marie Colvin and Harmoudi Saffar, 'Surge tactics to tame Ramadi, city of anarchy', *Sunday Times*, 25 February 2007.

84. Will Woodward, 'Upbeat Blair signals more troop withdrawals from Iraq', *The Guardian*, 19 February 2007.

85. Richard Norton-Taylor and Ewen MacAskill, 'Iraq: The British endgame', *The Guardian*, 21 February 2007.

86. Already the US-led coalition was continuing to unravel. Of the residual contingents of troops from various countries, most of which were small in number, many were anticipating withdrawal in the near future. These included troops from Armenia (a contingent of forty-six soldiers to be withdrawn by the end of 2007), Denmark (460 troops to be withdrawn by August), Moldova (eleven bomb-defusing experts returned home in January), Poland (900 non-combat troops to be withdrawn by the end of 2007) and South Korea (2,300 troops to be withdrawn by the end of 2007).

87. Thomas Harding and George Jones, '4,000 troops will stay in Iraq "for five years"', *Daily Telegraph*, 22 February 2007.

88. 'Iraqi cabinet agrees deal on sharing oil revenues', *The Guardian*, 27 February 2007.

89. Ibid.

90. Peter Beaumont, 'Radical Shia cleric withdraws backing for Iraq security drive', *The Guardian*, 26 February 2007.

91. The Iraqi Presidential Council is made up of the President and two Vice-Presidents. Each of them should represent one of Iraq's three largest groups: Sunni Arabs, Shi'ite Arabs and Kurds. At present the President is a Kurd and the two Vice-Presidents a Sunni Arab and a Shi'ite Arab respectively.

92. Tom Baldwin and Ned Parker, 'US ready to join Syria and Iran at "ice-breaker" talks', *The Times*, 28 February 2007; Suzanne Goldenberg, 'US invites Iran and Syria to talks on Iraq in reversal of Bush policy', *The Guardian*, 28 February 2007.

93. James A. Baker III and Lee H. Hamilton (co-chairs), *The Iraq Study Group Report* (New York: Vintage, 2006), Recommendation 9, pp. 51–2.

94. Joe Klein, 'What it really means to support the troops', *Time*, 19 February 2007.

95. Ibid.

Chapter 3: 'No moderate centre in Iraq'

1. There were many elements in Washington's attempt to reshape Iraqi politics that served to exacerbate the country's racial and sectarian divisions: for example, the effort to crush a political establishment that favoured sectarian Sunnis; the US-controlled

drafting of a constitution that created widespread resentment by prohibiting the participation of groups that had certain traditional ethnic and sectarian connections; and the creation of a so-called democratic party system, not on the basis of individual candidature but on the basis of slates of ethnic and sectarian groups. In addition, the total collapse of law and order inevitably plunged Iraqi communities into the arms of whatever racial and fundamentalist factions seemed to offer the most comfort and protection.

2. Simon Tisdall, 'US commanders admit: We face a Vietnam-style collapse', *The Guardian*, 1 March 2007.

3. The team, having a wide mix of combat experience and academic achievement, included Colonel Peter Mansoor, a former armoured division commander with a PhD in the history of infantry; Colonel H. R. McMaster, author of a well-known critique of Vietnam and an experienced counter-insurgency commander; Lieutenant Colonel David Kilcullen, a seconded Australian officer and expert on Islamism; and Colonel Michael Meese, son of the former US Attorney-General Edwin Meese, a member of the Iraq Study Group.

4. It was possible to argue about the *realpolitik* goals, such as the control of access to Iraqi oil and the consolidation of a permanent strategic presence in the country, but the declared goal of creating a liberal democracy sympathetic to free-market American values seemed more distant than ever. It was possible to consider also the advantages to Washington of maintaining a chaotic fragmented Iraq that was unlikely to develop as a coherent and unified ally of Iran and unable to present a strong challenge to American regional ambitions.

5. Tisdall, 'US commanders admit: We face a Vietnam-style collapse'.

6. Ibid.

7. Ibid.

8. In public, President Bush and other US politicians, saying that Basra was different to Baghdad, were not objecting to the emerging British policy on withdrawal, but it was obvious that the plan was causing headaches. It created the impression that the coalition was unravelling and posed fresh military problems.

9. Tisdall, 'US commanders admit: We face a Vietnam-style collapse'.

10. Lee Glendinning, 'Soldier killed defending patrol in ambush', *The Guardian*, 1 March 2007. Rifleman Coffey's death brought the number of British fatalities in Iraq since the start of hostilities to 133, of whom 102 had died in combat.

11. Yifat Susskind, *Promising Democracy, Imposing Theocracy: Gender-Based Violence and the US War on Iraq* (New York: MADRE, 2007). See Mithre J. Sandrasagra, 'Women's lives unraveling in occupied Iraq', Inter Press Service, 7 March 2007.

12. Sandrasagra, 'Women's lives unraveling in occupied Iraq'.

13. Susan J. Douglas, 'The Legacy of Tailhook: Supporting our troops at any cost overshadows holding them accountable for sexual assault within military', *In These Times*, June 2007.

14. Many other charities had already pulled out of the country. Three years before, Oxfam had stopped direct aid and switched to arm's-length work through local partners in Iraq. Care International closed its operations after the abduction and murder of Margaret Hassan, its director in Iraq. The Swiss-based International Committee of the Red Cross was still active in the country, providing medical aid and visiting detainees where possible to check on their welfare.

15. Sara Gaines, 'Lack of security forces out Save the Children', *The Guardian*, 1 March 2007.

16. Thomas Harding, 'My troops have little left to give, says Chief of Staff', *Daily Telegraph*, 7 March 2007.

17. Suzanne Goldenberg, 'US praised for diplomacy ahead of summit', *The Guardian*, 1 March 2007.

18. Ibid.

19. Alex Spillius and Damien McElroy, 'Iran stalls over attending talks to curb Iraq bloodshed', *Daily Telegraph*, 1 March 2007.

20. 'Rice changes tune on Iraq', *Morning Star*, 1 March 2007.

21. Ibid.

22. 'US policy foolish and dubious', *Daily Telegraph*, 2 March 2007.

23. Stephen Farrell, 'America's surge is starting to work – but can it last?', *The Times*, 3 March 2007.

24. Ibid.

25. Ibid.

26. Damien McElroy, 'US asks us to tidy up while the city is in ruins, says mayor of Baghdad', *Daily Telegraph*, 3 March 2007.

27. Ibid.

28. Marie Colvin, 'Theft of defence millions leaves Iraqis outgunned', *Sunday Times*, 11 March 2007.

29. American soldiers have frequently been badly treated when they have returned to the United States from foreign wars. See for example Richard Severo and Lewis Milford, *The Wages of War: When American Soldiers Came Home – From Valley Forge to Vietnam* (New York: Touchstone, 1990).

30. Dana Priest and Anne Hull, 'Soldiers face neglect, frustration at army's top medical facility', *Washington Post*, 18 February 2007; other articles would follow.

31. Quoted in Sarah Baxter, 'Squalor of the vets' hospital shocks US', *Sunday Times*, 4 March 2007.

32. Quoted ibid.

33. More than 200,000 Iraq and Afghanistan veterans had been treated at Veterans' Association hospitals by March 2007; and the estimated lifetime cost to the American taxpayer of supporting these veterans was $600 billion (Linda Bilmes and Joseph Stiglitz, *The Economic Cost of the Iraq War* (Cambridge, MA: National Bureau of Economic Research, 2006)).

34. See also Chapter 2, note 76.

35. Tom Baldwin, 'Bush acts to save face over care of troops', *The Times*, 7 March 2007.

36. Ibid.

37. Imre Karacs, 'Al-Qaeda group films execution of 18 Iraqi security troops', *Sunday Times*, 4 March 2007.

38. Tim Butcher, 'Iraqi PM risks Shia clash over reshuffle', *Daily Telegraph*, 5 March 2007.

39. Damien McElroy, 'Iraqi security forces "targeting Sunnis" in raids', *Daily Telegraph*, 6 March 2007.

40. Butcher, 'Iraqi PM risks Shia clash over reshuffle'.

41. 'Iraq probes raid by British soldiers', *Morning Star*, 6 March 2007.

42. 'Iraqi PM faces axe over oil law: US may torpedo Maliki regime', *Morning Star*, 15 March 2007.

43. Damien McElroy, 'The deserted mall where snipers hunt insurgents', *Daily Telegraph*, 6 March 2007.

44. United Nations Assistance Mission for Iraq, *Human Rights Report 1 January–31 March 2007*, Paragraph 12.

45. Ibid., Paragraph 13.

46. Ibid., Paragraph 17.

47. Ibid., Paragraph 43.

48. These detainees throughout Iraq were held by various bodies: the Multinational Force (17,898), the Ministry of Justice (9,965), the Ministry of the Interior (5,573), the Ministry of Defence (1,525), the Ministry of Labour and Social Affairs (502) and the Kurdistan Regional Government (2,178). Source: Iraqi Ministry of Human Rights; cited in United Nations Assistance Mission for Iraq, *Human Rights Report 1 January–31 March 2007*, Paragraph 66.

49. Ian Black, 'At least 110 pilgrims die in suicide attacks as US admits extra 7,000 troops may go to Iraq', *The Guardian*, 7 March 2007.

50. Ewen MacAskill and Julian Borger, 'Democrats demand troops out of Iraq by 2008', *The Guardian*, 9 March 2007.

51. Ibid.

52. Ewen MacAskill, 'Bush asks Congress for even more Iraq troops', *The Guardian*, 12 March 2007.

53. Alex Spillius, 'US plans withdrawal if Iraq surge fails', *Daily Telegraph*, 13 March 2007; Ewen MacAskill, 'Pessimistic Pentagon studies fallback options in Iraq', *The Guardian*, 13 March 2007.

54. In the 1980s and early 1990s the United States sent fifty-five advisors, members of the Green Berets, to support the pro-US government and security forces in El Salvador in a civil war (1981–92), where in fact the Salvadorian people were struggling against a fascist junta. Congress refused to allow the deployment of combat troops, and the operation was judged a success by Washington. In reality, by training 'interrogators' and by supplying weapons to a regime that enjoyed only minority support, the US was complicit in torture, the work of death squads and the frequent massacre of civilians.

55. MacAskill, 'Pessimistic Pentagon studies fallback options in Iraq'.

56. Ibid.

57. Steven Morris and Audrey Gillan, 'Soldiers cleared over ill-treatment of Iraqi prisoners', *The Guardian*, 14 March 2007.

58. Michael Evans, 'Last two soldiers acquitted of abusing Iraqis', *The Times*, 14 March 2007.

59. Ned Parker, 'US favourite tries to make a comeback', *The Times*, 14 March 2007.

60. During the reign of Saddam Hussein there had been frequent eruptions of tension on the Kurdish–Turkish border, largely because of the Kurdish separatist movement in Turkey – a situation that had often led to cross-border incursions by the Turks, the destruction of thousands of Kurdish villages and the temporary occupation of great swathes of Iraqi territory. Turkish depredations in Iraq were ignored by the West because Turkey was a NATO member being supplied with weapons by the United States.

61. Chlorine gas was first used as a weapon by the German army at the Battle of Ypres in April 1915.

62. Marie Colvin, 'Resilient Iraqis ask: What civil war?', *Sunday Times*, 18 March 2007.

63. The journalist Ghaith Abdul-Ahad ('Despairing and disregarded –

the daily quest to get out of Baghdad', *The Guardian*, 21 March
2007) described the plight of Iraqis struggling to obtain passports in
order to leave the country: the start of 'a surreal obstacle course';
desperate people queuing in the passport office yard in Baghdad;
officials considering applications for a single Baghdad district each
day; countless unsuccessful applicants having to wait a month until
the district comes up again; three different kinds of passport,
including the 'Rolls-Royce' G series; Ahmad, a Sunni, charging
$500 to help 'our brothers' who dare not venture into passport
offices controlled by the Shi'ite Ministry of the Interior; more
queues – 'outside western embassies for visas, asylum, reunion,
waving letters from relatives and university certificates . . . outside
the UNHCR for a document identifying them as refugees . . .
They queue for everything'; all the endless bureaucracy in
conditions of terror 'as Baghdad's civil war has escalated'.

64.   'Iraqis top list of asylum-seekers in Western world', *Morning Star*,
       24 March 2007.

65.   Sami Ramadani, 'In Iraq, public anger is at last translating into
       unity', *The Guardian*, 20 March 2007.

66.   Ibid.

67.   Audrey Gillan, 'Four years on: The regrets of the man who
       brought down Saddam', *The Guardian*, 19 March 2007.

68.   The figure of one million Iraqi fatalities is based on the calculations
       of Dr Gideon Polya – see Chapter 2.

69.   The police estimated the size of the Washington protest at between
       10,000 and 20,000; small pro-war demonstrations were also staged.

70.   'Protesters mark Iraq war anniversary', *Morning Star*, 19 March
       2007.

71.   Ibid.

72.   'World media gloom on Iraq anniversary', BBC News online, 20
       March 2007.

73.   James Hider, 'Car bombers kill their decoy children', *The Times*, 22
       March 2007.

74.   I include these reports regarding the terrorist use of children at face
       value, though I am aware that the US authorities have admitted
       planting material in the media as part of the propaganda war. False
       atrocity stories are commonly used in war propaganda, as for
       example with the reports that premature babies were taken from
       incubators and thrown on the 'cold, hard floor' by Iraqi troops
       during the occupation of Kuwait in 1990. In this connection, see
       for example John R. MacArthur, *Second Front: Censorship and*

Propaganda in the Gulf War (New York: Hill & Wang, 1992); Philip
M. Taylor, *War and the Media: Propaganda and Persuasion in the Gulf
War* (Manchester: Manchester University Press, 1992).

75. Ibid.; Michael Howard, 'Iraqi insurgents blow up car with children
    inside', *The Guardian*, 22 March 2007; 'Child decoys die in Iraq car
    bombing', *Daily Telegraph*, 22 March 2007.

76. James Hider, '45 bound and shot dead in revenge attack', *The
    Times*, 29 March 2007.

77. David Blair, 'Saudi king condemns US for its "illegitimate"
    occupation of Iraq', *Daily Telegraph*, 29 March 2007.

78. Ewen MacAskill, 'Bush warns of veto after vote for Iraq
    withdrawal', *The Guardian*, 24 March 2007.

Chapter 4: Talk of 'reposturing': British retreat?

1. Quoted in Graeme Wilson, 'Commons to investigate "appalling"
   treatment of injured returning troops', *Daily Telegraph*, 13 March
   2007.

2. Ibid.

3. Ibid.

4. According to an audit of US spending, some 34 per cent of the $21
   billion allocated for Iraqi reconstruction had been diverted to
   security – an increase from $4.56 billion to $6.31 billion. For
   private US contractors the cost of security in Iraq was running at
   around 12 per cent for each contract.

5. Quoted in David Pallister, '25% of Iraq aid budget goes to security
   firms', *The Guardian*, 2 April 2007.

6. See for example Geoff Simons, *They Destroyed Iraq and Called it
   Freedom* (London: Legacy, 2008), Chapter 6.

7. James Hider, 'Lorry bomb kills children in school', *The Times*, 3
   April 2007.

8. 'Six Iraqis die in gun attack on minibus near Kirkuk', *Morning Star*,
   5 April 2007.

9. There was a growing debate about the role of women in the British
   armed forces, stimulated in part by the experience of Faye Turney,
   taken prisoner along with fourteen other Royal Navy personnel by
   the Iranians and later released. There were about 1,600 female
   troops operating in Iraq and Afghanistan, many of them exposed to
   the routine dangers of roadside bombs and mortar fire.

10. Thomas Harding and George Jones, 'Blair links Iran to brutal act of
    terror', *Daily Telegraph*, 6 April 2007; Richard Norton-Taylor and

Michael Howard, "'The ugly reality of war'", *The Guardian*, 6 April 2007.

11. Jane's Information Group, quoted in Harding and Jones, 'Blair links Iran to brutal act of terror'.

12. David Blair, 'Why Teheran has such a vital interest in the future of Iraqi politics: Iran's role', *Daily Telegraph*, 6 April 2007.

13. Sean Raymont, 'Battle for Basra will be deadlier as forces pull back, officers warn', *Sunday Telegraph*, 8 April 2007.

14. In February one police chief had admitted that he could not trust a third of his officers because of their links to insurgents, and another senior officer said that he had been forced to hire 300 illiterate officers for tribal reasons. See Sean Raymont, 'Battle for Basra will be deadlier as forces pull back, officers warn', *Sunday Telegraph*, 8 April 2007.

15 James Hider, 'Insurgents transform US military jails into "terror training camps"', *The Times*, 7 April 2007.

16. Ibid.

17. Ibid.

18. Hala Jaber, 'Slaughter of a family by the death squads', *Sunday Times*, 8 April 2007.

19. Ibid.

20. Mark Kurkis, 'The small-town war', *Time*, 9 April 2007.

21. *Civilians without Protection: The Ever-Worsening Humanitarian Crisis in Iraq* (Geneva: International Committee of the Red Cross, 2007).

22. Ian Black, 'Red Cross details "unbearable suffering" of Iraqi civilians', *The Guardian*, 12 April 2007.

23. Quoted in Adrian Roberts, 'Iraq anguish increases by the day', *Morning Star*, 12 April 2007.

24. Quoted ibid.

25. *Civilians without Protection*.

26. Ibid.

27. Hala Jaber and Ali Rifat, 'Sunnis try to blast Al-Qaeda out of Iraq', *Sunday Times*, 1 April 2007.

28. Quoted in Tom Baldwin, 'Hurry up with Iraq Bill so I can veto it, says Bush', *The Times*, 4 April 2007.

29. Quoted ibid.

30. Quoted ibid.

31. The last similar deadlock between Congress and the White House occurred in 1995, when a funding dispute paralysed parts of the federal government. In the event, President Bill Clinton managed to win public support against the Republicans, headed by Newt

Gingrich, who were widely perceived as overreaching their mandate and putting politics before people.

32. Quoted in Tom Baldwin, 'Families caught up in battle over an end to the Iraq war', *The Times*, 9 April 2007.

33. On 11 April the *Wall Street Journal* declared in a leader: 'His [McCain's] support for the war and his appreciation of the stakes is [*sic*] one thing that keeps his candidacy alive, at least within the Republican Party.' In May 2006 McCain, speaking to jeers and boos, had said at a university graduation ceremony in Madison Square Garden that the 'benefits of success will justify the costs and risks', after 1,200 graduates had signed a petition objecting to his invitation to give the address. In April 2007 McCain was already running into 'war-chest' problems. It seemed likely that in the coming months, because of lack of financial support, he would abandon his run for presidential office.

34. Quoted in Suzanne Goldenberg, 'McCain rethinks his Iraq policy', *The Guardian*, 9 April 2007.

35. Quoted ibid.

36. Tom Baldwin, 'McCain goes for broke as he supports "a just war"', *The Times*, 12 April 2007.

37. Tim Reid, 'Bush tries to resolve war funds stand off', *The Times*, 17 April 2007.

38. Damien McElroy, 'Thousands of Iraqis in call for US to end its occupation', *Daily Telegraph*, 10 April 2007.

39. James Hider, 'Rally against US masks divisions in Mahdi Army', *The Times*, 10 April 2007.

40. Abu Haidar, quoted ibid.

41. Michael Howard, 'Moqtada rallies Shia to demand withdrawal of foreign troops', *The Guardian*, 10 April 2007.

42. Michael Howard, 'Al-Sadr followers quit cabinet over US presence', *The Guardian*, 17 April 2007.

43. Quoted in Thomas Harding, '20 Shia gunmen die in British fightback', *Daily Telegraph*, 12 April 2007.

44. Damien McElroy, 'Britain tarnished by war in Iraq, say three reports', *Daily Telegraph*, 12 April 2007.

45. *Iraq: A Conflict That Spares No One* (Geneva: International Committee of the Red Cross, 2007).

46. Quoted in Michael Howard, 'We'll be in control by end of 2007 says Maliki', *The Guardian*, 19 April 2007.

47. Quoted ibid.

48. Quoted ibid.

49. James Hider, 'British put the "Wild West" back under control of Iraqis', *The Times*, 19 April 2007.

50. Joshua Rozenberg, 'Does Basra have the right to life?', *Daily Telegraph*, 19 April 2007.

51. Peter Kilfoyle, a former defence minister, who admitted passing on details of the alleged plan to bomb Al Jazeera in Qatar, escaped prosecution.

52. Karen McVeigh, 'Two accused of leaking secret memo on Bush–Blair Iraq talks', *The Guardian*, 19 April 2007; Michael Evans, 'Blair aide "leaked classified Iraq memo"', *The Times*, 19 April 2007.

53. The judge warned the jury not to disclose any of the information: 'The information you heard in camera . . . remain [sic] confidential. It remains secret.'

54. The dead MPs were Mohammed Awad, a member of the hardline Sunni National Dialogue Front, which held eleven seats in the parliament and was critical of the Maliki government; Taha al-Liheibi, of the Sunni Accordance Front, which held forty-four seats and was part of the government; and Omar Ali al-Hussein, a member of the Kurdistan Islamic Union.

55. Quoted in James Hider, 'Bomber kills MPs in blow to heart of government', *The Times*, 13 April 2007.

56. Quoted ibid.

57. Damien McElroy, 'Suicide bomber kills Iraqi MPs in attack on the Green Zone', *Daily Telegraph*, 13 April 2007.

58. Quoted in Michael Howard, 'US admits Green Zone is no longer safe as suicide bomber strikes heart of government', *The Guardian*, 13 April 2007.

59. Quoted in McElroy, 'Suicide bomber kills Iraqi MPs in attack on the Green Zone'.

60. Quoted in Robert Watson and Aqeel Hussein, 'Bombing backfires by uniting Iraq's MPs', *Sunday Telegraph*, 15 April 2007.

61. Quoted in 'Iraq: New humanitarian crisis looms as more than three million Iraqis displaced by war', press release, Amnesty International, 16 April 2007; David Charter, 'UN pleads for world to help Iraqis trying to flee violence', *The Times*, 18 April 2007.

62. Dahr Jamail, 'Fleeing the killing', *Morning Star*, 21 April 2007.

63. Quoted in 'Iraq: New humanitarian crisis looms as more than three million Iraqis displaced by war'.

64. *Unjust and Unfair: The Death Penalty in Iraq* (London: Amnesty International, 2007). The report was based on Amnesty's

examination of hundreds of verdicts issued by the Central Criminal Court of Iraq (CCCI), as well as the testimonies of families of those convicted and their lawyers. It also includes a detailed analysis of Iraqi laws that undermine the right to a fair trial.

65. Quoted in 'Iraq: Televised "confessions", torture and unfair trials underpin world's fourth highest executioner', press release, Amnesty International, 20 April 2007.

66. Felicity Arbuthnot, 'Desperate measures: The ghettoisation of Baghdad', *Morning Star*, 26 April 2007.

67. Quoted in James Hider, 'Bombers kill 9 US troops as model town descends into bloody chaos', *The Times*, 25 April 2007.

68. Quoted in 'Iraq: Release Data on Civilian Deaths', press release, Human Rights Watch, 25 April 2007.

69. Quoted in Julian Borger, 'UN accuses Iraq of covering up rise in civilian deaths', *The Guardian*, 26 April 2007.

70. Quoted in Ewen MacAskill, 'Blow to Bush as top US commander warns of worse to come in Iraq', *The Guardian*, 27 April 2007.

71. Quoted ibid.

72. James Hider, 'Camp Cropper chief held for "aiding enemy"', *The Times*, 27 April 2007.

73. At the end of April 2007, since the invasion of March 2003 some 3,312 US military personnel had died in Iraq; up to 3 February 2007 there had been 26,188 wounded; 19.1 per cent of troops returning from Iraq reported mental health problems, compared with 11.3 per cent from Afghanistan and 8.5 per cent from other theatres of war; 4 per cent of troops were suffering post-traumatic stress syndrome after a month in Iraq, rising to 12 per cent after seven months; 4.4 per cent of troops were depressed after a month, rising to 9 per cent at seven months; 90 per cent of casualties in Iraq survived, compared with 69.7 per cent in the Second World War and 76.4 per cent in Vietnam; 20 per cent of survivors have serious head or spinal injuries, and another 6 per cent are amputees.

74. Quoted in Roger Boyes and David Bebber, 'Shell shock: the invisible scar from the trenches to the Gulf', *The Times*, 20 April 2007.

75. Quoted ibid.

76. Nick Britten and Bonnie Malkin, 'Stressed troops "at breaking point" in Iraq', *Daily Telegraph*, 28 April 2007.

77. *Channel 4 News*, 28 April 2007.

78. Quoted in Britten and Malkin, 'Stressed troops "at breaking point" in Iraq'.

79. Ewen MacAskill, 'Latest US solution to Iraq's civil war: a three-mile wall', *The Guardian*, 21 April 2007; 'Baghdad wall dispute grows: Maliki demand for halt rejected', *Morning Star*, 24 April 2007.

80. 'Baghdad wall dispute grows'.

81. Aqeel Hussein and Colin Freeman, 'Bomb victims' bodies held for ransom in Baghdad', *Sunday Telegraph*, 29 April 2007.

82. Hala Jaber, 'Doubly cursed: the Iraqi families both sides target', *Sunday Times*, 29 April 2007.

83. Andrew Sullivan, 'Republicans wriggle toward the war exit', *Sunday Times*, 29 April 2007.

84. The inspectors found bathrooms buckled by blocked drains and faulty wiring; faulty plumbing in special forces barracks; four large electrical generators, each costing $50,000, that were no longer working; a clogged sewer system in a maternity and children's hospital; needles, bandages and other medical waste in the sewer system; a new incinerator that was already out of order; a new sophisticated oxygen system that was only used as a back-up system; cleaning water being absorbed into hospital walls; excess water leaking from second-floor hallways and bathrooms to first-floor rooms, including critical patient care areas.

85. Ewen MacAskill, 'US report blames Iraqis for failing reconstruction', *The Guardian*, 30 April 2007.

Chapter 5: Eroding the politics of denial

1. Quoted in Steven Morris, 'First British soldier to be convicted of a war crime is jailed for ill-treatment of Iraqi civilians', *The Guardian*, 1 May 2007.

2. Jonathan Holmes, 'The legacy of Fallujah', *The Guardian*, 4 April 2007.

3. Jonathan Steele and Dahr Jamail, 'This is our Guernica', *The Guardian*, 27 April 2005.

4. Ibid.

5. Tony Lagouranis and Allen Michaelian, *Fear Up Harsh: An Army Interrogator's Dark Journey through Iraq* (New York: NAL, 2007), pp. 221–2.

6. David Blair, 'Envoys "warned of Iraq invasion nightmare"', *Daily Telegraph*, 2 May 2007.

7. Quoted ibid.

8. Richards retired in 2006 with a critical valedictory telegram, saying that the British Foreign Office, obsessed by management at the

expense of diplomacy and policy-making, was gripped by
'management speak' amounting to 'bullshit bingo'. He noted that
there were then '34 separate reviews being undertaken at the Foreign
Office . . . skills audits, capability reviews, zero-based accounting
reviews and so on . . . The staff cannot be expected to focus on
crucial policy questions, like how we clear up the mess in Iraq.'

9.   Brian Bennett, 'Last call in Iraq', *Time*, 7 May 2007.

10.   This ministerial summit was called the International Compact with
Iraq. Some sixty nations and twelve regional and international
organisations took part. The meeting appeared to be fragmented
and divisive, with the familiar enmities preventing constructive
dialogue.

11.   David Blair, 'Hopes of US–Iran talks dashed after attack over Iraq',
Daily Telegraph, 5 May 2007.

12.   Bush let it be known that he had signed the veto with a pen given
him by Robert Derga, whose son Dustin, a marine, had been killed
in Iraq two years before. (The Democratic leadership signed the bill
in front of television cameras to ensure maximum impact, and had
timed the measure to fall on the anniversary of George Bush's 2003
infamous appearance on an aircraft carrier under a massive banner
declaring 'MISSION ACCOMPLISHED', according to Senator
Hillary Clinton 'one of the most shameful episodes in American
history'.) This was Bush's second veto since he entered the White
House in 2001. In 2006 he vetoed a bill that would have provided
funds for stem cell research.

13.   Ed Pilkington and Ewen MacAskill, 'Bush vetoes Democrats'
attempt to set timetable for withdrawal of American troops from
Iraq', *The Guardian*, 2 May 2007.

14.   The US Troop Readiness, Veterans' Health, and Iraq
Accountability Act.

15.   'Generals express outrage at presidential veto', press release,
National Security Network, 2 May 2007.

16   Quoted ibid.

17.   Ibid.

18.   'President Bush is going against the advice of former generals',
National Security Network, 12 April 2007.

19.   Quoted in 'Generals express outrage at presidential veto'.

20.   Quoted ibid.

21.   Quoted ibid.

22.   Rose was a former SAS commander and head of the UN forces in
Bosnia. In 2006 he called for Blair to be impeached for going to

war on 'false pretences'. Speaking on BBC Radio 4's *Today* programme he said: 'To go to war on something that turns out to be false grounds is something that no one should be allowed to walk away from.'

23. General Sir Michael Rose, *Newsnight*, BBC2, 3 May 2007; Thomas Harding, '"Invaders" must leave Iraq, says SAS general', *Daily Telegraph*, 4 May 2007.

24. Rose, *Newsnight*.

25. Toby Harnden, 'Republicans warn Bush he risks being deserted over Iraq', *Daily Telegraph*, 11 May 2007; Suzanne Goldenberg, 'Republicans warn Bush of US fatigue over Iraq war', *The Guardian*, 11 May 2007; Tim Reid, 'Bush begs for more time as Republican revolt gathers pace', *The Times*, 11 May 2007.

26. Harnden, 'Republicans warn Bush he risks being deserted over Iraq'.

27. 'Iraq MPs call for US pullout', *Morning Star*, 11 May 2007.

28. *Iraq Occupation Focus Newsletter*, no. 69, 18 May 2007.

29. Ewen MacAskill, 'Iraq war strain leads troops to abuse civilians, survey shows', *The Guardian*, 5 May 2007.

30. Matthew Currier Burden, *The Blog of War: Front-Line Dispatches from Soldiers in Iraq and Afghanistan* (New York: Simon & Schuster, 2006.

31. Ibid. At the same time as the Pentagon was curbing military blogs, Colby Buzzell was awarded the £5,000 Lulu Blooker prize for *My War: Killing Time in Iraq* (New York: G. P. Putnam's Sons), voted the best book of 2007 based on a blog. It triumphed over 110 entries from fifteen countries (see Ed Pilkington, 'Iraq veteran wins blog prize as US military cuts web access', *The Guardian*, 15 May 2007).

32. 'Iraqi town simmers as US battles to restore services', AFP report, 12 May 2007.

33. 'Anger in Baghdad as Americans finish wall', *Daily Telegraph*, 3 May 2007.

34. James Hider, 'Bombs found hidden in walls of new school', *The Times*, 5 May 2007.

35. 'Iraq: Urgent appeal as two women face imminent execution', press release, Amnesty International, 10 May 2007.

36. Damien McElroy, 'Christians fleeing Iraq after death threats', *Daily Telegraph*, 8 May 2007.

37. It can of course be argued that free-enterprise capitalism is endemically tainted by criminal involvement – as, for example,

with the 'gangster capitalism' of Russia, the nefarious activities of the multinationals in the underdeveloped world, the involvement of mainstream corporations in corruption, money-laundering, the global drugs trade etc.

38. Other British teenage fatalities in Iraq included Private Eleanor Dlugosz (aged 19), Kingsman Adam Smith (19), Private Michael Tench (18), Kingsman Jamie Lee Hancock (19), Private Adam Morris (18), Signaller William Didsbury (18), Private Paul Lowe (19), Fusilier Gordon Gentle (19), Private Ryan Thomas (18), Private Andrew Kelly (19), Fusilier Kelan Turrington (18) and Trooper David Clarke (19).

39. Brinkley, quoted in Damien McElroy, 'Solution to ending insurgency is "Made in Iraq"', *Daily Telegraph*, 10 May 2007.

40. Sean Smith, 'Life in the "triangle of death"', *The Guardian*, 11 May 2007.

41. Ibid.

42. Suzanne Goldenberg, 'US general asks for more troops in northern Iraq', *The Guardian*, 12 May 2007.

43. Quoted ibid.

44. Quoted in Tom Baldwin, '"Scariest guy in town" stalks Bush over Iraq', *The Times*, 14 May 2007. The forgeries in question related to documentation stating that Saddam was trying to obtain quantities of uranium from Africa – asserted by President Bush in his State of the Union address in 2003 as something the 'British government had learned'. The principal British claims were subsequently discredited and others were withdrawn.

45. Uzi Mahnaimi, 'Al-Qaeda planning militant Islamic state within Iraq', *Sunday Times*, 13 May 2007.

46. Five US soldiers were charged with the rape and killing of Abeer Qassim al-Janabi and with the murder of her parents and younger sister in Mahmoudiyah, unquestionably a shocking atrocity. Three soldiers pleaded guilty.

47. Stephen Farrell and Tom Baldwin, 'Al-Qaeda group claims capture of three soldiers', *The Times*, 14 May 2007.

48. Quoted in Ian Black, 'Journalists removed from Iraq bomb site', *The Guardian*, 16 May 2007.

49. Ibid.

50. The main factions competing for power in Basra were: the pro-Iranian Mahdi Army, a loose alliance of Shi'ite militiamen, about half of which were connected to Muqtada al-Sadr's office in Najaf; the Fadhilla Party, an anti-Iranian Shi'ite militia organisation that

controls the oil business in Basra, parts of the security forces, the ports and customs; the Badr Brigade, the armed wing of the Supreme Council for the Islamic Revolution in Iraq, based in Iran for twenty years before the 2003 invasion; and about two dozen major tribes, demanding allegiance from their members above nationality, running smuggling operations and supporting politicians in the city.

51. Quoted in Ghaith Abdul-Ahad, '"Welcome to Tehran" – how Iran took control of Basra', *The Guardian*, 19 May 2007.

52. Quoted ibid.

53. Ammar, quoted ibid.

54. Quoted in Colin Freeman and Philip Sherwell, 'US surge is failing, says UK Iraq envoy', *Sunday Telegraph*, 20 May 2007.

55. Tim Shipman and Philip Sherwell, 'The relationship will become a little less special, Washington fears', *Sunday Telegraph*, 20 May 2007; Tim Shipman, Philip Sherwell and Patrick Hennessy, 'Bush gets ready for Iraq U-turn by Brown', *Sunday Telegraph*, 20 May 2007.

56. Quoted in Ed Pilkington, 'Bush presidency worst in history, says Carter', *The Guardian*, 21 May 2005; 'US ex-president attacks "subservient" Blair', *Morning Star*, 21 May 2007.

57. See for example *The Guardian*, 21 May 2007.

58. Quoted in Ed Pilkington, 'One building that's been built on time and on budget in Iraq', *The Guardian*, 21 May 2007.

59. Quoted ibid.

60. Stewart M. Powell, 'Bush could double force by Christmas', *San Francisco Chronicle*, 22 May 2007.

61. Ibid.

62. Ibid.

63. The ISG urged the creation of an 'Iraq International Support Group', which, according to Recommendation 5 in the group's report, would comprise Iraq, all the states bordering Iraq (including Iran and Syria), the key regional states (including Egypt and the Gulf states), the five permanent members of the UN Security Council and the European Union; and possibly also involve other countries – such as Germany, Japan and South Korea – 'that might be willing to contribute to resolving political, diplomatic, and security problems affecting Iraq'. Recommendation 7 of the report suggested that the support group call on the participation of the office of the UN secretary general, and that he should designate a special envoy as his representative.

64. Simon Tisdall, 'Bush may turn to UN in search for Iraq solution', *The Guardian*, 23 May 2007.

65. Ibid.

66. Quoted in Sarah Baxter, 'US plans to halve troops in Iraq on way to exit', *Sunday Times*, 27 May 2007.

67. Tim Reid, 'Democrats surrender to Bush over funding for Iraq troops', *The Times*, 24 May 2007.

68. Ann Wright, 'What Congress really approved: Benchmark No. 1 – Privatizing Iraq's Oil for US Companies', *Truthout*, 26 May 2007, www.truthout.org.

69. A principal concern of leading Democrats was that if they blocked funding for the war and troops were withdrawn, they would thereafter be blamed for the manifest defeat of US forces in the field. This had happened in the aftermath of Vietnam. Where politicians had been willing to continue the war it was eventually stopped by congressional pressure to withdraw funding. For years after, the Democrats were charged with responsibility for an American surrender.

70. On 24 May 2007 the total number of US deaths stood at 3,434 with 24,314 injured, many of them very seriously with brain damage, paralysis or amputation. The average number of US deaths per day before the troops surge was 2.2; after the surge it was 3.1 (source: Iraq Coalition Casualty Count, http://icasualties.org).

71. Ghaith Abdul-Ahad, Richard Norton-Taylor and Ewen MacAskill, 'Mahdi army vows revenge on British troops after Basra leader is killed', *The Guardian*, 26 May 2007.

72. Gareth Porter, 'Sunni resistance receptive to Sadr alliance', Inter Press Service, 24 May 2007.

73. Quoted in Toby Harnden, 'Clinton, Obama vote to axe Iraq funds', *Daily Telegraph*, 26 May 2007.

74. Philip Sherwell and Colin Freeman, 'British general tempts wary insurgents to negotiating table', *Sunday Telegraph*, 27 May 2007.

75. In mid-May 2007 ABC News carried a report that President Bush had signed a 'non-lethal presidential finding' that authorised a campaign of 'black' operations of 'propaganda, disinformation and manipulation of Iran's currency and financial transactions'. A short time later, CBS reported that the CIA had tried to sabotage Tehran's uranium enrichment efforts by tricking Iranian specialists into buying defective components.

76. Rupert Cornwell, 'Iraq is the only topic of conversation as the US and Iran finally meet', *The Independent*, 29 May 2007; Jonathan

Steele, 'Iraq and US see "positive" steps in first formal talks since hostage crisis of 1980', *The Guardian*, 29 May 2007.

77. 'Arabs laud US–Iran talks on Iraq but demand to be involved', *Morning Star*, 30 May 2007.

78. The regulation – Paragraph 11(a) of IAW Change 3, Department of Defense Directive 5122.5 – stipulates: 'Names, videos, identifiable written/oral descriptions or identifiable photographs of wounded service members will not be released without the service member's prior written consent.'

79. Quoted in David Carr, 'Not to see the fallen is no favor', *New York Times*, 28 May 2007.

80. Quoted ibid.

81. Tim Reid, 'US looks at option to reduce Iraq troop numbers', *The Times,* London, 29 May 2007.

82. Since 2003 some 300 foreigners and 5,000 Iraqis, including 250 doctors, had been kidnapped in Iraq. The foreign nationals kidnapped had experienced various outcomes: fifty-four had been killed, 147 released, four escaped, six were rescued and the fate of eighty-nine was unknown. By June 2007 around forty Iraqis were being kidnapped every day. About a quarter of all Baghdad residents had experienced a relative being kidnapped.

83. A security guard who preferred to remain anonymous described his work to the *Guardian* journalist Audrey Gillan and commented: 'I think the writing is on the wall for Baghdad. I think it is about to go ballistic. The Baghdad security plan is not going to work.' Private military companies, generally depicted as mercenaries, were exploiting a market worth billions of dollars. By June 2007 there were thought to be around 20,000 security personnel in Iraq, each earning at least $1,000 a day. Britain itself had spent £165 million on hiring mercenaries, amounting to about a quarter of the entire Iraqi aid budget. A further £43 million had been spent on mercenaries in Afghanistan.

84. Quoted in Audrey Gillan and Richard Norton-Taylor, 'Baghdad lockdown as troops hunt for Britons', *The Guardian*, 31 May 2007.

85. Quoted in 'Qaeda-led group claims downing of US craft in Iraq', Reuters, 30 May 2007.

86. Kirk Semple, 'U.S. and British Airstrikes Hit Iraqi Militia', *New York Times*, 26 May 2007.

87. 'Thousands flee upsurge in violence in Diyala province', IRIN, 14 May 2007.

88. Ahmed Rasheed, 'Iraqis in "besieged" city struggle to survive',

Reuters, 18 May 2007; 'Curfew begins to choke Samarra', Inter Press Service, 22 May 2007.

89.   'The occupation forces bombard wildly citizens' houses and orchards in Taji', Haq News Agency, 22 May 2007; 'US forces surround villages', Association of Muslim Scholars in Iraq report, 21 May 2007.

90.   Robert Verkaik, 'New claims of Army war crimes in Iraq', *The Independent*, 18 May 2007.

91.   Quoted ibid.

92.   Jamie Doward, 'Army must come clean on torture in Iraq, say MPs', *The Observer*, 27 May 2007.

93.   'Britons Blast Blair, Bush for Iraq War', Angus Reid Global Monitor, 26 May 2007.

94.   Quoted in Roland Watson, 'Iraq holds its breath for the vital summer ahead', *The Times*, 31 May 2007.

95.   Ibid.

Chapter 6: Coalition 'making things worse'

1.   In the event, Brown's premiership began with a shift in emphasis on Iraq, principally by virtue of government appointments that soon generated concern in the United States. Some of these appointments in turn led to anti-war comments – mainly by Douglas Alexander, the new International Development Secretary, and Mark Malloch Brown, the new Foreign Office minister of state – that would have been impossible under Tony Blair (see Chapter 7).

2.   The invasion of Iraq in March 2003 had involved 46,000 British troops in Operation Telic. By early June 2007 the figure had been reduced to 5,500, from 7,200 in January.

3.   Sean Rayment and Patrick Hennessy, 'MoD planning to pull troops out of Iraq within a year', *Sunday Telegraph*, 3 June 2007.

4.   It was heartening to be told by a minister close to the Chancellor's camp that 'Gordon will not do anything foolish' (quoted in Sean Rayment and Patrick Hennessy, 'MoD planning to pull troops out of Iraq within a year', *Sunday Telegraph*, 3 June 2007).

5.   Deborah Haynes, 'Iraqi minister puts pressure on Brown not to cut and run', *The Times*, 7 June 2007.

6.   Quoted ibid.

7.   Quoted ibid.

8.   Quoted in Tania Branigan and Rosie Lavan, 'UK and US must quit Iraq quickly, says former ambassador', *The Guardian*, 6 June

2007. Meyer was giving evidence to the Iraq Commission in London, set up by the Foreign Policy Centre think tank and Channel 4 to examine possible options for Britain's future role (see Chapter 7).

9. Julian Borger, Richard Norton-Taylor and Michael Howard, 'UK may seek Iranian help in finding Iraq hostages', *The Guardian*, 1 June 2007.

10. The Mahdi Army called for curbs on British forces after they had supported an Iraqi operation in which Abu Qadir, the militia's leader in Basra, had been shot dead.

11. Hala Jaber and Ali Rifat, 'Hostage gang in Basra demand', *Sunday Times*, 3 June 2007.

12. Unnamed security sources suggested that the four British security men may have broken basic security rules, such as varying their basic routine, not visiting dangerous buildings and posting a guard to warn of attack. Doubts had also been expressed about the suitability of their employer, GardaWorld, when it was granted a security contract in Iraq (Deborah Haynes and Richard Beeston, 'Britons seized in Baghdad "broke basic security rules"', *The Times*, 2 June 2007).

13. Quoted in Kim Gamel, 'US troop drive said faltering in Iraq', Associated Press, 4 June 2007.

14. Quoted ibid.

15. Anne Davis, 'Clinton in front as Democrats clash over Iraq', *The Age*, 5 June 2007; Leonard Doyle, 'Democrat rivals clash over Iraq and healthcare', *Belfast Telegraph*, 5 June 2007.

16. Davis, 'Clinton in front as Democrats clash over Iraq'.

17. Quoted in Doyle, 'Democrat rivals clash over Iraq and healthcare'.

18. Other items cited include: the hundreds of Iraqis going missing or being killed at checkpoints; a US staff sergeant, Justin Laughner, ordered to destroy pictures of Iraqi women and children killed by marines as part of a cover-up of twenty-four murdered civilians; cancer emerging as a major cause of death in southern Iraq; a mother, Adeela Harith, scavenging rubbish bins to feed her children; Baghdad as the 'city of garbage'; protests over power and fuel shortages; 10,000 Iraqi women imprisoned in Kurdistan, most of them suffering rape; and women being fired for security reasons. Sources are provided in *Iraq Occupation Focus Newsletter*, no. 71, 13 June 2007.

19. 'US reprises "shock and awe" campaign', *Morning Star*, 7 June 2007.

20. Charles J. Hanley, 'U.S. airpower dropping bombs on Iraq at twice last year's rate', Associated Press, 5 June 2007.

21.   The United States admitted launching cluster bombs through 2006, and 110,000 pounds of other types of bombs. A *Lancet* study found that through the first three years of the war, about 13 per cent of civilian casualties were caused by coalition air strikes, with about 78,000 Iraqis killed by bombs, missiles, rockets or cannon (see Nick Turse, 'The secret air war in Iraq', *Nation*, 11 June 2007).

22.   Numeir Horan, 'US warplanes pound residential area in Mosul', Voices of Iraq, 29 May 2007.

23.   Quoted in Anne Flaherty, 'Bush war advisor was skeptical on Iraq', Associated Press, 7 June 2007.

24.   Quoted ibid.

25.   Simon Jenkins, 'In Iraq's four-year frenzy, the allies have become the vandals', *The Guardian*, 8 June 2007.

26.   Ibid.

27.   Quoted in Damien McElroy, 'Move to depose me is foreign plot, says Iraq's prime minister', *Daily Telegraph*, 8 June 2007.

28.   Quoted ibid.

29.   Quoted in 'Iraq protests Turkey's cross-border shelling', Associated Press, 9 June 2007.

30.   Quoted in Damien McElroy, 'America "used forced labour to build Baghdad embassy"', *Daily Telegraph*, 9 June 2007.

31.   Ibid.

32.   Quoted in Patrick Seale, 'Withdrawal won't happen', *The Guardian*, 9 June 2007.

33.   Quoted ibid.

34.   Quoted in Nicholas Watt, 'UK forces in Iraq should stay in their bases, says ex-envoy', *The Observer*, 19 June 2007.

35.   Kim Sengupta, 'Navy chief "took private legal advice on Iraq"', *The Independent*, 11 June 2007.

36.   General Sir Mike Jackson, *Soldier: The Autobiography* (London: Bantam Press, 2007).

37.   Sengupta, 'Navy chief "took private legal advice on Iraq"'.

38.   William Rees-Mogg, 'Mr Blair extradited? Not as crazy as it sounds', *The Times*, 11 June 2007.

39.   Andrew Gimson, 'Beckett outgunned in a hopeless cause', *Daily Telegraph*, 12 June 2007; George Jones, 'Iraq rebels deliver final blow to Blair', *Daily Telegraph*, 12 June 2007.

40.   Ben Quinn, '11,000 troops go Awol since Iraq war', *Daily Telegraph*, 11 June 2007.

41.   'Ducking a fight', *Houston Chronicle,* 11 June 2007.

42. Mariam Karoumy, 'Iraq's parliament votes to replace "rude" speaker', Reuters, 11 June 2007.

43. George Jones, Rachel Sylvester and Alice Thomson, 'Brown attacks blunder over war in Iraq: Brown not even ready to talk about troops pull-out', *Daily Telegraph*, 12 June 2007; Graeme Wilson, 'Chancellor's subtle shifts on the war', *Daily Telegraph*, 12 June 2007.

44. Wilson, 'Chancellor's subtle shifts on the war'.

45. Deborah Haynes and Philip Webster, 'No change of policy over troop withdrawal, Brown tells Iraqis', *The Times*, 12 June 2007.

46. Richard Norton-Taylor, 'Single Basra base for British troops in Iraq', *The Guardian*, 13 June 2007.

47. Tony Perry, 'Commander's role in Iraq killings argued', *Los Angeles Times*, 12 June 2007.

48. Ewen MacAskill, 'US arms Sunni dissidents in risky bid to contain al-Qaida fighters in Iraq', *The Guardian*, 12 June 2007.

49. Statistics taken from the Pentagon's official website and from the Iraq Coalition Casualty Count.

50. Sources for all these items are given in *Iraq Occupation Focus Newsletter*, no. 72, 29 June 2007.

51. Ibid.

52. Tina Susman, 'Close and deadly contact', *Los Angeles Times*, 12 June 2007.

53. Quoted in Andrew Johnson, 'A bloody epitaph to Blair's war', *Independent on Sunday*, 17 June 2007.

54. Ibid.

55. Robert Fisk, 'A cry for justice from a good man who expected us to protect his son', *Independent on Sunday*, 17 June 2007.

56. *Iraq Occupation Focus Newsletter*, no. 72, 29 June 2007, cites these (with sources) and other details, including the following: most Baghdad residents were getting one hour of electricity a day ('This permanent electricity failure is just another way of giving Iraqis slow death' – Dr Umayma Salim); 24-hour waits at petrol stations; factories were closing and agricultural production was 80 per cent less than before the 2003 invasion; the New York-based Global Policy Forum declared that the US occupation was the principal cause of Iraq's current woes (the US–British occupation had 'utterly failed to bring peace, prosperity and democracy, as originally advertised. The United Nations and the international community must end the complicity of silence') and demanded an immediate withdrawal of foreign troops; a 117-page report, *War*

and Occupation in Iraq, released jointly on 19 June 2007 by thirty
NGOs, claimed that the US military and its allies were killing Iraqi
civilians, stealing Iraq's oil and destroying the nation's heritage with
total impunity; in a government-run orphanage, emaciated naked
children were covered in their own faeces and chained to beds
('There were three people that were cooking themselves food, but
nothing for the kids'); a thousand Iraqis were forced to flee Najaf,
living in temperatures of 50°C in a tented camp with no facilities
('We are dying in this camp . . . We have done nothing wrong.
Our only fault is that we are Iraqi Shi'ites'), and there were many
similar camps scattered across southern Iraq ('The most important
need is water' – Hicham Hassan, International Committee of the
Red Cross).

57. Joshua Rozenberg and Thomas Harding, 'British troops must fight
under Human Rights Act', *Daily Telegraph*, 14 June 2007; Richard
Norton-Taylor and Clare Dyer, 'Human rights law protects
prisoners of UK troops abroad, rule lords in landmark case', *The
Guardian*, 14 June 2007.

58. Damien McElroy, 'Al-Qa'eda launches new attack on shrine',
Daily Telegraph, 14 June 2007.

59. Alissa J. Rubin, 'Sunni mosque is destroyed in retaliation', *New
York Times*, 15 June 2007.

60. Deborah Haynes, 'Ominous calm as curfew and fear keep streets
clear', *The Times*, 15 June 2007.

61. Steven R. Hurst, 'American fighter jet crashes in Iraq', Associated
Press, 15 June 2007.

62. Michael Rowland, 'US Democrat declares he's lost confidence in
Iraq commanders', *World Today*, 15 June 2007.

63. Quoted ibid.

64. Charles J. Hanley, 'In an Iraq where people favor attacking US
troops, they're hanging those who do', Associated Press, 15 June
2007.

65. Quoted ibid.

66. Among those who had been condemned to execution were: an
Algerian who reportedly confessed to being a member of the
Islamic Army in Iraq, who had attacked the US military on various
occasions; a 'self-admitted member' of the 1920 Revolution
Brigades who reportedly confessed to mortar attacks on the Green
Zone; a foreigner of undisclosed nationality reportedly captured
with a suicide bomb vest and who 'admitted he was in Iraq to kill
Americans'; and other individuals reportedly found with

components or other evidence related to improvised explosive devices. Western-sponsored surveys had found that a majority of Iraqis favoured such attacks (see Charles J. Hanley, 'In an Iraq where people favor attacking US troops, they're hanging those who do', Associated Press, 15 June 2007).

67. 'Plight of refugees worsens as Syria, Jordan impose restrictions', IRIN, 17 June 2007.
68. Lara Jakes Jordan, 'General: stabilized Iraq may take decade', ABC News, 18 June 2007.
69. William M. Arkis, 'Petraeus' perspective on Iraq', *Washington Post*, 18 June 2007.
70. Quoted in Patrick Wintour, 'Iraq on verge of genocidal war, warns ex-US official', *The Guardian*, 18 June 2007.
71. Ibid.
72. Quoted in Anne Hull and Dana Priest, 'WP: Mental care falls short for vets', *Washington Post*, 17 June 2007.
73. Ibid.
74. See Geoff Simons, *They Destroyed Iraq and Called it Freedom* (London: Legacy, 2008), Chapter 8.
75. The official inquiry into the abuses at Abu Ghraib, ordered by Lieutenant General Ricardo Sanchez, yielded a comprehensive report, *US Army Report on Iraqi Prisoner Abuse*, prepared by Taguba. The report, including copious documentation and witness statements, records 'specific findings of fact', including 'that between October and December 2003 . . . numerous incidents of sadistic, blatant and wanton criminal abuses were inflicted on several detainees . . . The allegations of abuse were substantiated by detailed witness statements and the discovery of extremely graphic photographic evidence.'
76. Seymour M. Hersh, 'The general's report: how Antonio Taguba, who investigated the Abu Ghraib scandal, became one of its victims', *New Yorker*, 25 June 2007.
77. Quoted ibid.
78. Ibid.
79. Ibid.
80. Clare Dyer, 'Lords to look at legality of Iraq war', *The Guardian*, 18 June 2007.
81. Quoted in Richard Beeston, 'Battle rages after troops join forces to attack arms smugglers from Iran', *The Times*, 19 June 2007.
82. Quoted in Damien McElroy, 'US offensive in Iraq uses Vietnam tactics', *Daily Telegraph*, 20 June 2006; Simon Tisdall, '10,000 US troops attack insurgents', *The Guardian*, 20 June 2007.

83. Quoted in Richard Beeston, 'US ambassador demands a
     "diplomatic surge"', *The Times*, 20 June 2007.

84. Richard Beeston, 'America can't just walk away from the fight
     with al-Qaeda, US general insists', *The Times*, 21 June 2007.

85. Lynn Sweet, 'A different Hillary answers Iraq war protesters',
     Chicago Sun-Times, 21 June 2007.

86. The incidence of psychological trauma was rising with prolonged
     combat duty: 38 per cent of regular soldiers, 31 per cent of
     marines, 49 per cent of National Guard troops and 43 per cent of
     marine reservists had symptoms of post-traumatic stress, depression,
     anxiety and other psychological problems within three months of
     returning from active duty.

87. Simon Tisdall, 'Troops cracking under strain of combat in Iraq,
     Pentagon told', *The Guardian*, 22 June 2007.

88. Richard Beeston, 'In 2004 – with Saddam gone – 27 Iraqi students
     started their degree course full of hope. Today just 7 will sit their
     finals', *The Times*, 23 June 2007.

89. The partition option was discussed by two prize-winning writers,
     the reporter Ghaith Abdul Ahad and the author Rajiv
     Chandrasekaran, in *The Guardian* on 23 June 2007. *Chandrasekaran:*
     I see the situation as polarised . . . perhaps the only reasonable
     approach is to think about a degree of partition and accept the way
     things are headed. [. . .] *Ghaith:* But I just can't see it happening.
     [. . .] *Chandrasekaran:* But people are already voting with their feet.
     They're dividing themselves, people are moving from one
     neighbourhood to another in Baghdad . . . You may well have
     various cantons where one group predominates and has a degree of
     control, and [this is what I think] gives the Sunnis a sense of at least
     controlling some elements of their own destiny.

90. The Kurds make up about 20 per cent of Turkey and Iraq, and
     have a significant presence in Syria and Iran. The total Kurdish
     population is between twenty-five and thirty million, one of the
     world's largest ethnic groups without a country of its own. This
     fact has long been a cause of resentment – and ambition.

91. Rajiv Chandrasekaran, 'Lords of misrule still in charge at the
     Baghdad bubble', *Sunday Times*, 24 June 2007.

92. Tim Shipman, 'US must stop yelling at Iraqis, says general', *Sunday
     Telegraph*, 24 June 2007.

93. Ibid.

94. See Simons, *They Destroyed Iraq and Called it Freedom*, Chapter 10.

95. Quoted in Michael Howard, 'The end for Saddam's trusted cousin

and lieutenant: Chemical Ali sentenced to death', *The Guardian*, 25 June 2007.

96. Michael Howard, 'A town celebrates verdict but fears no one will be called to account for its suffering', *The Guardian*, 25 June 2007; Richard Beeston and Ali Hussein, 'Chemical Ali greets death sentence with a shrug as Kurds dance for joy', *The Times*, 25 June 2007.

97. Mark Thompson, 'The enemy's new tools', *Time*, 25 June 2007.

98. Ibid.

99. The victims included: Fassal al-Gawud, the former governor of Anbar and Sheikh of the al-Bu Nimir tribe; Sheikh Abdulaziz al-Fahdzawi of the Fahad tribe; Sheikh Traqi Saleh al-Assafi and Colonel Fadil al-Nimrawi, both leading tribal figures; Hussein Shaalan, an MP; and Rahim al-Maliki, a well-known poet.

100. Richard Beeston, 'Al-Qaeda takes its explosive revenge on tribal leaders who dared to fight', *The Times*, 26 June 2007.

101. Will Woodward, 'Iraq furore clouds Harman's first day', *The Guardian*, 26 June 2007.

102. Richard Owen, 'The Pope rebukes Blair over Iraq war', *The Times*, 25 June 2007.

103. Ellen Massey, 'Women resist return to sectarian laws', Inter Press Service, 25 June 2007.

104. Resolution 1325 recalls the UN Day for Women's Rights and International Peace (International Women's Day) of 8 March 2000, among other things, expresses concern about women and children adversely affected by armed conflict, stresses the need to implement international humanitarian human rights law protecting women and girls during and after conflicts, urges the training of all peacekeeping personnel on the rights of women and children, urges the secretary general to call for the appointment of women as special representatives and envoys, and expresses the need to incorporate a gender perspective into peacekeeping operations.

105. See Simons, *They Destroyed Iraq and Called It Freedom*, Chapter 6.

106. Nadje Sadig al-Ali, *Iraqi Women: Untold Stories from 1948 to the Present* (London: Zed, 2007).

107. 'Iranian influence in Iraq undimmed despite talks – US', Reuters, 27 June 2007.

108. Michael Howard, 'Turkey warns of plans to invade northern Iraq', *The Guardian*, 30 June 2007.

109. Richard Beeston, 'The old spirit stirs but the people of Baghdad have one wish: to get out', *The Times*, 30 June 2007.

110. Ibid.
111. Ibid.
112. In the week ending 26 June 2007 the US military had suffered at least 251 combat casualties, as total casualties reached at least 57,017. The total included 29,279 killed or wounded by 'hostile' causes and 27,738 dead and injured from 'non-hostile' causes, such as accidents, suicides and illness serious enough to require medical evacuation. Up to 31 March there were more than 12,971 dead and injured 'contractors' of American companies.
113. 'Republicans criticise Bush on Iraq', Al Jazeera, 27 June 2007.

Chapter 7: Judging a 'bankrupt' policy

1. 'Baghdad suburb residents flee after US raids', IRIN, 3 July 2007.
2. Quoted ibid.
3. Quoted in Sara Hashash, 'Baghdad anger as US kills 26', *Sunday Times*, 1 July 2007. The quote was also carried in the *Los Angeles Times*, 1 July 2007.
4. 'Village disputes story of deadly attack', BBC Online, 26 June 2007.
5. Ali al-Fadhily, '"Arrowhead" becomes fountainhead of anger', Inter Press Service, 10 July 2007.
6. Association of Muslim Scholars of Iraq reports, 2 and 3 July 2007.
7. 'Occupation soldiers kill a mom from Sunnis and amputate her baby leg in Qadiriyah', Haq News Agency, 6 July 2007.
8. Tom Baldwin, 'Washington uneasy over Brown's anti-war ministers', *The Times*, 2 July 2007.
9. Simon Jenkins, 'With one leap of courage, Brown could break the Iraq impasse', *The Guardian*, 1 July 2007.
10. Ewen MacAskill, 'US turns up heat on Iran by publicly accusing it of involvement in Iraq', *The Guardian*, 3 July 2007.
11. Quoted in Michael Evans, 'Manpower shortage as pressures of war drive troops to quit forces', *The Times*, 3 July 2007; Graeme Wilson, 'Troop exodus means Armed Forces "can no longer cope"', *Daily Telegraph*, 3 July 2007.
12. In early July 2007 the number of civilian personnel working in Iraq included at least 21,000 Americans, 43,000 'foreign' contractors and about 118,000 Iraqis – all funded by US tax dollars.
13. It is important to note that the United Nations declared against the use of mercenaries: see the International Convention against the Recruitment, Use, Financing and Training of Mercenaries (4

December 1989). The preamble of this 21-article convention emphasises that mercenaries are used for activities 'which violate principles of international law', including the 'perpetration of violent actions which undermine the constitutional order of States'. After defining *mercenaries* in Article 1, the convention declares that any person that 'recruits, uses, finances or trains mercenaries' commits an offence, and stipulates that state parties to the convention punish offenders 'by appropriate penalties which take into account the grave nature of these offences'.

14. Quoted in T. Christian Miller, 'Private contractors outnumber US troops in Iraq', *Los Angeles Times*, 4 July 2007.
15. Ibid.
16. 'Rights group reveals torture in Kurdistan', *Morning Star*, 4 July 2007.
17. Simon Tisdall, 'For most Americans the war in Iraq is already lost', *The Guardian*, 4 July 2007.
18. Journalist E. J. Dionne, quoted ibid.
19. Quoted ibid.
20. In coming to its conclusions the Iraq Commission was required to take into account: southern Iraq's security situation; the political and economic situation; the role of British troops; the UK's wider Middle East strategy; domestic considerations, such as the war's impact on social cohesion; the relevance of key strategic alliances; reconstruction and development in Iraq, including the role of the NGOs and other agencies; and long-term support for Iraq.
21. Lord Ashdown: 'One of the greatest international challenges of our time is bringing peace and security to Iraq. It is both in Britain's national interest, and a moral obligation, that a way forward is found for Iraq and its people.'
22. Baroness Jay: 'The Iraq Commission aims to produce a long-term strategy for Britain's role in Iraq – this will incorporate the challenges of reconstruction, rebuilding and humanitarian relief efforts as well as security for the Iraqi people and British troops.'
23. Lord King: 'The current situation threatens the stability of the region and has major implications for the world as a whole. It is up to the policy makers on all sides to consider how best to resolve it, and enhance the security of Iraq itself and the region.'
24. The nine commissioners, in addition to the co-chairs, were Professor Brian Brivati, Lord Hannay of Chiswick, Dr Rosemary Hollis, Sir Paul Lever, Lieutenant General Andrew Ridgway, Maeve Sherlock, Asim Siddiqui, Stephen Twigg and Sir Patrick Walker.

25. Richard Alleyne, Richard Savill and Richard Edwards, 'Doctor arrested after airport attack "was outraged by death of his friends in Iraq"', *Daily Telegraph*, 5 July 2007.

26. Richard Norton-Taylor and Ian Cobain, 'Bombs plot investigators look at al-Qaida cells in Iraq', *The Guardian*, 6 July 2007.

27. Seamus Milne, 'Denial of the link with Iraq is delusional and dangerous', *The Guardian*, 5 July 2007.

28. David Leppard, 'Iraq's Al-Qaeda linked to British car bombers', *Sunday Times*, 8 July 2007.

29. Howard Blume, 'A place to push impeachment', *Los Angeles Times*, 5 July 2007.

30. Ibid.

31. John Winn Miller, 'Hearts are Heavy this fourth of July', *Olympian*, 4 July 2007; Greg Mitchell, 'Paper with strong military readership calls for Iraq pullout', *Editor & Publisher*, 5 July 2007.

32. Miller, 'Hearts are Heavy this fourth of July'.

33. Andrew Sullivan, 'Emperor Bush unnerves the Republicans', *Sunday Times*, 8 July 2007.

34. David Owen, *The Hubris Syndrome: Bush, Blair and the Intoxication of Power* (London: Politico's, 2007), p. 131.

35. Justin A. Frank, *Bush on the Couch: Inside the Mind of the US President* (London: Politico's, 2006), p. 202.

36. Quoted in Brendan Nicholson, 'Coalition divided over the Iraq war', *The Age*, 6 July 2007.

37. Quoted ibid.

38. Ibid; Philip Coorey and Craig Skehan, 'Oil not reason for Iraq war, insists Howard', *Sydney Morning Herald*, 6 July 2007.

39. David Moberg, 'Iraqi unions fight the new oil law', *In These Times*, August 2007.

40. Aqeel Hussein and Gethin Chamberlain, 'Iraqi teachers are sacked in exam marking scandal', *Sunday Telegraph*, 8 July 2007.

41. Quoted ibid.

42. David Blair, 'Iraqi PM under pressure as bomb kills 130', *Daily Telegraph*, 9 July 2007.

43. Andrew S. Ross, 'Iraq: "Coming to grips with losing"', SF Gate, 9 July 2007.

44. Quoted ibid.

45. Philip Sherwell, 'Haditha massacre marines face fresh allegations of atrocities', *Sunday Telegraph*, 8 July 2007.

46. Quoted in Tina Susman, 'US has a duty to stay, Iraqi says', *Los Angeles Times*, 10 July 2007.

47. Quoted ibid.
48. Quoted in Deborah Haynes and Tim Reid, 'Iraq warns of catastrophe as Bush struggles with rising US rebellion', *The Times*, 10 July 2007.
49. Quoted in Sheldon Alberts, 'US morally bound to save Iraq, general says', CanWest News Service, 11 July 2007.
50. Quoted ibid.
51. 'White House in "Panic Mode" over Iraq', U.S. News & World Report, 10 July 2007.
52. Peter Baker, 'Bush plans to stress next phase in Iraq War', *Washington Post*, 10 July 2007.
53. Toby Harnden, 'Bush may be forced to pull out troops', *Daily Telegraph*, 10 July 2007; Ewen MacAskill, 'Republican revolt prompts Bush to rethink surge', *The Guardian*, 10 July 2007.
54. Tim Reid and Suna Erdem, 'Iraq plan needs time but pullout is aim, says Bush', *The Times*, 11 July 2007.
55. McClelland's suggestion of an enlarged UN role in Iraq to some extent anticipated the adoption in August of a new Security Council resolution on Iraq, proposing various ways in which UN activities in Iraq could be developed to encourage reconciliation and stability (see Chapter 8).
56. 'Labor urges govt on Iraq withdrawal plan', *The Age*, 11 July 2007.
57. This suggestion again anticipated the subsequent Security Council decision to agree an enhanced UN role in Iraq (see Chapter 8).
58. Toby Harnden, 'Republicans give Bush's aide tough time over Iraq troops', *Daily Telegraph*, 12 July 2007.
59. According to the White House report, unsatisfactory progress had been made on eight benchmarks: reverse de-Ba'athification (to correct the disastrous de-Ba'athification policies introduced by Paul Bremer); the distribution of oil revenues equally among all regions (this aim was no more than a smokescreen for handing over Iraq's oil reserves to foreign multinationals); the adoption of amnesty legislation (always problematic since it implied that insurgents would be tolerated); ensuring that the Iraqi security forces were accountable only to the government and loyal to the constitution (which involved disarming the militias – an impossible task for the ineffectual Maliki regime); giving Iraqi commanders authority to make military decisions without political interference; ensuring even-handed enforcement of the law; increasing the number of security units able to operate independently; and ensuring the Iraqi political authorities were not undermining the Iraqi security forces.

Some success had been achieved on paving the way for provincial elections and reducing the level of sectarian violence and militia activity. According to the report, success had been achieved in five areas: amending the constitution; forming semi-autonomous regions by law; providing three Iraqi brigades to give support in Baghdad; supporting the Baghdad security plan (linked to the US troop surge); rooting out outlaws, regardless of sectarian affiliation; establishing joint security stations in Baghdad; protecting rights of minority political parties; and spending $10 billion on reconstruction and infrastructure projects. Even the modest tallies of 'successes' could be challenged. For example, it was highly questionable how effective the Iraqi brigades were, and other US reports indicated that massive reconstruction funds had disappeared into a black hole of inefficiency and corruption.

60.   Quoted in Suzanne Goldenberg, 'Iraq war policy failing, says official report', *The Guardian*, 13 July 2007.

61.   Quoted ibid.

62.   Quoted ibid.

63.   Toby Harnden, 'Bush insists that progress is being made in Iraq', *Daily Telegraph*, 13 July 2007.

64.   Quoted in Patrick Cockburn, 'Bush's optimism is impossible to square with the situation in Iraq', *The Independent*, 13 July 2007.

65.   Ibid.

66.   It was yet to be reported that the United States had lost track of vast amounts of weaponry and other equipment destined for the Iraqi security forces (see Chapter 8).

67.   'Iraq report card not accurate: Maliki', ABC News (Australia) website, 14 July 2007.

68.   Quoted in 'Republicans press Bush over Iraq', BBC News Online, 14 July 2007.

69.   Tom Baldwin, 'Destructive power is no measure of a country's might, Britain tells US', *The Times*, 13 July 2007.

70.   Ibid.; Patrick Wintour and Julian Borger, 'Brown message to US: it's time to build, not destroy', *The Guardian*, 13 July 2007.

71.   Philip Webster and Tom Baldwin, 'Cabinet is ordered to toe the line on US', *The Times*, 14 July 2007.

72.   Even in these rapidly deteriorating circumstances few British parliamentarians were prepared to support an early withdrawal of UK forces from southern Iraq. By 16 July 2007 only fourteen MPs had signed Early Day Motion (EDM) 335, calling for the immediate withdrawal of all British forces from Iraq; and only

twenty-seven had agreed EDM 1777, 'call[ing] upon the new
Prime Minister to announce as his first act in office a timetable for
the withdrawal of British troops from Iraq'.

73. Jim Rutenberg, 'Parts of Iraq report are grim where Bush was
upbeat', *New York Times*, 15 July 2007.

74. George Bush, radio address, quoted on *Dawn* website, 15 July
2007.

75. Sarah Baxter and David Cracknell, 'America stares at failure in
Iraq', *Sunday Times*, 15 July 2007.

76. 'Reuters photographer and driver killed in Iraq', Reuters, 13 July
2007; 'Two Reuters men die in "random American bombardment"',
The Guardian, London, 13 July 2007. Six Reuters employees had
been killed in Iraq since the US-led invasion of 2003.

77. Chris Hedges and Laila al-Arian, '"The carnage, the blown-up bodies
I saw . . . Why? What was this for?"', *The Guardian*, 13 July 2007.

78. Quoted ibid.

79. Quoted ibid.

80. Quoted ibid.

81. Quoted ibid.

82. Ibid.

83. Quoted ibid.

84. Quoted ibid.

85. The *Iraq Occupation Focus Newsletter* was continuing to record, with
full documentation, the impact of the war on Iraqi civilians: on 12
July an AP report noted that US helicopters had killed women and
children in Baghdad's Amin district; on 13 July the *New York Times*
reported that US forces had killed six Iraqi policemen; on 22 July
the *Los Angeles Times* reported that US helicopters had attacked
homes in Husseiniyah, survivors finding body parts of women and
children in the rubble – according to one witness, Hazim Hussein,
'a war against civilians'; also on 22 July American troops executed
three citizens in front of their families in Samarra; on 26 July US
F-16 aircraft bombed the home of Ramzi Abdul Dulaimi in
Diwaniyah, killing fourteen family members; on 27 July at least
seventeen people, including two women, were killed when US and
Iraqi forces battled Shi'ite militia members in Kabala; the citizens of
Dora, now ringed with concrete slabs, were complaining that the
US military had turned their neighbourhood into a prison – one
woman, Um Mohammed, said that conditions were deteriorating
with every passing day ('We have become almost like detainees in a
prison camp. There is no water and there is no electricity and no

fuel to run the standby generators'), and Falah Hassan said that the
US soldiers were taking ordinary men and women to their
barracks, chaining them and humiliating them before they were
released. (*Iraqi Occupation Focus Newsletter*, nos. 74 & 75, 26 July &
4 August 2007.)

86. Deborah Haynes, 'Soldiers of the surge: the vital battle to win
hearts and minds', *The Times*, 14 July 2007.

87. Britain had 5,500 troops serving in Iraq, and suffered 23 fatalities
between 5 February and 24 June 2007 (4.1 fatalities per 1,000
troops). The United States had 165,000, and had lost 463 troops
over the same period (2.8 per 1,000).

88. Sean Rayment, 'British death rate in Iraq now worse than
America's', *Sunday Telegraph*, 15 July 2007.

89. Ian Griggs and Jonathan Owen, 'They pay with their blood and
limbs. Surely we owe them more than this: More casualties,
horrific injuries and inadequate care at home', *Independent on
Sunday*, 15 July 2007.

90. Thomas Harding, 'Brown urged to plan Iraq withdrawal', *Daily
Telegraph*, 16 July 2007.

91. 'The war in Iraq', editorial, *Pittsburgh Tribune-Review*, 15 July 2007.

92. Max Hastings, 'Yes, Iraq is a calamity, but military intervention can
be a very good thing', *The Guardian*, 17 July 2007.

93. Patrick Cockburn, 'From Baghdad to Kirkuk, the dead bodies
show failure of the "surge"', *The Independent*, 17 July 2007.

94. Ibid.

95. Quoted in Tim Shipman, 'Iraq war has helped al-Qa'eda, says Bush
ally', *Daily Telegraph,* 18 July 2007.

96. Quoted ibid.

97. Timothy Garton Ash, 'America is just starting to wake up to the
awesome scale of its Iraq disaster', *The Guardian*, 19 July 2007.

98. Tim Reid, 'Stubborn President still has the power to stand firm
over Iraq', *The Times*, 19 July 2007.

99. Thom Shanker and David S. Cloud, 'US generals ask for more time
before judging Iraq policy', *International Herald Tribune*, 20 July
2007. Lieutenant-General Raymond Odierno, the number two
commander in Iraq, said that it would take 'at least until November'
to judge with confidence whether the surge was working.

100. The opposition to the oil bill was supported by many protest
groups worldwide, including the US Green Party.

101. Quoted in 'Baghdad's call for basic services', *Morning Star*, 19 July
2007.

102. Seumas Milne, 'Insurgents form political front to plan for US pullout', *The Guardian*, 19 July 2007. Three of the groups (comprising the 1920 Revolution Brigades), in their first interview with the Western media, said in Damascus that they would continue their armed resistance until all foreign troops were withdrawn from Iraq, and at the same time denounced al-Qaeda for sectarian killings and suicide bombings against civilians.

103. Deborah Haynes, 'Al-Qaeda faces rebellion from the ranks', *The Times*, 23 July 2007.

104. Richard Norton-Taylor, 'RAF deaths expose Basra vulnerability', *The Guardian*, 21 July 2007; Catherine Philp, 'Welcome to Basra – get ready to hit the deck ten times a day', *The Times*, 21 July 2007.

105. Richard Norton-Taylor, 'Defence committee: British troops in Iraq face "nightly suicide missions"', *The Guardian*, 25 July 2007.

106. In early August 2007 a federal appeals court in San Francisco issued a strong rebuke to the VA department in ordering payment of retroactive benefits to Vietnam War veterans who had contracted leukaemia through exposure to Agent Orange. The opinion from the 9th US Circuit Court of Appeals declared that the performance of the VA had 'contributed substantially to our sense of national shame'. The backlog of disability payments was between 400,000 and 600,000 with delays of up to 177 days to process an initial claim and 657 days to process an appeal (*Morning Star*, 24 July 2007). Melissa Kasnitz, the managing attorney of Disability Rights Advocates, said that it was the veterans 'who risk their lives for our country' who were suffering the consequences of the VA's dismal record.

107. 'Voters, in online forum, challenge Democrats on military draft, Iraq war, minimum wage', Associated Press, 24 July 2007.

108. Michael R. Gordon, 'U.S. is seen in Iraq until at least '09', *New York Times*, 24 July 2007.

109. Quoted by Al Pessin, Voice of America, 24 July 2007.

110. Quoted in Toby Harnden, 'Iraq pullout plan "is a priority"', *Daily Telegraph*, 27 July 2007.

111. Quoted in Sarah Baxter, 'US braced for bloody pull-out', *Sunday Times*, 29 July 2007.

112. Quoted ibid.

113. Quoted ibid.

114. Quoted in David Swanson, '300 towns, cities, states oppose Iraq occupation', After Downing Street website, 31 July 2006.

115. NCCI and Oxfam, *Rising to the Humanitarian Challenge in Iraq* (Oxford: Oxfam International, 2007); Jonathan Steele, 'Iraq is

turning into a humanitarian disaster, a new report shows', *The Guardian*, 30 July 2007; Jonathan Steele, 'Children hardest hit by humanitarian crisis in Iraq', *The Guardian*, 30 July 2007.

116. 'Amnesty demands Iraqi refugee help: US slammed for allowing in only 7,000 Iraqis', *Morning Star*, 27 July 2007; Suzanne Goldenberg, 'Saved by the bonds of war, "lucky" Iraqis trickle into US', *The Guardian*, 24 July 2007.

117. Ewen MacAskill and Patrick Wintour, 'Brown US agenda balances praise for alliance with hopes of an early pull-out from Iraq', *The Guardian*, 30 July 2007.

Chapter 8: Rebirth of the Vietnam syndrome

1. In 2003, when Lawrence Lindsey, one of President Bush's top budget advisors, estimated that the entire Iraq war could cost as much as $200 billion he was fired for producing an inaccurate and alarmist estimate.

2. Quoted in Bryan Bender, 'Budget office analysis says war could cost $1 trillion', *Boston Globe*, 1 August 2007.

3. Jeremy Scahill, *Blackwater: The Rise of the World's Most Powerful Mercenary Army* (London: Serpent's Tail, 2007).

4. Ibid., pp. xviii–xix.

5. Matt Spetalnick, 'Cheney admits was wrong about "last throes" in Iraq', Reuters, 1 August 2007, reported in *The Times,* London, 1 August 2007.

6. 'Iraq violence: monitoring the surge', BBC website, 3 August 2007. Data compiled by Mona Mahmoud.

7. Ibid.

8. Ibid.

9. Polly Curtis, 'Iraq veterans suffer stress and alcoholism', *The Guardian*, 3 August 2007.

10. Quoted in 'Gates glum as Iraq crumbles', *The Australian*, 4 August 2007.

11. Quoted ibid.

12. Jonathan Steele, 'Good news from Baghdad at last: the oil law has stalled', *The Guardian*, 3 August 2007.

13. The federation was also known as the Iraqi Federation of Oil Unions or IFOU. The letter from Sweeney to al-Maliki included the following words: 'The IFOU has been at the forefront of the struggle to preserve public ownership and control of Iraq's oil resources in the face of a concerted effort by the US government,

the IMF and multinational oil companies to . . . privatize ⅔ or more of Iraq's oil . . . The IFOU has, with the support of four other labor federations in Iraq, declared that it will resist this raid on the national heritage of Iraqis, including by work stoppages and strikes if necessary.'

14. Washington and London had always represented the oil law as a means of achieving reconciliation by guaranteeing that the various ethnic and sectarian communities would have an equal share of revenue from the country's energy resources, but only one of the law's forty-three articles mentions revenue-sharing, and then only to propose a separate 'federal revenue law'. The main aim of the law, in effect drafted and approved in Washington and London, is to establish arrangements for the operation of foreign oil companies in Iraq, terms that are much more favourable to the companies than those in any other oil producing state of the region, including Kuwait and Saudi Arabia. Platform, an oil industry watchdog, warns that the oil law could 'sign away Iraq's future'. Iraq's massive unexploited oil reserves, which could amount to 200 billion barrels, 'would go to foreign companies' (Steele, 'Good news from Baghdad at last').

15. Quoted in Michael Howard, 'The struggle for Iraq's oil flares up as Kurds open doors to foreign investors', *The Guardian*, 7 August 2007.

16. Leon Wofsy, 'The "Surge": buying time for whom and for what?', Leon Wofsy's Op-Ed website, 3 August 2007. In his 2004 campaign for the Senate, Obama said that the US might have to launch missile strikes on Iran and Pakistan to stop extremists getting control of nuclear bombs (David Mendell, 'Obama would consider missile strikes on Iran', *Chicago Tribune*, 25 September 2004).

17. Felicity Arbuthnot, 'Britain's child soldier shame', *Morning Star*, 4 August 2007.

18. Tony Allen-Mills, 'Listen up maggot, we can win this', *Sunday Times*, 5 August 2007.

19. Mike Drummond, 'At US base, Iraqis must use separate latrine', McClatchy website, 3 August 2007.

20. Aqeel Hussein and Colin Freeman, 'Suicide bombers destroy last peaceful district of Baghdad', *Sunday Telegraph*, 5 August 2007.

21. Kidnappers, not wishing to be captured, had hit upon the novel idea of leaving homing pigeons on the doorsteps of their victims' homes. The relatives were then expected to attach cash to the birds' legs, whereupon they would deliver the ransom to the

kidnappers' hideouts. One family attached $10,000 in $100 notes to the legs of five homing pigeons, which they found in a cage on their doorstep with an attached note giving instructions. Ziad al-Fatlawi's kidnapped twelve-year-old son Firas was released as soon as the pigeons arrived.

22. Quoted in Steven Hurst, 'Power cuts worsen as Iraqi grid nears collapse', *The Guardian*, 6 August 2007.

23. Quoted in Damien McElroy, 'US troops beat ambushes by sending robot warriors into battle', *Daily Telegraph*, 6 August 2007.

24. Government Accountability Office, *Stabilising Iraq: DOD Cannot Ensure That US-Funded Equipment Has Reached Iraqi Security Forces*, August 2007.

25. Ibid, quoted in Ewen MacAskill, 'The US arsenal lost in Iraq', *The Guardian*, 7 August 2007.

26. MacAskill, 'US arsenal lost in Iraq'.

27. Deborah Haynes, 'Abandoned: the 91 Iraqis who risked all', *The Times*, 7 August 2007; Deborah Haynes, 'Interpreters beg for asylum as militants show them no mercy', *The Times*, 7 August 2007. On 16 August Dominic Asquith, the British ambassador in Baghdad, paid a tribute to Iraqis who had worked for the British, saying that some local employees were under 'very severe threat' (Deborah Haynes, Richard Beeston and Michael Evans, 'Britain has a moral duty to Iraqi staff, says Baghdad envoy', *The Times*, 17 August 2007). One former interpreter had blows from a metal pipe rained down on him and cigarettes stubbed out on his head (Deborah Haynes, 'Sectarian militias seek revenge on interpreter's family and friends', *The Times*, 21 August 2007). On 23 August it was reported that the government had accepted privately that interpreters who face danger for helping UK troops in Iraq should be given sanctuary in Britain (Martin Fletcher and Deborah Haynes, 'Britain ready to back down on asylum for its interpreters in Iraq', *The Times*, 23 August 2007).

28. Francis Elliott, Greg Hurst and Michael Evans, 'Brown intervenes over the Iraqi interpreters denied political asylum', *The Times*, 8 August 2007.

29. Damien McElroy, 'America accuses Iran as Baghdad talks open', *Daily Telegraph*, 7 August 2007.

30. Quoted in Ewen MacAskill, Julian Borger and Patrick Wintour, 'US uneasy as Britain plans for early Iraq withdrawal', *The Guardian*, 8 August 2007.

31. Anthony Lloyd, 'Death in Basra: the British under siege', *The Times*, 9 August 2007.

32. MacAskill *et al.*, 'US uneasy as Britain plans for early Iraq withdrawal'.

33. *Iraq Occupation Focus Newsletter*, no. 76, 20 August 2007.

34. This prohibition was introduced by Paul Bremer soon after the 2003 invasion and subsequently left in place by the Iraqi government, to US approval.

35. 'UFPJ update on Iraq oil laws', United for Peace & Justice website, 9 August 2007.

36. In 2003 a bomb killed UN envoy Sergio Vieira de Mello and twenty-one other staff at the United Nations headquarters in Baghdad.

37. 'The UN disconnect in Iraq', editorial, *Newsday*, 12 August 2007.

38. Damien McElroy and Tim Butcher, 'Overstretched US cuts support to Israel', *Daily Telegraph*, 9 August 2007.

39. Solomon Hughes, writing in the *Morning Star* (10 August 2007), highlighted how the US surge in Iraq reflected the tactics employed by the British in Malaya. Sir Robert Thompson, one of the officials in charge of British forces in Malaya, had written: 'Much can be learnt merely from the faces of the population in villages that are subject to clear-and-hold operations . . . Faces . . . are full of cheerful welcoming smiles. The people know who is winning.' General Petraeus wrote: 'The Malaya insurgency provides lessons applicable to combating any insurgency.' In Malaya hundreds of thousands of people were confined in 'barbed-wire villages' in order to consolidate colonial control, directly analogous to the Petraeus implementation of 'population control measures' that included walled and gated communities, curfews and a pass system operated by the security forces. Hughes's article includes a photograph of a smiling British soldier holding in each hand the severed head of an 'insurgent'. Thomas Bell (*Daily Telegraph*, 31 August 2007) quoted Najib Razak, Malaysia's deputy Prime Minister, as saying that the British counter-insurgency operation in Malaya 'set the benchmark for such actions'. Here it was acknowledged that 500,000 villagers, mostly ethnic Chinese, were rounded up and put into 'concentration camps'. Thousands of families were rounded up at the crack of dawn and resettled behind floodlit barbed-wire and chain-link fences. Allegations that the British forces were collecting insurgents' heads were raised in Parliament. The Malayan model was also adopted with the 'strategic hamlets' set up by the Americans in the Vietnam War.

40. The fact that the horrors of the Iraq War were not being reported prompted the film director Brian de Palma to make *Redacted* (see Chapter 9).

41. Michael Evans, 'Blogs and chat rooms out of bounds in MoD gag order on troops', *The Times*, 10 August 2007. One British soldier, Sergeant Dan Mills, managed to beat the gag order by publishing *Sniper One: The Blistering True Story of a British Battle Group under Siege* (London: Michael Joseph) in August 2007. The book sold 11,000 copies before publication and Michael Joseph arranged to pay the author's earnings into an account where they will wait until Mills leaves the army in 2009 (Michael Smith, 'Sniper beats gag with siege story', *Sunday Times*, 19 August 2007).

42. Quoted in Michael Evans, 'Blogs and chat rooms out of bounds in MoD gag order on troops', *The Times*, 10 August 2007.

43. Toby Harnden, 'White House considers return to conscription', *Daily Telegraph*, 11 August 2007.

44. Sean Rayment and Philip Sherwell, 'US prepares to plug hole left by withdrawal of British troops', *Sunday Telegraph*, 12 August 2007.

45. Tim Butcher, 'Al-Qa'eda blamed for Iraq's worst terrorist atrocity', *Daily Telegraph*, 16 August 2007. The Yezidi of Celle in Germany, numbering about 7,000, are the largest group of their sect outside Kurdish Iraq. Their religion exhibits features of Hinduism (belief in reincarnation), Mithraism (the sacrifice of bulls), Christianity (the practice of baptism), Zoroastrianism (facing the sun in prayer) and Sufism (reverence for mystical experience). Opponents accuse them of devil worship. On or around 7 April 2007 Du'a Khalil Aswad, a seventeen-year-old girl, was stoned to death over a period of about thirty minutes by members of her family and others in punishment for her relationship with a Sunni Muslim teenager. In reprisal, a Sunni armed group killed two dozen Yezidi workers on 22 April 2007. Members of the Iraqi security forces were reportedly present at the stoning and failed to intervene. The search for bodies in the muddy remains of the clay homes demolished by the bombs revealed more dead and wounded (Michael Howard, 'Grim search for bodies continues as death toll from Iraq suicide bombings tops 250', *The Guardian*, 16 August 2007).

46. Peter Beaumont, 'Fatigue cripples US army in Iraq', *The Observer*, 12 August 2007.

47. Ibid.

48. Audrey Gillan, 'We've been neglected and let down, say combat troops', *The Guardian*, 15 August 2007.

49. Quoted in Tim Reid, 'Petraeus paves the way for US troop withdrawals next year', *The Times*, 16 August 2007.

50. Marie Colvin and Sarah Baxter, 'US pays insurgents to fight Al-Qaeda', *Sunday Times*, 9 September 2007.

51. Congress was growing increasingly uneasy about the scale of government expenditure on the war. US officials said there was a need to spend $750 million to fly thousands of armoured troop carriers to Iraq to protect troops against what were assumed to be Iranian-made roadside bombs. The Pentagon was also being asked to speed up deployment of the new Mine Resistant Ambush Protected (MRAP) vehicle, designed with a raised V-shaped hull to withstand explosive projectiles. The army had ordered 8,000 MRAPs at a cost of $12 billion, with officials saying that 3,400 would be supplied by the end of 2007.

52. In 2007 the length of service in Iraq was extended from a year to fifteen months, which was particularly disruptive for the National Guard, part-time soldiers who have to take temporary leave from civilian employment. Their jobs were supposed to be protected by law but many were returning home to find that they had been passed over for promotion or even discharged. The figure of ninety-nine suicides in 2006 compared with eighty-eight in 2005, sixty-seven in 2004 and sixty in 2003. The suicide rate for women serving in the wars was twice that of women who were not sent to war.

53. Richard Norton-Taylor, 'As the death toll continues to rise, how do experts view the possible exit strategies?', *The Guardian*, 16 August 2007.

54. Quoted ibid.

55. Sarah Baxter, 'Americans doubt "General Betraeus" over troop surge', *Sunday Times*, 19 August 2007.

56. This suspicion was subsequently confirmed by a British officer (see Chapter 9).

57. Sarah Baxter and Michael Smith, 'Britain faces Iraq rout, says US', *Sunday Times*, 19 August 2007. In the event the British withdrawal from Basra Palace to the airport was carried out without casualties, suggesting that the UK military had negotiated a deal with the Mahdi Army – an effective surrender (see Chapter 9). It remained to be seen how and when the British would leave the airport, totally vacating the country. Biddle was arguing that the British would not be able to 'pull all its troops out through the airport, which is why they will have to fight their way out' (Michael Smith and Sarah Baxter, 'Army chiefs fear Iraq exit will be Britain's Saigon moment', *Sunday Times*, 19 August 2007).

58. Quoted in Smith and Baxter, 'Army chiefs fear Iraq exit will be Britain's Saigon moment'.

59. Quoted ibid.

60. Quoted in Tim Shipman, '"The Brits have lost Basra. What they are doing there is of no value"', *Sunday Telegraph*, 19 August 2007.

61. Quoted ibid.

62. Raymond Whitaker and Robert Fox, 'Military commanders tell Brown to withdraw from Iraq without delay', *Independent on Sunday*, 19 August 2007.

63. *Christian Science Monitor*, 3 August 2007.

64. AFP, 1 August 2007.

65. Leila Fadel, 'Despite violence drop, officers see bleak future for Iraq', McClatchy website, 15 August 2007.

66. 'Rise in corruption cases after US crackdown', *Independent on Sunday*, 19 August 2007.

67. Paul Lewis, 'Recruiting for Iraq War undercut in Puerto Rico', *Washington Post*, 18 August 2007.

68. 'Military Recruiting 2005', National Priorities Project website, 7 September 2006.

69. Christine G. Appy, 'Class Wars', in Lloyd C. Gardner and Marilyn B. Young (eds), *Iraq and the Lessons of Vietnam: Or, How Not to Learn from the Past* (New York: New Press, 2007), pp. 136–49.

70. In August 2007 AAEI launched 'Iraq Summer' – 'to help end the war by making it politically toxic for Republicans to support it' (Katrina Vanden Heuvel, 'Americans against Escalation in Iraq', *Nation* website, 14 August 2007).

71. Items, provided with sources, taken from *Iraq Occupation Focus Newsletter*, no. 77, 5 September 2007.

72. Michael Howard, 'Kurds flee homes as Iran shells villages in Iraq', *The Guardian*, 20 August 2007.

73. Thomas Harding, '450 rocket attacks in 3 months on base in Basra', *Daily Telegraph*, 20 August 2007. In 2004 there were twenty-six attacks on the air base, the following year fifteen, and in the last quarter of 2006 nearly 200; by mid-August 2007 there had been 177 attacks, most of them in the previous three months.

74. Ibid.

75. 'British army declares "progress" in Iraq', *Morning Star*, 21 August 2007.

76. Thom Shanker and Mark Mazzetti, 'Two senators call for new leader in Iraq', *New York Times*, 21 August 2007.

77. This comment was ironic in view of the fact that the United States

had contrived the removal of al-Maliki's predecessor, Ibrahim al-Jaafari (despite his notionally democratic mandate), to enable al-Maliki to take his place.

78. Some observers were suggesting that national unity in Iraq would not have been welcomed in the United States. A united pro-Iran Islamic Iraq, hostile to Western interests, was the last thing Washington wanted. And the cliché 'divide and rule' sprang to mind.

79. Again it was ironic that the United States could complain, apparently seriously, about 'foreign' intervention in the sovereign state of Iraq.

80. Shanker and Mazetti, 'Two senators call for new leader in Iraq'. According to one senior US official the new intelligence report, 'Prospects for Iraq's Stability', had 'more fire in its assessments' than the Bush administration had had in its own: 'It leaves you with the sense that what we've been doing hasn't been working, but we can't let up, or it'll get worse.'

81. Charles Bremner, 'Paris vacates the moral high ground to give Washington a helping hand', *The Times*, 22 August 2007.

82. 'Iraqi President welcomes French visit but says Iraq solving its own problems', Associated Press, 22 August 2007.

83. Peter Allen, 'France calls for new Iraq Prime Minister', *Daily Telegraph*, 27 August 2007.

84. Louise Nousratpour, 'Army general calls for more troops in Iraq', *Morning Star*, 23 August 2007; Thomas Harding and Tony Helm, 'US general blames Britain for crisis in Basra', *Daily Telegraph*, 23 August 2007. Also on 23 August *The Independent* graphically depicted the escalation of the US forces in Iraq from March/April 2003 to August 2007 set against the gradual reduction of UK forces in the country over the same period. The British were being 'accused of fleeing from victorious insurgent forces'.

85. Thomas Harding, 'Troop numbers fall as strain tells on armed forces', *Daily Telegraph*, 24 August 2007.

86. When I was researching for my book *Vietnam Syndrome: Impact on US Foreign Policy* (Basingstoke: Macmillan, 1998) I was amazed to discover how much of the language of psychiatry was used to describe the effects of America's defeat and humiliation in southeast Asia. Paranoia, trauma, shock, amnesia, panic, emotional collapse – all were used to describe a national mental state. It is not always realised how much America's later wars were viewed through the prism of Vietnam. When, for example, the US was

escalating its 'low-intensity warfare' in El Salvador there were copious media references to Vietnam – for example, 'The Vietnam shadow over policy for El Salvador' (*Business Week*, 16 March 1981), and 'El Salvador, Vietnam and Central American policy' (*Wall Street Journal*, 4 March 1982). President George H. W. Bush declared, after evicting Saddam Hussein from Kuwait in 1991: 'The spectre of Vietnam has been buried forever in the desert sands of the Arabian peninsula . . . By God, we've kicked the Vietnam syndrome once and for all.' He was wrong.

87. Tim Reid and Martin Fletcher, 'Bush invokes Vietnam to justify staying in killing fields of Iraq', *The Times*, 23 August 2007; Leonard Doyle and Kim Sengupta, 'The vanishing coalition: Bush invokes Vietnam as splits emerge with Iraq allies', *The Independent*, 23 August 2007; Alex Spillius, 'Iraq pull-out would be disaster like Vietnam, warns Bush', *Daily Telegraph*, 23 August 2007; Massimo Calabresi, 'Bush's risky Vietnam gambit', *Time*, 23 August 2007; Christopher Hitchens, 'To invoke Vietnam was a blunder too far for Bush', *The Observer*, 26 August 2007.

88. Robert S. McNamara, *In Retrospect: The Tragedy and Lessons of Vietnam* (New York: Times, 1995).

89. Lawrence J. Korb, '11-step program for Iraq failure: the Bush team is repeating the mistakes the US made in Vietnam', *Los Angeles Times*, 3 May 2004.

90. McNamara, *In Retrospect*, p. xvi.

91. Lloyd C. Gardner and Marilyn B. Young (eds), *Iraq and the Lessons of Vietnam: Or, How **Not** to Learn from the Past* (New York: New Press, 2007).

92. Tim Reid, 'Bush ally breaks ranks with call for troop pullout', *The Times*, 24 August 2007.

93. Paul Harris, 'America divided over Iraq surge', *The Observer*, 26 August 2007.

94. Even the propaganda of the Bush administration was not claiming that Iraq was now a democracy. At best it was a 'burgeoning democracy', a 'nascent democracy' etc. Even these more modest claims were belied by the Iraqi constitution, the character of the electoral process, and the absence of judicial and other checks and balances.

95. Alex Spillius, 'Iraq: Democracy is not essential, says the US', *Daily Telegraph*, 24 August 2007.

96. Damien McElroy, 'Saddam's party "ready to help US withdrawal"', *Daily Telegraph*, 24 August 2007.

97. Quoted in Ed Pilkington, 'Bush threatens to confront Iran over alleged support for Iraqi insurgents', *The Guardian*, 29 August 2007.
98. Ewen MacAskill, 'US failing to meet most benchmarks in Iraq, says study', *The Guardian*, 31 August 2007.
99. Steven Lee Myers and David S. Cloud, 'Bush fights back on Iraq reports', *New York Times*, 31 August 2007.
100. 'Mahdi army "seizes base as British quit"', *Daily Telegraph*, 27 August 2007.
101. The British armed forces were reportedly lacking thousands of specialised soldiers, sailors and airmen crucial to the wars in Iraq and Afghanistan: the Blair government had cut the forces by 30,000 at a time when wars were being waged on two fronts. The pressure of inadequate resourcing, as with the US military, was compelling London and Washington to make strategic decisions independent of any assessment of events 'on the ground' in Iraq and Afghanistan. This is turn was feeding the tensions between the two allies.
102 Ian Black and Ed Pilkington, 'US pressure forces move to reconciliation', *The Guardian*, 27 August 2007.
103. Ibid.
104. Quoted in Martin Fletcher, 'Baghdad runs out of energy as scorching heat adds to misery', *The Times*, 25 August 2007.

Chapter 9: Withdrawal: UK now, US later?

1. Martin Fletcher, 'Welcome to the new US embassy', *The Times*, 1 September 2007.
2. Jane C. Loeffler, 'Fortress America', *Foreign Policy*, September–October 2007.
3. Ibid.
4. Fletcher, 'Welcome to the new US embassy'.
5. Alex Spillius, 'Marine leader "killed five unarmed men"', *Daily Telegraph*, 1 September 2007.
6. General Sir Michael Jackson , *Soldier: The Autobiography* (London: Bantam Press, 2007); Con Coughlin and Neil Tweedie, 'Army chief attacks US over Iraq', *Daily Telegraph*, 1 September 2007; Fran Yeoman, 'Former army chief condemns US for "short-sighted" policy on Iraq', *The Times*, 1 September 2007. It is interesting to note that Jackson seemingly lacked confidence in the judgements of Prime Minister Tony Blair and Attorney General Lord Goldsmith, for, to avoid being arraigned for war crimes, he

felt the need to satisfy himself that the existing Security Council
decisions justified invading Iraq by studying the relevant UN
resolutions: 'Having had some part to play in putting Slobodan
Milošević into a cell in The Hague, I had no wish to be his next-
door neighbour.'

7.   Quoted in Rupert Hamer, 'Second general attacks "flawed" U.S.
     Iraq policy', *Sunday Mirror*, 2 September 2007.

8.   Mary Dejevsky, 'Shame they were so quiet when we went to war',
     The Independent, 4 September 2007.

9.   The refugees in Syria and Jordan were, for the most part, not housed
     in makeshift camps but had been accommodated in civil society.
     This inevitably put immense extra burdens on such facilities as
     education, health care, food distribution, water availability and
     sewage treatment – at a time when international aid was insufficient
     and Britain was struggling to return the few Iraqis who had managed
     to reach the United Kingdom. The problems facing Syria and Jordan
     made it likely that the two countries would soon close their borders
     to refugees, further compounding the tensions inside Iraq.

10. Quoted in Aislinn Simpson, 'Anger in forces over 1,500 left
     waiting for casualty payments', *Daily Telegraph*, 1 September 2007.

11. It was the case in America also that, unlike during the Vietnam
     War, the public was largely shielded from the horrors of the war.

12. The title of the film refers to the editing or 'blacking out' of
     material for legal or other reasons, advertising De Palma's claim that
     censorship was preventing the American public from seeing the
     reality of the war. He uses a variety of devices: blogs, YouTube
     posts, videologs on the internet and the video diary that one of the
     soldiers is shooting. There are several references to the
     shortcomings of the mainstream media in reporting the war.

13. 'De Palma stuns film festival with horrors of Iraq war', *Daily
     Telegraph*, 1 September 2007.

14. Ibid.

15. David Gritten, review, *Daily Telegraph*, 1 September 2007.

16. Marie Colvin, 'An odd surge of hope in Baghdad', *Sunday Times*, 2
     September 2007.

17. Colin Freeman, 'Iraq to free 6,000 Sunnis in bid to avert political
     collapse', *Sunday Telegraph*, 2 September 2007.

18. Quoted in Alex Spillius, 'America ready to move into Basra when
     British troops move out', *Daily Telegraph*, 1 September 2007.

19. Michael Smith and Sarah Baxter, 'UK troops poised to quit Basra',
     Sunday Times, 2 September 2007.

20. Ian Black and Michael White, 'British forces withdraw from Basra Palace base', *The Guardian*, 3 September 2007; Michael Evans and Martin Fletcher, 'Under cover of darkness, British troops pull out of their last base in Basra city', *The Times*, 3 September 2007; Thomas Harding, 'British forces quit centre of Basra in huge night operation', *Daily Telegraph*, 3 September 2007.

21. Al-Fireji was nominally in charge of all Iraqi security forces in southern Iraq, and was regarded as the 'man of the hour', much needed to add credibility to the British withdrawal. Officials would comment 'General Mohan will sort this out' or 'General Mohan has decided'. He was supposedly secular and untainted by corruption, and had been imprisoned for eleven months by Saddam Hussein in the mid-1990s. He said: 'At the end torture is pointless, people will confess to anything to avoid further pain. I know I did.'

22. Thomas Harding, Damien McElroy and Aqeel Hussein, 'City fears bloodshed as, flags flying and heads held high, British troops pull out', *Daily Telegraph*, 4 September 2007.

23. Ibid.

24. Peter Beaumont, 'The road from Basra: to some a handover, to many a retreat', *The Guardian*, 4 September 2007.

25. Quoted in Ed Pilkington, 'A tale of three cities: Basra, London and Washington', *The Guardian*, 3 September 2007.

26. Paul Krugman, 'Snow job in the desert', *New York Times*, 3 September 2007.

27. This reinforced Dr Gideon Polya's calculation that the war had caused around one million deaths (see Chapter 2).

28. Sources for this paragraph and the next are given in *Iraq Occupation Focus Newsletter*, no. 78, 18 September 2007.

29. Martin Bell, 'As the British escape Basra, a proper enquiry must begin', *The Guardian*, 4 September 2007.

30. Ibid.

31. 'Britain will pay "blood price" – Blair', BBC News Online, 6 September 2002.

32. The twelve points comprised: 1. Resolve issues through non-violence; 2. Prohibit use of arms while in talks; 3. Form independent disarmament commission; 4. Accept the results of negotiations; 5. End international interference (did this mean Iran or the US?); 6. Commit to protect human rights; 7. Assure independence of the courts; 8. Ensure full participation of all parties in governance; 9. Take steps to end violence, displacement and damage to infrastructure; 10. Establish independent body to unite

the nation; 11. Protect Iraq's unity and sovereignty; 12. Commit to
principles as complete set of rules.

33.   Mario M. Cuomo, 'War and the constitution', *Los Angeles Times*, 3
      September 2007.
34.   Barbara Lee, 'Time for Congress to take a stand', *San Francisco
      Chronicle*, 4 September 2007.
35.   Martin Fletcher, 'US ready to take over in Basra if Britain
      withdraws all troops', *The Times*, 5 September 2007.
36.   Quoted in Suzanne Goldenberg, 'US commander hints at Iraq
      rollback next year', *The Guardian*, 5 September 2007.
37.   Quoted in Martin Kady II, 'Anti-war Dems fight for timeline',
      Politico, 7 September 2007.
38.   Quoted ibid.
39.   Quoted in 'Government urged to admit Iraq oil meddling',
      Morning Star, 7 September 2007.
40.   Martin Fletcher, 'Amputations, torture, brutal cruelty: the bloody
      reality behind the statistics', *The Times*, 7 September 2007.
41.   Ibid.
42.   Ibid.
43.   Martin Fletcher and Richard Mills, 'Are they guardians or
      Ghazaliyah? Or is the US giving guns to a sectarian gang?', *The
      Times*, 6 September 2007.
44.   Daniel Flitton, 'Iraq drowns out APEC's other issues', *The Age*, 8
      September 2007.
45.   Bin Laden said that there were two ways to end the war: either to
      escalate the killing or to abolish the US democratic system of
      government, which merely serves the interests of the major
      corporations.
46.   Paul Krugman, 'Time to take a stand', *New York Times*, 7
      September 2007.
47.   Leila Fadel, 'Setbacks outweigh successes in Iraq since surge began',
      McClatchy website, 8 September 2007 (Laith Hammoudi,
      Mohammed al-Dulaimy, Sahar Issa, Jamal Naji and Ali Omar
      contributed to the article).
48.   Quoted in Suzanne Goldenberg, 'Petraeus tells troops: surge has
      not worked out as we had hoped', *The Guardian*, 8 September
      2007.
49.   Quoted ibid.
50.   Richard Norton-Taylor, 'British to step up detainee release after
      militia talks', *The Guardian*, 8 September 2007.
51.   Michael Smith, Hala Jaber and Sarah Baxter, 'US generals to "lay

off" Britain as Mahdi Army claims it forced Basra truce', *Sunday Times*, 9 September 2007.

52. Tom Baldwin, 'Military leaders cross swords over "surge"', *The Times*, 10 September 2007.

53. Marilynn Marchione, 'Thousands of GIs cope with brain damage', Associated Press, 9 September 2007.

54. Quoted ibid.

55. Thomas Harding, 'US "delayed the Basra pull-out"', *Daily Telegraph*, 10 September 2007.

56. This was widely seen as a reliable poll with a margin of error of plus or minus 2.5 per cent.

57. 'Iraq poll September 2007: in graphics', BBC News Online, 10 September 2007.

58. Tom Baldwin, 'Turning point for America in Iraq', *The Times*, 11 September 2007.

59. Suzanne Goldenberg, 'Washington: the surge is working – Baghdad: the lottery of life goes on', *The Guardian*, 11 September 2007; Leonard Doyle, 'The view from Washington: Petraeus offers hope of success to a war-weary America', *The Independent*, 11 September 2007; Kim Sengupta, 'The view from Baghdad: mounting death toll which makes a mockery of US optimism', *The Independent*, 11 September 2007.

60. Peter Baker, 'Petraeus backs partial pullout', *Washington Post*, 11 September 2007.

61. 'Buying time for Bush, Britain and the Iraqi factions', *The Guardian*, 11 September 2007.

62. Krugman, 'Time to take a stand'.

63. Andrew Sullivan, 'Petraeus lets slip the ugly truth of this war', *Sunday Times*, 16 September 2007.

64. Quoted in Gerard Baker, 'It's odd that this soldier should be getting such flak', *The Times*, 11 September 2007.

65. Quoted in 'Reality check shows Iraq hanging in the balance', *Indianapolis Star*, 14 September 2007.

66. Quoted in Alissa J. Rubin and Damien Cave, 'US envoy glosses over Iraq issues', *International Herald Tribune*, 12 September 2007.

67. Jeff Zeleny, 'Obama's Iraq speech', *New York Times*, 12 September 2007.

68. Jennifer Hunter, 'No radical thinking on Iraq: Obama's disappointing speech lacks fresh ideas', *Chicago Sun-Times*, 13 September 2007.

69. The seven men, seeing the Washington debate as 'surreal', wrote:

'Four years into our occupation, we have failed on every promise. When the primary preoccupation of average Iraqis is when and how they are likely to be killed, we can hardly feel smug as we hand out care packages . . . Armed Sunni tribes [in Anbar province] have indeed become effective surrogates, but the enduring question is where their loyalties would lie in our absence. We operate in a bewildering context of determined enemies and questionable allies.' (Quoted in Suzanne Goldenberg, 'US troops who criticised Iraq war strategy killed in Baghdad', *The Guardian*, 13 September 2007.)

70. This was reminiscent of the Vietnam War, when US soldiers used to mail home body parts for their wives and girlfriends. This activity reached such a pitch that General William Westmoreland wrote an instruction prohibiting the practice.

71. The commission included nineteen other senior military and police officers, who visited seventy sites across Iraq and interviewed 200 individuals. The report also recommended: flying the Iraqi flag from military and police bases, including those under US or British control, to emphasise the sovereignty of the Iraqi government; allowing sectarian groups to police their own communities; reform of the 'dysfunctional' Shi'ite-dominated Interior Ministry; creation of a 'transitional headquarters' to oversee the handover of security to Iraqis; recruitment of 3,000 international police advisors; and dissolution of the 20,000-strong auxiliary national police, plagued by sectarianism (Henry McDonald, 'Iraq security: Belfast-style walls recommended for Baghdad', *The Guardian*, 14 September 2007).

72. 'Baghdad residents protest at wall', BBC News Online, 13 September 2007.

73. This whole episode had been questioned as a charade. (See Krugman, 'Time to take a stand').

74. Martin Fletcher and Tom Baldwin, 'Bush vows "enduring role" in Iraq as Sunni ally dies in roadside attack', *The Times*, 14 September 2007; Suzanne Goldenberg, 'Bush appeal undercut by killing of Sunni ally', *The Guardian*, 14 September 2007; Damien McElroy and Alec Spillius, 'Bush denounces murder of Iraq ally', *Daily Telegraph*, 15 September 2007. The investigative journalist Greg Palast claimed that the entire story of Sheikh Abu Risha had been concocted for propaganda purposes: 'Sheikh Abu Risha wasn't a sheikh. He wasn't killed by al-Qaeda. The new alliance with former insurgents in Anbar is as fake as the sheikh – and a murderous deceit . . . Abu Risha was the PR hook used to sell the "success" of the surge.' According to Palast he was bribed with

millions of dollars to play the Americans' mendacious game (Greg Palast, 'Bush's fake sheikh whacked: the surge and the Al-Qaeda bunny', Information Clearing House website, 17 September 2007).

75. Deborah Haynes, 'Exiled interpreters left in limbo as they wait for salvation from Britain', *The Times*, 21 September 2007. See also Chapter 8, note 27.

76. Martin Fletcher, 'Get out or die, security force chief tells interpreters for British army', *The Times*, 14 September 2007.

77. Martin Fletcher, 'Dragged to death for helping the British', *The Times*, 17 September 2007.

78. Quoted in Maura Reynolds, 'White House caps week with Iraq report', *Los Angeles Times*, 15 September 2007.

79. In the event Senate Republicans blocked the bid. The measure needed sixty votes to pass in the Democrat-controlled Senate but received only fifty-six, with forty-four against. Defense Secretary Robert Gates denounced the measure as a back-door attempt to pull troops off the battlefield.

80. Philip Sherwell and Tim Shipman, 'Move troops to Iran border, Brown told', *Sunday Telegraph*, 16 September 2007.

81. Tim Reid and Philip Webster, 'US commander to meet Brown as pullout from Basra frays ties', *The Times*, 13 September 2007.

82. Quoted in Catherine Drew, 'US commander presents plan for drawdown in Iraq', Voice of America website, 19 September 2007.

83. Quoted in David Blair, 'British may be out of Basra in weeks, claims US general', *Daily Telegraph*, 19 September 2007.

84. Michael Evans, 'British withdrawal from Basra has led to drop in violence, says US general', *The Times*, 19 September 2007.

85. Richard Norton-Taylor, 'US agrees further British withdrawal from Iraq', *The Guardian*, 19 September 2007.

86. Jeremy Scahill, *Blackwater: The Rise of the World's Most Powerful Mercenary Army* (London: Serpent's Tail, 2007).

87. Alex Spillius and Damien McElroy, 'Security firms face inquiry after death of 11 Iraqis', *Daily Telegraph*, 19 September 2007; Richard Beeston, 'Blackwater deaths prompt security review', *The Times*, 19 September 2007. Jeremy Scahill noted in *Blackwater* that the mercenaries in Iraq were not accountable to any legitimate authority in the country and could not be disciplined by the US Army. A court martial of a private sector employee could be challenged on constitutional grounds, and, following edicts delivered by Paul Bremer, the Iraqi courts did not have jurisdiction to prosecute foreign contractors without US permission. A

Congressional Research Service report issued in July 2007 concluded: 'It is possible that some contractors may remain outside the jurisdiction of US courts, civil or military, for improper conduct in Iraq.'

88. David DeVoss, 'Iraq's "Dirty Harrys"', *Los Angeles Times*, 23 September 2007; Tony Allen-Mills, 'A battle too far for Bush's private army', *Sunday Times*, 23 September 2007.

89. Ewen MacAskill, 'Maliki insists Blackwater must pay for shootings', *The Guardian*, 24 September 2007.

90. 'Iraq says draft law on private security firms will go to parliament', *International Herald Tribune*, 25 September 2007.

91. *Today*, BBC Radio 4, 2 October 2007.

92. Quoted in Tom Baldwin, 'Blackwater denies rogue mercenary charge', *The Times*, 3 October 2007; Ewen MacAskill, 'Iraq security firm denies trigger-happy charge', *The Guardian*, 3 October 2007.

93. MacAskill, 'Iraq security firm denies trigger-happy charge'.

94. *Newsnight*, BBC2, 2 October 2007; Ben Van Heuvelen, 'The Bush administration's ties to Blackwater', Salon website, 2 October 2007.

95. Van Heuvelen, 'Bush administration's ties to Blackwater'.

96. Ari Berman, 'HRC's Blackwater Connection', Nation website, 5 October 2007.

97. Bryan Pearson, 'Iraq vows to punish Blackwater guards', AFP, 8 October 2007.

98. David M. Herszenhorn, 'House's Iraq bill applies U.S. laws to contractors', *New York Times*, 5 October 2007.

99. Marie Colvin, 'Tide turns as inmates hand over jail radicals', *The Guardian*, 23 September 2007.

100. Ibid.

101. See Chapter 8, note 45.

102. Deborah Haynes and Richard Beeston, 'Al-Qaeda suicide bomb fears spark pleas for a British return to Basra', *The Times*, 28 September 2007.

103. 'Iraqi "hatred" of occupiers', *Morning Star*, 22 September 2007.

104. Sara Hashash, 'Criminal gangs "control Iraq ministries"', *Sunday Times*, 23 September 2007.

105. Conn Hallinan, 'U.S. secret air war pulverizes Afghanistan & Iraq', AlterNet website, 14 September 2007.

106. Patrick Wintour, 'Miliband: we have alienated millions of Muslims over Iraq', *The Guardian*, 26 September 2007.

107. Richard Norton-Taylor, 'Brown to pave way for further cutback of troops in Iraq', *The Guardian*, 3 October 2007.

108. Bob Ainsworth, interview by Jeremy Paxman, *Newsnight*, BBC2, 2 October 2007.
109. Brendan Carlin, 'Britain "in Iraq for decades"', *Daily Telegraph*, 26 September 2007.

Chapter 10: A successful surge?

1. Ahmed Ali, reporting for Inter Press Service (5 November 2007), cited 'well-informed estimates' that at least five million Iraqis had been driven from their homes. The UNHCR acknowledged more than 4.4 million displaced Iraqis, a figure that many workers among refugees found conservative. In early November 2,000 Iraqis were fleeing their homes every day, most having received direct threats from death squads or militias.
2. *Iraq: Human Rights Abuses against Palestinian Refugees* (London: Amnesty International, 2007).
3. 'Iraq:Palestinian refugees caught in the crossfire', press release, Amnesty International, 1 October 2007.
4. Ibid.
5. Jonathan Petre, 'Archbishop highlights human cost of Iraq', *Daily Telegraph*, 6 October 2007.
6. See Geoff Simons, *They Destroyed Iraq and Called it Freedom* (London: Legacy, 2008), Chapter 6.
7. Quoted in Conn Halliman, 'The algebra of occupation', Foreign Policy in Focus website, 27 November 2007.
8. Interviews and court transcripts revealed that US snipers were under pressure to produce a high body count, a Vietnam War measure disavowed by the Pentagon over Iraq. Thus in their zeal to get more 'kills' out of snipers, officers of the 1st Battalion, 501st Infantry Regiment allegedly adopted a programme of leaving weaponry as 'bait', and allowing snipers to kill anyone who came to pick the items up (Ned Parker, 'Sniper team tells of pressure from above', *Los Angeles Times*, 5 October 2007).
9. 'Murder charges unlikely for Haditha killings: Iraq atrocity prosecution takes "major blow"', Morning Star, 6 October 2007.
10. 'Diyala operation killed 25 civilians, eyewitnesses claim', Voices of Iraq, 7 October 2007, quoted in *Iraq Occupation Focus Newsletter*, 18 October 2007.
11. 'UN calls for US to publish facts on Iraqi deaths', *The Guardian*, 12 October 2007.

12. Fanny Carrier, 'Abu Ghraib prisoners accuse US companies of torture', AFP, 3 October 2007.

13. 'Child prisoners abused and tortured, say activists', IRIN, 25 October 2007.

14. Salam Faraj, 'Outraged Iraqis condemn killings by foreign guards', AFP, 10 October 2007; Sarmad al-Waali and Deborah Haynes, 'Daughters' anguish at funeral of mother killed by private guards', *The Times*, 11 October 2007.

15. Suzanne Goldenberg and Ewen MacAskill, '15 Iraqi civilians killed as US aircraft target al-Qaida leaders', *The Guardian*, 12 October 2007.

16. Joshua Partlow, 'UN reports a "humanitarian crisis"', *San Francisco Chronicle*, 12 October 2007 (full UN report available at www.uniraq.org).

17. 'Hundreds forced to scavenge for food in garbage bins', IRIN, 17 October 2007.

18. Ahmed Ali, 'Corruption adds to Baquba's problems', Inter Press Service, 18 November 2007.

19. Quoted ibid.

20. Peter Spiegel, 'US official won't discuss Iraq corruption', *Los Angeles Times*, 5 October 2007.

21. Sarah Baxter, 'Iraq's ousted corruption buster', *Sunday Times*, 21 October 2007.

22. 'Deadly month in Iraq dulls US claims of progress', AFP, 2 November 2007.

23. Tina Susman, 'Conflicting accounts of an Iraq clash', *Los Angeles Times*, 17 November 2007.

24. Suzanne Goldenberg, 'US soldier's family brings legal action against British private security firm', *The Guardian*, 30 October 2007.

25. Doug Smith and Saif Hameed, 'Army convoy is accused of firing without provocation', *Los Angeles Times*, 19 November 2007.

26. 'US commander: Iraq is "nightmare"', *Sunday Telegraph*, 14 October 2007.

27. Ewen MacAskill, 'Mystery over $1bn of Iraq funding', *The Guardian*, 24 October 2007.

28. 'US forces kill more civilians in Iraq', *Morning Star*, 22 October 2007.

29. Tom Baldwin, 'America suffers an epidemic of suicides among traumatised army veterans', *The Times*, 15 November 2007; Penny Coleman, '120 war vets commit suicide each week on average', AlterNet, 26 November 2007.

30. Matthew Taylor and Esther Addley, 'Undiagnosed brain injury –
    the hidden legacy of Iraq', *The Guardian*, 27 October 2007; Esther
    Addley and Matthew Taylor, 'One soldier's father calls it the silent
    injury. Now Britain's forces centre is braced for an influx of cases',
    The Guardian, 27 October 2007.
31. 'Wars may cost trillions by 2017', *Los Angeles Times*, 25 October
    2007.
32. Richard Norton-Taylor, 'Brown to make deep cuts in troop
    numbers and offer asylum deal', *The Guardian*, 8 October 2007.
33. Richard Norton-Taylor and Patrick Wintour, 'Troops may be
    home sooner than predicted', *The Guardian*, 9 October 2007;
    Philip Webster, 'All British troops may leave Iraq next year', *The
    Times*, 9 October 2007.
34. Michael Smith, '850 more troops in Iraq before Christmas', *Sunday
    Times*, 28 October 2007.
35. Michael Evans, 'Government "gave public false hopes" on
    achieving Iraq goals', *The Times*, 8 October 2007.
36. Gethin Chamberlain, '"We are tired of firing at people – get us out
    of here"', *Sunday Telegraph*, 28 November 2007.
37. Ibid.
38. Michael Evans, 'MoD rebuffs general's claim that troops are
    devalued and angry', *The Times*, 19 November 2007.
39. Ibid.
40. Kimberley Helfing, 'Veterans make up 1 in 4 homeless in US', *San
    Francisco Chronicle*, 7 November 2007.
41. Michael Evans, 'Iraq is damaging forces' readiness for full-scale
    war', *The Times*, 22 October 2007.
42. Carl Hulse, 'Democrats tie Iraq spending bill to a pullout goal',
    New York Times, 9 November 2007; Anne Flaherty, 'Senate blocks
    Iraq war money', Associated Press, 16 November 2007; Andrew
    Taylor, 'Congress back to budget, Iraq battles', Associated Press,
    2 December 2007.
43. Barbara McMahon, 'Rudd sets date for Iraq pull-out', *The
    Guardian*, 1 December 2007.
44. Quoted in Ewen MacAskill, 'Upbeat US military claims it has
    forced al-Qaida out of Iraqi capital', *The Guardian*, 9 November
    2007.
45. Ibid.
46. Ali Fadhily, 'Fewer deaths bring no reassurance', Inter Press
    Service, 9 November 2007.
47. Ibid.

48. Ghaith Abdul-Ahad, 'When night falls, the assassins gather in Hayaniya Square', *The Guardian*, 17 November 2007.

49. Lauren Frayer, '6,000 Sunnis join pact with US in Iraq', Associated Press, 29 November 2007.

50. Hala Jaber, 'American-backed killer militias strut across Iraq', *Sunday Times*, 25 November 2007.

51. James Hider, 'Shoot-out between Saddam's spy and al-Qaeda brings life back to streets', *The Times*, 30 November 2007.

52. Jaber, 'American-backed killer militias strut across Iraq'.

53. Colin Freeman, 'I will talk to those with blood on their hands, says British general', *Sunday Telegraph*, 11 November 2007.

54. In mid-November 2007 Abdul Samad Sultan, Iraq's displacement and migration minister, claimed that 1,600 Iraqis were returning every day. Both the UNHCR and the Red Crescent expressed scepticism about the government figures (Ian Black, 'Iraqi refugees start to head home', *The Guardian*, 22 November 2007). In a report released on 22 November the UNHCR, having interviewed Iraqis in Syria, found that 14 per cent of respondents were returning to Iraq because they thought the security situation had improved, as opposed to 70 per cent who cited visa and financial reasons.

55. Quoted in Jonathan Steele, 'Refugees celebrate first bus back to Iraq', *The Guardian*, 28 November 2007.

56. Quoted in Michael R. Gordon and Stephen Farrell, 'Iraq lacks plan on the return of refugees, military says', *New York Times*, 30 November 2007.

57. Stephen Collinson, 'Iraq "progress" shifts US political sands', AFP, 18 November 2007.

58. On 29 November 2007 this focus was echoed by John Negroponte, deputy Secretary of State, who urged Iraq's leaders to build on the security gains by making more political progress. On 5 December Defense Secretary Robert Gates visited Iraq with the same message.

59. Al Pessin, 'US military: Iran-backed Shiites continue attacks in Baghdad, despite reduced violence', Voice of America website, 26 November 2007.

60. Damien Cave, 'At least 35 dead in Iraq violence', *New York Times*, 27 November 2007; Salam Faraj, 'Women killed in US firing as Iraq mulls role of American forces', AFP, 27 November 2007; Ali al-Tuwajri, '10 killed as Qaeda raids Iraq village', AFP, 1 December 2007.

61. Jonathan Steele, 'Iraqi insurgent regrouping, says Sunni resistance leader', *The Guardian*, 3 December 2007.

62. Article 58, Section 4 of the Iraqi constitution says that the Council of Representatives (the parliament) has to ratify 'international treaties and agreements' negotiated by the Council of Ministers (the Cabinet): 'A law shall regulate the ratification of international treaties and agreements by a two-thirds majority of the members of the Council of Representatives.'

63. Alex Spillius and Graeme Baker, 'Iraqi government failures "greater threat than al-Qa'eda"', *Daily Telegraph*, 16 November 2007.

64. Ibid.

65. Quoted in Paul Tait, 'Iraq forces better but not ready yet – US general', Reuters, 29 November 2007.

66. This development, a pattern that was commonplace through the 1990s, was presenting fresh problems for the US. Turkey, a NATO member, was using US-supplied arms to attack Iraq, supposedly protected by the US, supplying it with arms and training.

67. Quoted in Ewen MacAskill, 'Turkey launches biggest bombing raid on Kurdish rebels in Iraq', *The Guardian*, 17 December 2007.

68. Ibid.

69. Quoted in Ian Black, 'US pleads for calm after Turkish troops pursuing PKK enter Iraq', *The Guardian*, 19 December 2007; Deborah Haynes, 'Turkey's cross-border raid mars Rice's upbeat visit', *The Times*, 19 December 2007.

70. Quoted in Deborah Haynes, '"I came to rid Basra of its enemies, I now hand it back to its friends"', *The Times*, 17 December 2007.

71. Quoted in Colin Freeman, 'Ready or not, Basra back in Iraqi hands', *Daily Telegraph*, 16 December 2007.

72. Ibid.

73. Ibid.

74. Quoted in Mona Mahmoud, Maggie O'Kane and Ian Black, 'UK has left behind murder and chaos, says Basra police chief', *The Guardian*, 17 December 2007.

75. Ibid.

76. Marie Colvin, 'I felt a new terror on Basra's streets', *Sunday Times*, 16 December 2007.

77. Ibid.

78. Quoted ibid.

79. Quoted ibid.

80. Patrick Cockburn, 'Britain bows out of a five-year war it could never have won', *The Independent*, 17 December 2007.

81. Richard Edwards, 'Morale of troops "hit by spin"', *Daily Telegraph*, 15 December 2007.

82.   Damien McElroy, 'US troops "may be sent to Basra after British withdrawal"', *Daily Telegraph*, 14 December 2007.

Chapter 11: Psychology, lies and the wider world

1.   Letter to the Honorable William J. Clinton from the Project for the New American Century, signed by Elliott Abrams, Richard L. Armitage, William J. Bennett, Jeffrey Bergner, John Bolton, Paula Dobriansky, Francis Fukuyama, Robert Kagan, Zalmay Khalilzad, William Kristol, Richard Perle, Peter W. Rodman, Donald Rumsfeld, William Schneider, Vin Weber, Paul Wolfowitz, R. James Woolsey and Robert B. Zoellick.

2.   The central point, that Clinton resisted pressure for regime change in Iraq, should not disguise the fact that he authorised frequent bombing raids against the country, sometimes including cruise missiles, and in particular the massive Operation Desert Fox assault in 1998. In addition, he maintained what many observers came to see as a genocidal sanctions policy.

3.   The questionable tactics that led to the election of George Bush extended far beyond arranging for the Supreme Court to block the Florida recount in 2000. They included phone-jamming, faulty machines and ballot-rigging on a massive scale (see Robert F. Kennedy Jr, 'Was the 2004 election stolen?: Republicans prevented more than 350,000 voters in Ohio from casting ballots or having their votes counted – enough to have put John Kerry in the White House', *Rolling Stone*, 1 June 2006; Sasha Abramsky, 'Just try voting here: 11 of America's worst places to cast a ballot (or try) – machines that count backwards, slice-and-dice districts, felon baiting, phone jamming, and plenty of dirty tricks', *Mother Jones*, September–October 2006). This is all highly relevant to judging the credibility of a Bush government seeking to impose its concept of democracy on Iraq.

4.   Wilson–Johnson telephone conversation, 11 February 1965, PREM 13/692, National Archives (UK).

5.   Louis Heren, *No Hail, No Farewell* (London: Weidenfeld & Nicolson, 1970), p 231.

6.   Quoted in Jonathan Coleman, 'Harold Wilson, Lyndon Johnson and the Vietnam War 1964–68', American Studies Today Online website, 28 November 2005.

7.   For Britain's various contributions to the American military effort in Vietnam, see John W. Young, 'Britain and "LBJ's War" 1964–68',

Cold War History vol. 2, no. 3, pp. 63–92; Mark Curtis, *Web of Deceit: Britain's Real Role in the World* (London: Vintage, 2003).

8. When London asked for a meeting between Wilson and Johnson, the President responded: 'We got enough pollution around here already without Harold coming over with his fly open and his pecker hanging out, peeing all over me.' (Quoted in Alex Danchev, '"I'm with you": Tony Blair and the Obligations of Alliance – Anglo-American Relations in Historical Perspective', in Lloyd C. Gardner and Marilyn B. Young (eds), *Iraq and the Lessons of Vietnam* (New York: New Press, 2007), p. 56.)

9. Bob Woodward, *60 Minutes*, CBS, 18 April 2004.

10. 'God told me to invade Iraq, Bush tells Palestinian ministers', BBC press release, 6 October 2005.

11. Quoted from an 'author source' by Barbara Victor, *The Last Crusade: Religion and the Politics of Misdirection* (London: Constable, 2005), p. 5.

12. Quoted in Richard T. Cooper, 'General casts war in religious terms', *Los Angeles Times*, 16 October 2003.

13. Quoted in Victor, *Last Crusade*, p. 13.

14. Justin A. Frank, *Bush on the Couch: Inside the Mind of the US President* (London: Politico's, 2006), p. 61. There are precedents for 'remote psychoanalysis', even when the subject has died: see Sigmund Freud and William C. Bullitt, *Thomas Woodrow Wilson, Twenty-Eighth President of the United States: A Psychological Study* (London: Weidenfeld & Nicolson, 1967).

15. Peter W. Galbraith, *The End of Iraq: How American Incompetence Created a War without End* (London: Simon & Schuster, 2006), p. 83.

16. Diary, *The Guardian*, 28 June 2005.

17. 'Oh dear . . .', *The Guardian*, 8 September 2007.

18. Quoted in Robert Draper, *Dead Certain: The Presidency of George W. Bush* (New York: Free Press, 2007).

19. James Fallows, 'Bush on disbanding the Iraqi military', Atlantic website, 2 September 2007.

20. See for example David Cracknell and Isabel Oakeshott, 'The madness of King Tony', *Sunday Times*, 4 February 2007; Matthew Parris, 'Are we witnessing the madness of Tony Blair?', *The Times*, 28 March 2003; 'Is Tony Blair crazy?', Royal Society of Medicine media release, 27 November 2003; Tim Radford, 'Blair mad? That's a barmy idea', *The Guardian*, 1 December 2003. It is of course a familiar ploy to denounce a political opponent as insane. Niall Ferguson could not write an article on North Korea's Kim

Jong Il ('This time, Crazy Kim has upset the wrong country: China', *Sunday Telegraph*, 9 July 2006) without including phrases such as 'looks like an escaper from a lunatic asylum', 'a raving mad regime', 'a madman as both a neighbour and a dependant' and 'crazy Kim'. In the same vein Andrew Sullivan (*Sunday Times*, 9 July 2007) declared that Kim was a 'loopy dictator'. There was no evidence that Kim was mad.

21. David Owen, *The Hubris Syndrome: Bush, Blair and the Intoxication of Power* (London: Politico's, 2007).

22. Charles Tripp, 'Militias, vigilantes, death squads', *London Review of Books*, 25 January 2007, quoted ibid.

23. It scarcely needs to be suggested that Christian faith (or declaration of Christian faith) does not guarantee virtue. On 12 April 1922 Adolf Hitler gave a speech in Munich which included the words: 'My feelings as a Christian point me to my Lord and Saviour as a fighter . . . How terrific was His fight against the Jewish poison . . . I recognise more profoundly than ever before . . . that it was for this that He had to shed His blood upon the Cross.'

24. Alan Deutschman, 'Is your boss a psychopath?', *Fast Company*, July 2005, p. 44.

25. See for example Dilip Hiro, *Secrets and Lies: The True Story of the Iraq War* (London: Politico's, 2004).

26. For decades the United States had allowed Pakistan to acquire highly restricted nuclear technology. President Pervez Musharraf became essential to US plans, and so the Bush administration tolerated Pakistan's nuclear programme, in line with traditional American policy: see Adrian Levy and Catherine Scott-Clark, *Deception: Pakistan, the United States and the Global Nuclear Weapons Conspiracy* (London: Atlantic, 2007).

27. William Clark, *Revisited – The Real Reasons for the Upcoming War with Iraq: A Macroeconomic and Geostrategic Analysis of the Unspoken Truth'* (Roslindale, MA: Rat Haus Reality Press, 2003, revised 2004); Roy Carson, 'Venezuelan move to replace US$ with the euro upsetting Washington more than Saddam's euro conversion last November', VHeadline website, 18 June 2003.

28. Carson, 'Venezuelan move to replace US$ with the euro upsetting Washington more than Saddam's euro conversion last November'.

29. William Clark, 'The real reasons why Iran is the next target: the emerging euro-dominated international oil market', Global Research website, 27 October 2004.

30. I have included chapters on civilians and torture elsewhere: see

Geoff Simons, *They Destroyed Iraq and Called it Freedom* (London: Legacy, 2008), Chapters 6 and 8 (respectively), and there is a substantial supporting literature.

31. Naomi Klein, 'Erasing Iraq: In search of a "Model" for the Middle East', in *The Shock Doctrine: The Rise of Disaster Capitalism* (London: Allen Lane, 2007), pp. 326–40.

32. Ibid.

33. Quoted ibid.

34. Eric Olson, 'Operation Iraqi Freedom Journal', p. 42; quoted in Michael Gordon and Bernard Trainor, *COBRA II: The Inside Story of the Invasion and Occupation of Iraq* (London: Atlantic, 2006), p. 382.

35. Simons, *They Destroyed Iraq and Called It Freedom*, Chapter 6.

36. 'The whole world is watching us die', International Action Center website, 2 April 2003.

37. Simons, *They Destroyed Iraq And Called It Freedom*, Chapter 8.

38. Alfred W. McCoy, 'Torture in the Crucible of Counterinsurgency', in Gardner and Young, *Iraq and the Lessons of Vietnam*, p. 230. In support of his argument, McCoy cites *The 9/11 Commission Report: Final Report of the National Commission on Terrorist Attacks upon the United States* (New York: W. W. Norton, 2004), pp. 90–3.

39. *US Army Report on Iraqi Prisoner Abuse* (Taguba report). See also Chapter 6, note 75.

40. Taguba report, pp. 17–18.

41. Tony Lagouranis and Allen Michaelian, *Fear Up Harsh: An Army Interrogator's Dark Journey through Iraq* (New York: NAL, 2007), p. 50.

42. Ibid, p. 113.

43. Ibid, pp. 127, 129.

44. 'UN deplores Iraq torture', *Morning Star*, 22 September 2006.

45. Scott Shane, David Johnston and James Risen, 'Secret U.S. endorsement of severe interrogations', *New York Times*, 4 October 2007.

46. The 'dark side', favoured by Cheney, even found its way into mainstream British television. A BBC documentary, *Taxi to the Dark Side* (8 October 2007), explored how torture spread like a virus from Bagram in Afghanistan to Abu Ghraib and Guantanamo.

47. Damien McElroy, 'Iraq Prime Minister "using Saddam's tactics"', *Daily Telegraph*, 28 September 2007.

48. Vikram Dodd, 'Briton held in Iraq as terrorist claims he was tortured', *The Guardian*, 17 September 2007.

49. Stephen Grey, *Ghost Plane: The True Story of the CIA Torture Program* (New York: St Martin's Press, 2006), p. 21.

50. Grey presents detailed, well-sourced information putting the matter beyond doubt. There has been speculation that this sort of material might be used in war crimes trials of US officials and CIA personnel in the future.

51. The pure Arabic version of the Koran is allegedly held as a divine copy in heaven. The word *daraha* in Arabic (Sura 4, Verse 34) has been variously translated – for example, as 'hit', 'strike', 'scourge', 'chastise', 'tap', 'beat' and 'spank'. Whatever translation is preferred, the meaning is unambiguous: women are subservient to men and should be controlled by them, through physical abuse and humiliation if necessary. It is widely acknowledged that Muslim feminists (if this is not an oxymoron) are deeply perplexed by Koranic texts that permanently enshrine the inferior social position of women. One female Muslim academic concludes: 'A modern reading . . . of the corpus of Islamic laws which regulate the lives of women cannot but see them as inequitable, infantilising and unacceptable in today's world': see Ghada Karmi, 'Women, Islam and Patriarchalism', in Mai Yamani (ed.), *Feminism and Islam: Legal and Literary Perspectives* (London: Ithaca Press, 1996), pp. 69–85. The supposed inferiority of women is enshrined also in the other two main Abrahamic religions.

52. See the sources for this paragraph in Simons, *They Destroyed Iraq and Called It Freedom*, Chapter 6.

53. Authorisation for Use of Military Force (Enrolled Bill), September 18, 2001.

54. A second joint resolution, adopted by Congress on 2 October 2002 and authorising the use of the US armed forces against Iraq when the preparations for war were well under way, simply rubber-stamped Bush's decision to invade Iraq – a decision taken months if not years before.

55. Tim Shipman, 'Britain "on board" for US strikes on Iran', *Sunday Times*, 7 October 2007. The *New Yorker* magazine was quoted: 'The bombing plan has had its most positive reception from the new government of Britain's Prime Minister Gordon Brown.'

Bibliography

Al-Ali, Nadje Sadig, *Iraqi Women: Untold Stories from 1948 to the Present* (London: Zed, 2007).

Al-Khalil, Samir, *Republic of Fear: The Politics of Modern Iraq* (London: Hutchinson, 1989).

Ali, Ayaan Hirsi, *The Caged Virgin: An Emancipation Proclamation for Women and Islam* (New York: Free Press, 2004).

Ali, Kecia, *Sexual Ethics and Islam: Feminist Reflections on Qur'an, Hadith, and Jurisprudence* (Oxford: Oneworld, 2006).

Ali, Tariq, *The Clash of the Fundamentalisms: Crusades, Jihads and Modernity* (London: Verso, 2002).

Anderson, Jon Lee, *The Fall of Baghdad* (New York: Penguin Press, 2004).

Anderson, Liam and Gareth Stansfield, *The Future of Iraq: Dictatorship, Democracy, or Division?* (New York: Palgrave Macmillan, 2004).

Arnove, Anthony, *Iraq: the Logic of Withdrawal* (New York: New Press, 2006).

Arnove, Anthony (ed.), *Iraq under Siege: The Deadly Impact of Sanctions and War* (London: Pluto Press, 2000).

Baird, Jay W., *From Nuremberg to My Lai* (Lexington, MA: D. C. Heath, 1972).

Baker, James A. III and Lee H. Hamilton (co-chairs), *The Iraq Study Group Report* (New York: Vintage, 2006).

Baker, Nancy, *General Ashcroft: Attorney at War* (Lawrence: University Press of Kansas, 2006).

Bates, Stephen, *God's Own Country: Tales from the Bible Belt* (London: Hodder & Stoughton, 2007)

Blix, Hans, *Disarming Iraq: The Search for Weapons of Mass Destruction* (London: Bloomsbury, 2004).

Bobbitt, Philip, *The Shield of Achilles: War, Peace and the Course of History* (London: Allen Lane, 2002).

Boehlert, Eric, *Lapdogs: How the Press Rolled Over for Bush* (New York: Free Press, 2006).

Bremer, L. Paul and Malcolm McConnell, *My Year in Iraq: The Struggle to Build a Future of Hope* (New York: Simon & Schuster, 2006).

Chandrasekaran, Rajiv, *Imperial Life in the Emerald City: Inside Baghdad's Green Zone* (New York: Alfred A. Knopf, 2007).

Chehab, Zaki, *Iraq Ablaze: Inside the Insurgency* (London: I. B. Tauris, 2006).

Clark, Ramsey and others, *War Crimes: A Report of United States War Crimes against Iraq* (Washington, DC: Maisonneuve Press, 1992).

Cliffe, Lionel, Maureen Ramsay and Dave Bartlett, *The Politics of Lying: Implications for Democracy* (Basingstoke: Macmillan, 2000).

Cockburn, Patrick, *The Occupation: War and Resistance in Iraq* (London: Verso, 2006).

Cole, David and James X. Dempsey, *Terrorism and the Constitution: Sacrificing Civil Liberties in the Name of National Security*, 3rd ed. (New York: New Press, 2006).

Danner, Mark, *Torture and Truth: America, Abu Ghraib and the War on Terror* (New York: New York Review, 2004).

Dershowitz, Alan M., *Why Terrorism Works: Understanding the Threat, Responding to the Challenge* (New Haven, CT and London: Yale University Press, 2002).

Diamond, Larry, *Squandered Victory: The American Occupation and the Bungled Effort to bring Democracy to Iraq* (New York: Times, 2005).

Dobbins, James, John G. McGinn, Keith Crane, Seth G. Jones, Rollie Lal, Andrew Rathmell, Rachel M. Swanger and Anga R. Timilsina, *America's Role in Nation-Building: From Germany to Iraq* (Santa Monica, CA: Rand Corporation, 2003).

Dodge, Toby, *Inventing Iraq: The Failure of Nation-Building and a History Denied* (New York: Columbia University Press, 2003).

Draper, Robert, *Dead Certain: The Presidency of George W. Bush* (New York: Free Press, 2007).

Etherington, Mark, *Revolt on the Tigris: The Al-Sadr Uprising and the Governing of Iraq* (Ithaca, NY: Cornell Univeristy Press, 2005).

Feldman, Noah, *What We Owe Iraq: War and the Ethics of Nation Building* (Princeton: Princeton University Press, 2004).

Frank, Justin A., *Bush on the Couch: Inside the Mind of the US President* (London: Politico's, 2006).

Fukuyama, Francis, *After the Neocons: America at the Crossroads* (London: Profile, 2006).

Galbraith, Peter W., *The End of Iraq: How American Incompetence Created a War without End* (London: Simon & Schuster, 2006).

Gardner, Lloyd C. and Marilyn B. Young (eds), *Iraq and the Lessons of Vietnam: Or, How **Not** to Learn from the Past* (New York: New Press, 2007).

Gordon, Michael and Bernard Trainor, *COBRA II: The Inside Story of the Invasion and Occupation of Iraq* (London: Atlantic, 2006).

Graham-Brown, Sarah, *Sanctioning Saddam: The Politics of Intervention in Iraq* (London: I. B. Tauris, 1999).

Greenberg, Karen J. and Joshua L. Dratel (eds), *The Torture Papers: The Road to Abu Ghraib* (New York and Cambridge: Cambridge University Press, 2005).

Grey, Stephen, *Ghost Plane: The True Story of the CIA Torture Program* (New York: St Martin's Press, 2006).

Grosscup, Beau, *Strategic Terror: The Politics and Ethics of Aerial Bombardment* (London: Zed, 2006).

Hazelton, Fran (ed.), *Iraq since the Gulf War: Prospects for Democracy* (London: Zed, 1994).

Hersh, Seymour M., *Chain of Command* (London: Penguin, 2005).

Human Rights Watch, *Iraq's Crime of Genocide: The Anfal Campaign Against the Kurds* (New Haven, CT and London: Yale University Press, 1995).

Isikoff, Michael and David Corn, *Hubris: The Inside Story of Spin, Scandal, and the Selling of the Iraq War* (New York: Crown, 2006).

Jackson, General Sir Mike, *Soldier: The Autobiography* (London: Bantam, 2007).

Juhasz, Antonia, *The Bush Agenda: Invading the World, One Economy at a Time* (London: Duckworth, 2006).

Kaplan, Esther, *With God on Their Side: How Christian Fundamentalists Trampled Science, Policy, and Democracy in George W. Bush's White House* (New York: New Press, 2004).

Kennedy, Helena, *Just Law: The Changing Face of Justice – and Why It Matters to Us All* (London: Chatto & Windus, 2004).

Klein, Naomi, *The Shock Doctrine: The Rise of Disaster Capitalism* (London: Allen Lane, 2007).

Klein, Naomi and others, *No War: America's Real Business in Iraq* (London: Gibson Square, 2005).

Lagouranis, Tony and Allen Mikaelian, *Fear Up Harsh: An Army Interrogator's Dark Journey through Iraq* (New York: NAL Caliber, 2007).

Laufer, Peter, *Mission Rejected: U.S. Soldiers Who Say No to Iraq* (White River Junction, VT: Chelsea Green, 2006).

McCarthy, Rory, *Nobody Told Us We Are Defeated: Stories from the New Iraq* (London: Chatto & Windus, 2006).

Nakash, Yitzhak, *The Shi'is of Iraq* (Princeton: Princeton University Press, 1994).

Norton-Taylor, Richard and Nicolas Kent, *Called to Account: The Indictment of Anthony Charles Lynton Blair* (London: Oberon, 2007).

Olson, Kim, *Iraq and Back: Inside War to Win the Peace* (Annapolis, MD: Naval Institute Press, 2006).

Omaar, Rageh, *Revolution Day: The Human Story of the Battle for Baghdad* (London: Viking, 2004).

Owen, David, *The Hubris Syndrome: Bush, Blair and the Intoxication of Power* (London: Politico's, 2007).

Packer, George, *The Assassins' Gate: America in Iraq* (New York: Farrar, Straus & Giroux, 2005).

Phillips, David L., *Losing Iraq: Inside the Postwar Reconstruction Fiasco* (New York: Westview Press, 2005).

Pintak, Lawrence, *Reflections in a Bloodshot Lens: America, Islam and the War of Ideas* (London: Pluto Press, 2006).

Polk, William R., *Understanding Iraq: A Whistlestop Tour from Ancient Babylon to Occupied Baghdad* (London: I. B. Tauris, 2006).

Poole, Oliver, *Black Knights: On the Bloody Road to Baghdad* (London: HarperCollins, 2003).

Priest, Dana, *The Mission: Waging War and Keeping Peace with America's Military* (New York: W. W. Norton, 2003).

Ramesh, Randeep (ed.), *The War We Could Not Stop: The Real Story of the Battle for Iraq* (London: Faber & Faber, 2003).

Ricks, Thomas E., *Fiasco: The American Military Adventure in Iraq* (London: Allen Lane, 2006).

Ritter, Scott, *Endgame: Solving the Iraq Problem – Once and for All* (New York: Simon & Schuster, 1999).

Ritter, Scott, *Iraq Confidential: The Untold Story of America's Intelligence Conspiracy* (London: I. B. Tauris, 2005).

Ritter, Scott and William Rivers Pitt, *War on Iraq: What Team Bush Doesn't Want You to Know* (London: Profile, 2002).

Riverbend, *Baghdad Burning: Girl Blog from Iraq* (London: Marion Boyars, 2005).

Robertson, Geoffrey, *Crimes against Humanity: The Struggle for Global Justice*, 2nd ed. (London: Penguin, 2002).

Rogers, Paul, *Iraq and the War on Terror: Twelve Months of Insurgency 2004–2005* (London: I. B. Tauris, 2006).

Rose, Michael, *Washington's War: From Independence to Iraq* (London: Weidenfeld & Nicolson, 2007).

Sands, Philippe, *Lawless World: America and the Making and Breaking of Global Rules* (London: Allen Lane, 2005).

Scahill, Jeremy, *Blackwater: The Rise of the World's Most Powerful Mercenary Army* (New York: Nation, 2007).

Scheuer, Michael, *Imperial Hubris: Why the West is Losing the War on Terror* (Washington DC: Brassey's, 2004).

Schumacher, Gerald, *A Bloody Business: America's War Zone Contractors and the Occupation of Iraq* (St Paul, MN: Zenith Press, 2006).

Short, Clare, *An Honourable Deception?: New Labour, Iraq and the Misuse of Power* (London: Free Press, 2004).

Simons, Geoff, *Future Iraq: US Policy in Reshaping the Middle East* (London: Saqi, 2003).

Simons, Geoff, *Iraq: From Sumer to Post-Saddam*, 3rd ed. (Basingstoke: Palgrave Macmillan, 2004).

Simons, Geoff, *Iraq: Primus inter Pariahs – A Crisis Chronology*

1997–98 (Basingstoke: Macmillan, 1999).

Simons, Geoff, *The Scourging of Iraq: Sanctions, Law and Natural Justice*, 2nd ed. (Basingstoke: Macmillan, 1998).

Simons, Geoff, *Targeting Iraq: Sanctions and Bombing in US Policy* (London: Saqi, 2002).

Stewart, Rory, *Occupational Hazards: My Time Governing Iraq* (London: Picador, 2006).

Suskind, Ron, *The One Per Cent Doctrine: Deep Inside America's Pursuit of Its Enemies since 9/11* (New York and London: Simon & Schuster, 2006).

Timmerman, Kenneth R., *The Death Lobby: How the West Armed Iraq* (Boston: Houghton Mifflin, 1991).

Victor, Barbara, *The Last Crusade: Religion and the Politics of Misdirection* (London: Constable, 2005).

Wallis, Jim, *God's Politics: Why the Right Gets It Wrong and the Left Doesn't Get It* (San Francisco: HarperSanFrancisco, 2005).

West, Bing, *No True Glory: A Frontline Account of the Battle for Fallujah* (New York: Bantam, 2005).

Williams, Kayla, *Love My Rifle More than You: Young and Female in the US Army* (London: Weidenfeld & Nicolson, 2006).

Woodward, Bob, *Bush at War* (New York: Simon & Schuster, 2002).

Woodward, Bob, *Plan of Attack* (New York: Simon & Schuster, 2004).

Woodward, Bob, *State of Denial: Bush at War, Part III* (New York: Simon & Schuster, 2006).

Yamani, Mai (ed), *Feminism and Islam: Legal and Literary Perspectives* (London: Ithaca Press, 1996).

Index